Giants Of The Sea

Ships & Men Who Changed The World

The fascinating story of the colossal cargo ships
that make today's world trade possible
& the pantheon of nine visionary
titans who created them

For Pam —

Best wishes,

John D McCown

Sept 2021

John D. McCown, Jr.

Library of Congress Cataloging-In-Publication-Data
Names: McCown, Jr., John D., author
Title: Giants Of The Sea
Description: First edition
LCCN: 1-08-790276-2
ISBN: 978-1-0879-0276-0
1. Shipping 2. Transportation 3. Business History 4. Trade 5. Economy

Front cover: OOCL Hong Kong, a 21,100 TEU container ship that is among the largest container vessels in the world. Fully loaded, the total cargo value approaches $1 billion. Top close-up photo licensed via Getty Images. Bottom wide-angle photo by kind permission of Martin Bott.

Back cover: The nine individual giants most responsible for the modern cargo shipping industry.

Typography: Text set in Garamond, 12 point

Manufactured in the United States of America
First Edition

For Malcom

You launched a great idea that changed the world forever. Containerization turned strangers into trading partners and enriched all countries. Your genius continues to benefit billions all around the globe. It was my great honor and distinct pleasure to work with you. My hope is this book will make the world more aware of the incredible contribution you made to mankind.

Contents

Author's Preface

Like many young boys, I had an early fascination with large moving objects. This was kindled by a father who would load five pajama-clad children into his 1962 Impala convertible and, after an ice-cream cone stop, tour fire stations in Mobile, Alabama. Each of us was figuratively allowed to adopt one fire truck as our own. Commentary invariably centered on which of us had the largest fire truck, a position I coveted as the oldest. These outings would also often include a drive past the local docks.

It is on one of these excursions that I first saw a cargo ship. I was in awe of its size and peppered my father with questions about it for days. My dad had worked for a cargo shipping company for a couple of years after the war and he patiently answered my many questions. My interest led him to begin sharing many of his own maritime related experiences.

Those experiences my dad shared included his time as second mate aboard the tall ship *Danmark*. When Germany invaded Denmark, this large full-rigged sailing ship was in New York City to participate in the World's Fair and the U.S. Coast Guard requisitioned it. My father, a Coast Guard lieutenant during World War II, was assigned to the ship which engaged in patrols and training exercises along the New England coast. I grew up hearing stories of his experiences on that ship.

Ironically, decades after I had first heard of this grand sailing ship, I would get the opportunity to go aboard it even before I began my career in shipping. This occurred in 1976 when 16 tall sailing ships came to New York to participate in the bicentennial celebration in New York. I had just moved to New York to work for a bank and my father was visiting over the July 4th weekend. By virtue of its former service in the U.S. Coast Guard, the *Danmark* was second in the parade of tall ships just after the *Eagle*, the Coast Guard's sail training ship. Given my father's history with the *Danmark*, we managed to make our way to where it was tied up in lower Manhattan. After talking to the sailor manning the gangplank, he sought out an officer and we were eventually introduced to the captain. Surprisingly, he was the son of the Danish captain aboard the *Danmark* when my father served on it during World War II! The captain invited us onboard and gave us a tour of his ship that was almost exactly as my father remembered it.

I would come to learn that my hometown of Mobile was a large port city with a proud maritime heritage. Among other things, the world's first submarine was developed and built in Mobile some 150 years ago. It is generally accepted today that modern ballistic missile submarines are the most important strategic element of our navy. These underwater vessels are probably a key reason the world has avoided a nuclear conflict. There is an interesting anecdotal story you will here about later that links these key strategic naval assets with the segment of the shipping industry with which I spent the greatest amount of time. I would also grow up to learn that the Mobile based cargo shipping company my father worked for briefly after the war was the predecessor of the company that developed the new shipping sector in which I spent most of my career.

My first actual experience at sea was as a 12-year old accompanying my father on a day trip on the aircraft carrier *USS Lexington*, based in nearby Pensacola, Florida, as part of a Navy League outing. I was amazed at the size of that massive ship. I besieged my dad with questions about that ship and ships in general. From then on, he would routinely pass along to me his copies of Seapower, a quarterly Navy League magazine filled with articles and information on naval ships.

That fascination for large moving objects continued as I grew up. As a 15-year old I was mesmerized by the crawler-transporter I saw moving Apollo XI at Cape Canaveral in 1969. I was then awestruck by the subsequent launch of the first moonshot during an unforgettable trip with my father, brother and closest cousin. Several years later, I would go on to spend three summers during college as a pilot of the 171' Mark IV monorails at Walt Disney World. My interest in large moving objects seemed to grow as I grew. My guess is that this fascination is one of the things that drew me to spend most of my career in and around the shipping industry, where the largest movable objects ever built by mankind reside.

In addition to early experiences that likely played a role in channelling me into shipping, I've recently learned that I may have even been genetically preordained to take this path. One of the Christmas gifts from our children was a DNA analysis of our genetic ancestry. From that test, I learned that 8% of my genes go back to Nordic areas once dominated by the Vikings. As detailed elsewhere, for several centuries the Vikings were indeed the most proficient maritime traders in the world. Perhaps my shipping life was hard wired in and was always my destiny based on genes.

This book results mainly from my accumulated experience and knowledge of the shipping sector. Multiple primary data sources have been accessed to get precise up-to-date numbers. Key among them is the Bloomberg terminal's BMAP function that allows a real-time sort using various criteria. Since 2002 by international treaty, all commercial vessels worldwide are required to be equipped with a transceiver that continuously broadcasts various information including the identification, position and speed of the vessel. I used Bloomberg's BMAP function to develop tables showing break downs of vessels by segment and along various attributes. This extensive database includes vessels under construction as well as older vessels no longer in operation. Care was taken to exclude such vessels to arrive at a census of the world's merchant marine in service or capable of being in service. The final sort refreshed all the data relating to number of vessels and various size characteristics based on those that were actually operating on January 4, 2018.

In effect, this book is a complete census of the world's merchant marine fleet on that date. There is no other vessel census or compilation that I'm aware of that is as thorough or as detailed as what is presented here.

In addition to this vessel database, macro statistics on world trade and economic activity were obtained from a variety of data sources. Included among those is information from the United Nations Conference on Trade and Development, Container Trades Statistics, the World Bank and the U.S. Bureau of Transportation Statistics. Container Trades Statistics is a cooperative of all the major container vessel operators who provide it with container volume data that it aggregates into information on loaded container trade flows worldwide.

All of the numbers in this book have been reviewed and doublechecked to ensure that they accurately reflect the activity or segment being reviewed or discussed. I'm a quantitative person and you will see lots of numbers here. However, I won't compound that tendency, and bog down your reading, with the details of how various numbers and relationships were determined and calculated. There are detailed worksheets backing up all the numbers and analytics. I would be pleased to provide additional information and backup for any of the numbers in the book and can be reached at the email address included at the end of this chapter. The bibliography includes a listing of various sources of primary data that were researched in developing sections of this book.

More so than in most other industries, there are terms and jargon specific to shipping that are often unclear and confusing to outsiders. There is so much jargon in shipping that I sometimes think that is rooted in an actual desire to make the sector opaque to outsiders. This text will, however, minimize the use of those industry terms and jargon and use everyday terms. An over-riding goal is to increase the understanding of the cargo shipping industry.

Individual chapters on each of the nine individuals most responsible for the postwar revolution in shipping efficiency will follow an overview of the cargo shipping industry cargo. There will then be chapters on each of the major ship categories where they will be reviewed in detail as they exist today. Each category has its own characteristics and differing metrics. Following that are chapters on topics and issues that apply to all vessel categories.

The bibliography also includes many books on shipping. These were particularly helpful in expanding the chapter related to the early history of cargo shipping. I've enjoyed reading many books on shipping but have always found them to typically be long on sailing and short on cargo.

The majority of the thousands of shipping books written focus on our maritime past and the adventures and discoveries that can be tied directly to shipping, mostly of the sailing variety. It is most certainly a glorious past. Vivid reminders of that are captured in the wonderful paintings of sailing ships on display in offices and homes across America. Indeed, Alex Brown & Sons, the investment bank that took the shipping company I co-founded public, started life as a shipping company and its logo was based on the company flag all of their vessels flew. That same investment bank also underwrote the first initial public offering in the U.S., the B&O Railroad. My company was the last initial public offering they did prior to losing their separate identity when acquired by a large bank.

Another serendipitous coincidence relates to an organization that epitomizes the sense of adventure and discovery that marked the height of the sailing age. Outward Bound is an organization that benefits some 200,000 people each year that participate in their programs. Its very name comes from the term used to describe when a ship leaves a protected harbor and ventures out on a journey that typically includes points unknown. Outward Bound's mission is to give young people the skills and ability to deal with harsh conditions and the metaphors with early life at sea are numerous. Students are referred to as crew and Outward Bound's logo is a compass rose. The programs teach confidence, tenacity, perseverance and teamwork and are universally applauded for their effectiveness.

NYC Outward Bound, an affiliate of the larger national organization, is focused on fulltime secondary education within the larger Outward Bound framework and manages a dozen public high schools with exceptional performance statistics. One of those schools, The Gaynor McCown Expeditionary Learning School, is named after my younger sister, a teacher and leader in the field of education who died way too young. Gaynor left a mark and made a difference in the education world. It is always a great pleasure to attend the school's graduation ceremony each June where some 100 crewmembers mark what is really the beginning of their own life's journey.

Many people toil for decades in sectors that in the grand scheme of things have little actual utility or genuine relevance to the world around us. While they may be passionate about the razor blades or potato chips they make or the cable or credit card service they provide, the basic fact is that most manufacturing and service companies and sectors simply don't serve a fundamental requirement and are easily replaceable or substitutable. Under closer scrutiny, you realize that the products or services of many sectors are more related to convenience than to necessity. That is, however, certainly not the case with the cargo shipping industry. I suspect that an underlying reason others and I were drawn to the shipping industry was to be part of something that we all knew was meaningful and that really made a difference.

I've had the great fortune to spend most of my career associated with a herculean industry that literally carries the economy of the world on its shoulders. There is simply no substitute for what cargo shipping does. The shipping industry matters in a fundamental way unmatched by almost any other industry. This was a book that I thought needed to be written for a number of reasons, not the least of which was to make this grand industry more recognized by the public.

Many colleagues and friends who became aware of my book project have provided encouragement and advice and I'm grateful for all the comments they have made. One catalyst for my moving ahead with this project was an oft-hand comment by a colleague at the hedge fund where I worked that he found it interesting to read about large cargo ships. That was a further indication to me that there could be an interest in this book that goes beyond a narrow audience and I hope that proves to be the case.

I'm particularly grateful to Charles Cushing, noted naval architect and longtime friend, for his thoughtful reading of the manuscript. He provided many helpful suggestions and comments. One of the pleasures of my association with the shipping industry is the hundreds of thoughtful and interesting personalities I have been fortunate to meet and know and Charles epitomizes those qualities.

Life is a journey and as fellow Alabama native Forrest Gump said, it is full of surprises. Mine has certainly been that and thankfully most of the surprises have been to my benefit. A close friend of mine who has heard most of my best stories once remarked that I was a real life Forrest Gump based on the people I met along my journey. More through happenstance than anything else, I have shaken hands with Presidents Carter, Reagan, Bush and Clinton, Pope John Paul II, Mikhail Gorbachev, Fidel Castro and presidential nominees and leading Senators Bob Dole and John McCain. I've also met hundreds of business and government leaders along the way.

None of these gentlemen, however, have captured my interest and fascination as much as Malcom McLean and the other individual giants profiled herein. I suspect this is rooted in my awareness of the very tangible and beneficial effect the actions of these people are having on the world. The shipping industry has more than its fair share of people who are leaving a mark and making a difference. This book is my capstone project and my attempt to make a difference in the way people think of the shipping industry and its impact on the world.

I'm appreciative of all the input and suggestions I received from many people on this project. However, any errors or omissions are and remain mine alone. I hope you find this book both informative and enjoyable. Please feel free to share any feedback with me by sending me an email at john.d.mccown@gmail.com. Thank you.

"A modern fleet of ships does not so much make use of the sea
as exploit a highway"

The Mirror of the Sea, 1906
Joseph Conrad, Polish-born author & English novelist, 1857-1924

1. Introduction

The giant cargo vessels of the 21st century are the prime movers of global commerce. This book focuses on the thousands of ships that connect and enrich the world. It is also about the pantheon of nine individual giants whose vision set in motion their development. The physical giants that constitute this incredible network and the individual giants whose insight produced this remarkable worldwide conveyance system have benefited everyone.

Almost every type of tangible good – food, clothing, innumerable finished products, raw materials, fuel – moves by vessel. In 2017, these vessels collectively moved $11.7 trillion in goods representing 15% of the 2017 gross world product. Considering that more than three-fifths of that gross world product is represented by services, the net result is that cargo moved by vessels equalled 41% of tangible worldwide goods. In other words, almost half of what can be touched in the entire global economy makes its way to where it is consumed in whole or part on one of these vessels. World trade as we know it today simply couldn't exist without these efficient leviathans.

Today's large world trade is a post World War II phenomenon in terms of it having a major economic impact in most countries. In the postwar period the U.S.'s trade with foreign countries has increased almost 800-fold. All countries have experienced geometric increases in the absolute and relative importance of trade in their economies with some showing even more growth than the U.S. A shared characteristic everywhere has been the central and irreplaceable role of shipping. Trade has revolutionized the world's economy and lifted hundreds of millions out of poverty. The prime catalyst for that has been the revolution in shipping cost economics through both scale and specialization. Shipping costs relative to cargo value went from being a meaningful or prohibitive percent to an exponentially lower and sometimes almost inconsequential percent, minimizing the barrier of distance. With that fundamental structural change, world trade exploded.

The worldwide impact of these giant ships – the largest moving objects ever built by man – extend beyond commerce. The economic benefits incurred from these giant vessels may be met by their political benefits. A case can be made that today's relative peace across the globe is directly tied to world trade. The more economically bound countries are, the less likely they are to engage in conflict. It could be argued that the navy most responsible for world peace today is the thousands of merchant vessels quietly empowering commerce and growth around the globe. These ships effectively represent a massive logistics matrix that binds countries and delivers ever increasing economic and political benefits to the world every day.

If these giant vessels are the physical "big fish" of our seas, the nine pioneering visionaries behind them are the mental "big fish" of world trade and commerce. The development and growth in size and number of these giant cargo ships can be traced directly to them. Their ingenuity and entrepreneurism produced legacies that continue to benefit billions of people worldwide.

Economists refer to the shipping industry as a near perfect market, the best example of supply and demand factors coming together to determine pricing. The supply demand dynamic drives everything related to the economic performance of shipping. By definition, the primary assets in the industry are readily re-deployable to wherever demand arises across the globe. These factors result in a high degree of volatility encompassing various economic and cost factors that frame and underpin the risks and rewards to both the industry and the world at large.

Almost everyone intersects with the shipping industry in ways you may not even realize. Despite playing a more central role in economies than ever before, ironically it has receeded from public view and is now a largely invisible network to the public. It is a fascinating industry with its own complexities. We'll avoid getting bogged down on details and focus on what these giant cargo ships do and the visionaries most responsible for the modern cargo shipping industry.

Malcom McLean invented container shipping and is rightly known to history as the Father of Containerization. But that title hardly describes the effect his farsighted innovation has had and continues to have on the world. Everyone on the planet has benefited in some way from Malcom's genius.

D.K. Ludwig is to large tankers moving crude oil what Malcom McLean is to container ships. The two had a decade's long business and personal relationship. Ole Skaarup, also well known to McLean, was the person most responsible for the development and advancement of modern bulk carriers as a special purpose type of vessel.

McLean, Ludwig and Skaarup comprise the triad of pioneers whose insight directed the development of containerships, tankers and bulk carriers, respectively, the three major types of ocean-going cargo vessels today. Their fingerprints are all over the world economy and will be for the foreseeable future.

Six other gentlemen profiled in the pages that follow are Henry J. Kaiser, Stavros Niarchos, Aristotle Onassis, Y.K. Pao, C.Y. Tung and Maersk McKinney Moller. All left indelible marks in the shipping world that benefits trade and commerce today.

Three Americans, two Danes, two Greeks and two Chinese. This globe-spanning group of nine great men wrote the history on the development of modern cargo shipping. In response to the age-old debate of whether men make history or history makes men, in this industry the record shows that it is clearly the former. Except for the Americans, all of these men can coincidently be linked to past cultures with a strong maritime trade tradition. The Danes can be linked to the Vikings traders, the Greeks can be linked to the Phoenician traders and the Chinese can be linked to the maritime traders of the Han dynasty.

There is a thread that runs throughout the history of cargo shipping up until this day and the interconnections are fascinating. That filament not only connects many of these individual giants with previous maritime cultures, but also connects them in multiple ways with each other and today's modern shipping network. While all of the non-Americans can be connected with their own countries vivid maritime past, the Americans are most linked with the future and what resulted from their ideas.

The birthplace of modern cargo shipping is inevitably linked to America. It is there that the ideas and processes that created modern shipbuilding and all three of the modern shipping segments were developed. While the building and operation of those segments was initially typically American, both migrated to other countries for structural reasons but you can still see the path leading back to America.

These nine visionaries, all bold entrepreneurs, not surprisingly shared many similar traits. Most displayed strong entrepreneurial inclinations at a very early age. They were all broad thinkers with a constant eye on what would unfold long term. All of them were strong analytical thinkers who were particularly comfortable and very adroit with numbers and finance. Each of them recognized and appreciated the benefits of size and scale. They were all born within a relatively narrow range. Their work ethic was exceptional and their focus tended to be exclusively on larger strategic goals. All were optimists about both their and the world's future. They all developed an appreciation for their own judgment and counsel and moved ahead with confidence after they had made a decision.

Fundamentally, they were all builders of hard assets and companies. When they had made a decision on something, they were not timid in implementing that decision. They backed up their convictions with their own capital and their personal economics were directly tied to the success of their ships.

They were all true giants. While their accomplishments weren't generally well known to the public at large, each was held in high regard by almost all of those near and around them. The majority of these men were frequently referred to just by their initials. In their companies, when someone said MPM, DK, MMM, YK or CY, everyone knew who they were talking about. The use of initials to refer to someone is typically a demonstration of the highest respect for someone who you work for. While you are familiar with that person, to refer to him in talking with others by his first name was viewed as inappropriate for someone held in such high admiration. Likewise, both due to respect and the time in which they lived, their colleagues almost always addressed these individuals in person with the honorific Mr.

The confidants of these giants best knew their extraordinary accomplishments. In today's age filled with business folks whose promotional skills often outdistances their actual accomplishments, each of these giants were most focused on pushing the envelope in their particular spheres. They were generally indifferent, if not outright disdainful, to promoting their business accomplishments in the media. The ethos of these pioneering men was a constant search for new and better ways of doing things. They were always pushing ahead to develop innovative tangible assets and processes, following their own counsel and risking their own capital.

Despite the enormous wealth most of them accumulated, their personal tastes were often simple. These men led with their actual accomplishments and those accomplishments were the primary reward they sought. That is not to say that at least a couple of these gentlemen didn't have colorful personal lives that were often regaled by the media.

The careers of the nine pioneers broadly coincided with the explosive growth in trade after World War II. In 1940 prior to the war, U.S. exports and imports combined were $6.6 billion, an amount equal to 6.5% of total U.S. gross domestic product of $101 billion. Some seventy-seven years later in 2017, U.S. trade with foreign countries had increased by a factor of 788 times to $5.2 trillion. On a relative basis, trade in 2017 was 27% of U.S. gross domestic product of $19.0 trillion.

The more than four-fold post-war increase in trade relative to GDP in the U.S. is a pattern that has been followed throughout most of the industrialized world. In some countries, particularly in Asia, the relative growth in exports and imports was even higher.

In researching the lives of these individual giants, it is also striking how many of them left a mark in fields outside of shipping. I saw firsthand the broader insight and effect Malcom McLean had and wasn't surprised to learn that this was a shared characteristic among most of these gentlemen. Shipping involves significant investments in long-lived assets requiring broad awareness and strong macro thinking. Those same skills were also deployed in other areas and examples include advances by Henry Kaiser in healthcare, Malcom McLean in modular housing, C.Y. Tung in education and Y.K. Pao in diplomacy.

The collective legacy of these nine men is extraordinary. Their innovations related to shipping were in fact the prime movers that paved the way for the postwar trade revolution. Modern cargo shipping is the very tool that makes world trade, and hence world prosperity and peace, possible. There is no industry that can point to a group of its pioneers that have left behind such an encompassing and beneficial legacy. In addition, every day millions derive tangible benefits from the continuing work of their foundations and bequests. In the fullest sense, these men were entrepreneurs who gave back more to the world than they received.

The fact that transportation is an enabling factor for trade is magnified when considering the cost revolution that has occurred in sea transportation due to the men that are profiled here. If the three most important factors in real estate are location, location and location, then the three most important factors in trade are shipping cost, shipping cost and shipping cost. Ever since David Ricardo developed the theory of comparative advantage in the early 1800's to explain why countries trade, economists have focused on labor and resource production costs and generally ignored transportation costs. In the real world, whether transport costs are 50% or 5% or less than 1% of the value of the product being shipped, that cost will exponentially affect the amount being shipped. The historical data shows that trade is highly elastic to shipping costs relative to cargo value. As this ratio has dropped sharply, world trade volume has exploded. In many cases shipping costs are the chicken and trade is the egg.

Trade is fundamentally an arbitrage. The extraordinaryly efficient sea conveyance system that developed after World War II is the lubricant that moved world trade into high gear. Shipping is more cause than effect in world trade. More so than any sector, shipping has been at the forefront of global development and, in fact, is the basic enabler of world trade.

McLean, Ludwig, Skaarup, Kaiser, Niarchos, Onassis, Pao, Tung, Moller. Each played a role in this transition. They were all driven to develop and operate the bigger and better ships that made possible the exponential growth in trade. They were risk-takers and builders in the classic sense. The term shipping magnate applied to many of them. One of the first recognized billionaires in the world, D.K. Ludwig who was shown number one in the inaugural Forbes 400 listing in 1982, came from their ranks. While they typically made and occasionally lost fortunes, the innovations in shipping they left behind are their enduring legacy.

Because of them, there is a physical world wide web comprised of a network of thousands of large vessels. Instead of packets of electronic information, this network brings billions of people almost half of the tangible products they buy. An article entitled "The 20-Ton Packet" in a 1999 issue of Wired magazine described the container shipping industry as the biggest real-time data-streaming network in the world. The analogies between the physical network of thousands of giant cargo ships and the electronic networks embedded in computer systems are numerous.

The most tangible part of this physical network, what puts it in motion, is a legion of cargo ships. Large cargo ships are beautiful in form and elegant in function. The following pages include details on their size and aspects of their operation that illuminate both their form and function. The cover of this book is pictures of what is currently one of the largest container ships in the world, a magnificent vessel that is so efficient in moving almost $1 billion in cargo halfway around the world that the shipping cost is almost inconsequential.

The raw amount of material and goods these workhorse vessels move is awe-inspiring. For people who like fun facts, the shipping sector is a fertile area. Many of the statistics presented are shown in terms of how they relate to other better known metrics. Certainly they are thought provoking.

The simultaneous right brain and left brain attraction of cargo vessels was eloquently captured by novelist Joseph Conrad. He wrote "fifty hulls, at least, molded on lines of beauty and speed, moored all in a row, stern to quay, as if assembled there for an exhibition not of a great industry but of a great art". Cargo shipping is art with utility. A great, beautiful conveyance matrix without which we wouldn't recognize the world we have today.

It's worth highlighting that the catalyst for the Age of Discovery that led to Christopher Columbus opening up the New World was mercantile in nature. When Vasco da Gama sailed around the southern tip of Africa, the Portuguese opened up a shipping trade route between Europe and Asia. The Age of Discovery began. The Spanish were not content to cede this new trade to their rival. In underwriting Columbus's voyage, Spain was focused on developing a shipping trade route that would best their main rival and benefit their economy. Da Gama's voyage around Africa and Columbus's discovery of the Americas were evolutionary turning points for mankind. These events placed a premium on knowledge and innovation. It's been noted that advancement in both science and the humanities resulted in the First Enlightenment.

Naval and merchant ships accomplished the projection of power and influence by European countries around the globe. The deployment and activities of those ships wrote much of world history from the 1500's through the 1800's. The pattern of establishing mercantile relationships with far-flung overseas locations was a shared one among countries. Whether it was the Spainards in the 1500's, the Dutch in the 1600's, the French in the 1700's or the British in the 1800's, the successive countries that dominated the earliest beginnings of what we now call globalization followed a similar model. While they all acted in what they viewed as their own best economic interests, these countries and their ships figuratively and literally opened up the entire world.

As the age of the sail and the related adventures and discoveries receded, those classic ships were eclipsed by great cargo vessels whose importance to mankind is incalculable. Although cargo shipping is geometrically more linked to everything today, the industry it not well known by the public at large. There was a time when the arrival of a clipper ship was big news and many individuals knew people who made their livelihood from shipping. Not surprisingly, cargo shippers were among the largest companies in all seaports.

Over time many companies with roots in shipping morphed into large industrial and financial powerhouses. For instance, Royal Dutch Shell, now the largest company in the world in terms of revenues, started life as a small shipping company. It became the first to move crude oil through the Suez Canal in 1892 in a vessel holding less than 1% of the crude oil that moves in its behemoth tankers today. Among leading financial firms in New York City, it's more the rule than the exception to have a heritage linked to shipping as highlighted by reception areas festooned with paintings of grand sailing ships.

Shipping's past is glorious, but its present is even more remarkable now. Collectively, the shipping sector has never been more important to mankind and the world than it is today.

Shipping is one of the single most important industries in the world, providing a service that cannot be displaced or substituted. Without cargo ships, world trade and the world economy would simply grind to a halt. How many other industries are so critical and irreplaceable? If there were no internet or carbonated beverages or fast food restaurants, all sectors dozens of times bigger economically than the marine cargo shipping sector, alternatives for communicating, drinking or eating would still be readily available and the world economy would continue.

However, there is simply no viable substitute for the 63.9 trillion ton-miles of tangible goods moved by cargo vessels in 2017. That number underscores the staggering amount a cargo moved by the largely invisible network of cargo ships. To put that figure into perspective, it is useful to compare it to more visible freight networks with which most people are familiar. The 63.9 trillion ton-miles of cargo moved by merchant vessels is 34 times larger than the freight moved by all the U.S. railroads and 32 times larger than the freight moved by all the U.S. trucking companies.

Much has been written about the interconnected global economy that developed and became recognizable to all over the last several decades. Until just recently, most political leaders around the world broadly embraced globalization. The underpinning of this acceptance was the view that competition across borders resulted in giving consumers everywhere choices of products at the lowest costs. With countries focusing on producing products where they have relative comparative advantages, most economists believe that the collective benefits to the world can be measured in trillions of dollars each year. Whatever the benefits, how they are distributed between and within countries is increasingly being challenged, particularly by individuals in sectors experiencing disruption due to globalization.

The pros and cons of globalization have become an active part of recent public discussions around the world. Even with all this discussion, the role of shipping as a catalyst for globalization hasn't received much attention. During a July 2016 press conference, President Obama connected "the mobility of cargo container ships and global supply chains" to the existence and growth of globalization. That insight was both unusual and on point for a political leader. Just as progress is inevitable, when it comes to trade, the advent of container shipping was geometric progress on a world scale.

There is nothing that has been more of a catalyst to globalization than the efficiency of modern shipping. By consistently reducing the cost and time barriers which historically acted as friction in preventing trade, shipping made and continues to make globalization possible.

The collective benefits of globalization are irrefutable. This is borne out by World Bank statistics that show a significant drop in poverty levels around the globe just in the recent past. In 1990, some 1.85 billion people or 35% of the world's population lived in poverty, which is defined as income less than $1.90 per person per day. Just over a quarter of a century later in 2015, poverty levels had been reduced to 768 million people, or 10% of the world's population. That is a staggering reduction in poverty levels and the most rapid relative improvement that the world has ever experienced.

There is no other causal relationship to explain the tectonic shift in world poverty levels that would be anywhere near as important as world trade, which increased geometrically over that period. Without the magnificent and efficient distribution network resulting from those thousands of giant cargo vessels, the level of world trade we are currently experiencing simply would not exist.

The Cato Institute recently established an affiliate known as Human Progress with a mission to chronicle noteworthy advancements. Part of that effort involves profiling individuals they refer to as a Hero of Progress based on key accomplishments that benefited mankind. Dozens of individuals have been recognized, including many that invented vaccines, and their shared characteristic was that their personal efforts have clearly made the world better. Human Progress identified the 17th Hero of Progress as Malcom McLean and so far he is the only businessman to be so honored. In recognizing him, they drew a direct link between the invention of container shipping and the trade it made possible and the reduction in world poverty levels resulting from that trade. This was an appropriate and insightful recognition of a world changer who has literally improved the lives of billions of people living in the world today.

2. The World's Ocean Highways

How prophetic Joseph Conrad was more than a hundred years ago when in one of his books he wrote "A modern fleet of ships does not so much make use of the sea as exploit a highway". The seas were relatively underutilized roads then, infrequently connecting major ports. Today, they are more like four-lane super highways connecting every navigate-able part of the globe.

Oceans, seas and gulfs comprise 71% of the surface area of the earth. The 139.4 million square miles of ocean has an average depth of 2.3 miles. That works out to 321 million cubic miles of salt water, representing 97% of all the water on Earth, which paves the world's remarkable ocean highways. That is the vast domain across which cargo ships traverse. Big oceans, big ships, big numbers.

In thinking about cargo ships, it is clear that length is typically the most readily understood dimension. Tons, particularly deadweight tons which is the weight a ship can carry and the sum total of all cargo, fuel and stores onboard, is also a measure that is understood and meaningful. One frame of reference that most Americans can readily visualize is the length of a football field, 100 yards or 300' in total. To many people, cargo ships that long would not necessarily be considered giant in terms of vessel size today. But two times that, or a total length of 600', would meet almost everybody's definition of a large vessel. In these pages, that length is used as a reasonable cutoff to separate smaller vessels from the larger cargo vessels. While many vessels in the 300' to 600' range are also often involved in long ocean voyages, almost all 600' and longer vessels are exclusively engaged in long ocean voyages typically moving cargo five thousand or more miles.

To put 600' into historical perspective, that length is over one-third longer than the 441' long Liberty ships built during World War II. Those thousands of ships, with a deadweight capacity of 10,856 tons, were large vessels at that time. After their herculean duty as the logistical supply lines that won the war, they went into commercial service to begin a process that ushered in the geometric growth in postwar world trade.

On January 4, 2018, there were 17,546 cargo ships in service in the world over 600' in length, the equivalent of more than two football fields. If lined up end to end, this ribbon of steel would stretch out 2,766 miles. Add the 13,699 vessels that are from 300' to 600' long and those 31,245 vessels in total equate to a ribbon of steel that is 3,934 miles, long enough to connect New York and most ports in Northern Europe. Each day two additional vessels are added to the world's merchant fleet, resulting in a net increase of 116 miles each year of ships if lined up end to end.

As large as this incredible freight armada is, if the vessels over 600' in length were evenly spread across the world's oceans today, each would occupy 7,945 square miles of ocean, no closer than 89 miles to each other. If the larger group of vessels over 300' were spread out evenly, each would occupy 4,462 square miles of ocean and be no closer than 67 miles to each other. In reality, cargo ships are not evenly dispersed across the oceans and certain areas and routes are concentrated. However, the overriding point is that the oceans are expansive and a cargo ships time at sea is often lonely. Most of these ships spend 80% of their time at sea, often without seeing another vessel on their horizon.

Despite their relative isolation, these cargo vessels move 10.6 billion tons of cargo annually, which is worth some $11.7 trillion. Across all vessel classes, that works out to an average cargo value of $1,105 per ton or some 49 cents per pound. The latter figure is a good approximation for the across the board average value of all the tangible items produced and consumed by individuals across the globe.

The $11.7 trillion total value of trade moving by vessel is equal to 70% of the $16.7 trillion of annual world trade. In terms of weight, vessels move more than 95% of international trade. Excluding the services component of the gross product of the world, the $11.7 trillion in tangible products moved by vessel are equivalent to 41% of the remaining gross product of the world. In other words, today almost half the tangible products produced in the world make their way to consumers via cargo vessels.

The sharp increase in the portion of the world's economy moving on vessels has been matched by a continuous shift in the mix of merchant vessels versus naval vessels populating the seas and oceans. At all times through the sailing age, a meaningful number of vessels were partially or fully armed. Ships were focused on exploration or military objectives. To the extent there were ships at sea, navy ships dominated those seas. Today that reality is inverted. When ships pass at sea, those ships are almost always cargo vessels. Today's ocean highways pave the way for commerce rather than conflict.

The current merchant fleet of 17,546 large vessels spread across the world's oceans is almost twenty times the total 915 principal surface combatant ships now operated by all the navies in the world. Those naval vessels are also much shorter than the cargo vessels focused on here. Indeed, except for aircraft carriers, all naval vessels are less than 600' in length. For instance, the U.S. Navy's Ticonderoga class guided missile cruisers, probably the most powerful warships in the world today, are 567' long. Using the 600' length metric chosen here to define a giant vessel, there are only 19 naval ships in the world that fit that category. All are aircraft carriers. Of the 19 aircraft carriers now in service, 10 are U.S. aircraft carriers. In other words, the current merchant fleet of 17,546 large vessels is more than 900 times the number of naval vessels in the same overall length category. Despite the impressive length of those aircraft carriers, there are thousands of merchant vessels that have greater lengths than the largest aircraft carrier.

Except in dire circumstances, naval vessels provide protection but are not fully activated. The larger merchant navy, however, is at work every day in a network that binds the world. In doing its primary job of moving cargo, this merchant navy also acts to reduce the likelihood of conflict. It is the embodiment of the concept of world peace through world trade.

Day in, day out, these cargo ships crisscross the globe, quietly and efficiently carrying some 1.7 billion tons of cargo at any given time. In 2017, the typical vessel traveled 74,752 nautical miles, an average of 8.53 knots, or nautical miles per hour, including total time in port loading and discharging. A nautical mile is the distance spanned by one minute of latitude along a meridian of the Earth and is equivalent to 6,076 feet or approximately 115% of a statute mile. With an average of 6.19 roundtrip voyages annually, this endless floating conveyor belt now moves a total of 10.6 billion tons each year of a wide range of cargoe consumed across the planet. Those shipments move on average 6,034 nautical miles from where they are loaded to where they are discharged. In total, these vessels move 63.9 trillion ton-miles of cargo each year.

To put that extraordinary ton-mile figure into greater perspective, the U.S. Bureau of Transportation Statistics estimates that total domestic freight in the U.S. across all modes was 5.3 trillion ton-miles in 2014, the last year for which actual data is available. Domestic truck and rail were the largest modes at 2.0 and 1.9 trillion ton-miles, followed by pipeline (.9) and domestic water (.5). Domestic air is not a meaningful factor at .01. In other words, this network of thousands of giant vessels at sea currently moves 32 times the amount of freight that moves on America's highways and 35 times the amount of freight that moves on America's railways.

To personalize these staggering ocean cargo figures, consider that the numbers average out to every person on the planet having 509 pounds of cargo on vessels at sea at any given time. Over the course of a year, this incredible vessel network moves an average of 3,153 pounds of cargo almost one-third the way around the globe for every inhabitant of the planet. That works out to an amazing 19 million pound-miles of cargo per person per year. Another way to visualize that cargo on a more granular level is to think, for example, of 1,352 pounds of iron ore, 1,056 pounds of gasoline and 746 pounds of products from local retailers are delivered to every individual in the world each year. The actual movement of physical goods is a monumental logistical task made possible by this highly efficient shipping network. Without that herculean conveyance system, life as most people on the planet are now experiencing it simply could not exist.

Joseph Conrad's observation over one hundred years ago was prescient, but even he would undoutedly be amazed at what exists today. The pioneering visionaries and the giant cargo ships that have resulted from their initiatives have resulted in an irreplaceable physical conveyance system. They have turned the oceans into the greatest and most important highway in the world.

3. Early Cargo Ships & Trade

Egypt, widely known as the cradle of civilization, was also the cradle of cargo shipping. Based around the Nile River, Egypt was the first to develop sailing ships. The Nile was a perfect highway for waterborne commerce. In vessels first built of papyrus reeds bundled together and then covered with short wood planks, crews would sail south and drift or row north with the current.

The first noteworthy cargo vessels were barges built 5,000 years ago by Egyptian pharaohs to move granite downriver from Aswan for building pyramids. The cargo capacity of these barges was initially up to 50 tons of granite stone. The voyage on the Nile from the quarries in Aswan to the harbor in Giza where the granite was unloaded was 600 miles. While the current provided most of the propulsion, oars were sometimes used for rowing in addition to steering.

Queen Hatsepsut, who ruled Egypt from 1478 BC to 1458 BC, was the only woman pharaoh of Egypt and the world's first female ruler. Historians often refer to her as the first great woman in history. Under her reign, Egypt built barges 200' to 300' long to transport obelisks, the largest of which was 97' long and weighed 350 tons.

Queen Hatsepsut later introduced Egypt to cargo shipping outside the Nile with a series of vessels for trade with Pont (now Somalia) on the Red Sea. These 85' vessels with 15 oars on each side were rowed on the Nile to a point where they would be beached, dismantled and moved across land to the Red Sea. The vessels would then be rebuilt and rowed south on the Red Sea and around the Horn of Africa to modern day Somalia. An inscription on a temple in Thebes describes "the loading of the ships very heavily with marvels of the country of Pont" and lists myrrh, ebony, ivory, wood, animals, animal skins and incense as among the cargo carried.

From Egypt, shipping then progressed to the Mediterranean Sea. From 800 BC on, Greece was a dominant maritime power, but with a focus on military vessels. For merchant vessels and trade in the Mediterranean, however, the Greeks were no match for the Phoenicians. Located on the eastern end of the Mediterranean in modern day Lebanon, Phoenicia produced the most notable maritime traders of the time and was the first country whose economic activity was dominated by maritime trade. The Vikings, the Venetians, the Portuguese and the Dutch would later employ this model of building an economy around maritime commerce in different degrees.

The merchant marine dominance of the Phoenicians was rooted in the cedar trees of Phoneica. Ships were built with wood and tall, wide and straight hardwood trees were required for planks and masts. Blessed with this superior timber, the Phoenicians quickly became the most able shipbuilders on the Mediterranean. On their square sailed merchant ships, the Phoenicians traveled throughout the Mediterranean and even into the Atlantic. There is evidence that the Phoenicians may have circumnavigated Africa from east to west while searching for new trading opportunities. Their ships were broad to allow them to export large quantities of wood, linen, dyed cloths, embroidery, metalwork and glasswork and to import papyrus, ivory, ebony, silk, amber, spices, incense and precious metals.

One by-product of active trading throughout the Mediterranean was the spread of the Phoenician alphabet. A phonetic script that enabled understandable written communication was essential to the growth of trade. This script was a significant improvement in the hieroglyphics that were previously used. Following their conquest by the Persians in 540 BC, the Phoenicians gradually lost their identity and were absorbed into the Greek empire when Alexander the Great defeated Persia in 333 BC.

Around 300 BC, the Far East saw the beginning of maritime trade in India and China. Initially focused on trade routes first developed along large rivers, it then expanded to include coastal and regional routes. Around the beginning of the Han dynasty in 202 BC, the Chinese began using ships with a stern mounted rudders and masts and sails. Known as junks, these ships sailed into the South China Sea and established trade routes to India and what is now known as Vietnam, among other destinations. These unique ships and their larger descendants would be the main type of cargo vessel used by the Chinese for the next two thousand years.

The Romans developed the next step up in cargo shipping. At its height around 400 AD, Rome was an enormous city inhabited by approximately one million people. It was the most populous city in the world and was a large market that needed to be fed. This resulted in the building of specialized vessels to ensure adequate food supplies for Rome. Just as all roads led to Rome, in those days most merchant ships delivered their cargo to Rome.

The Roman merchant ship traditionally had a rounded hull to maximize its capacity for grain, the primary product. While the largest of these vessels could move 1,200 tons of cargo, the primary size was a "ten-thousander" able to carry that number of sacks of grain or amphoras of wine (about 400 tons). These Roman ships had square sails on up to three masts. The main trade route was between Alexandria where grain from the Nile Valley was loaded and shipped to Rome. To put into perspective how active this trade route was, each year Rome imported 420,000 tons of grain. That translated into 1,200 shiploads of grain per year or an average of five vessels each with 350 tons of grain per day after excluding the non-navigable winter months.

An early Roman emperor built a large artificial inland harbor on the north bank of the Tiber River that would serve as the main port of ancient Rome for more than 500 years. Called Portus, the Latin word for harbor or haven, it consisted of a 97 acre hexagonal basin connected to the Tiber River and other points through a series of canals. It addition to grain shipments, Portus was the gateway for shipments of glass, ceramics, marble and even wild animals coming from Africa for spectacles in the Colosseum.

The amphora, a wheel thrown terracotta container, was the standard marine shipping container of the Roman era and was used in vast numbers. While primarily used to move wine and olive oil, amphoras were also used for grain, fish, nuts, spices, olives, grapes and other commodities. A typical amphora was tall with a slender neck and two opposing handles on each side of the neck. The most popular size was around 18 inches high, but ranged up to 5 feet in height requiring several handlers. Amphoras had a pointed base allowing upright storage on land by embedding in soft ground. This shape also facilitated marine transport. The ships had wooden racks that allowed the amphoras to be placed upright. Ropes tied to the handles prevented shifting.

Amphorae were cheap and plentiful and typically just used for one voyage and not returned, so they were broken up at their destination. An indication of how widespread the use of this utilitarian container was exists today in the form of a breakage site in Rome close to the Tiber

River. At that site, the fragments created a hill now known as Monte Testaccio, which is 150' high with a diameter of 1,000'.

In a fascinating example of something from the past helping with the present and future, lead recovered from a Roman merchant ship is playing a role in the search by physicists for dark matter that is believed to make up 83% of the universe. The instrumentation used to detect dark matter is extraordinarily sensitive and the background radiation emitted from all objects can affect experiments. To minimize this, physicists shield their measurement devices with lead, which blocks this background radiation. Even lead, however, emits a low level of background radiation that can impact experiments. To mitigate this, lead recovered from ancient Roman shipwrecks is ideal because after two thousand years most of its unstable isotopes have decayed away. In addition, the sea has shielded it from cosmic rays that add to its radioactivity. Recently, lead ingots recovered from a Roman cargo vessel that sunk off the coast of Sardinia have been melted down and recycled for use in protecting instrumentation physicists are now using to better understand the universe.

As the Roman Empire declined, so did a vibrant grain trade between Egypt and Rome. It would be a thousand years later in the sixteenth century before vessels of similar cargo tonnage would ply the Mediterranean waters again. The seven seas (Mediterranean, North, Adriatic, Aegean, Black, Red and Arabian) continued to experience growth in all types of sailing ships but the predominant focus was military or naval vessels rather than cargo vessels.

The names of several of the famous seven seas actually tie with the nomenclature used in maps from antiquity. In those maps, it was customary to include a compass where the directions were shown in different colors. Black represented north, red represented south, white represented west and yellow represented east. Their directional orientation relative to most cartographers is how the Black Sea and the Red Sea got their names. In many early maps, the Mediterranean was actually referred to as the White Sea as most of it lied to the west of the mapmakers. However, it would eventually become known to all as the Mediterranean Sea. That name was derived from the latin terms medius (for middle) and terra (for land, earth). That name fit with the view that much of the civilized world was on the coast of that great sea.

The Viking Age began around 800 AD and lasted some 300 years. While most known for voyages of exploration and plunder, the Vikings were also very astute traders. In fact, it was in Scandinavia that the first towns focused on trading were developed. With their distinctive longships often over 100' long, the Vikings traded all over Europe and the Mediterranean. These graceful shallow draft vessels were designed for speed, going 6 knots with oars and up to 15 knots with sail under favorable conditions. The longships had symmetrical bows and sterns, allowing them to reverse direction quickly without turning. They had large rectangular sails on a single mast coming up from the middle of the ship. Longships typically had dragonheads at the top of their upsweeping bows and sterns. These ships represented the epitome of naval power at the time and they came to be known as dragonships throughout Europe. It must have been a terrifying sight when 600 dragonships attacked Hamburg in 845.

The broad influence of the Vikings in trade and commerce across the entire European continent is not as well known, perhaps in large part due to the brutal raids so associated with them. With more than one hundred recorded raids across Europe, the pillaging and plummeting by Vikings is what stands out in history. Less known is that the Vikings also developed trade routes that extended throughout the continent and that the influence of the Viking culture for centuries was significant. The Viking influence on Russia was great. Sailing as far as the Black Sea and Caspian Sea, a group of Swedish Vikings known as the Rus entered the area today known as Russia. At the time, disorganized Slavic tribes occupied the area. The Rus brought order to the region and under a Rus chieftain all the tribes became unified and eventually fully assimilated. The Rus lended their name to what would become a major empire.

As with the Phoenicians before them, a key reason for the dominance of the Vikings on the sea was their shipbuilding skill, which was in large part a consequence of the region's natural resources. For many centuries, the Vikings were the preeminent shipbuilders in the world, in no small part due to the plentiful large oak and other hardwood trees in Scandinavia. They were particularly adept at metalworking and they developed iron tools that assisted in their shipbuilding. Their early vessels were multi-purpose, but as their shipbuilding skills improved, the Vikings developed specialized ship designs. Short wide hull designs were developed to transport cargo while long narrow hull designs were used to carry armed raiding parties.

Another key maritime related reason for the spread of the Vikings was their expertise in refining their vessels and sails to get the most speed from wind power. While sails had been used for centuries, the Vikings revolutionized sail technology resulting in the fastest ships the world had ever known. Their longships were light and flexible and built from the keel up, only later adding internal framework and support. The rectangular sails used by the Vikings were larger, relative to the size of the ship, than any sails used before. When these light ships were combined with large sails, the Viking longships were the fastest vessels on the water by a large margin.

The Vikings developed several major trading centers at ports on the Scandinavian coast that linked with shipping routes extending throughout all parts of Europe. Viking traders sold fur, wood, leather, wool and iron and bought goods such as spices, silk, wine, wheat, pottery and glass. They established a bullion economy where weighed silver was used as the means of exchange. Everywhere they went, the Vikings also bought and sold slaves.

Viking settlements in Greenland became an important source on some of the goods and materials traders sold. Historians have recently discovered that a key aspect of this trade with Europe related to walrus tusks. Because these tusks could be carved into elegant figures, it was a luxury item sought after by churches and wealthy individuals. From statues to chess pieces, items carved from walrus tusks were treasured for centuries across Europe. These tusks originated from Scandinavian countries around 500 AD and, until recently, historians believed that remained the primary source. Based on detailed research confirmed by DNA tests of various figures, historians have now concluded that after the Vikings settled Greenland, almost all of the walrus tusks came from Greenland. The Vikings must have determined that the supply of walruses in Greenland and the related cost to harvest the tusks was lower than the similar factors in the Scandinavian countries. In that respect, the transition of the walrus tusk trade to Greenland is arguably the first tangible example of globalization.

Around 1000 AD, Leif Erikson landed in a place he called Vinland because he said it had grapevines and self-sown wheat fields. Vinland is what is now known as Newfoundland, making Erikson the first European to set foot in North America, almost five hundred years before Columbus. The Vikings elected not to return to Vinland, presumably because they believed it offered nothing more than what they could obtain to trade from other closer settlements. That epic voyage, however, is testimony to the Vikings skill as both traders and shipbuilders.

For almost three hundred years starting in the 13th century, maritime commerce throughout all of the seven seas was dominated by the Venetians. Venice built a large national shipyard in the late 1100's and the warships it produced allowed it to take control of the Eastern Mediterranean and eventually gain additional territories with the partitioning of the Byzantine Empire in 1204.

The success of the Venetian empire was fundamentally really built on a foundation of salt. The lagoons surrounding Venice were key sources of salt and in 1200 there were 119 local salt works providing this preservative and seasoning. As demand for salt increased, Venice augmented its local production by importing salt from areas where its merchant ships traded. At one point, a rule was put in place requiring that all ships returning to Venice must return with salt onboard as ballast. Large warehouses were developed to store salt in Venice. As a result of these efforts, Venice developed a virtual monopoly on the salt trade, which served it well in extending and expanding its trade activities. Salt became a store of value and Venice's control of the production and sale of this "white gold" throughout the Mediterranean was powerful. It is interesting to note that the word "salary" comes from the Latin word for salt.

With salt acting as the figurative and literal base cargo of its growing fleet, Venice became the merchant capital of Europe. The state recognized how central its own ships were to that role. Initially these merchant vessels were built at Venice's flourishing private shipyards. They were referred to as round ships because the beams were a third of the length. With a capacity of up to 600 tons, these broad merchant ships brought back to Venice wine from Crete, sugar, cotton and grain from Europe and silver, copper and woolen cloth from as far away as England.

Various spices became a natural progression of Venice's monopoly of the salt trade. The spice trade was the first meaningful intercontinental trade and it would grow to involve large parts of Europe, Africa and Asia. Spices like pepper, cinnamon, ginger and cumin initially moved completely overland and Muslin traders in the Middle East were secretive about the true sources of spices they obtained mainly in Asia that became treasured in Europe. These spices had no underlying nutritional value, but did improve the taste and enjoyment of a wide variety of foods.

The Venetians opened maritime routes for the spice trade from the Eastern Mediterranean to multiple European destinations that resulted in tremendous growth. The spice trade was in fact another early example of what today is referred to as globalization. To improve the speed of their merchant fleet, the Venetians developed a new vessel that was as long as their war galleys but wider and deeper in order to carry cargo. These vessels, known as great galleys, were all built at the national shipyard and were 132' long with a beam of 23'. The Venetians were quick to appreciate what a merchant ship that was as fast as a warship could do for their trade networks. From their introduction in the early 14th century and for the next two hundred years, these great galleys dominated Venetian trade, carrying the merchandise that was the most valuable part of Venice's growing commerce.

The Venetian maritime trade routes were divided into seven major routes from Venice that were covered by an annual voyage comprised of a convoy of standard sized ships. The most important was the Alexandria route, which sometimes had two voyages annually. On the Alexandria route, great galleys carrying silver bullion and gold coins exchanged them for spices, silks and dyes from the East that had made their way to Egypt. This route was bringing back 2,500 tons of spices annually, most of which would then be redistributed across Venice's trade network. The second convoy moving eastward was the Beirut route, which traded for spices that reached the coasts of Syria and Palestine from inland points. The Romanian route sailed into the Black Sea where it traded for furs, silks and slaves. The Barbary route traded in ports along the pirate infested shores of North Africa and then traveled north to the Moorish Coast of Spain. The convoy of the Northeast African route first sailed to Tripoli and then split into two. One unit travelled to Alexandria and the other unit to Beirut. The convoy of the Southern France route sailed along the coasts of Italy and Southern France, primarily selling merchandise from the Far East that had flowed into Venice's trade network. Finally, the most difficult convoy was the Flanders route, where ships sailed outside of the Mediterranean and on to England and what is now Belgium, with an en-route port call in Lisbon. In all, these seven trade routes formed a web of some three dozens ports that were regularly connected with Venice by these merchant ships.

Initially, trade between China and Italy moved over land on the route first taken by Venetian Marco Polo that became known as the Silk Road. Some 135 years after his journey, much of that trade transitioned to a maritime Silk Road established in 1405 by Chinese Admiral Zheng He. Born in what is now Mongolia, Zheng He was captured by the Chinese as a boy and placed in servitude with a ruling family. He eventually gained the confidence of leaders within the Ming dynasty. Trade via the Silk Road had expanded Chinese knowledge of the world and resulted in the Ming dynasty sponsoring a series of ocean voyages to increase both knowledge and trade. Zheng He was in charge of these multi-year voyages, seven of which occurred between 1405 and 1433.

The Chinese had developed a maritime tradition focused around its two large rivers and coastal areas well before the major exploratory voyages of Zheng He. One proof of that was the invention of the compass by the Chinese in 200 BC. The compass allowed ships to navigate away from the coast for the first time. The Chinese were also the first to invent dry-docks which they did in 1000 AD, some 500 years before dry-docks were used in Europe. During the Ming dynasty, the Chinese were the first to build ships with watertight compartments. They were also the first to build ships with a stern post and a balanced rudder positioned before the stern post, innovations that allowed the Chinese to build much larger ships.

The pioneering shipbuilding processes that China developed made Zheng He's voyages possible. Between 1403 and 1407, the Chinese built 1,681 ocean-going vessels, primarily at shipyards in Suzhou, near modern day Shanghai, and Longjiang, in the southern province of Guangdong. An estimated 30,000 people were living and working in these shipyards as carpenters, ironsmiths, caulkers and rope and sail makers. The scope of this project, even by today's standards, was massive. It was by far the largest shipbuilding project ever at the time and it would really be more than 500 years before that record was broken.

Admiral Zheng He's fleets visited ports throughout Southeast Asia, India, much of the east coast of Africa and the Arabian Peninsula, dispersing and receiving goods along the way. On the horn of Africa, he connected with traders bringing goods from Europe. There is even a group of scholars who point to a Chinese 1418 world map that presents all the major continents with a precision that wouldn't be seen in European maps for more than a century. Those scholars see that as evidence that Zheng He may have even traveled to parts of North and South America.

In exchange for gold, silver, porcelain, silk and horses, Zheng He received spices, ivory, exotic animals and numerous goods new to China. The size of the fleets and his largest ships suggest that the volume of trade and cargo moved must have been significant. Records show that his first expedition consisted of 27,800 men on 62 large treasure ships supported by 190 smaller ships.

The treasure ships were large nine-masted square rigged ships with four decks that could carry a massive amount of cargo and accommodate up to 500 people in what would be considered luxurious style at the time. The ships had dragon eyes on the prow and brightly painted hulls. Vessel dimensions were "44 zhang 4 chi long and 18 zhang wide'. The 444 was considered symbolic and lucky, with four being the symbol of the earth and its four corners. There were also four seas, four cardinal directions, four seasons and, according to Confucianism, four bonds or virtues: propriety, integrity, righteousness and modesty. Given the conversion factor of 10.5 feet per zhang, if those dimensions for the treasure ships are accurate, they would have been 466 feet long and 189 feet wide. That would make these the largest wooden ships in history and their cargo carrying capacity would not be eclipsed until iron hulls hundreds of years later.

Accompanying Zheng He's flagship treasure ships were horse ships, supply ships and troop transport ships. The horse ships were eight-masted, 339 feet long and carried horses which were a key trading currency. The supply ships were seven-masted, 257 feet long and carried most of the food and provisions for these multi-year expeditions. The troop transport ships were six-masted, 220 feet long and carried soldiers. The treasure ships and some of the other ships had cannons, but there is no record of any military activity on any of Zheng He's voyages. Of course, just the sight of such a massive fleet and potential fighting force would have dissuaded any country visited from aggression. Zheng He's fleets developed an elaborate system of sight and sound signals in order to communicate at sea. When they were in port, they relied on hundreds of translators who sailed with them to facilitate communications with local people.

In addition to increasing trade, Admiral Zheng He's expeditions were intended to show to others the greatness of China's civilization. It must have been a staggering sight in any port when a fleet of 300 ships holding some 30,000 men dropped anchor. This outward projection of power by China came to an end with Zheng He's death at sea during his seventh expedition in 1433.

The logistics of supporting such massive expeditions, with hundreds of ships and thousands of men, and the related costs and planning required must have been extraordinary. Not having confidence in anyone else to lead such expeditions, and increasingly preoccupied with problems along its northern borders, China turned inward. Given the clear superiority of Chinese shipbuilding and the size and scale of an ocean-going fleet that was far ahead of European vessels, history undoubtedly would have unfolded very differently if China had not withdrawn and turned inward at that time.

It would be almost six centuries before China turned again to outward directed initiatives such as the Zheng He expeditions. Perhaps because of this, Chinese leaders highlight the history of Zheng He today. In China's current global infrastructure program known as One Belt, One Road, the Road refers to the maritime route stretching from Southeast Asia across the Indian Ocean to the Middle East, Africa and Europe, almost the same maritime route Zheng He pioneered six hundred years ago.

The European sailing ships that crossed the oceans of the world at the start of the Age of Discovery in the late 1400's initially transported men and information. These vessels, the subject of countless books and movies that cemented their legacy in world maritime history, initially were voyages of exploration and adventure. That exploration was rooted in the desire to discover new trading partners and products. Like the Viking five centuries earlier, the Venetians two centuries earlier and the Chinese a century earlier, these were voyages with clear commercial objectives. Based on what was learned on these voyages along with the exotic items that were brought back to Europe, these expeditions were the catalysts for what would later become meaningful cargo movements by ship.

In 1488, a Portuguese expedition led by Vasca da Gama sailed around Africa via the Cape of Good Hope and proceeded to Asia. Da Gama's circumnavigation of Africa was the beginning of meaningful intercontinental trade by vessel. With this and later voyages that continued on to India and parts of Asia, an active maritime spice trade with Europe opened up. Spices such as cinnamon, cassia, cardamom, ginger and pepper became prized in Europe. While a limited amount of spices had previously reached Europe either completely overland or via Venice where it moved by ship from the Eastern Mediterranean, the establishment of a much more cost efficient all-water marine alternative sharply increased the spice trade to Europe.

Portugal initially dominated the trade and the wealth resulting from the spice trade underpinned much of that country's growth. As the search for new spices such as nutmeg which existed only in the Banda Islands heated up, the spice trade continued to expand. The discovery of the Pacific Ocean and the first circumnavigation of the globe occurred as a result of Ferdinand Magellan's epic expedition. Like many other voyages of discovery, this was driven by the search for new marine routes to obtain spices.

It is interesting to note that the discovery of the Americas was a direct result of the maritime spice trade. The sole reason that Spain underwrote Christopher Columbus's 1492 voyage was to find a new route in order to break Portugal's dominance of the maritime spice trade. The discovery of the Americas was really a subset of the first transatlantic commercial voyage. The movement of spices by ship from Asia to Europe created the first major maritime cargo lane. Volumes shipped would soon be eclipsed by another commodity cargo.

By the mid-1500's voyages of discovery were increasingly supplanted by voyages of trade. Spanish and Portuguese galleons were the dominant participants in trade routes between those countries and their newly established colonies in the Americas. When it was learned that the Japanese could make firearms on a large scale, the spice trade was augmented by new trade routes to Asia. Portuguese and Dutch merchants began direct trade by sea of fine porcelain from China to Europe during the Ming dynasty, dominating the movement of a popular product that had previously moved overland. Porcelain originated in China over a thousand years earlier and as such variations of the dinnerware used across the world are still referred to as china. However, the Asian trade by sea was nowhere near the first meaningful intercontinental trade brought about by the discovery of the Americas. For the first couple of hundred years, that trade could be reduced down to one word: sugar.

Europe quickly realized that the climates in Brazil and the islands in the Caribbean were well suited to grow sugar cane. Large plantations developed to satisfy the demand for sugar in Europe, whether it was for tea in England, cakes in Amsterdam, molasses for rum or numerous other products that could utilize this sweet ingredient. Other outbound products such as tobacco and cotton would eventually supplement the sugar shipments that dominated the early commerce between the Americas and Europe. These shipments and the areas in which they could be grown were given such priority that the area that now includes the U.S. was relatively ignored by much of Europe.

An early determinant of where settlements in the New World were established was what areas and islands offered the best natural harbors. Trade could only occur when sailing ships could first be safely moored and safely loaded. The ideal places were inlets near the ocean with narrow passages that opened up to larger bodies of water protected by natural breakwaters. These inlets often were found in or near rivers that flowed into larger bodies of water. Ports at the mouths of rivers were among the more common New World ports. They were protected from turbulent ocean waves and, due to the self-dredging action of the flowing river, had deep water near land.

Geological formations in the form of natural harbors played significant roles in the actual discovery and development of the Americas. Where a ship could find a safe harbor was a key catalyst for much of the civilization that would follow. Early on, Havana, Cuba became the epicenter of Spain's New World empire because it offered unparallel protection in its natural harbor. So did the harbor San Juan, Puerto Rico. This important center of Spanish trade was so highly regarded as a rich port that it was given that Spanish name. The island itself was called San Juan in memory of the catholic saint. Through a mistaken reading of an early map, the names for the city and the island were inverted and to this day the city is called San Juan while the entire island is called Puerto Rico.

The wealth accumulated by Portugal from its early dominance of the maritime spice trade with Asia made it the envy of all countries in Europe, especially its archrival Spain. In its quest to develop a western maritime route, Spain claimed many new lands where it established commercial and trading activities. In the Americas, those activities would expand into areas beyond sugar and related products. Spain's conquest of Mexico and Peru resulted in tremendous wealth. Spain plundered the gold and silver holdings of the indigenous people and then forced them to mine additional precious metals. The gold and silver that moved into the Spanish treasury in the mid-1500's made it not only the richest country on the Iberian Peninsuala, but the richest country in Europe. The treasure ships that moved that cargo to Spain also became the favorite targets of pirates operating in the Caribbean.

Mexico, which was known as New Spain at the time, played a key role in another important maritime trade route developed by Spain. Among the other settlements by Spain during its voyages to establish a western trade route was the Phillipines. By the mid-1500's, Manilla had a large Spanish presence and commerce with China and other parts of the Far East had begun. To fund increasing amounts of trade, ships loaded with silver sailed from the West Coast of Mexico to the Phillipines. Spain established a mint in Mexico where silver coins with serrated edges were produced. These edges prevented a common practice of chipping off portions of a coin by making the chipping obvious. These coins, known as Pieces of Eight, were the first verifiable currency. They were well received and resulted in an increase in trade between the Spanish in the Phillipines and China. The coins were used to buy porcelain, silk, ivory, spices and an assortment of exotic goods from China.

The Chinese products that Spain purchased sailed from the Phillipines to Mexico on the return leg of the merchant ships that brought the Pieces of Eight. This Manilla to Acapulco voyage took advantage of Pacific tradewinds in a clockwise loop, the eastbound leg more northernly and the westbound leg more southernly. From Acapulco, the Chinese goods moved overland to the East Coast of Mexico for shipment to Spain aboard a treasure ship also moving precious metals. The Phillipines to Mexico trade route grew to such importance that a special class of merchant ships called Manilla galleons was developed to serve the route.

The Manilla galleons sailed the Pacific for 250 years. They were built in Manilla using Phillippine hardwoods, another example of the key role of local trees in early shipping. The galleons were the largest of the day with an average capacity from 1,700 to 2,000 tons and lengths approaching 175'. The vessels carried up to 300 passengers and crew in addition to cargo. The eastbound leg had the most cargo, but in addition to the silver coins on the westbound leg, tobacco, cocoa and various other food products from the Americas made its way to the Far East. The westbound leg even included some goods transhipped from Europe such as wine and olive oil. From 1565 to 1815, Spain, which controlled the Phillipines, built 108 galleons to serve this important trade route. It is estimated that at least one-third of the silver that was mined in Mexico and Peru made its way to China on the Manilla galleons. Not until the advent of steamships and the development of the Suez Canal did the long run of the Manilla galleons came to an end.

Prior to that, for over four hundred years, Spain developed a trade network connecting the Far East, the Americas and Europe with its Manilla galleons. In a similarity to modern cargo networks, Spain's network included overland movements and transhipments. With the maritime and overland route, Spain had the ability to move much sought after goods from the Far East to Europe, although hardly as efficiently and timely as Portugal with its all water trade route around Africa.

Spain's motivation for explorations that resulted in these and other trade routes was driven by and rooted in its mercantile interests. The Treaty of Tordesillas that Spain entered into with Portugal in 1494 also necessitated those explorations. Terms of the treaty prohibited Spain from sailing from Europe to the Far East via Africa's Cape of Good Hope. Spain effectively gave Portugal exclusive access to the most efficient route over which to conduct trade between Europe and the Far East.

Spain continued efforts to find a better maritime route to the Far East, but never succeeded. Those efforts, however, achieved even greater discoveries than finding a new maritime route to the Far East. It's a tangible reminder that the journey is often more important than the destination. The subsidiary benefits from Spain's expeditions of discovery are simply incalculable. Beyond the significant wealth accumulation, they literally opened up a New World. There were even subsidiary benefits within the trade routes that developed as a result of the voyages of discovery. For example, the first exploration by Spain of modern day California was to scout out possible stopoff points for weary Manilla galleons prior to reaching Acapulco.

A vivid reminder of the early trade irrelevance of the North American mainland can be seen in old maps. A 1762 print of the West Indies by Thomas Kitchin, a London-based cartographer to King George III, shows the islands of the Caribbean accurately as they exist today, while Florida and portions of the southeast U.S. are inaccurate and almost unrecognizable. At that point in time, the Caribbean was vastly more important to Europe than the rest of North America. As part of an international treaty at the same time, France and England effectively swapped Canada for Grenada. Today nobody could comprehend such a trade as involving comparable values, but at the time the prominence of the sugar trade made it so.

World history can be traced, in part, through trade involving various commodities. That is certainly the case with the sugar trade. This trade originated in Brazil and it spread out across many of the Caribbean islands. A triangular shipping trade developed among the Americas, Europe and Africa. Ships would move sugar, rum and other commodities from the Americas to Europe, textiles and manufactured goods from Europe to Africa and slaves from Africa to the Americas. It was the need for labor to plant and harvest sugar cane in the Americas that drove the demand for slaves.

The actual volumes of sugar shipments to Europe during this period were large for the time, but inconsequential relative to modern drybulk movements. Brazil's sugar production was concentrated in the Pernambuco region in the northeast where shipments between its port city of Recife and Amsterdam, the main sugar refining center, peaked in the 1640's at 24,000 tons per year. An entire year's export could readily fit within just one hold of thousands of modern bulk carriers that exist today. Because Brazil was not able to keep up with the demand from Amsterdam refiners for raw sugar, more sugar plantations were established throughout the islands of the Caribbean. Even with this expansion, the available production data from various islands suggests that total sugar exports from the Americas to Europe never exceeded 50,000 tons per year.

None of the Caribbean islands was a busier shipping center than the Dutch possesion of St. Eustatius, a small island in the northern portion of the Leeward Islands. In the mid-1700's, St. Eustatius was effectively the economic hub of the Americas. By 1760, St. Eustatius was recording almost 3,000 ship arrivals each year at its port. Almost 20,000 merchants, sailors and slaves were crowded on a small island that acted as a relay point to many other Dutch controlled islands in the Caribbean. Plantations on St. Eustatius produced just 300 tons of sugar annually. Because its warehouses collected sugar produced on other islands, it exported 10,000 tons annually to Europe. The island also acted as a transshipment hub for tobacco, cotton and manufactured goods that came and left by ship. St. Eustatius was the foremost conduit through which the American colonists obtained guns and gunpowder from Europe required for the revolution. Nearly half of the wartime supplies used by the colonists came via this route. At the time, the British viewed St. Eustatius as one of the main reasons they were unable to achieve a quick victory.

Of interest is the historical footnote that St. Eustatius was the site of the first formal recognition by a foreign government of what would become the U.S. On November 16, 1776, a merchant ship flying the flag of the Continental Congress entered the port. On the orders of the governor, the guns of the local garrison fired a welcoming salvo, becoming the "first salute". The Dutch governor desired to trade and engage in commerce with that merchant ship.

From the 1500's through the early 1900's, the wooden barrel was the standard marine shipping container for transporting cargo. Typically made of wooden staves bound by wooden or metal hoops, the traditional barrel had a liquid capacity of 42 gallons. Barrels were ubiquitous and moved almost everything. Liquids such as rum and wine as well as a large array of dry goods and commodities moved in barrels. The major reason barrels were effective containers was that the round shape allowed it to be rolled by one man. This could be done when it was upright by rolling along the bottom edge or when it was on its side where only the small midsection touched the ground. The barrel shape made for efficient loading and unloading on a ship via a plank. While the weight of a loaded barrel would vary based on what it held, on average seven barrels would typically hold one ton of cargo.

This same wooden barrel also became the first container that was frequently interchanged between transport modes with the advent of the steam age. The barrel put on a steam train or Erie Canal barge would then be put on one of Fulton's steam powered paddlewheel ships. Hundreds of millions of wooden barrels were made. Coopers, the term for the craftsmen who constructed barrels with wooden staves and metal loops, made up one of the largest occupations from the 1500's through the 1800's. The wooden barrel would remain the main method of moving a wide assortment of goods on ships through the early 1900's before they were replaced with cardboard boxes.

The industrial revolution in the early 1800's triggered an increase in trade, first via sail and then via the revolutionary technology of steam power. Both the fast clipper ships and the faster steamships, combined with an explosion in migration and communal living, which in effect made the world smaller, made trade more viable. These advances in transport technology eroded what some historians have referred to as the tyranny of distance. It is interesting to note that steam powered cargo ships did not immediately replace sail powered cargo ships. Initially, early steamships focused on passengers. Their primary cargo was mail. A series of progressive improvements in steamship technology changed that, in time for an outside event to usher in the larger transition of cargo from sail to steam.

The industrial revolution began in England. With England's resulting economic dominance, it is not surprising that the largest trading lane in what has been referred to as the first age of globalization was between England and Asia. Trade between Asia and both Europe and the Americas quickly followed. Even after steamships were used on other routes, the Far Eastern trade was still dominated by fast sailing ships. Few steamships could carry enough coal to go around Africa enroute to Asia. The opening of the Suez Canal in 1869 immediately changed that dynamic. Steamships could readily handle that significantly shorter voyage. As a result, the canal opening was the death knell for moving cargo via sail.

The apex of trade via sailing ships with Asia would occur in the 1800's in the form of Clipper ships. There has never been ships so directly and completely associated with cargo movements as the Clipper ships. They were so named based on their ability to "clip along" and get as much speed as possible from available wind. This usually translated into speeds of 12 knots or better for ships that typically carried 800 to 1,000 tons of cargo.

The number of Clipper ships crested in 1852 when there were some 200 in service. American and British shipyards were the dominant builders of Clipper ships. Trade routes to and from China involved celebrated clippers like the *Cutty Sark, Sea Witch, Thernopylae* and *Pride of Baltimore*. Clipper races were key news items of the day and captivated the public. It was the Clipper ships of the Americans that ruled the seas.

In 1849, the *Sea Witch* sailed from Hong Kong to New York in just 74 days. That record would stand for over 150 years until it was surpassed recently by only a slight margin by a modern sailboat with obvious navigational and communications advantages. The skipper of that modern sailboat is a friend. His accomplishment in beating the long standing sailing record is significant, but he also has complete respect for the sailing abilities of the captain and crew of the *Sea Witch* for what they accomplished.

A granular insight into the actual cargo moved on these grand cargo sailing ships came from research inspired by a beautiful print I have in my study of the *City of Mobile*, an American clipper ship named after my hometown. When that ship arrived in London in 1845, an article on it appeared in the Illustrated London News. The article said that it arrived at the East India Docks with the largest cargo of wheat to ever leave America or enter London, or ever enter any port in the world, as well as a significant quantity of barreled flour and stores. The quantity of wheat was described as equal to 9800 quarters. That imperial measure is equivalent to 28 pounds, which means that this world-record wheat cargo shipment was equivalent to some 137 tons. While the article didn't say what the wheat was stored in, it was most likely either in burlap bags or in the barrels a diverse range of other cargo was stored in. We know it must have been a wide range of cargoes as the ship was described as being equal to 1,734 net registered tons with three decks for cargo and passenger accommodations on the top deck. The article said the ship would sail next for Liverpool in what was no doubt the first of many additional ports of call in Europe. While the ship was in London, it was inspected by the most respected captains in the port and pronounced to be the best-built and fastened ship ever to enter the port of London. Given that London was then the maritime capital of the world, that pronouncement underscores the allure of the fast clipper ships.

The most important port in the U.S. during the clipper ship era in the early to mid 1800's was Baltimore, which had a well-protected natural harbor. Second to Baltimore was Boston, another city with a great harbor whose commerce also benefited from its proximity to Nantucket Island, the whaling capital of the world at that time. The shipping and commerce in both Baltimore and Boston at that time handily eclipsed the shipping and commerce of New York City.

While New York City also had an extraordinary natural harbor that was the bedrock of its own development, it would take another maritime event to propel it well ahead of all its rivals. With the opening of the Erie Canal in 1825, New York City became the port with a direct and cost efficient water link to much of the Midwestern states. The Erie Canal provided an all-water route from the Great Lakes to the Hudson River, which then flowed down to New York City. The commerce that new route directly produced and the multiplier effect it had on the development of New York City was significant. The canal allowed the transport of goods for one-tenth the previous cost and less than half the previous time. The Erie Canal is an excellent example of the economic prime mover effect of shipping. With the beneficial effects of the Erie Canal, New York City quickly eclipsed both Baltimore and Boston as the center of shipping and was transformed into the commercial capital of the country.

Shortly after the peak of the clipper ship era, faster, more reliable steamships increasingly displaced sailing ships. Robert Fulton had in 1807 developed a commercially successful steamboat that moved passengers from New York City to Albany and back, a round trip of 300 miles, in 62 hours. Fulton would go on to improve designs for steamboats that changed the transportation landscape of the U.S. It was Fulton's initial innovation that played a key role in the industrial revolution that swept the U.S. and Europe as manufacturing processes transitioned from hand to machine. While Fulton wasn't the inventor of the steam engine or even steamboats, which were first used in England, his high profile adaption of both captured the attention of the public. Steam engines like the one Fulton used to power steamboats were soon being adapted for industrial uses to manufacture products. As steam engines became larger, they were put on ships that would venture across the oceans.

The *Savannah,* an American built and owned hybrid sailing ship and sidewheel steamer, was the first steamship to make a transatlantic crossing in 1819. The *Savannah* was a small ship with a 98' length and gross registered tons of 320. The steam engine that turned the sidewheels was rated at 90 horsepower. President James Monroe was in Savannah, Georgia and the vessel owner made him aware of his plans and invited him to tour the ship. President Monroe took a short excursion aboard the *Savannah* and later dined aboard the ship, expressing enthusiasm for the prospect of an American steamship being the first to cross the Atlantic. The vessel departed Savannah the next day and arrived in Liverpool just under 30 days later. Upon leaving port and at several key points along the way, it passed other ships. Those who saw volumes of smoke coming from the vessel assumed they were witnessing an historic crossing. The *Savannah* was, in fact, the first ship with sidewheels to cross the Altantic. However, her steam engine had operated for a total of only 80 hours during the crossing, or only 11% of the time. The large majority of the power for the *Savannah* to make her historic crossing had been provided by the wind. It would be almost twenty years before another ship would make a transatlantic crossing using steam power alone.

Even after the appearance of steamships, clipper ships grew in relative importance. The peak of the clipper ship era was more than 30 years after the historic transatlantic voyage of the *Savannah*.

The transition from sail to primarily steam took more than five decades. A key leader in that transition was the British Royal Navy. With the advent of steam propulsion technology, the British Navy recognized the operational benefits steam power offered. Steam powered warships were faster with more consistent speeds. They were also less subjected to the weather in transiting the seas and less dependant on wind conditions. Of great importance, they had better access to inland waterways.

Employing this new technology required that the British Navy had sufficient access to coal to fuel its steam engines. England's vast coal resources made getting coal in its homeports easy. To ensure that its ships would have access to coal around the globe, the British Navy systematically supported the establishment of coal bunkering facilities at strategic ports around the world. The catalytic role of establishing this infrastructure would, in turn, play a role in the transition from sail power to steam power among cargo ships.

In 1838, the British vessel *Great Western* became the first purpose-built steamship to regularly cross the Atlantic. Isambard Brunel, who also played a key role in developing England's railroads as well as its bridge and tunnel infrastructure, designed the ship. Brunel's designs revolutionized public transport and modern engineering earning him recognition as one of the most ingenious engineers in history. The *Great Western* was an iron strapped, wooden, side-wheel paddle steamer that was 252' long and documented at 1,700 gross registered tons. She had four masts to hold sails that were not just used for auxiliary power, but also used in rough weather to reduce rolling in order to ensure that both paddles remained in the water.

As she was being built, critics claimed that the *Great Western* was simply too big. However, Brunel, who also headed up the investor group that owned the *Great Western,* was both an extraordinary naval architect and an astute businessman. Brunel knew that the carrying capacity of a ship increases as the cube of its dimensions, while the water resistance only increases as the square of its dimensions. Larger ships, therefore, were much more cost efficient per unit of cargo carried.

These simple principles, embraced first by Brunel, become the key catalyst in the development of modern cargo ships. The *Great Western* met and exceeded expectations in its transatlantic service. That success quickly resulted in the development of additional paddle steamers. In its initial two years of service, the *Great Western's* average westbound crossing to New York took 16 days for an average speed of 7.9 nautical miles per hour, or knots. The eastbound crossing to Bristol took 13 days for a 9.6-knot average speed.

Based on the initial success of the *Great Western,* Brunel and his investor group sought growth. Keenly aware of the scale economics of larger ships, Brunel designed what would be the world's largest vessel. He first determined that this ship would have an iron hull rather than the traditional wooden hull. The industrial revolution made iron more cost effective. Iron hulls were not subject to dry rot, were less bulkly, and had greater structural strength. The practical limit on the length of a wooden hull ship was some 300', but that was not the case with iron hulled ships. Brunel embraced iron-hulled technology and each draft design of his new vessel was bigger than the draft design before. When construction of the new ship, which was to be named the *Great Britain,* began, Brunel's plans called for it to be 320' long with a capacity of 3,400 tons, making it 42% larger than any ship in existence.

As the *Great Britain* was being built, Brunel made a major design change. He abandoned the side-wheel paddle engines, already half constructed, for new engines built around a propeller propulsion system. Only months earlier the first screw propelled ship had gone into service. Brunel focused on ways of improving the efficiency of *Great Britain's* paddle wheels and immediately became interested in the new propeller technology. After making arrangements to conduct tests with the propeller ship using different propeller designs, he became convinced of its superiority as a propulsion system. To his investor group Brunel argued that, even with the increase in cost and construction time, the design change was well worth it.

Brunel reasoned that a screw propeller offered six distinct advantages over side-wheel paddles. Screw propulsion machinery was lighter, thereby improving fuel economy. The machinery could be placed lower in the hull, which lowered the ship's center of gravity and kept the vessel stable. Because they required less room, propeller engines allowed more cargo to be carried. By eliminating the bulky side-wheel paddles, the ship met with less water resistance and was more maneuverable. Unlike paddle wheels whose water depth was changing constantly depending on waves at sea and cargo onboard, a propeller was always completely submerged and operating at full efficiency. Finally, screw propulsion machinery was actually less expensive than side-wheel paddle machinery in comparisons involving both as original alternatives. Brunel's arguments were persuasive and the *Great Britain* was built with the new propeller technology. The building of the *Great Britain* by Brunel, the man who was effectively the first naval architect focused on cargo ships, would have far reaching consequences. Wood was replaced by iron and propellers allowed the real power of steam engines to be harnessed.

In 1843, the *Great Britain,* the longest and largest capacity ship in the world, was launched amid much fanfare. The biggest steam engines ever built provided it with power. Due to all of its superlatives and because it embraced new technology and many engineering firsts, some of which had yet to be actually tried, the *Great Britain* was viewed with a combination of both awe and skepticism. One leading British newspaper referred to it as "the greatest experiment since Creation". The ship was christened before thousands of spectators by Prince Albert, who arrived on a royal train from London conducted by Brunel, and the launching of the *Great Britain* was covered by newspapers around the world.

After further refinements by Brunel on the size and shape of the propeller, the *Great Britain* generally achieved speeds in the 10 to 11 knot range in transatlantic service. The large iron hull proved more than satisfactory. Brunel had designed it with massive redundant strength by including ten longitudinal iron girders installed along the keel. This technique paved the way for the larger iron vessels to come. The *Great Britain* embodied the replacement of both wood by iron and paddle wheels by propellers. The 1846 grounding would curtail the transatlantic service of the *Great Britain* but not the type of ship that it had ushered in. Today, the *Great Britain* floats alongside the dock in Bristol as a museum ship. In a 2002 poll of the one hundred greatest Britons in history, Isambard Brunel was ranked second after Winston Churchill and ahead of Charles Darwin, William Shakespeare and Sir Isaac Newton.

The difference in how power is translated into propulsion as ships transitioned from paddle wheels to propellers is highlighted by the prefix that comes before a vessel's name. Most people assume that the prefix *SS* before a vessel's name refers to *steam ship*. That is only partially correct as *SS* actually refers to *screw steamer*. The initial steamships had the prefix of *PS* for *paddle steamer*

Recreational sailing remains to this day an activity enjoyed by millions of people around the world. While technology has resulted in enhancements, the basic mechanics of using wind power to propel a sailboat are largely unchanged for thousands of years. To be on a small sailboat offshore is one of the most intensive interactions one can have with nature with the energy of the water below you and the power of the wind above you. Its interesting to note that recreational sailing was a passion of Albert Einstein's throughout his life. He craved sailing in his spare time and it is easy to believe he sorted out some of his groundbreaking thoughts while sailing. After all, the elemental natural forces that make sailing possible are directly linked to the elemental forces that Einstein's genius recognized as binding the universe together. He once told a reporter that "atomic power is no more unnatural than when I sail my boat on Saranac Lake."

The advent of steam engines displaces sailing vessels, initially at a slow pace via paddle wheels and later at an accelerated pace as propeller based propulsion systems were developed and refined. The steel hull, screw propeller driven prototype general cargo ship that was introduced by the *Great Britain* would effectively be the preferred model for the next one hundred years. Similar vessels consistently got a little bigger, eventually growing to about four times the capacity of the *Great Britain* based on the simple principle that Brunel had realized, namely that vessel capacity was a cube function while vessel construction and operating costs were a square function. This principle resulted in larger ships that reduced overall costs per cargo unit. That same principle later moved into overdrive during the post-World War II period as specialization gave birth to the modern cargo vessel age and ships exponentially bigger than Brunel could ever have imagined were built.

Moving a diverse range of cargoes from and to dozens of ports was how cargo was transported, whether by clipper ships or by steamships. Despite the difference in size of the vessels, how cargo moved in them and how they were loaded and unloaded was fundamentally the same –

unspecialized and inefficient. A picture in my study is a constant reminder of this. It shows a Waterman Steamship vessel in the 1930's with dozens of large wooden barrels on the pier waiting to be loaded one by one on the vessel. This operation was fundamentally not too different than the loading operation of smaller vessels four hundred years earlier.

One of the first commercial shipments of oil was from the U.S. to Europe in 1861 aboard a conventional sailing ship when kerosene was moved in wooden barrels. Oil and related products continued to move in barrels and cans. As trade in oil expanded, the cost of moving it in barrels and cans promoted the development of bulk transport of oil, which occurred in the early part of the twentieth century. With that development, tankers became the first example of a special purpose ship.

Much of the oil trade towards the end of the 1800's involved moving Russian crude oil on small early tankers from the Black Sea to the Far East. Initially these vessels were not allowed to transit the Suez Canal as they were deemed to be a fire or explosion risk. However, an enterprising importer asked the Suez Canal Company for the specifications of a tanker it would allow through the canal. Three early tankers with separate compartments for moving oil and a deadweight capacity of 5,010 tons were constructed. These were the first tankers of the Tank Syndicate, a startup company that eventually morphed into the Royal Dutch Shell Company, the giant integrated oil company that is currently the largest corporation in the world in terms of revenues. In 1892, one of those vessels became the first tanker to transit the Suez Canal.

The relative smallness of the early tanker sector in 1907 was evident by the fleets of the two largest oil companies in the world. Royal Dutch Shell had 24 steam driven oil tankers and Standard Oil, the forerunner of Exxon and many other oil companies, had 20 tankers, 16 of which were sail powered. Most of these early tankers were small and involved mainly in coastal trade. The international oil trade remained fairly insignificant until World War II.

By the beginning of the twentieth century, most cargo ships were steam powered. Few vessels traveled at more than 10 knots. The British Empire had been built largely on the strength of the British Navy, which still ruled the seas. Great Britain was also the world leader in terms of both its merchant marine fleet and shipbuilding industry. In 1915, the worldwide merchant marine fleet totaled 49 million tons. With an average of around 6,000 tons per vessel, the world's merchant fleet was comprised of slightly more than 8,000 vessels. Of this tonnage, 44% were British flag, 12% were American flag, 10% were German flag and 5% were French flag. All of the other registries combined totaled only 29% of the world's merchant marine fleet.

The breakout of World War I was a catalyst for shipbuilding activity by the Allies, particularly in the U.S. By early 1917, over 200 Allied merchant marine ships per month were being destroyed by Germany's unrestricted submarine warfare. The U.S. built over one thousand cargo ships, providing as much tonnage for the war effort as the British shipyards. Large parts of the hulls of many of those ships were built with wood. An estimated 40% of the ships were sunk. At the end of the war, many of the ships in better condition were laid-up as a ready reserve fleet to be used should another crisis develop. As a consequence, the impact that cargo ships built during World War I had on the world's merchant marine fleets after the end of the war was fairly minimal.

No ships were more directly and completely associated with cargo movements and world trade prior to the post World War II period than the Clipper ships. Throughout much of the nineteenth century they dominated the economic activity of many coastal cities in the U.S. The southern tip of Manhattan was full of clipper ships unloading their goods onto horse drawn wagons. Boston and Baltimore and San Francisco were similar hubs of marine commerce and activity. Local newspapers would report on their front page what ships were expected and from where they were coming from. Almost everyone was aware of the comings and goings of these magnificent sailing vessels. The public would turn out in large numbers to see them.

During the clipper ship era, shipping and everything related to it was America's largest industry other than agriculture by millions of small farmers. Shipping was the first industry with large scale within a sole enterprise. Many large companies that exist in America today can and do translate their heritage back to a shipping company in early America. The key point is that cargo shipping two centuries ago had a significantly higher profile with the American public than it does today.

Yesterday's much celebrated clipper ships are dwarfed in any comparisons with their much lesser know modern day counterparts. The capacities of those famous cargo ships do not move the needle compared to the capacity of today's cargo ships. Even at the top of the Clipper ship era, the collective cargo capacity of those ships was just .01% of the cargo capacity of today's cargo ships.

The reason for this dichotomy is simple and complex at the same time. Relative to today's trade levels, there was not much world trade prior to World War II. This dearth of trade was not for lack of a large number of steam powered cargo ships. In 1936, there were almost five thousand general cargo vessels. But with an average of just $1/13^{th}$ of the cargo capacity of a typical vessel today and geometrically less efficient processes for loading and unloading vessels, this much smaller merchant fleet could handle only a small fraction of the volume of cargo that can be moved with today's fleet. Changes in vessel size and productivity of moving cargo revolutionized shipping efficiency in the post World War II period.

The term revolution is often overused, but is an appropriate description of what occurred in cargo shipping post World War II. The changes that took place following World War II was more far reaching than anything since cargo first moved by ship 5,000 years ago in Egypt. The men profiled in this book were at the forefront of technological advances in building ships, process advances in loading and unloading ships and business practice advances in how those ships were deployed and operated. Collectively, the advances spawned by these entrepreneurs resulted in the development of the modern cargo shipping industry that would be the major driver in the sharp growth of world trade.

In 1936 the U.S.'s total total trade was $4.2 billion. By 2017 the U.S.'s total total trade had grown to $5.2 trillion. This extraordinary growth in postwar trade, equivalent to a 9.1% annual rate over the entire 81-year period, is well known. What is broadly unappreciated is the direct role modern cargo vessels played as a catalyst for the explosion in world trade by exponentially improving on the cost efficiency of moving cargo.

World War II was the catalyst that laid the groundwork for the modern cargo shipping era. Economists know that war is a great economic prime mover. It was that and more with regard to cargo shipping. The war initiated a staggering increase in the metrics of cargo shipping.

This revolution in cargo shipping started in the U.S. with the building of the Liberty ships. In the 10 years prior to 1940, the U.S. built a total of 23 cargo ships. In the next 5 years, that number increased by a factor of more than 200 times as the U.S. built over 4,600 cargo ships. Those ships and the techniques developed in building them, and the refinements inspired by them, gave birth to the modern cargo shipping era.

The world's pre-war merchant marine fleet was dominated by British, American, French, Italian and Japanese vessels. These vessels were typically in the 6,000 deadweight ton range. Today's largest vessels carry more than 60 times as much cargo as those vessels. As a result of giant leaps in cargo handling productivity as a function of specialized design, today's ships are also typically in and out of port in less than a day compared to days or even weeks required by previous vessels.

The marine cargo that moved pre-war was prosaic. It had little to do with relative costs and more to do with products that were not available otherwise. Key exports by the U.S. were grain, cars and tractors while key imports were wine from France, marble from Italy and coffee from Brazil. The products that were shipped were typically viewed as unique and differentiated. Marble from Italy arrived in the U.S. with a hefty freight charge. The concept of outsourcing and transferring production to another location to take advantage of labor or other input costs simply did not exist at that time.

Early cargo ships differed in two fundamentally important ways from modern cargo ships. Early vessels were small and generally lacked specialization. Their smallness and their design as general cargo vessels translated into much higher cargo costs. Marine transportation results in significant cost economies of scale as vessels get larger. Specialization by cargo type results in better utilization of available vessel space and also sharply reduces the time and cost involved in loading and unloading vessels, both of which contribute to better cost economics. Containerization was where specialization would have the most pronounced impact. It was the great equalizer, allowing a wide variety of cargo to move in the most efficient manner.

These early cargo vessels would spend weeks in port loading a broad array of cargo. Liquids in barrels, a variety of other types of cargo in barrels, cargo in an endless variety of boxes and crates and grain in bags would all be manhandled aboard in a time consuming and costly loading operation involving cargo boons and shipboard winches. Nothing was unitized and there was very little similarity from winching aboard one net of cargo to the next. Each presented its own issues and challenges. Carpenters were needed constantly to construct wooden bulkheads to both separate cargo and prevent dangerous shifting while the vessel was at sea.

Dozens of men engaged in backbreaking manual labor would be swarming all over the vessel. Muscle power alone was involved in the tedious job of stowing and securing cargo. Large gangs of longshoremen were needed throughout a ships time in port. In many respects, up until the 1950's vessels were loaded and unloaded in ways similar to how they had been fifteen hundred years earlier by the Romans. Each barrel or box or crate or bag would be moved from a warehouse and placed in cargo nets or on pallets or cargo trays to be winched aboard. An equally time consuming process of moving the crate or bag or barrel to where it would be stowed on the ship occurred when it was onboard.

Besides vessel size, the main difference between the 1950's and earlier times, even going back to the Roman era, was how those barrels, boxes, crates or bags got on and off vessels. For hundreds of years, a man walking up a plank carried each item. The limit to what could be loaded each time was what a man could carry. This was basically the limit for thousands of years. Various rigging was developed that allowed multiple items to be swung on a vessel in a cargo net, but the items still had to be individually put in the net and stowed on the vessel. With the advent of steamships, that rigging took the form of derricks on the deck that could be adjusted to winch cargo onboard. When these derricks were combined with wire cable and powered winches, the weight of cargo that could be swung onboard was increased. However, it still remained an intensely laborious task with each individual item generally handled multiple times as the vessel was being loaded. Manual labor and muscle power were still the primary ingredients to loading and unloading cargo vessels.

Determining where and when to load each ports unique mix of cargo to avoid damage from the effect of either other cargo or the occasional ingress of sea water required great care amd skill. For instance, before the development of modern fertilizers, one of the larger cargoes was dried manure shipped to farmers. Most workers tasked with loading and unloading vessels, known as longshoreman or dockers, knew that water degraded that cargo and created a bad smell. To avoid this problem, bundles of dried manure were marked "Stow High In Transit". The resulting acronym found its way into popular language as an expression of something unpleasant.

A cargo vessel earns its revenue at sea by moving something from the origin port to the destination port. Port time is an inefficient use of vessel time. Despite loading only a very small fraction of the amount of cargo in today's modern vessels, early cargo vessels always took much longer to load and unload. Cargo handling practices of the time and their lack of specialization resulted in inefficient use of the vessel, expensive stevedoring operations and high shipping costs.

As large as the difference from stevedoring and other inefficiencies was, an even larger cost disadvantage, compared to modern vessels, resulted from the small shipment sizes and the lack of scale economies evident in today's vessels. Like Brunel recognized, as ships and cargo sizes get larger, costs do not rise much, resulting in ever decreasing shipping costs per equivalent unit. Those scale economies are significant and their absence burdened early cargo vessels.

The overall cost of shipping anything from one country to another is a built-in barrier to trade between those countries. Even if something can be produced in one country for less cost, shipping costs can make it non-competitive in another country. Prior to the modern era of large, specialized cargo vessels, total shipping costs were often equal to 50% or more of the value of the product being shipped. This large additional cost acted as a tangible barrier to trade between countries. Where shipping costs relative to product value was most important involved substitutable products that could be made in multiple locations. In those cases, relatively low shipping costs could energize trade.

In addition to the high direct cost of shipping, early cargo vessels also suffered cargo losses due to damage and pilferage. More damage resulted from the multiple times the cargo was handled as well as the lack of vessel specialization. Early cargo vessels also typically experienced more water damage at sea. Because of the large number of people involved in loading and unloading operations along with warehousing activities, pilferage and cargo theft was difficult to police.

Depending on the cargo, theft losses could be significant. Food and alcohol shipments were particularly tempting targets. It was not unusual for dockworkers to engage in on-board consumption of fruitcakes, candy or whiskey, which was particularly hard to prevent. Elaborate methods to steal scotch and other whiskey products existed. In New Jersey, for example, women were known to sew special pockets into the inside of their husbands jackets sized to allow a whiskey bottle to be concealed and not detected when they exited the vessel. The incidence of such theft almost always increased around Christmas and other holidays. Another indirect cost of cargo vessels was imprecise schedules, owing to inefficient cargo operations, which made it difficult to plan a precise timetable for exports and imports.

Between the high relative direct cost of shipping and the vagaries that resulted from damage, pilferage and imprecise schedules, prior to the modern vessel era moving cargo by sea was just for the intrepid. The vision of the nine individual pioneers chronicled in later pages would change that forever.

The September, 1937 edition of Fortune Magazine, the pre-eminent business periodical, was dedicated entirely to reviewing the U.S. flag shipping industry. It included specific shipping cost data that put the issue of relative costs then versus now into sharp perspective. That issue stated that the total cost to ship copper wire from New York to Brazil was $20.75 per ton in 1936. According to an inflation calculator available at the U.S. Bureau of Labor Statistics, that amount would be equivalent to $353.40 per ton in 2014. Today copper wire would be moved in a 20' container where 38,000 pounds of wire, equal to 19 tons, could be loaded. That same 20' container could be moved to Brazil today for $1,135, or the equivalent of $59.74 per ton. In other words, the relative cost of shipping today is just 1/6th of what it was. This random example is typical of the exponential advances in shipping cost efficiency across a myriad of cargoes.

That geometric reduction in the relative cost of shipping has rippled through the economies of the world and made trade possible now that was not possible in the past. Where that is most important is in the thousands of products that flow from one country to another seeking out the lowest costs in labor and other inputs. In those cases, shipping efficiency has resulted in countless arbitrages that have been a primary catalyst in increasing world trade. Today marine shipping has become so efficient that a product can be moved halfway around the world for less than it would cost to move that same product domestically. For example, a 40' container of electronics can be moved from Shanghai to New York for $2,000 or approximately 1% of the value of the shipment. To move those same products domestically from Austin, Texas to New York would cost approximately $3,000. In that example, the international shipping costs are almost inconsequential. Shipping efficiency has made the manufacturing world smaller. Transport costs that were a barrier to world trade are now an enabler of world trade. The modern cargo shipping industry has energized David Ricardo's two centuries old Theory of Comparative Advantage by significantly reducing trade friction in the form of shipping costs.

Paradoxically, the shipping industry was better known and a larger industry in relative terms prior to the efficiency of the modern vessel era. The September, 1937 edition of Fortune had a cover emblazoned with the smokestack logos of some 40 U.S. flag shipping companies. The 200-page issue noted that the annual revenue of the U.S. shipping companies was approximately $210 million, an amount that was similar to the entire soft-drink industry at the time. At that time, the U.S. flag shipping companies engaged in both domestic and foreign trade with the 953 cargo vessels they operated. Those vessels represented one-fifth of the world's merchant marine fleet. However, those vessels were miniscule in size relative to today's cargo ships. Today, the shipping industry is a more important cog in the world's economy than it has ever been but ironically its profile and relative fortunes have diminished considerably.

Another aspect of shipping that increased its profile in the past was passenger shipping as a means of actual transport. In 1936, an estimated 679,000 people made transatlantic passages and an equal number went to other destinations. Passenger shipping as a means of transport has all but disappeared today, having been displaced by the speedier and more efficient airplane.

Despite this increase in efficiency, or in part because of it, in times past the shipping industry was better known to the public than it is today. The increased efficiency of the industry has resulted in its fading from the public view as ships spent less time in port and more time at sea where they were out of sight.

World War II was the line of demarcation for both world trade and the modern cargo vessel era. It all started with Henry Kaiser's Liberty vessels and their transition to merchant marine use. The immediate availability of thousands of breakbulk ships at relatively low prices energized shipping and started the industry on the path of bigger and better ships. The construction techniques that were developed in building Liberty ships, as well as the use and conversion of the vessels themselves, were the catalysts that spurred the development of specialized and larger vessels. Breakbulk vessels that moved most types of cargo on their multiple decks gave way to specialized vessels, the most important ones of which were container ships, bulkers and tankers. As vessel designs and shipyard capabilities became more refined, ships grew larger and delivered economies of scale. The lower overall costs of those vessels made trade possible where it was not possible before due to shipping costs. The vessels were the chicken and world trade was the egg, not vice versa. Shipping costs went from 50% or more to 1% or less of the value for some products, and products that were not even moved before are now moved in great quantities.

Ships were trending up in average size prior to and during World War II, but the shipping pioneers profiled in this book drove the real increase in size during the postwar period. While there are now 17,554 cargo ships longer than 600', there was not even a single cargo ship in that category at the end of the war. That was not for lack of engineering capability. After all, what are still some of the tallest buildings and biggest dams had been built by then. The limitation was on the demand side and the ships were right sized for the trade occurring at the time. The lack of specialization resulted in significant port time and that was also a constraint on size. As specialization took hold with the new container and bulk carrier categories and became broader within the tanker category, that constraint was reduced. The transition from an industrial shipping model driven by long term contracts to a supply driven model would also play a role. It was, however, the insight and actions of these extraordinary men that set in motion a relentless climb in ship sizes across categories. As vessels got bigger, owners would often chose to match that size with new orders just to stay competitive. More often than not, this led to an over supply of vessel capacity that would push down rates. Chronic excess supply is certainly bad for the economic results of the shipping industry, but the rates that result from it are a further positive catalyst for trade volume.

There is a void in the historical account of the role played in world affairs by these giant ships and the individual giants who created them. These efficient leviathans have been the greatest prime mover of world trade. Without them, world trade would be a small fraction of what it is today and the achievement of world peace would be eminently more challenging. The revolution that has occurred quietly and over decades in the postwar period has benefited mankind immensely.

4. Overview of Ship Types Today

Today there are three primary categories of cargo vessels - container ships, tankers and bulk carriers. There is also an array of general multi-purpose and specialized vessels that do not fit squarely into one of the three primary categories. Prior to World War II, most cargo vessels fit into the general multi-purpose category. Of today's three primary categories, the only one that existed on a much smaller scale then was the tanker category. Both container ships and modern bulk carriers were yet to be invented.

Container ships primarily move finished goods that were loaded at the point of origin into steel containers, typically measuring 40' long by 8' wide by 8.5' high. These containers move inland on chassis pulled by trucks or via railroad to the port, where they are loaded onto vessels with large gantry cranes and unloaded the same way. The customer pays an all-inclusive amount per container for this service. Strings of vessels provide a regularly scheduled service between the same series of ports and are often referred to as liner operators. Due to the integrated focus of this business, the profit and loss statements include much more than just the activities of the vessels. The establishment of a liner service typically requires an investment in multiple vessels, container equipment, cranes and terminals to build an integrated transportation system.

No transportation segment is as directly involved with and responsible for world trade as container ships. While it is the smallest of the three primary sectors in terms of cargo weight at 1.8 billion tons in 2017, it leads the way with cargo value. In 2017, container ships moved 161.7 million twenty-foot equivalent units, or TEU's, the metric used to measure volume. Those container units represented $7.0 trillion worth of goods in 2017, equal to 60% of the total value of world trade moving by water.

Container ships are the primary supply chain for world trade and the main catalyst for globalization. A strong argument can be made that globalization was born on April 26, 1956 when Malcom McLean, who invented container shipping, first sailed the vessel *Ideal X*. Coincidentally, in that same month the first Toyota was imported into the U.S., a precursor to the wave of imported cars that would follow in what became the first sign of globalization to most Americans. Today, Americans buy millions of cars each year that are made overseas, but the majority come into the U.S. as components in containers which are then put together in assembly plants as just one example of complex multi-country manufacturing that is globalization today.

In 2017, container ships handled the equivalent of $933 worth of goods annually for every person on earth. That is a staggering per capita economic contribution and is driven by the much higher cargo value on container ships compared to other sectors. On an overall basis, the average value per ton of cargo moved on container ships is 7.4 times and 24.7 times more valuable, respectively, than the average value per ton of cargo moved on tankers and dry-bulk vessels. An interesting metric that takes into account these relative differences but that also telegraphs something about pricing dynamics is a comparison of cargo value to newbuilding cost for the largest vessels in each category. The largest container ships in the world today carry 21,413 TEU's and were built for $159 million each. Fully loaded, those ships would be carrying $931 million worth of goods, almost six times their construction cost.

Tankers typically move a single cargo comprised either of crude oil or some refined petroleum product such as gasoline. These liquid bulk cargoes are loaded via pipeline by pumping from nearby tanks on shore and unloaded the same way. Tankers are contracted out by the vessel owner on a single voyage basis, known as a voyage charter, or for a defined period of time, known as a time charter. In a voyage charter, the vessel owner is paid a lump sum to move a full shipload between two ports and is responsible for all costs. With a time charter, the vessel owner is paid an agreed amount per day for the vessel and its crew with all other expenses, including vessel fuel and port expenses, paid directly by the charterer who also directs where the vessel goes. A variant of a time charter is a bareboat charter where the owner provides the vessel with the charterer providing and paying for the crew. These bareboat charters are for a longer period than a time charter. The profit and loss statement of a tanker is comprised primarily of charter income and direct vessel expenses. Entry into the tanker business can be attained through the purchase of a single vessel.

The tanker segment moved 3.5 billion tons of crude oil and various petroleum products in 2017. That movement was the equivalent of 73% of the 97 million barrels per day of petroleum products that are consumed around the world. No end market is so dependent on shipping as the various markets served by tankers. Given this, it is not surprising that the tanker segment was the first to experience the significant progression in vessel size that resulted in increased efficiency through scale economies.

In 2017, tankers delivered $256 worth of crude oil and petroleum related products for each person on the globe. The amount shipped was equivalent to 145 gallons per capita, enough fuel for 7.5 billion people to each drive a car almost four thousand miles. The typical VLCC built today has a 307,356-ton deadweight capacity, carries almost 2.3 million barrels and has a new construction cost of $105 million. Fully loaded with crude oil, the $135 million worth of cargo on that VLCC is worth 1.3 times its construction cost.

Bulk carriers, often referred to as dry-bulk ships or bulkers, typically move a single dry commodity cargo such as iron ore, coal, wheat, corn or some other mineral or food related product. They are loaded via conveyor belt or gravity chute connected to nearby storage facility and unloaded by cranes with buckets or special pneumatic devices. Like tankers, bulkers are typically contracted out on a voyage charter basis or a time charter basis. With a voyage charter, the vessel owner gets a lump sum to deliver a cargo to a specific destination and is responsible for all vessel costs. In a time charter, the vessel owner is paid an agreed amount per day with all other expenses, including vessel fuel and port expenses, paid directly by the charterer who also directs where the ship goes. The profit and loss statements of a bulker is also comprised primarily of charter income and direct vessel expenses and this business can be entered through the purchase of a single vessel.

Bulk carriers are the workhorses of the industry and they are the largest segment in terms of tons moved and the one with the most ships. The 4.5 trillion tons of dry-products they moved in 2017 represent the majority of total worldwide consumption of those products.

In 2017, bulk carriers moved a staggering 1,352 pounds of various commodities for every person on the planet. Due to the relatively low value of most of what is moved on bulk carriers, the per capita value of cargo moved in 2017 was just $102. The largest VLOC or Very Large Ore Carrier have a deadweight capacity of 400,000 tons and are built for $130 million. If fully loaded with iron ore, the cargo value on those vessels would be $20.4 million, equivalent to just one-sixth of the vessel construction cost.

Outside of those three primary types, there are other general multi-purpose ships along with very specialized vessels such as car carriers, refrigerated ships, livestock carriers, heavy-lift ships, drill ships and other types involved with the offshore exploration and storage of petroleum related cargoes. In total, they moved 748 billion tons of cargo in 2017. Collectively, they do not move nearly as much cargo as each of the three primary categories. However, the cargo they move is relatively high value and includes new vehicles and a broad array of manufactured items and merchandise goods. It is still a third below the value per ton of cargo typically moved on container ships. In 2017, this overall category of vessels moved the equivalent of $265 worth of cargo for everyone on the globe.

The characteristics of the various types of cargoes have a pronounced effect on the design of the vessels that have been developed to move those specialized cargoes. A primary distinction relates to the weight of the cargo as that is directly related to the capacity and stability characteristics of the vessel. Dense, heavy cargoes need less space than lighter, more volumetric cargoes and all of this is reflected in the design of the hull and its cargo carrying components.

This distinction can be reduced down to whether the product being moved is considered a weight cargo or a measurement cargo. The former is determined by actual weight, typically expressed in metric tons. The latter is determined by dividing the occupied space in cubic feet by 40 to get the measurement tons. The benchmark of 40 cubic feet per ton is the line of demarcation between what is considered a weight cargo and what is considered a measurement cargo. Crude oil, the biggest commodity moved by tankers, is a weight cargo and 31 cubic feet of crude oil are needed to weigh in at one metric ton. Iron ore, the biggest commodity moved by bulk carriers, is almost three times heavier and only 11 cubic feet are needed to weigh in at one metric ton. Container freight, on the other hand, is a measurement cargo with 131 cubic feet of typical container freight needed to weigh in at one ton.

This basic difference of whether something is a weight cargo or a measurement cargo affects many of the physical characteristics of the vessel such as how deep in the water it moves and how much cargo it can safely carry. Those physical characteristics then impact and directly influence the cost and economic aspects of the different vessel types. There is a tension between the natural elements that impact vessel design and economic performance and that is why regulations exist and vessels are routinely inspected.

Suffice to say the engineering that goes into a modern cargo vessel to ensure that it can safely accommodate the cargo it was designed to carry is significant. As the largest moving objects ever built by man, the stresses that vessels experience are considerable and complex. Furthermore, those stresses are dynamic rather than static as vessels move through the sea in all conditions with waves leading to movement in all directions.

We selected an overall length of 600', equivalent to two football fields, as the cutoff for determining a giant cargo vessel. Mandatory electronic identification information all vessels are required to broadcast shows there were 17,546 vessels in that category on January 4, 2018. In addition to location, speed and recent voyage history, certain characteristics including vessel length are available from various databases. Most of the vessel statistics in this text come from one such database maintained by Bloomberg.

The individual sections on vessel types will include breakdowns of the vessels into categories in which they are more typically known. Here we will focus on length, a metric that is easy to understand and to visualize. All of the 17,546 vessels over 600' in length are primarily involved in long ocean voyages. Our ocean highways are also actively utilized by thousands of smaller vessels. For instance, there are another 13,699 vessels of all types between 300' and 600' in lenght. However, as a group, vessels greater than 600' long have an average length of 832' and an average deadweight of 91,546 metric tons. Deadweight is the total weight of cargo, stores and fuel that can be safely transported on a vessel. The cargo deadweight of vessels is typically 95% of total deadweight tonnage.

If we use 300' in length, still a big vessel, as the cutoff, our universe of large vessels grows to 31,245 currently. Lined up end to end, that line of ships would stretch 3,934 miles. Those vessels could form a literal bridge between the U.S. and Europe, on which an individual could hypothetically walk between continents without ever touching water. But such a bridge could move nothing relative to the trillions of tons of cargo that the world's merchant fleet moves efficiently and quietly each year.

The table below summarizes the major types of vessels as of January 4, 2018 in 300' increments of total length. Each column shows cumulative data for the ships in that category. For instance, in the 600' plus category, there are 17,546 ships that would stretch 2,766 miles if lined up end to end based on their average length of 832'. The table also includes data for vessels in the range up to the next size. For example, there are 12,926 vessels ranging from 600' to 900' in length, 4,324 vessels in the 900' to 1200' range and 296 vessels in the over 1200' in length category.

Type	Ships > 300'	Ships > 600'	Ships > 900'	Ships > 1200'
Container	4,932	3,048	1,562	294
Tanker	9,766	4,810	1,353	2
Bulk Carriers	9,420	7,849	1,542	0
Other	7,127	1,830	163	0
Total	31,245	17,546	4,620	296
Ships In Range	13,699	12,926	4,324	296
Overall Miles	3,934	2,766	930	70
Average Length	665'	832'	1,063'	1,250'
DWT (000's):				
Total In Range	194,398	808,510	749,817	47,937
Container	253,487	225,736	163,322	47,054
Tanker	647,997	566,549	290,344	883
Bulk Carriers	751,793	721,272	305,421	0
Other	147,385	92,706	38,667	0
Total Overall	1,800,661	1,606,263	797,753	47,937

DWT/Ship:				
Total In Range	14,191	62,549	173,408	161,948
Container	51,396	74,060	104,559	160,046
Tanker	66,352	117,786	214,593	441,573
Bulk Carriers	79,808	91,893	198,068	0
Other	20,680	50,411	237,220	0
Total Overall	57,630	91,546	172,674	161,948

As the table shows, in the 600' plus category, bulk carriers constitute the largest number and represent 44.7% of all vessels that long. They are followed by tankers, which represent 27.4% and container vessels, which represent 17.4%. The other categories outside of the three main categories, comprised of vehicle carriers, passenger vessels, vessels involved in offshore energy exploration and general cargo vessels, represent 10.5% of vessels with a 600' plus length.

The number of vessels, however, is just one metric by which the different categories can be compared. The varying size, capacity and speed of the vessels, along with characteristics of the cargo such as value, among others, provide additional ways to compare and contrast the different categories of vessels as well as the different classes of vessel within each category.

The table summarizes the deadweight tons and average deadweight tons both within the various length ranges and for all vessels overall equal to or above each length range. Note that as the metrics in the table above includes all categories of vessels, that results in an anomaly in the deadweight for the highest length range. Because that length is mainly container ships while the prior range includes high deadweight bulk carriers and tankers, the average deadweight does actually decrease. Deadweight is not a particularly useful metric for container ships both because their cargo is relatively light and almost half of the containers are typically loaded on deck.

When making comparisons across all ship categories, deadweight tonnage has some limitations but it is still the best across the board metric to use, especially as compared to other tonnage measures. As the above table shows, the total deadweight capacity of all cargo vessels more than 300' long is currently 1,800,661,482 tons, or an average of 57,630 tons at the 31,245 ships. Based on the January 4, 2018 world population of 7,530,103,737 people, that average works out to an average of 536 pounds of deadweight capacity for each person on the planet. That is a static measure that approximates the per capita carrying capacity at any given time of the world's merchant marine fleet. Today the typical cargo vessel makes 6.19 roundtrip voyages per year. By extension and with the simplifying assumptions that cargo is moved on only one leg of each voyage and capacity is reached at 95% of deadweight, which translates into this merchant marine fleet having a capacity to move 3,153 pounds of cargo for each person annually. That statistic is worth reflecting on as it is breathetaking and highlights the significant but largely invisible role cargo ships play in everyone's daily lives. Reducing it down to a daily figure, each day cargo ships in effect deliver 8.6 pounds worth of tangible commodities and goods to each of the earth's 7.5 billion residents. Shipping affects every person's life every day.

These same broad measures can be used to chart the extraordinary long-term growth in overall merchant marine shipping capacity. In 1915, the total deadweight capacity of the world's merchant marine fleet stood at 49 million tons. This was comprised of 8,210 ships with an average capacity of approximately 6,000 tons. Based on the 1915 world population of just over 1.9 billion persons, the average per capita capacity equalled 57 pounds. In the ensuing one hundred years, the number of vessels grew almost in lock step with the population growth over the period. However, owing to the ever-increasing size of the typical cargo ship, the growth rate in per capita shipping capacity was well above that figure. While world population over the period grew at compound annual growth rate of 1.36%, total merchant marine deadweight tonnage grew over the period for a compound annual growth rate of 3.59%. By definition, this is a real growth rate unaffected by inflation and that is high growth rate over a one hundred year period.

Comparing shipping capacity to population growth, the net effect is that per capita deadweight capacity is 9.3 times higher today than it was slightly more than one hundred years ago. This proxy for the growth in trade intensity actually understates the change since it is a static measure. When the faster vessel speed at sea and the quicker turnaround in port due to extraordinary terminal efficiencies is taken into account, it is reasonable to say cargo ships travel at least 50% more miles per year compared to a century ago. This increase in per vessel productivity translates into the tangible vessel data indicating an increase of more than 14 times in terms of trade intensity over the period. There are many other metrics that show similar geometric changes in trade intensity.

There is an extraordinary irony in the various measures showing the world's trade intensity today versus anytime in the past. That irony is that, despite the exponential growth in world trade made possible by merchant ships, those ships are more invisible to the general public than they ever have been. A goal of mine is to increase the awareness of these ships, the trade they make possible and the individuals most responsible for the development of the modern cargo shipping industry.

5. Henry J. Kaiser

The Father of Modern Shipbuilding.

It started with the ships a man described as America's boldest, most spectacular entrepreneur built. The Liberty ships Kaiser efficiently built helped to win the war and then become the workhorses of the world's merchant fleets. The efficient processes he pioneered are still used today and this consummate builder paved the way for the post-war growth in trade.

Henry John Kaiser was born on May 9, 1882 in Sprout Brook, New York, a hamlet in the middle of New York 60 miles west of Albany. The son of German immigrants Franz and Marie Kaiser, he was the youngest of four children and all of his siblings were girls. His father was a shoemaker and his mother worked in a cheese factory while also being a part time nurse. When Kaiser was seven, his family moved to the outskirts of the larger city of Utica, New York.

Kaiser left school at the age of 13 to take a job as a sales clerk in a hardware store where he made $1.50 per week. He was a hard worker and this and his thriftiness was evident in this first job. He walked four miles to work each day, returning four miles back in the evening, in order to save the bus fare.

Kaiser was very close to his mother and that would be the most influential relationship of his childhood. In later years, he would credit his mother as the inspiration for his developing the strong work ethic and determination that stayed with him his entire life. Kaiser was devastated when, at the age of sixteen, his mother died in his arms due entirely to the lack of accessible medical care.

In 1899, Kaiser took a job as an apprentice photographer. He was fascinated by the technology in this relatively new profession and learned everything he could about photography. His interest in this area had him relocating 150 miles north to Lake Placid, where he was running a small photography studio on his own by the time he was twenty.

It was in Lake Placid that he would meet his future wife, Bess Fosbough, when she came into his photography shop to buy film. They began to see each other frequently and were clearly attracted to each other. It wasn't too long before marriage was being discussed. However, Fosbough's father demanded that Kaiser demonstrate that he was more financially stable before he would consent to their marriage.

Motivated to do just that, Kaiser sought and obtained a sales job with a hardware company that had a position in Spokane, Washington. Moving across the country in 1906, Kaiser prospered in the same field where he had his first job ten years earlier. He returned ten months later. He had saved money and was able to demonstrate an increasing income trend. Upon outlining these facts, his father-in-law's concerns were placated and he gave his approval. They were married on April 8, 1907 and Kaiser returned to Spokane with his wife. Their first son, Edgar, was born in 1908 and their second son, Henry Jr, followed him shortly thereafter.

Kaiser's return to the West Coast was driven not only by the specific job that he had, but also by a realization that this part of the country was growing faster. With that growth, he thought it offered a broader range of opportunities no matter what path his career took. By this time, Kaiser was exhibiting the sort of action oriented business acumen that would eventually mark him as one of the greatest industrialists in history. We can readily assume that he progressed through the ranks at the hardware retailer where he worked.

Our research was not able to determine what exactly the catalyst was for Kaiser transitioning to the construction area in which he first became well known. However, it is fair to say that he was influenced by his experience. Anyone who worked in the hardware business as long as he did must have had a growing appreciation for how the right tool made a job easier. Likewise, his photography experience likely instilled an appreciation for technology and how it could change things quickly. Those ingredients, combined with a growing region and his considerable business acumen, must have kindled at some point a strong belief that there would be opportunities for a company focused on fulfilling government construction contracts.

In 1914 at the age of 32, Kaiser founded a paving company that concentrated on road construction and other large paving jobs. His company was one of the pioneers in the use of heavy construction equipment. With that equipment and the cost advantages it provided, Kaiser was able to bid successfully on one paving job after another and grew to be the largest such contractor in the region.

The awarding of a $20 million contract in 1927 to build 200 miles of roads and 500 bridges across Cuba resulted in a significant expansion of his company. By the early 1930's, Kaiser's company was one of the prime contractors in building the Hoover dam on the Colorado River and the Grand Coulee dam on the Columbia River. His partners on these major dam projects included Steve Bechtel and Harry Morrison whose own companies would go on to become two of the largest construction companies in the world.

Kaiser's transition from road and dam builder to ship builder is obviously interesting. It is not, however, as circuitous as it seems as there was a common thread in those disparate activities. Henry J. Kaiser was a man of boundless energy and enthusiasm. Large construction projects excited him and he viewed building in all of its forms as the noblest of human activities.

Kaiser completed the Grand Coulee dam, considered by some as an impossible project at its onset, years ahead of schedule and under budget. He was known for constantly challenging the accepted way of doing things. This frequently lead to results that were "more, better and faster" than anyone had thought possible. Those words became his company's motto. The spirit that appeared to motivate how he went about all his projects is captured by his favorite poem, "The Bridge Builder" by Will Allen Dromgoole.

Years later, when Kaiser was asked to testify before a Congressional committee reviewing his stellar wartime production achievements, he asked for the opportunity to preface his remarks by reciting this poem which is shown below.

An old man going a lone highway,
Came, at the evening, cold and grey,

To a chasm vast and deep and wide.
The old man crossed in the twilight dim,
The sullen stream had no fear for him;
But he turned when safe on the other side
And built a bridge to span the tide.

"Old man," said a fellow pilgrim near,
"You are wasting your strength building here;
Your journey will end with the ending day,
You never again will pass this way;
You've crossed the chasm, deep and wide,
Why build this bridge at evening tide?"

The builder lifted his old, gray head;
"Good friend, in the path I have come," he said,
"There followed after me today
A youth whose feet must pass this way.
This chasm that has been as naught to me
To that fair-haired youth may a pitfall be;
He, too, must cross in the twilight dim;
Good friend, I am building this bridge for him!"

Kaiser's first intersection with shipbuilding was in 1940. Already involved in producing cement for his dam projects, Kaiser reasoned he could also make a profit on cement produced in California and sold in Hawaii if he developed a more efficient way to ship cement. At the time, cement was loaded in hundred pound bags onto pallets which were then stacked in cargo holds in a laborious, high-cost operation that made it unprofitable to ship cement to Hawaii.

Kaiser believed that if he could just pour bulk cement into a ship's hold and unload it using pneumatic hoses, he would sharply reduce loading and unloading costs. The so-called experts scoffed, saying that bulk cement would absorb moisture at sea and harden. Kaiser and his team were convinced their method would work. They bought two ships to test their idea and proceeded to have them modified into early versions of what would later be called bulk carriers. With the first shipment of cement to Hawaii, Kaiser was proven right and the business venture was a commercial success. More importantly, however, was his introduction to Todd Shipyards where the vessels were modified.

In the course of the modification, Kaiser got to know John Reilly, the dynamic President of Todd, a company with multiple shipyards whose roots went back to the nineteenth century. In discussions, the two men agreed that the looming hostilities would be a boon to shipbuilding. Reilly expressed concern that he lacked the men and equipment to take advantage of the growth.

While Kaiser had no experience in the sector, he did have a large well-trained workforce available as the Grand Coulee dam project was winding down along with much of the heavy equipment that could be put to work. Kaiser and Reilly agreed to explore how they might work together on shipbuilding projects.

In July 1940, a delegation from Britain arrived in the U.S. with $96 million to spend on 60 cargo vessels. Kaiser was determined to turn his concepts into an action plan to bid for and win that contract.

When Kaiser met with U.S. Navy personnel, they gave him 18 minutes to make his presentation on shipbuilding and then promptly turned him down based on his lack of experience. However, through his friend A.P. Giannini, President of California's Bank of America, Kaiser obtained an introduction to President Roosevelt. The presentation to FDR must have gone better as it resulted in Kaiser obtaining a contract to build the first 50 Liberty class ships.

Kaiser established Kaiser Shipyard in Richmond, California. There was no shipyard there before and he systematically built it from the ground up along with the processes it would follow. He made active use of many of the project construction techniques that had worked so well for him in projects such as the Grand Coulee Dam.

With his well thought out plan, Kaiser got his Richmond shipyard up and running to produce Liberty ships. His production efficiency in building ships impressed the government and it asked him to establish additional shipyards. All of the processes that worked at the initial shipyard in Richmond were replicated and expanded at other shipyards that Kaiser established and operated.

In addition, shipyards operated by other companies adopted Kaiser's processes and they too began to efficiently produce Liberty ships, which were later supplemented by the larger Victory class general cargo ships. The Kaiser shipyards and the other shipyards that adopted its processes also produced T-2 tankers for the war effort. The common thread with all of these ships is that they all resulted from and flowed out of Kaiser's production process genius.

A key innovation of Kaiser's shipyards was the use of prefabrication and modular construction techniques to build ships. Prior to World War II, ships had essentially been built in the same piece by piece method for centuries, starting with the keel and building up. When he built the Grand Coulee Dam, Kaiser made use of a new type of crane known as a whirley crane. It allowed a boom and A-frame to rotate 360 degrees. The mobility of these cranes allowed dam subassemblies and conduits to be built and moved into position to be attached to the dam.

Kaiser reasoned that that the use of whirley cranes at shipyards would allow for prefabrication and modular construction, with large pre-assembled components lifted and moved into place. He had six such cranes that were used on the Grand Coulee Dam project disassembled and moved to three of his shipyards.

The whirley cranes proved to increase efficiency just as much as Kaiser expected, and more cranes were built specifically for the shipyards that worked even better. The ability to build multiple sections of a ship at the same time and then move those components via crane so they could be welded to the ship proved to be an extraordinary revolution in both cost efficiency and the time it took to build a ship.

No longer were ships built from the keel up which was laborious and time consuming, but individual modules and subassemblies were built at the same time and then joined together. This technique of modular construction is fundamentally the same process that shipyards around the world follow to this day.

The extraordinary shipbuilding productivity that resulted from Kaiser's new and different approach to producing ships is dramatically highlighted by the before and after production statistics. In the 10 years before 1940, the U.S. built a total of 23 cargo ships. In the 5 years after, the U.S. built over 4,600 cargo ships.

The transition from rivets to welding in the construction of ships was another key development pioneered by Kaiser. While rivets were the traditional method, Kaiser was aware that welding was being used in auto manufacturing and other industries and surmised that it could be utilized in shipbuilding. The productivity increase was at least two-fold, as one man could weld whereas two men were always needed for riveting. The overall productivity gain, however, was much more as now unskilled laborers could be taught to weld. Rosie the Riveter actually related to aircraft construction. Wendy the Welder was used for ship construction, but it never really caught on with the public.

The U.S. shipbuilding industry played a direct role in winning World War II with the thousands of cargo ships it built. Many of those ships would go on to populate the merchant marine fleets of the world.

Those ships and the pioneering shipbuilding techniques that were developed to build them became important catalysts for the modern cargo shipping network that exists today. While the U.S. is no longer a major builder of cargo ships, it remains the most sophisticated shipbuilder of complex naval vessels in the world and elsewhere we discuss the continuing impact of this superiority.

The techniques that Kaiser developed geometrically shortened the time it took to build a ship. From the first ship he built in 1940 at his Richmond shipyard, he would rapidly expand the operations of his company to a total of 18 shipyards. In total, his shipyards would build 1,490 ships, mostly general cargo Liberty and Victory ships but also T-2 tankers.

The modular construction and welding techniques that Kaiser pioneered were quickly copied by other U.S. shipyards and the thousands of ships they produced with record efficiency can also be linked directly with Kaiser. Towards the end of the war, it was taking only several weeks to produce a ship. In one well-publicized case, a Kaiser shipyard produced a 10,500 ton Liberty ship in a total of just 4 days, 15 hours.

The extraordinary efficiency of the shipbuilding revolution that Kaiser created became well known to most Americans and was a great source of pride. In his typical matter-of-fact style, Kaiser eschewed the notoriety that came his way from newsreels and magazine articles. He did, however, understand the enormity of what he had accomplished as he said more than once "When your work speaks for itself, don't interrupt".

In another indication of the high regard Kaiser was held in at the time, President Roosevelt seriously considered picking him to be his vice president in the 1944 election. However, he ended up selecting Harry Truman after it was determined that Kaiser might be viewed as too progressive. Kaiser had just been named as the most popular civilian in the U.S. in a Gallup poll, and another poll shortly thereafter had Kaiser ranked third in terms of a list of people Americans thought should be president, trailing only Generals Douglass MacArthur and Dwight Eisenhower.

The wartime effect of the Liberty ships that Kaiser produced is hard to overstate but has been well chronicled by historians. More than one general has said that World War II couldn't have been won without the Liberty ships. Less known, however, is the impact these ships first had as commercial cargo ships in ushering in the growth in world trade in the postwar era and the impact that the shipbuilding processes and techniques that Kaiser introduced would have in producing today's giant cargo ships.

Kaiser can aptly be called the father of modern shipbuilding in addition to the numerous accolades he has received. It is difficult to think of any other businessman in history whose legacy raises to equal Kaiser in terms of what his efforts produced for his country.

Following the war, Kaiser would go on to found Kaiser Motors, Kaiser Steel and Kaiser Aluminum, all large corporations in their respective fields. His interests in the automobile sector would include Willys-Overland, the manufacturer of the Jeep line of utility vehicles. That company was eventually sold to American Motors Corporation which resulted in Kaiser owning 22% of that major car manufacturer.

In addition to his pioneering industrial efforts, Kaiser was ahead of the times in his view of the health care coverage that employers should provide. At his shipyards, he provided what in effect was the first large-scale health maintenance organization. His interest in providing health care was rooted in his mother's sudden death for want of basic medical care when he was a young boy.

A significant legacy of his bold health care initiative continues to exist today in the form of Kaiser Permanente, a health maintenance organization covering 11 million people. In addition to being one of the largest HMO's in the world, Kaiser Permanente just announced another first with its plans to start its own medical school.

At Kaiser's death in 1967, President Johnson said, "Henry J. Kaiser embodied in his own career all that has been best in our country's tradition. His own energy, imagination and determination gave him greatness – and he used that greatness to give unflaggingly for the betterment of his country and his fellow man."

6. Malcom P. McLean

The Inventor and Father of Container Shipping.

Trade simply wouldn't exist at current levels without the extraordinary cost efficiencies that resulted from Malcom's genius. Almost everyone has daily exposure to products they consume, wear or otherwise use that made the way to them via container. No other individual is more responsible for the global trade phenomena than this giant among giants.

Malcom Purcell McLean was born on November 14, 1913 in Maxton, North Carolina, a town with a population of 1,300 that was 70 miles southeast of Charlotte, North Carolina. Originally called Shoe Heel, Maxton was a farming community settled more than a century earlier by Scottish immigrants. In testimony to its roots, the local paper was the *Scottish Chief.*

Malcom had six siblings, split evenly between three brothers and three sisters. He was the second oldest among a close-knit group of children. Malcom would remain close to all his siblings, most particularly to one brother and one sister. His father was a farmer who supplemented his income by delivering mail on a rural postal route. Malcom was named after his father who used the more traditional spelling of Malcolm. While Malcom spelt his name that way initially, at a later point in his life he would decide to change it. He would recall that his spelling simply fit better with the way his name was actually pronounced.

The Scottish heritage in the area of North Carolina that Malcom grew up in was according to sociologists a catalyst for the unusual entrepreneurial activity that would come out of the area. North Carolina had become the most popular destination for people migrating from Scotland. In large part, this was due to encouragement in the 1700's by the royal governor of the colony, a Scotsman himself. These immigrants came from a culture rooted in hard work and industriousness, not surprising given that the same culture produced Adam Smith, the father of capitalism. It's reasonable to speculate that those basic traits were exacerbated in Scotsmen who elected to cross the Atlantic to settle in North Carolina.

Thousands of Highland Scots, descendents of the Celts who settled in northern Scotland, migrated in large organized groups to North Carolina by the late 1700's. They farmed the land and found that they could plant their crops without removing the tall straight longleaf pine trees. By removing a ring of bark, the tree died and all its needles fell, letting the sun reach the crops. Many Scottish farmers also went into the naval store business of producing products from the sap of those pine trees. Pitch and tar were important products at the time, in large part because they were needed to protect the hulls and rigging of wooden sailing ships.

How much this strong Scottish heritage played a role with young Malcom is unclear, but what is clear is that he began to exhibit diligent work habits and strong entrepreneurial skills even as a child. Before and after school, he had multiple farm chores that he performed meticulously.

After finishing his chores after school, Malcom would grab his shoeshine kit and go into town, moving from store to store where he would hawk his services. Initially getting a nickel to shine a pair of shoes or boots, as his performance reputation and sales abilities increased, he was often able to get a dime. Malcom remembered a story of returning to Maxton for a visit decades later. Walking along the sidewalk, he came across an elderly gentleman who recognizing him, smiled and said, "shine for a dime", repeating Malcom's often repeated sales pitch as a fourteen-year-old child.

Malcom graduated from high school in 1931 in the depths of the depression and promptly got a job stocking shelves in the local grocery store. His innate analytical skills were beginning to show and he quickly completed any tasks involving numbers. Within months, he was in the front of the store handling checkouts where he impressed the owner and his customers with his courteous and very efficient service in addition to his obvious math skills.

It didn't take long before Malcom was confident he could manage his own retail business. Upon learning that a gas station in nearby Red Springs was looking for a manager, Malcom actively pursued and got that job. He studied and quickly learned the economics related to cash coming in and cash going out in that business.

In what would be the first of many initiatives he would undertake to differentiate his product with customers, he came up with a unique marketing promotion. Malcom thought his car traffic would increase if he gave drivers a memorable experience that would make them always want to come back to his gas station. Taking a page from organ grinders that were popular in various urban areas at the time, Malcom bought a monkey that he put on a leash attached to his gas pumps.

Customers, particularly those with children, embraced this attraction and gas sales at the station shot up sharply. Malcom did, however, have to modify the housing situation for the monkey who was initially locked inside the office at night. When Malcom opened up one morning, he found the office in disarray with papers scattered throughout. He quickly built a new enclosure outside that would become the new home for the monkey.

Malcom was always reviewing his receipts and disbursements and making various calculations of what could be done to improve the numbers. When he ordered a truckload of gasoline, he became aware that the trucker got $5 for moving that load from Fayettville, a larger town 28 miles away. His calculations lead him to believe he could do that himself and save a large amount of money. Talking the station owner into letting him use an old tank trailer in the back of the station, he did just that.

With $120 Malcom had saved from pumping gas, he bought a used tractor to pull the tank trailer. By moving his own gasoline, Malcom was able to sharply reduce his transport costs. As he moved more loads, his actual experience became a further input for refining his calculations. Even after factoring in full costs for equipment and his time, Malcom saw savings. He made inquiries of other businesses in town regarding what they paid for trucking and began developing his next business plan.

In 1934, Malcom formed McLean Trucking Company. He was the sole driver moving gasoline to the service station he continued to run. In addition to the savings he achieved there, he had determined that trucking offered nice profits if managed correctly.

Looking around for more opportunities in trucking, Malcom bought a used dump truck from a local man who agreed to accept installment payments over time. He immediately entered into a contract to haul dirt for the WPA, the federal public works program. Malcom hired a driver and that venture was immediately profitable from the beginning. With the cash he made there, he bought a new truck to haul vegetables for local farmers. Each successful contract gave rise to another opportunity. Malcom left his position at the gas station to focus exclusively on his growing trucking business.

Within a year of starting his trucking business, 22 year old Malcom owned two trucks and one tractor trailer and also employed nine drivers who owned their own tractor trailers. He brought in his brother Jim and his sister Clara to help him. In a framework that would work well for all of them for decades, Jim focused on day to day operations, Clara handled administrative tasks and Malcom focused on revenue growth and the future. It was a team and a division of labor that proved to be very effective.

To say that Malcom was hands-on is an under-statement and doesn't adequately capture his constant focus on the basics of moving freight from one point to another. During the heady growth that would occur over the next decade, Malcom would often be seen behind the wheel driving one of his rigs. His granular approach resulted in observations that assisted in both reducing costs and increasing revenue.

In 1937, Malcom married Margaret Sykes, his girlfriend who lived in a nearby North Carolina town. They bought a house in Winston-Salem and began starting a family. Their first child was a daughter, Nancy, and their son, Malcom Jr., and another daughter, Patricia, would follow later.

Malcom shared with me numerous stories of his experience as a driver and how that informed his insight into the freight business. Each time he drove, he was aware of the cargo he was moving and its various attributes. He paid attention to how it was loaded and unloaded, how much it weighed and what its value was, among other things. Malcom would always take whatever time was needed to observe how cargo was put in and taken out of his trailer, where it was moved from and where it was initially placed after unloading. He was naturally curious and embodied the concept of management by walking around.

As he was driving, Malcom would reflect on all the characteristics of the cargo that he was moving. As he would say many times, when you're driving, you've got plenty of time to think. Malcom chose always to be thinking about the movement of freight from one point to another. Combined with his keen skills of observation, these traits and habits would serve him well for the rest of his life.

There was one early experience that Malcom had as a driver that stands out as the catalyst for his greatest initiative. Before getting to that, however, it's worth recounting a couple of other experiences he had as a driver that were reflective of the business principles he was developing.

In the early days of McLean Trucking, Malcom continued to drive and preferred to handle new business as that allowed him to see the cargo being loaded and unloaded and meet the people that were involved. His natural curiosity and polite southern manner lead to constructive conversations, whether on the loading docks or in the offices, that often would result in additional business with that new customer. Malcom was a man with many skills. While my view is that his rigorous focus on relative costs, supported by a very sharp quantitative mind, was his top skill, he was also an excellent salesman.

One of Malcom's frequent trips as a driver was from North Carolina to New York. Between furniture, tobacco and a variety of other goods, his home state was a solid generator of truck freight. On one such trip that involved delivering cargo for several key accounts in the New York area just before Thanksgiving, Malcom came up with an idea that he thought could result in more business with those customers.

He was going to personally deliver live turkeys to decision makers at each of those accounts. Going to a local North Carolina turkey farm, he picked out three nice turkeys and indicated his plans. The farmer put each turkey in its own large burlap bag which he tied at the top, assuring Malcom they could breathe and would arrive in fine shape. Malcom then put the bagged turkeys in the cab of his tractor and setoff for New York. The first half of the trip was uneventful, although the turkeys got increasingly louder.

One by one, however, the turkeys managed to peck holes in their burlap bags and free themselves. Between hopping around the cab to pecking at each other and occasionally pecking on Malcom's right arm, it became quite a menagerie. Stopping at tollbooths was particularly eventful, as the turkeys would attempt to escape through his rolled down window. Malcom devised a way to roll down his window just enough to allow him to pass cash to the toll taker, but not enough to allow a twenty-pound turkey to flee. Of course, this made for a hilarious scene at all of the tolls.

With the burlap bags in tatters and Malcom determining that stopping would just prolong the situation, he pressed on all the way to New York. He literally hand delivered the live turkeys to his contacts in New York. The drama and acknowledgement that came with this differentiated act resulted in increases in business with each of those accounts.

Malcom's analytical mind was intuitively always comparing one thing to another. Indeed, one of his favorite expressions was "if you don't have something to compare, you don't have anything". Malcom saw this as a doctrine that really influenced almost every decision he made or action he took. He would note that every day starts off with the innate comparison of whether it is light or dark before you even decide to get out of the bed.

His awareness on the value of comparisons was borne out in another one of his trips to New York that involved delivering chairs to a theater in the Broadway district. This shipment, like many shipments at the time, was setup for the trucking company to be paid cash upon delivery. As was his habit, Malcom assisted in unloading the chairs and then went to the manager's office to get the freight amount due paid in full.

The manager, however, handed over an envelope containing only 80% of the total amount, coming up with some rationalization related to why he was short-changing the bill. Upon hearing this, Malcom turned to the manager's secretary and politely asked her if she was paid for everyday she worked the previous week or just four out of the five days she worked. When she answered in the affirmative, Malcom rhetorically said if she is being paid for all the work she did, why isn't he being paid for all the work he did?

That comparison resonated with the manager, who reached into his drawer and paid the balance. Malcom was a man of absolute business integrity and he viewed the transaction between carrier and customer as something that should be completely fulfilled by both sides.

As McLean Trucking grew, Malcom would spend less time behind the wheel of a tractor. Luckily, however, he was behind the wheel in 1937 when he had time to make some observations that would be recalled and implemented years later. Malcom was driving a full truckload of cotton bales from Fayetteville, North Carolina to an export dock in Hoboken, New Jersey. He had learned that his shipment was eventually destined for Europe. Malcom had never delivered freight alongside a ship and was looking forward to what he could observe and learn from that new experience.

He arrived early and was told by a tall Irish dock supervisor to wait until he was called. As he waited for hours, he watched as each truck pulled alongside the ship and gangs of men first unloaded the truck and then placed the goods in cargo nets to be winched onboard the vessel. He saw that a similar process in reverse was occurring on the ship. The same slow, laborious process unfolded with one truck after another.

Malcom was struck by the inefficiency he was witnessing as the same cargo was literally manhandled multiple times to get it onboard. Late in the afternoon he asked the dock supervisor when his truck would be unloaded, and when the response was if he didn't get some cash he wasn't sure when he would be unloaded, Malcom also got another firsthand insight into how things typically worked on the dock.

Decades later he would reflect on his takeaways from that day. "I had to wait most of the day to deliver the bales, sitting there in my truck, watching stevedores load other cargo. It struck me that I was looking at a lot of wasted time and money. I watched them take each crate off the truck and slip it into a sling, which would then lift the crate into the hold of the ship. Why not just lift the trailer and put it on the ship without its contents being touched?" Malcom tucked away what he had seen and learned in Hoboken. Nineteen years later, he would implement a revolutionary business plan, the genesis of which came from his direct observations that day.

Malcom applied his insightful approach to all elements of his growing trucking business. By 1940, he was operating some thirty tractor trailer rigs that produced annual revenue of $230,000. While he was no longer behind the wheel, he was constantly reviewing and analyzing all of the typical costs from pickup to delivery. Wherever Malcom was his yellow pad and pencil were close by. His favored approach was to cost out in longhand any situation he was reviewing. This habit would stay with him for the rest of his life and ensured that he had a granular understanding of the cost economics of his businesses.

The underpinning for Malcom's initial focus on costs was the regulatory nature of trucking at the time. With the passage of the Motor Carrier Act of 1935, interstate trucking was brought under the authority of the Interstate Commerce Commission, or ICC. The ICC had regulated railroads since 1897. The ICC had almost total control of trucking companies that offered services to the public.

Truckers could only haul goods that the ICC allowed them to move on routes approved by the ICC and at ICC approved rates. This highly regulated environment made expansion into new routes difficult and this protected existing carriers. While it limited competition, the overriding goal of the ICC was to keep the transportation industry stable.

Consistent with this goal of stabilizing trucking services, the ICC would allow a trucking company to expand into a new route only if it could show that was in the public interest and the rate offered would be profitable. The only meaningful way a trucking company could attract new business was by offering lower rates than competitors offered. The regulatory framework made this a difficult needle to thread as lower rates without lower costs were deemed to be destabilizing by the ICC.

Malcom wanted to grow and he realized that the regulatory framework effectively meant that he couldn't offer lower rates, the only way to grow fast, unless he also had lower costs. Malcom's obsessive focus on costs was therefore rooted directly in that regulatory framework.

Malcom took advantage of the public filings with the ICC to learn everything that he could about competitor's rates and their financial performance. He was constantly making comparisons between his company and other companies to learn where he had the largest advantage and where he should focus on expanding. He developed a process for calculating the revenue, cost and profit for each individual shipment handled and used that as a tool to improve his overall performance. By 1945, McLean Trucking was operating 162 tractor trailer rigs and generating $2.2 million in annual revenue, ten times the level just five years earlier.

As McLean Trucking grew, so did Malcom's cost-saving innovations. The company opened one of the first automated terminals in the industry with a facility in Winston-Salem that used conveyor belts to move freight from one truck to another, saving labor costs. For less than truckload shipments, terminal expenses where cargo was sorted and consolidated involved significant labor costs and this early automation gave Malcom's company a noteworthy competitive cost advantage.

Of even more cost impact, during a time when most trucking fleets used only gasoline engines, McLean Trucking was the first to fully convert his fleet to diesel engines. While diesel engines were starting to be offered by General Motors and other tractor manufacturers, they weren't popular because drivers didn't like their acceleration characteristics. Malcom, however, had done a detailed analysis on all the numbers on the initial test diesel engine in one of his tractors. He saw firsthand that it resulted in significantly lower fuel cost per mile. Malcom quickly converted exclusively to tractors with diesel engines.

Because all trucking companies had to file detailed income statements breaking out fuel costs with the ICC that were publicly available, other trucking companies eventually saw the results and began to copy McLean Trucking's use of diesel engines. Malcom would say years later that, luckily for him, most of his competitors weren't looking nearly as closely at his costs and financial statements as he was at their costs and financial statements. Malcom was obsessed with costs and constantly involved in comparisons of his costs and performance with other trucking companies.

Related to fuel, he sought and obtained discounts at various service stations along the company's key routes and required that his drivers only fuel at those stations. While that seems obvious and is the situation throughout the trucking industry today, it was unique at the time as drivers typically bought fuel wherever they chose.

As Malcom analyzed the various factors that effected fuel consumption, he specified that new trailers should be constructed with sides that were crenellated and not smooth. He got this advice from experts at the University of North Carolina who told him that crenellation would reduce wind drag and therefore fuel consumption.

As these various cost reduction initiatives took hold, the gap between costs at McLean Trucking and the rest of the industry widened. With this cost advantage, Malcom could offer lower rates on new routes and still prove to the ICC that these rates were profitable. This relative cost advantage was a meaningful edge that allowed the company to sharply grow its business. Cost reduction and volume growth became a virtuous circle for McLean Trucking.

In addition to growing this way, McLean Trucking also acquired several smaller trucking companies and indoctrinated them into the company's way of doing business. Another route of growth involved leasing routes from other trucking companies. All these various approaches resulted in significant growth at McLean Trucking. By 1950, it was operating some 800 tractor trailer rigs and the company was five times bigger than it was in 1945 with annual revenue approaching $15 million.

With his own experience behind the wheel, Malcom understood the key importance of the driver and the multitude of decisions he made every day. Holding down insurance and repair costs meant having drivers who were safety conscious. McLean Trucking had one of the first systematic driver-training programs where novices were paired with senior drivers on key runs such as Winston-Salem to Atlanta. If the novice made it through his first year without an accident, the senior driver got a bonus equal to one months pay.

Recognizing that safety was often coincident with a driver who was calm and deliberate in his actions, Malcom had his driver recruiters hang out at diners frequented by truck drivers. They would approach drivers who calmly ordered meals and avoid drivers who were loud and belligerent. This approach was grounded in Malcom's own experience in diners as a driver and another example of a keen sense of observation that was always on.

Malcom clearly understood the power of monetary incentives for drivers. For instance, one year he had a nice new house built on a road that most drivers would pass on approaching the main terminal in Winston-Salem. He then announced that house would be given to the driver with the best safety record at the end of the year. Not surprisingly, McLean Trucking was at the top of the industry in safety performance and that in turn was reflected in lower costs.

McLean Trucking began hiring young college graduates in the early 1950's and put them through what was the first formal management training in the trucking industry and among the first such programs in the country. Their first task was to learn how to drive a truck. After six months behind the wheel, they were then sent to terminals where they spent a few months loading and unloading freight into trailers. After learning these core aspects, they then spent several months at the head office where they learned the commercial aspects of trucking.

A key aspect of this was learning the McLean Trucking approach to making a proposal to a potential customer. Not surprisingly, this was driven by a cost analysis which compared the shippers current freight cost per unit to what it would be with McLean Trucking. After a year, these trainees had a solid grasp of both the operational and commercial aspects of the trucking business and were dispatched to sell freight in cities up and down the East Coast.

A relentless focus on costs and relative competitiveness was an obsession with Malcom and it was reflected at all levels of the company. The salesman who managed the account completed forms showing the anticipated profit for each shipment and copies were passed along to both the driver and the terminal manager. This way, everyone was on the same page with regard to the commercial impact of the shipment and the information was also used to prioritize truck dispatching and routing.

The accounting department also consolidated this profit per load information into various reports that were scrutinized by management and by Malcom in particular. He used these reports to move the company towards the more profitable loads and to move away from the less profitable loads. With the detailed insight that came from these reports, Malcom also established for the sales force a minimum profit percentage that any new business would need to have.

Even when it had become a large trucking company, Malcom could often be seen walking around his terminals, talking to drivers and other workers, and observing everything that was going on. His version of management by walking around and the granular feel and insight he got from this approach aided his business immensely. Decades later I would personally see firsthand countless examples of his keen sense of observation.

One of Malcom's favorite things to do even after McLean Trucking had become a large company was to spend a couple of hours in the gatehouse where drivers got their dispatching orders. At the gatehouse, the truck was weighed and sealed and the drivers were given specific instructions on which route to take. Malcom liked to observe the systematic processes he had developed and always had his eyes and ears open for observations and suggestions for improvement.

When he was in the gatehouse, he would typically ask the driver to show him his profit per load form. On one weekend evening when he did this, he noticed that while a particular load was profitable, it was below the minimum profitability level that was in effect at that time. Malcom knew which salesman was associated with the account and picked up the phone and called him at home.

Malcom indicated to the salesman that because the load was below the minimum profitability standard, he had instructed it to be returned to the shipper. When the salesman said that the shipper was a big, important shipper, Malcom said that was good and they would therefore understand. That was one of the last times he came across a freight shipment that didn't meet the minimum profitability standards in effect. As it would turn out, that shipper whose load was returned did in fact become an even larger customer of McLean Trucking.

This story underscores an aspect of Malcom's business philosophy regarding costs, rates and profit. While his strongest focus was on developing freight businesses that had lower costs, he was resolute that you had to see a profit in each and every freight transaction, just as the regulators believed. Malcom thought that some of the lower cost should be passed along to the customer to get the business, but that his company should retain as much as possible of that lower cost to achieve higher profits.

The costs in the trucking industry are primarily variable and this no doubt played a role in Malcom developing a strong view that each load or transaction had to be profitable on a full cost basis. The regulatory framework at the time requiring that new rates would only be approved if they were deemed to cover all costs certainly reinforced this approach.

Malcom's focus on profits was captured in a short poem he authored and shared at a meeting of all the salesmen at McLean Trucking. The poem Malcom recited for me decades later is shown below.

May the sun never rise
On the day in a driver's run
When cargo isn't a prize
And freight is hauled for fun

Malcom would take this philosophy with him to a shipping industry that was anything but a variable cost business. With a much larger percentage of fixed costs than the trucking industry, the shipping industry lent itself to rates sometimes focused more on incremental costs than the full cost of the shipment.

While Malcom would rail against this, at the same time he would recognize the dynamics of real world situations in the shipping industry and the leverage cargo providers often had. Malcom would frequently observe that the easiest thing in the world to do is a cut a rate. Referring to situations where he himself was involved, he noted that sometimes you didn't need to do anything but sit in a shipper's office and "the rate would decline almost by itself".

By the early 1950's, McLean Trucking had grown to be the largest trucking company in the south and the fourth largest trucking company in the entire country. It owned and operated 1,776 tractor trailer rigs across a network of 37 terminals spanning most of the eastern U.S. The company had dozens of major routes, but few were as important to its business as the long haul freight moving between New York and Texas and Florida.

With this growth, Malcom was a large purchaser of tractors and became one of the largest customers of General Motors. By now, the entire trucking industry had switched to diesel engines, but Malcom remained focused on specifications that would result in the most cost efficient tractors. His insightful views on tractors, and his importance as a customer, resulted on his being asked to be on an advisory board that would meet a couple of times each year in Detroit with senior management at General Motors.

The subject of one of those meetings in 1953 was a freewheeling discussion of what the future held. Malcom painted an optimistic picture regarding freight demand and highlighted what he saw as key factors related to tractors going forward. He then volunteered that he anticipated that more automotive buyers would eventually embrace the operating cost focus of the trucking industry. When that happens, Malcom saw that clearly favoring the production of small cars like the ones he knew were starting to be made in Japan. Referring to rough calculations he had done on his yellow pad the night before, he came up with a meaningful estimated difference in the operating cost of those small cars compared to a typical General Motors car.

Malcom was asked to share his views about small cars with the General Motors board of directors, which was meeting the next day. After outlining those views, one director said "Americans don't want small cars and it will never be more than 3% of the market, which we'll leave to Nash". A few years later in the same month and year Malcom would launch his revolutionary business idea, Toyota would import its first car into America, beginning a shift in average new car size that continues to this day. Several decades later, General Motors would belatedly recognize that small cars would become the large majority of the new car market. Malcom's observations relating to the future of the car business were prescient, but unfortunately nobody at General Motors cared to listen to him.

Despite success underscored by having the second highest profits of any trucking company in the country, Malcom was constantly looking for ways to further improve his costs. As he reflected on his business in 1953, he found himself going back to his observations on the Hoboken dock back in 1937. The instant catalyst was a growing concern that domestic ship lines, able to buy surplus Liberty ships from the government for low prices, might be able to encroach on his important long haul business even with their laborious traditional breakbulk loading and unloading methods.

As he thought more about it, his concern about those existing domestic ship lines lessened, but he became intrigued with the costs that would result from implementing his idea from sixteen years ago of more efficiently moving full-loads on vessels. Weeks of his own longhand analysis on his ever-present yellow pad got him even more excited. While everything he was doing on paper was new, his decades of analyzing costs in granular detail put him in position to accurately model this new approach. Indeed, it is hard to imagine that anyone was in a better position than Malcom to estimate those costs.

In addition to what he believed his idea could do with costs, it addressed an increasing concern he had about highway congestion on many of his key routes and the adverse effect it was beginning to have on his costs. It is worth remembering that the beginning of the Interstate Highway System was still three years away at that time.

The sporadic congestion that trucks experienced in 1953 on long hauls between, for example, Florida and New York was significant without the network of arterial four lane highways we have today. Malcom's concept not only involved taking advantage of a lower cost marine highway, but of linking that with trucks he controlled on both ends so that a single company handled the entire freight movement from initial pickup to final destination.

The initial implementation planning of Malcom's idea revolved around putting truck trailers on vessels and ferrying them between North Carolina and New York and Rhode Island, bypassing the worst highway congestion areas. By the end of 1953, Malcom had developed a plan to build waterfront terminals where trucks would drive up ramps in order to place their trailers on the decks of vessels. A real estate firm working for McLean Trucking began looking for terminal sites.

The timing of Malcom's property search coincided with an initiative by the Port Authority of New York and New Jersey to find a new tenant for its under-utilized docks in Newark, New

Jersey. Malcom visited the proposed site and liked that it had plenty of space to marshal trailers, was adjacent to the newly opened New Jersey Turnpike and was a short trip to most freight locations in the New York City area. He outlined his concept to port authority officials who embraced the idea and became early proponents of his plans. An agreement to lease the site was quickly reached and the port authority began preparing the facility with its own funds.

Malcom was now focused on buying S.C. Loveland, a small barge operator, to get their coastal operating rights and begin service by putting his trailers on barges that would be towed along the East Coast. Like the trucking business, the domestic marine business was highly regulated at the time. Among other regulations, you needed to have operating rights to serve specific U.S. ports.

Key among those regulations was the Jones Act that required that movements between U.S. ports must be on U.S. built, crewed and owned vessels. Malcom had developed plans to build new larger roll-on, roll-off vessels which he anticipated could be largely financed through an available government loan guarantee program. However, he first wanted to prove his concept with the Loveland barges.

While Malcom was in discussions to buy Loveland, he was also studying the shipping industry in detail. In reviewing Moody's financial manual in 1954, he came across Waterman Steamship Corportation, a large traditional shipping company based in Mobile, Alabama whose stock was publicly traded. In learning more about that company, he became intrigued that its Pan-Atlantic Steamship subsidiary might be a better platform for him to begin his new service.

Pan-Atlantic had coastal operating rights to serve 16 ports and had four ships in coastwise voyages between Boston and Houston. The more he looked at and analyzed the Waterman numbers, the more Malcom became convinced this was the way to go. The plan he came up with involved getting Pan-Atlantic by first buying all of Waterman Steamship Corporatation and then selling the parts he wouldn't utilize.

The acquisition of Waterman bears close examination not only for what it set in motion related to the shipping industry, but also as an extraordinary example of Malcom's financial acumen. This was a trait shared by many of the shipping pioneers. Given the capital-intensive nature of the shipping industry, a comfort with finance and a strong analytical ability was a required skill.

What particularly attracted Malcom to Waterman Steamship Corporation was its balance sheet. The company had no debt and its assets included 37 ships, most in services to Europe and Asia, along with $25 million in cash. Malcom's preliminary inquiries had him believing that all of Waterman could be purchased for $42 million. Malcom was confident he could finance much of the purchase. He also thought that by disposing of assets he didn't envision using, he could effectively reduce his cost basis in the assets he would utilize. While that type of financial engineering approach is fairly typical today, it certainly wasn't in the mid-1950's.

Malcom was now committed to transitioning all of his business interests to his new integrated truck-ship service. With agreements in principal in place in late 1954 to buy Pan-Atlantic and Waterman, Malcom turned his attention to financing the acquisition and taking other preparatory steps related to the transition. An initial matter that he had to deal with was the legal structure as the ICC encouraged modal separation and wasn't expected to waive a regulation that precluded a trucking company from also owning a domestic shipping company.

While McLean Trucking was a publicly traded company at the time, Malcom and his siblings Jim and Clara owned the large majority of the stock and controlled the company. To address this, they all placed their stock in a trust where the independent trustees were authorized to take all actions, including selling the stock. With this move, Malcom effectively severed his ties with the extraordinarily successful trucking business he had built over the previous twenty years, in order to start an entirely new transportation business. This was a brazen entrepreneurial move, but one that Malcom's own analysis of the underlying costs had him highly confident that his next business would be even more successful than McLean Trucking.

At the same time he moved away from S.C. Loveland, Malcom moved away from his plan to use complete trailers and instead decided his vessels would just carry the trailer bodies without the wheels and landing gear. Like everything, this resulted from his detailed analysis of what process would result in the lowest costs. By stacking just the truck bodies, he could get more units on a given sized vessel.

Malcom was also already envisioning a second generation of larger vessels and realized that new purpose-built vessels to accommodate lots of regular highway trailers would cost more than various ways of converting existing ships he had already mapped out for moving just the truck bodies. With that change, however, Malcom needed to develop his own truck bodies, or containers, as nothing presently existed that would fit his needs.

A review of various trailer manufacturers resulted in his circling in on Brown Industries, a Spokane, Washington based company that specialized in building unique and custom containers. A meeting was scheduled and Keith Tantlinger, Brown's chief engineer, flew across country to meet with Malcom. Outlining his plan in a level of detail that impressed Tantlinger, Malcom said he wanted containers that were 33' long and 8' wide. Those dimensions fit with the then current maximums allowed with highway trailers. In addition, that length fit with the planned deck space on the T2 tankers Malcom had identified as ideal. That space would be evenly distributed on a metal framework that would be constructed above the myriad of piping on the two tankers that would be converted.

Having determined that the initial route will be between Newark and Houston, Malcom planned to also carry crude oil on the northbound leg. To secure the containers to the framework and to each other, Malcom outlined his idea of attaching six pieces of foot long steel, each with a hole in the bottom, to the sides of each container. These pieces would fit into slots in the framework and a rod would then be inserted through the holes to lock the container in place. With some minor refinements that Tantlinger recommended, Brown immediately began building two prototype 33' containers based on Malcom's basic design.

Simultaneously, Malcom was actively pursuing financing to close on the Waterman acquisition. Those discussions led him in late 1954 to meet Walter Wriston, a 35 year-old Assistant Treasurer at First National City Bank of New York. Wriston had just been put in charge of the bank's nascent shipping loan division. Malcom outlined his ideas to Wriston who saw it as viable. He was also impressed with Malcom's analytical approach and justification of the concept with straightforward comparisons of his costs to traditional ways of moving freight. Malcom also highlighted Waterman's debt free balance sheet and considerable asset value in a matter of fact way that made the banker realize this entrepreneur was financially savvy. After a couple of initial meetings,

Wriston was sold on the concept and Malcom indicated he would come back to him with a specific proposal on the financing he wanted the bank to consider.

With a net worth of some $25 million at the time, Malcom was a very wealthy man. However, information regarding stock holdings and personal wealth was quite limited back then. There was little about Malcom's manner that telegraphed this and he was then and always would be loath to talk about his personal finances. Just as he had in the past, Malcom would use this to his advantage in one financial negotiation after another. He had adroitly used debt financing while he was in the trucking industry, and he would make even more use of it when he transitioned into the much more capital intensive shipping industry.

This episode telegraphed a view on negotiation and financial privacy that Malcom had developed and that would be evident for the rest of his career. It is best summed up by his expression of "don't count someone else's money". While I suspect this was in part reflected his annoyance at people asking and talking about his wealth, it was primarily driven by his direct approach to business matters that focused on his position and making a solid presentation to the other party. Any speculation on the other party's position, just like an estimate of their finances, would often draw Malcom's rebuke.

Malcom of course already had a specific financing request in mind that he refined further and presented to Wriston. A new McLean Industries entity would be setup and capitalized primarily with $7 million in preferred stock. Malcom agreed to personally backstop that issue by buying any preferred stock that couldn't be placed with outside investors. First National City Bank would then loan McLean Industries $42 million, which would fund the acquisition of Waterman. As security, the bank would have first mortgages on all 37 Waterman vessels and UCC filings giving it a security interest in all other Waterman assets.

Immediately after the closing, Waterman would declare a large dividend to McLean Industries, which would be used to payoff more than half of the loan. Systematic sales of other assets would then commence to further reduce the loan balance over the near term. In addition, the cash flow from Waterman's existing operations as well as the projected cash flow from the new truck-ship service was more than sufficient to meet regularly scheduled loan payments.

Wriston analyzed the proposal and indicated that he anticipated the bank would be willing to move ahead as he had concluded that the bank's interests would be fully protected. There is no doubt that his favorable impression of Malcom, his track record and his new concept also played a key role in reaching that determination. A closing date was scheduled for the financing and Malcom turned his full attention to other issues related to the pending acquisition that needed addressing. Among those were several legal obstacles that had been thrown up along the way.

The most serious one involved several railroads who were protesting with the ICC, claiming that the McLeans would effectively control McLean Trucking and Waterman in violation of the law requiring separation of the modes. Malcom was no stranger to fighting with the railroads at the ICC and that experience had influenced the trust structure he and his team created. The court supported that structure and ruled that the acquisition of Waterman wouldn't violate the law. Not long after the court's decision, the subject was made moot when the trustees sold the McLean Trucking stock. With that sale, Malcom realized some $20 million in cash.

Shortly before the scheduled closing on the Waterman purchase, Malcom received a disturbing call from Wriston who said the transaction was getting some pushback from superiors of his at the bank and he should come downtown. Malcom immediately went to the bank's headquarters where he met with two of Wriston's superiors.

Malcom expressed surprise that there were further questions, as he indicated he had already addressed those questions with Wriston who had given his approval to the transaction. In response, one of the vice presidents said, "Wriston is just a clerk around here". Taken aback, Malcom responded that "Wriston may just be a clerk, but he's going to be the boss of both of you pretty soon". Malcom then went on to address all of their questions and they too became supporters of the loan and of Malcom.

With the financing now fully committed, the closing occurred a few days later in Mobile on May 6, 1955. As there was a rumor of a competing bidder interested in Waterman, it was decided to move quickly and simultaneously close on the loan and the acquisition. One problem that came up was that they lacked a quorum for the Waterman board to take various corporate actions. This was solved by one of Malcom's lawyers rushing outside and offering a passerby $50 for less than an hour of work.

With a quorum now in place, the $42 million loan was drawn and that amount was paid to acquire Waterman. The Waterman directors were then replaced by Malcom's nominees and the new Waterman board authorized a $25 million dividend to its new McLean Industries parent, which immediately used that dividend to reduce the amount outstanding on the loan. Just as all the transactions had been completed and the meeting was breaking up, lawyers for the opposing bidder served papers to prevent the dividend, but they were too late.

Malcom's financial engineering skills had resulted in him acquiring one of the largest shipping companies in the country where his total personal investment was only $10,000. Many decades later similar such transactions would be referred to as leveraged buyouts. The Waterman transaction was not only ahead of its time, but also near the top in terms of the actual return on investment.

Walter Wriston became not only the boss of those two vice presidents in quick order, but eventually the boss of everyone at the bank when he became the CEO of what became known as Citibank in 1967. In his fourteen-year tenure leading what became the largest commercial bank in the world, Wriston oversaw the introduction of numerous innovations including automated teller machines, interstate banking, negotiable CD's and multiple firsts related to its pioneering pursuit and growth in credit card. Wriston is widely regarded as the single most influential commercial banker during the second half of the twentieth century.

Malcom and Wriston would remain friends for the rest of their lives. On reflecting on the Waterman transaction, Wriston would later be quoted as saying, "In a sense, Waterman was the first LBO". His regard for Malcom's business judgment was such that in the early 1980's when he was contemplating who he would recommend as his successor, he met privately with Malcom as an independent sounding board. Outlining the various candidates and their respective merits, Malcom strongly recommended the man he had read about who had revolutionized back office operations and knew the cost of processing a check to five decimal points. This in fact was the person who became the next CEO.

As an aside, I would see this same sort of situation play out again and again as CEO's and board members referred to Malcom would seek out his advice on major strategic decisions of companies both within and outside the transportation industry. Through word of mouth, Malcom's judgment and insight became something that was actively sought by leading businessmen across the country.

With Waterman now his, Malcom moved full steam ahead with all the preparations related to implementing his concept. Two T-2 tankers went into Baltimore's Bethlehem Steel shipyard to be converted to carry containers on deck as per plans put together by Malcom's engineers. Because what Malcom wanted to do was so radical and unheard of, traditional naval architects weren't particularly useful at this point. Indeed, one shipyard naval architect volunteered that putting that amount of cargo weight on deck would most likely result in the ship capsizing.

Malcom brought on some key people whose operational experience and judgment he valued. Many of these folks had experience with innovative initiatives that Malcom had implemented at the trucking company, so they were accustomed to doing something different. Cecil Egger, who was in charge of all maintenance activities at McLean Trucking, brought a practical approach to refining the design of the load bearing framework on the vessel where the containers would be put on the vessel.

As the shipyard conversion work was being performed, the two prototype containers were delivered to the shipyard. Keith Tantlinger had assured Malcom that his design had enough strength in the aluminum sides and roof that loaded containers could be stacked on top of each other. While Malcom appreciated the lightweight of the aluminum, he still had a nagging concern that the thin roof might not stay rigid under pressure and that this could result in the failure and buckling of the container.

Prior to Tantlinger arriving at the shipyard one morning, Malcom decided to perform his own test. When Tantlinger arrived, he saw Malcom, Jim McLean, Cecil Egger and several additional associates jumping up and down on the roof of the container. Despite their best, prolonged efforts at disproving Tantlinger's confidence, the roof remained rigid. With this highly practical yet no doubt humorous test passed, Malcom immediately ordered 200 containers just like the prototypes. Now totally convinced of his technical skills, Malcom then made Tantlinger a job offer to be the chief engineer of his new company, which he accepted.

There was a myriad of innovations that occurred throughout 1955 as Malcom and his team prepared to launch the pioneering service. Because almost everything they were doing was new, they had to rely on their own judgment to come up with practical solutions.

Typical shipboard winches could not lift loaded twenty-ton containers, so they obtained large land based revolving cranes and moved them to Newark and Houston for dockside installation. After reinforcing the dock to accommodate the added weight, the cranes were mounted on rails allowing them to move alongside the vessel. Between that mobility and the 72' boom on the cranes, they could reach any position on the vessel. Tantlinger devised a spreader bar paralleling the size of the container that positioned the crane. Special attachments on the spreader engaged the corners of the container, eliminating labor and making the actual loading and unloading of containers fairly automated.

Throughout 1955, the terminal facilities in Newark and Houston were being prepared. Unlike traditional terminals that primarily involved dockside warehouse space where breakbulk cargoes were stored, Malcom wanted flat, paved areas where the only obstruction would be light towers in order to work at night. Containers waiting to be loaded would be in one area and containers that have been unloaded and are waiting to be picked up by a truck for final delivery would be in another area. All containers in the terminal would be on a chassis, a steel framework with wheels.

When a container is mated with a chassis, it looks very similar to a highway trailer. However, no such chassis existed at that time and they had to be designed and built. While this was a new product, the experience of Malcom and his team with trailers was significant. Their development of the chassis rotated around deconstructing the trailer and adding some reinforcing beams.

For Malcom, the space and layout of these new marine terminals had broad similarities to the trucking terminals they knew so well and so they had a clear guide to follow. Indeed, a defining characteristic of Malcom's philosophy then, and for the rest of his career, is that he saw himself more in the trucking business than in the shipping business.

As the conversion work on the ships neared completion and the other equipment needed was put in place, Malcom hoped to start Pan-Atlantic's new service in late 1955. However, two government agencies weren't moving as fast as Malcom. The Coast Guard wanted proof that the vessel was seaworthy and that the stacked containers wouldn't come off in heavy seas, presenting a danger to both the crew and other ships at sea. Tantlinger orchestrated a test where two containers filled with coke briquets, a cargo of average density and little value, were loaded on top of each other on the first vessel to be converted. Tantlinger went to a local toy store and bought out all the modeling clay they had. He then cut it into small pieces and wedged them between the containers such that indentation would show movement. That vessel then sailed between Newark and Houston and back, with the Coast Guard checking the loads after each voyage. At no time, including after one leg when the vessel encountered heavy seas, did the containers shift or move at all.

With that actual test, the Coast Guard signed off on the seaworthiness of the vessels. That approval in turn resulted in the American Bureau of Shipping, a classification society that set standards for maritime insurers, to also approve the vessels. The ICC also had to approve Pan-Atlantic's new service and the hearings related to that went on for months. The objections of the railroads, however, were overruled by the ICC, which gave its formal approval in late 1955.

Malcom's plans were getting increasing attention in the media as word spread about a successful businessman jettisoning his former business for an untested startup. One of the inquiries he received came from Helen Bentley, a 32 year-old reporter for the Baltimore Sun. Bentley exclusively covered maritime and waterfront issues for the newspaper and also hosted a local Baltimore television program entitled *The Port That Built a City*. Becoming aware of Malcom's plans through her contacts at the Bethlehem Steel Shipyard, she tracked Malcom down by phone to learn more. As Malcom would recall decades later, the knowledgeable maritime reporter opened the conversation with the pointed question of "Are you for real?" After answering with a laugh that he thought he was, Malcom went on to explain his concept in detail. That no doubt would be a recurring thought that many would have, as they became aware Malcom's various initiatives in the decades to follow.

That conversation began a close friendship that would bridge 46 years. Bentley would go on to be appointed Chairman of the Federal Maritime Commission, where she was the highest-ranking woman in the Nixon administration. She then went on to serve five terms in Congress where she was a staunch advocate for U.S. flag shipping interests and the city and port of Baltimore. Her support for the latter was so effective and outstanding that the official name of the port, one of the busiest in the country, was officially renamed the Helen Deliche Bentley Port of Baltimore.

Bentley was also a strong advocate for women and in a dozen or so industry events I attended where she was the main speaker, she always started with "I'm pleased to be with you here in _____, the year of the woman", where the blank represented whatever year we were in. She was a trailblazer for the advancement of women and I suspect would have been even more recognized nationally if she had been a Democrat and not a Republican. Coincedentally, my daughter Caroline's college years were spent in Baltimore at Johns Hopkins University. On the night before her freshman orientation, we had a memorable dinner with Helen Bentley. I was delighted that my daughter could meet and hear firsthand the advice from such an extraordinary female role model.

With the vessels, equipment and terminals in place in early 1956, a precise schedule was established that called for the first sailing from Newark on April 26, 1956. The vessel that would be used was a T-2 tanker built in 1945 at the Marinship shipyard in Sausalito, California. Originally named *Potrero Hills*, Malcom renamed the vessel *Ideal X*.

Many decades later Malcom would share with me the two factors that he was thinking of when he came up with that particular name. The first was fairly straightforward, as he believed his new service was the ideal way of moving merchandise freight between Newark and Houston. The second factor, however, came from Malcom's view that the concept was experimental, so he appended the X that was being used by the military to designate experimental aircraft, such as the X-15, at that time.

The *Ideal X* had been converted to carry 58 33' containers on deck while retaining the ability to carry 15,000 tons of bulk petroleum products in its tank holds. Customers for whom McLean Trucking had moved cargo from New York to Houston were lined up. By offering an attractive rate compared to trucking that could readily be justified to the ICC, all 58 slots were booked. What had made traditional shipping unattractive compared to trucking at the time was the cost and time involved in the loading and unloading, so it was those metrics that Malcom was most focused on as the inaugural sailing approached.

In large part due to media coverage and promotional activities on the new service by the port authority, almost one hundred people including many government dignitaries were present on the morning of April 26. As the *Ideal X* was tied up alongside berth 26 in Port Newark, they watched firsthand as one container after another was loaded every 7 minutes by the crane. A couple of hours after a luncheon hosted by the port authority, the vessel was completely loaded and preparing to sail. In less than eight hours of cargo activity, the new process had loaded the same amount of cargo that it would have taken some three days to load with the traditional breakbulk loading process.

Throughout the day, Malcom was intently watching the loading operation and all the various processes related to moving the loads from the terminal and positioning them under the crane. Walking up and down the ship, he was looking at alignments and clearances and making mental notes on what could be done to refine and improve the processes. He was doing much of this by himself and, as a still generally unknown figure, his observations went unnoticed. The crowd largely dissipated after the luncheon was completed.

Shortly thereafter, however, Malcom noticed a man stationed up on the fly bridge of the *Ideal X*, closely watching the loading operation. Seeing that he was still in the same place thirty minutes later, Malcom climbed up the ladder to the fly bridge. He was curious as to the observations of someone else who was clearly paying attention. Coming up alongside and leaning on the rail next to him, Malcom said "So, what do you think about this?" Not knowing whom the stranger asking this question was, without looking at Malcom he immediately replied "I think we ought to sink this sonna bitch right here and right now".

Malcom chose not to engage him in any further conversation. He would find out later that day that this man was a top official for the International Longshoreman's Association, the union that represented the dockworkers. Except for Malcom, that gentleman had more insight than anyone into what the future held based on what occurred on April 26, 1956.

The successful loading operation without any glitches and in one-tenth of the time it would have previously taken was the main event that reinforced and proved Malcom's concept. The uneventful sailing from Newark to Houston also affirmed that all the engineering calculations were correct and the containers on deck did not make the vessel unstable. While Malcom was confident about both based on his painstaking analysis and planning, even he breathed a sigh of relief as everything rolled out as he had thought it would.

Apparently he wasn't the only one, as while the inaugural sailing from Newark to Houston was fully booked a week before, there was still available space on the return voyage from Houston to Newark. However, as word spread about everything working as expected, it and subsequent voyages quickly began to fill up with bookings. Malcom and his key executives flew to Houston and were there when the *Ideal X* arrived five days after leaving Newark and saw a repeat of successful cargo operations.

Malcom and his team were pleased with what they saw, but Malcom anxiously awaited the final actual cost numbers of the cargo operation. Based on previous analysis, they had already benchmarked the total cost of loading loose breakbulk cargo on a typical ship at $5.83 per ton in 1956. The actual cost of loading the *Ideal X* in Newark came in at 15.8 cents per ton. With cost savings of 97% on a key activity related to shipping, any doubt that container shipping didn't have a very bright future was completely removed. While that view was initially just held by Malcom and his team, over the next couple of decades it would become a view held by everyone in the shipping business.

The expansion and technical improvement from that initial sailing proving the concept was rapid and continuous. The two converted T-2 tankers would be joined in late 1957 by six general cargo ships transferred from Waterman to Pan-Atlantic and converted to each carry 226 containers. By both putting containers in the hold of the vessel and stacking higher on deck, they would have a capacity more than four times the capacity of the *Ideal X*.

The containers would now be 35' long, two feet longer than before and in line with the new regulations related to maximum trailer length on the highway. A number of innovative engineering solutions were developed during this heady period to go along with what would be the first pure container ships. For instance, a framework of cell guides made from ninety-degree angle steel was developed to guide the containers into the hold that is fundamentally the system still used today. With a crane loading and removing a container at various angles and various instruments to measure stress and clearance, Tantlinger spent weeks determining the best spacing for the cell guides. To make the vessels self sufficient, shipboard gantry cranes that moved on top of the vessel on rails were designed and installed. New container chassis were designed with sloping edges so that a container being deposited by crane would be guided into place. Those chassis now had locking system that could be engaged by moving a handle at each corner of the chassis.

The new 35' containers were built with heavy steel posts at the corners to handle the additional weight, as they would now be stacked up to six high in the holds of ships. These containers had steel castings with an oblong hole on all eight corners. The gantry cranes now had spreader bars, which included couplings that could be automatically twisted into the casting to lift the container. These castings would also accept a specially designed twist lock that would secure the containers to one another. Those key inventions are effectively the same as what is still being used today. Refrigerated containers to handle perishable products were designed and built.

All of these various technical improvements shared the characteristic of reducing the labor necessary to load and unload container ships. With the delivery of the first four converted vessels, additional ports and sailing frequencies were added to Pan Atlantic's coastwise network.

Malcom's research of potential new routes had resulted in his turning his attention to Puerto Rico, an island economy which was tied to the mainland for most of what it consumed as well as the market for most of what it produced. As a U.S. commonwealth, Puerto Rico is covered by the Jones Act which requires that its imports and exports to the mainland move on U.S. flag vessels. Malcom knew his container ships could move cargo much more efficiently than existing traditional shipping companies serving Puerto Rico. He earmarked the last two of the converted vessels to begin his first offshore service in March 1958.

When the first ship arrived in Puerto Rico, what Malcom wasn't prepared for was the reaction of the longshoremen on the island. The longshoreman in San Juan simply refused to provide any labor to unload the initial shipment of containers. Because the local union chapter had a lock-hold on the port, the first ship and then the second ship sat alongside for weeks and then months as discussions continued.

Malcom's coastwise services on the mainland weren't popular with the longshoreman, but there had been no work stoppages. Even though the requests for labor were well below what would be requested for a similar sized traditional ship, perhaps because those services were still a small percent of total activity, they weren't a priority and no action was taken. In Puerto Rico, however, presumably the longshoreman there decided they needed to nip this in the bud or it may quickly spread across their particular universe.

After four months of the two loaded ships being tied up alongside in San Juan, with the delay costing millions of dollars, Pan-Atlantic agreed to the longshoreman's demands to use a minimum of 24 men to work his container ships in Puerto Rico. This minimum gang size, regardless of whether that many men were actually needed, would become a precedent in Puerto Rico and then on the mainland that would mitigate some of the cost advantages of the new container shipping process.

However, the savings compared to traditional shipping were still significant and this compromise with labor had no impact on the time difference. Pan-Atlantic's new Puerto Rico service with two full container ships providing weekly service quickly took off with customers. Instead of competing against the rail and trucking modes like the coastwise services, here Malcom was competing against traditional shipping companies and his underlying cost advantage allowed him to offer rates they simply could not match. One of his ships at full capacity could be turned in San Juan in less than a day, whereas a similar sized traditional ship would need a week in port.

The initial problems in Puerto Rico had Malcom realizing that Pan-Atlantic was still too rooted in a maritime culture. He thought the company was too bureaucratic without as much of the entrepreneurial qualities that had helped McLean Trucking grow. From what he could see, the U.S. shipping industry was populated by managers who eschewed competition and looked to the government and its legislative support and subsidies as the prime economic driver.

On Malcom's first trip to Washington, D.C. to attend a conference of all of the U.S. flag ship operators just after he purchased Waterman, he would see this attitude firsthand. After a full day of listening to speeches, during the Q&A period, Malcom said "I've heard lots of talk about what the government should do for us, but I've heard nothing about what we should do for ourselves". Malcom got his response when he heard from the back of the room someone say "Who is that fool?" More than ever, he recognized an overhaul of the culture at Pan-Atlantic was needed to maximize the benefits and expansion of container shipping.

That observation by Malcom would come to epitomize the way I would see years later that he consistently approached business situations. After looking and observing, he would come up with ideas and plans for improvement. He was constantly pushing and stretching his companies, even when that in effect meant competing with and disrupting his own assets. Status quo was a condition that didn't sit easily with Malcom and he always turned inward to see what constructive steps he could take.

In June 1958, Malcom moved Pan-Atlantic's headquarters from Mobile to a warehouse near the Newark docks. Pan-Atlantic was now just operating container ships and Waterman, still operating traditional breakbulk ships, remained headquartered in Mobile. To inject more aggressiveness and initiative into Pan-Atlantic, he turned to the trucking industry. He reasoned that the pure ship part of Pan-Atlantic's business was now relatively small and the cargo handling, terminal and inland transportation parts of the business were more similar to trucking. Besides, with all the new and different approaches being implemented by Pan-Atlantic, the experience of traditional shipping folks in those areas wasn't even relevant.

Malcom's sister Clara and his brother Jim moved to New Jersey and were given responsibility for administration and day to day operations, respectively. In enlisting the skills that had worked so well at McLean Trucking, they helped shift the focus away from the ship and towards moving freight from end to end for the lowest cost. The involvement of these trusted lieutenants also freed up Malcom to focus on improving and growing the new system. Malcom established a lean and flat corporate structure that suited his desire to walk around the office, getting the information he wanted firsthand. New hires mostly from the trucking industry came in and brought with them the aggressiveness and creativity that Malcom wanted.

Key new hires by Malcom included Paul Richardson, Ken Younger, Bernie Czachowski, Charles Cushing, Ron Katims and Ken Johns. Richardson joined McLean Trucking out of college years earlier and was one of the first to go through its management training program. A Boston native with an outgoing personality, he quickly rose to be one of the best performing salesman at the trucking company. Malcom hired him away as New England sales manager and within six months put him in charge of all sales. Younger was hired from Roadway Express to run the Puerto Rico service and in short order also was put in charge of cargo operations at all of the terminals. Czachowski came from McLean Trucking and in his new role managed the key relationships with all the independent truck lines that Pan-Atlantic contracted to pickup and deliver loads between customer locations and the terminals. Cushing was hired after getting an advanced degree in naval architecture from MIT. Malcom wanted to have someone in-house who he could talk with about a range of vessel conversion possibilities and who could provide engineering and architectural context to the array of ideas he was developing. Katims came out of Cornell University where he majored in civil engineering. He was the land-based equivalent of Cushing and someone Malcom could bounce the further ideas he had regarding terminal layouts, shoreside cranes, container and chassis equipment and the interactions of all of those components. Johns was hired upon graduating from Auburn University where he was a star player on their football team. One of the first to go through a management training program patterned after what Malcom had established at McLean Trucking, Johns quickly became a key contributor in all areas of the company. All of these talented men would advance through the organization and would eventually lead their own companies.

Malcom would develop close professional relationships with all of these key new hires. They all became staunch disciples of container shipping and Malcom himself. This would be the core team around which the company would refine and expand its unique freight system. From moving cargo in containers through its Newark terminal totaling 228,000 tons in 1957, over the next two years it quadrupled its volume to 1.1 million tons 1959.

With all of the initial customers, using Pan-Atlantic's new service was a radical change. Whether their cargo had previously moved by truck, rail or traditional steamship line, the switch to what was effectively a new mode needed to be laid out in an easy to follow manner. Working with Richardson, Malcom developed a form called the "Total Transportation Cost Analysis" which became a required document for salesmen to present at each meeting.

This form was a side by side comparison of the cost of moving the customer's product by truck, rail, traditional ship and container ship. It included not only the carrier rates, but also the local pickup and delivery costs, warehousing costs, insurance costs and any other costs involved in the entire movement.

Looked at that way, Pan-Atlantic's overall cost was always lower than whatever the mode the potential customer was using. The salesmen were instructed to highlight the savings per load and to multiply it by yearly volume to show the annual savings. Those annual numbers were typically significant and memorable.

This straightforward, analytically driven sales approach proved quite effective. In addition to the savings involved in total transportation costs, as Pan-Atlantic moved cargo in containers, customers saw firsthand the very low incidence of cargo damage or theft and this became increasingly recognized as an added benefit.

The success Malcom was having implementing his new transportation concept was getting noticed. Media accounts even got the attention of the White House and an event was scheduled where Malcom would be recognized by President Eisenhower as an example of an innovative startup that was making the economy more efficient. The story of what happened on the way to this event is anecdotal evidence of Malcom's fertile mind and its constant focus in always thinking about more efficient ways of moving freight.

On the morning of the event scheduled for that afternoon, Malcom and his wife Margaret took the train from New York to Washington. He had his yellow pad out and was going through several pages of calculations, explaining to his curious wife that he was estimating what the cost per container would be if this same train moved containers rather than people. On his pad, Malcom had developed two different cost per container mile estimates. One was based on moving individual containers on flatcars and the other was based on stacking containers two high. This was based on Malcom's view that special lower flatcars could be developed so the train didn't exceed height restrictions due to the various overpasses he was observing as the train headed to Washington.

When the train reached Union Station, upon exiting Malcom immediately went down on his hands and knees to get a better look at the clearance to see how much lower the flatcars could go. Getting his answer, when he got up his wife was more than a little bit upset to notice that his inspection had resulted in a small tear in his suit pants. With no time to have that fixed and certainly not wanting to be late, they proceeded immediately to the White House. Apparently the tear wasn't noticed, but this story underscores that on that day, Malcom really was more focused on this freight idea and the related analysis than in being honored by the President at the White House.

With the potential of containers moving on railroads, his interest was driven by what the railroads might be able to do to compete with his new service. As a trucker who had spent years in competitive battles with the railroads, he gave little thought at the time to separately developing an idea where a platform wasn't available to him. More importantly, he had satisfied himself that his new service offered costs that couldn't be matched by the railroads. In particular, his further research underscored the hundreds of overpasses that would need to be raised for the more efficient two containers high method to have broad domestic coverage.

It would be almost three decades before the railroads would see what Malcom saw in 1959 and begin moving double stacked containers. That straightforward concept played a large role in revitalizing the rail industry and it would revolutionize domestic transport in the U.S. Indeed, it was the transition of more freight moving from road to rail due to the cost efficiency of double stacking that was one of the catalysts that attracted famed investor Warren Buffet to Burlington Northern Sante Fe. After initially investing in the railroad, in 2009 Buffet reached an agreement to purchase all of the remaining shares in what was his biggest investment ever.

In 1960, Malcom changed the name of Pan-Atlantic to Sea-Land Service to better describe the integrated end to end transportation it was providing to customers in its coastwise and Puerto Rico routes. That name fit squarely with Malcom's straightforward and direct way of describing something as it was in fact a new service that moved freight on sea and land. However, Malcom was more creative in the Sea-Land logo that he designed. Only a handful of people knew what the real inspiration for the red and black logo dominated by a stylized "S" in the middle. Malcom would confide in me that he viewed the logo as a graphic representation of a dollar sign.

The 1960's would be periods of halcyon growth in container volume at Sea-Land. It would become the dominant carrier to Puerto Rico, as traditional ship lines simply couldn't compete on either a cost or time basis. Sea-Land's service was credited with helping to ignite a manufacturing boom in Puerto Rico as manufacturing went from 18% of the economy in 1955 to 25% in 1970.

Sea-Land started a new service to Alaska that followed a similar upward trajectory and displaced traditional operators. A new intracoastal service connecting the East Coast and the West Coast was also started by Sea-Land with much success. Additional coastwise routes and frequencies were added to the company's growing domestic freight network. As each new route unfolded, initially skeptical shippers and competitors were turned into converts and the container revolution began to spread throughout the domestic U.S. Jones Act markets.

For the additional container ships to move this cargo, Sea-Land was redefining the number of ways existing ships could be converted to meet its needs. By inserting new mid-bodies, existing ships were lengthened and made even more cost efficient. Extensions were developed that widened the space where containers could be loaded on deck. The bridges on ships were relocated or raised to improve line of sight visibility and allow containers to be stacked higher on deck. The first several generations of container ships, each much bigger than the ones before, all resulted from significant physical conversions to existing ships.

Sea-Land became the experts in vessel conversion and established its own shipyard on the Gulf Coast to do much of this work. At the same time they were refining and improving the vessel assets used in their system, they were doing the same with the equipment and terminals used in their system. It was a period of constant innovation and refinement. The entire Sea-Land team was focused on putting in place hard assets that allowed cargo to be moved from one place to another more efficiently.

The first ten years of Malcom's container shipping system was exclusively within the domestic Jones Act markets. As the new system spread from one domestic market to another, there were many naysayers consistently indicating why it wouldn't work. Initially they said it wouldn't work in any market. Then they said it would only work coastwise and not in any offshore market. When Puerto Rico and Alaska were successful, they said it would only work in domestic U.S. markets and couldn't work in international markets.

In each market Sea-Land entered into, the strongest proponents ended up being the customers that moved containers on the new services. As they monitored their overall costs and compared them to prior costs, they saw tangible and meaningful savings. When they became more accustomed to using containers, they became better at loading them and using more of the cubic space available in the container, which made the savings even greater. This leaning curve experience was fairly consistent across markets and resulted in early customers becoming very loyal customers and strong proponents of using containers.

In 1965, Malcom began planning to launch a transatlantic service that would be the first international container route. By this time, his domestic services were all successful and expanding. Sea-Land had some twenty container ships operating, all of which were conversions, typically of Waterman general cargo ships.

There was a dozen additional conversion projects in progress, including one that would result in his largest container ships yet for a transatlantic service. Malcom knew that he would be going up against large traditional shipping companies with his transatlantic initiative and was determined to reinforce Sea-Land's financial condition and liquidity. He did this be entering into two outstanding financial transactions.

The first involved selling $10 million of stock in Sea-Land's parent McLean Industries to Daniel K. Ludwig, a major tanker owner who also owned American-Hawaii Steamship Company. Beyond the additional equity capital that also allowed more borrowing, by bringing Ludwig in Malcom pre-empted American-Hawaii's plans to build its own container ships and put them in a domestic intercoastal service.

Malcom would recount decades later the lunch meeting he had with Ludwig where he initially outlined his proposal. Ludwig was ambivalent over lunch and the discussion continued as Ludwig walked to an awaiting car outside the restaurant. Getting in the car, Ludwig said, "I don't want to do it. I've made too many mistakes recently". Malcom then immediately responded "Don't let this be your biggest mistake". When Ludwig asked him what he meant by that, Malcom said he was as confident about his next steps as anything he had ever done and that this had him believing that Ludwig's investment will come back to him many times over. Driven by Malcom's confidence, Ludwig committed to the investment, beginning a close business relationship that would last for more than three decades.

The second transaction Sea-Land entered into was a sale and leaseback of nine container ships for $28 million with Litton Industries, a large conglomerate that owned Ingalls Shipyard on the Mississippi Gulf Coast. As part of the transaction, Ingalls would also be building and inserting mid-bodies and performing other conversion work on vessels formerly operated by Waterman.

In addition, Litton Industries agreed to convert certain notes it held from Sea-Land for previous shipyard conversion work into McLean Industries stock. With this series of transactions, Malcom was getting the larger ships he wanted for the new transatlantic service along with the liquidity to weather whatever initial startup problems he may have. The unexpected issues he had with the startup of his Puerto Rico service was top of mind and he wanted to be fully prepared for any startup hiccups that may unfold.

Sea-Land launched its transatlantic service in 1966. On the first voyage, the majority of the containers were booked by the military, which had significant ongoing shipments to supply the American troops based in Europe. The military had previously used Sea-Land for domestic and Puerto Rico shipments and was willing to be an early user of the new international service.

Indeed, at each leg in the expansion of container shipping, the military was there. In addition to being a large shipper, moving supplies is a core part of the military's mission and this had them analyzing the cost and time of shipmnets in detail and always on the lookout for better methods. This attitude had previously resulted in the military developing something called the conex box. Conex, which stood for container express, was an 8' x 6' x 6' steel box developed in 1952 during the Korean War. With a capacity of 9,000 pounds, it was filled with various supplies. The box was then loaded as another item of breakbulk cargo on a traditional ship. These mini-containers weren't stacked on each other and lacked many other attributes, but from using them the military was undoubtedly more receptive to Malcom's innovations.

The receptivity of international commercial shippers to Sea-Land's new transatlantic service was a different matter and wasn't universal. While customers who had successfully used Sea-Land's domestic services were onboard, companies that hadn't used it were generally circumspect of the new shipping method. Their concerns were exacerbated by traditional shipping companies' active campaign to discredit Sea-Land's new service. When Sea-Land threw a party in Rotterdam to introduce its new service when its first ship arrived, many of the guests booed. The head of Holland-America Line, one of the largest traditional shipping lines in the transatlantic, told Sea-Land's Paul Richardson "You come back with the next ship and take all those stupid containers home".

The shipping companies that were resisting the introduction of container shipping in the transatlantic were following a pattern frequently seen across businesses when an innovator disrupts the status quo. Existing participants in almost all industries don't like change because it tends to devalue their existing assets and business models. It is for this reason that most innovation results from outsiders who don't have this installed base issue.

This is particularly the case in the capital-intensive shipping industry where long-lived multi-decade assets make the installed base issue even more pronounced. A ship owner who just invested in a series of general cargo ships it expected to use for twenty-five years had little interest in swapping that for a new system. In that sense, the traditional shipping companies that fought the introduction of container shipping weren't really questioning the method, which most likely recognized as superior. They were against it solely because they saw it disrupting their own assets and business.

Because Malcom was such a disrupter himself, he was always on the lookout for what could potentially disrupt his businesses and never developed a similar concern. He had and would continue to take steps that effectively had him disrupting his own businesses. Malcom would say in later decades that if you weren't open to competing with yourself with better assets, other people would. A favorite saying of his was that you "had better not stand in the way of progress".

Shortly after Sea-Land launched its transatlantic container service, both Moore McCormack Lines and U.S. Lines launched transatlantic container services themselves. As U.S. flag carriers, they had followed closely the success of Sea-Land in its various domestic services and were concerned about the competitive effect if they didn't have a similar offering in a market they were both already involved.

While Sea-Land's transatlantic service had more frequent sailings and had more efficient cargo operations owing to their experience, all three carriers and their customers reported sharp efficiencies in terms of both cost and time. In addition to the military cargo that was large eastbound volume for all three carriers, the container carriers immediately gained large volumes of liquor shipments on the westbound return leg. In addition to direct freight cost savings, the liquor companies embraced the security that came with moving their valuable products in locked containers. These companies had long complained of the systematic pilferage that occurred on the docks as their products moved on and off traditional breakbulk vessels.

The speed with which container shipping spread over the next couple of years was amazing. From three lines offering container service in early 1966, there were a dozen offering some form of container service in mid-1967. Traditional shipping companies that had initially resisted learned that customers were demanding the new system and they really had little choice. For these new entrants, moving containers on breakbulk ships gave way to moving containers on converted ships, which then gave way to moving containers on the first full container ship newbuildings.

By 1968, there were ten transatlantic container sailings a week and total annual volume was 200,000 TEU's, four times the volume in 1967. Sea-Land, still operating converted ships which were also the largest vessels in the trade, was at the top of the pack both in terms of revenue and cost efficiency.

With Sea-Land's Europe volume growing and more of it originated or destined in the Midwest, Malcom developed a plan to build his own rail yards and put containers two high on his own specially designed railcars. He envisioned contracting with a railroad to pull these dedicated all-container trains between his docks in Elizabeth, New Jersey and the Midwest.

Malcom knew that on relatively long inland movements, the rail system he had in mind would be lower cost than moving the containers on the road via truck. The discussions on implementing this with one railroad ended when it merged with a railroad that opposed the plan. It would be another two decades before the railroads implemented unit trains moving just double-stacked containers in initiatives that would revolutionize domestic transport.

As meaningful as the experience in the transatlantic trade was as a catalyst to expand container shipping internationally was, at around the same time there was another catalyst developing on the other side of the world that would have even more effect. That catalyst was another initiative driven by Malcom and it related to military cargo moving to Vietnam.

The buildup of American soldiers in Vietnam starting in 1965 resulted in significant logistical problems in unloading and dispatching the growing amounts of cargo. By late-1965, there were 45 ships being worked by the military in Vietnam with another 75 ships waiting off the coast or in the Philippines to be unloaded. The problems only got worse as the months went by and this issue was getting attention at the highest levels of government. Changing how supplies were ordered, having ships unload all their cargo at a single port rather than going to multiple ports and using more conex boxes mitigated the issue, but major logistical problems remained.

Secretary of Defense Robert McNamara invited shipping executives to Washington and sought their input. Malcom immediately saw it as an opportunity to demonstrate what container shipping could do to solve the problem. After meeting with defense department officials, Malcom flew to Vietnam with Ron Katims to visit various ports and get additional briefings directly from the military on the problems they had along with key freight needs and goals. Convinced more than ever that container shipping could be made to work in Vietnam, Malcom lobbied the Pentagon to give him the opportunity to prove what he could do.

Sea-Land's first foothold was an April 1966 contract to run a trucking operation to distribute cargo from the port of Saigon. While this had nothing to do with containers, Sea-Land managed it well and gained increasing support within the military. Malcom had several high-ranking military people championing using containers for Vietnam cargo, but there was still very strong resistance from factions that would be displaced if this occurred.

As an aside, when I joined his holding company McLean Securities in 1980, there were only around ten people in our small suite of offices in New York City. It was fairly clear to me what everyone's role in supporting Malcom was except for an older gentleman named Harry Jetay. A delightful man, who knew a little bit about everything, I would learn that Jetay occasionally worked on special projects for Malcom. More importantly, I became aware that Jetay had managed that initial trucking operation in Vietnam. His recounting hiding under a jeep as Viet Cong were attacking an inland trucking depot was a chilling reminder of the dangers even civilians faced. In a measure of Malcom's loyalty, when Jetay was later laid-off from Sea-Land, he was placed on Malcom's personal payroll even though there was no real job that he performed.

In May 1966, Sea-Land got a contract to run three container ships between Oakland and Okinawa, a Japanese island that was a large staging point for cargo moving on to Vietnam. In short order, Sea-Land was able to demonstrate that it could move the same amount of cargo with half the number of ships and one-sixteenth as much labor at traditional breakbulk ships. In July 1966, Sea-Land was awarded a contract to move containers to Subic Bay, a major naval base in the Philippines and another staging area for Vietnam. By this time, there was a general acknowledgement that container service directly to Vietnam should be implemented, but the timetable kept getting pushed back, mainly by the military unit overseeing current port operations.

However, Secretary McNamara's visit to Vietnam in October 1966 where he spent much of his time visiting ports and seeing firsthand the backlog had the effect of moving things into high gear. That same month, a contract was awarded to Sea-Land to not only move containers directly to Vietnam from the West Coast, but to also operate the terminals and provide trucking service under a fixed priced contract. Sea-Land's willingness to provide service under a fixed price contract instead of the usual cost plus arrangement underscored Malcom's confidence in what they could do.

Sea-Land began direct service to Vietnam in March 1967. Using seven container ships in total, with three large ships and four smaller feeder ships, this network began improving the logistical bottlenecks in Vietnam immediately. The success was well beyond even what Sea-Land had expected. In short order, three linehaul ships would replace more than a dozen general cargo ships.

Because container shipping was solving such a high profile problem, its success quickly became widely known and written about. Shipping companies and their customers who had been ambivalent were now onboard. An overriding view was that if container shipping could do what it did in Vietnam with its unique challenges, imagine what its potential in other areas and trade lanes without those challenges.

Malcom would be the first one to exploit what could be done in one of those other trade lanes. In spite of the significant cost savings the military was getting, Sea-Land was generating a solid profit with its Vietnam service even with his three large ships returning with empty containers to the West Coast. As a trucker at heart, Malcom abhorred empty miles.

Looking at the map, Malcom reasoned that they should approach Asian manufacturers to solicit their interest in shipping products back to the U.S. in containers. In a whirlwind business trip to Japan in 1967, Malcom received commitments from Mitsubishi and several other large shippers. The initial shipments they made met or exceeded expectations. As these manufacturers compared the actual total costs and time of moving products in containers versus in general cargo ships, they wanted to move all of their products by container. The late 1960's saw Sea-Land grow exponentially in eastbound container shipments in the pacific as one shipper after another saw the benefits in moving their manufactured products in containers.

Sea-Land's success with both its transatlantic and transpacific services was quickly copied by other companies as word on the effectiveness of this new system spread. Some dozen years after the advent of container shipping as a domestic conveyance system, it was now rapidly morphing into the international conveyance system that has shown extraordinary growth ever since.

The international expansion of container shipping was aided by Sea-Land relinquishing patents it had obtained and not pursuing other patents it could have likely obtained. Malcom knew that standardization would assist in the progression of container shipping and he willingly passed on the technology that he and his company had invented.

Almost all of the new assets and processes that made container shipping possible were developed by Sea-Land. It was an amazing lab of innovation during those halcyon early years. Besides passing along its technology, the shipping companies that converted to container shipping were meaningfully assisted in doing so by former Sea-Land employees. In populating the industry, these managers passed along the operating know-how and experience that allowed container shipping to expand geometrically in the late 1960's and beyond.

Had Malcom's sole focus been wealth accumulation, he would have acted differently in a number of ways. Instead, he was both internally and externally the strongest proponent for the adoption of container shipping. Whether meeting with his own team, shippers, port authority officials or government leaders, he was constantly attempting to help others see the future that he saw. His focus was directly on container shipping itself and not solely on the peripheral monetary aspects.

I had a firsthand example decades later when he was talking about one of his early trips to Japan and referred to an opportunity he had to buy 200 acres of what was then rundown dock land in Tokyo. Pulling out a map from an ever-present stack of atlases in his office, he roughly outlined the land in question and tasked me with coming up with an estimate of the current value of that land. Returning to his office a couple of hours later, I said the developed property was worth in the tens of billions, which would certainly put the land value alone in the billions. Malcom smiled, saying that he knew the $2 million that could have bought the land would have been a great investment. However, he said that just wasn't his business and his capital was focused on ships and equipment.

In 1969, on the heels of strong growth and financial performance at Sea-Land, R.J. Reynolds acquired the company for $530 million. Even though that is a relatively small acquisition by today's standards, it was one of the largest acquisitions ever at that time. It was driven by the desire of the large tobacco company to diversify itself.

Much of the acquisition price was in the form of a new class of convertible preferred stock. With Malcom owning some 40% of Sea-Land at the time of the acquisition, he became a board member and the largest shareholder at R.J. Reynolds with close to 10% ownership. The $10 million that Ludwig invested a few years earlier was now worth $100 million. Malcom's siblings Jim and Clara each received almost $50 million in value from the acquisition.

Malcom served on the R.J. Reynolds board through the mid-1970's. He championed the 1970 acquisition of Aminoil, an oil exploration company based in Kuwait, as both a good investment and a hedge against Sea-Land's fuel cost. It was a prescient call, as Aminoil would be sold for $1.7 billion in 1984, some thirty times the original purchases price.

Sea-Land continued to grow and in 1972 built its first new container ships, the eight SL-7 vessels. With a capacity of 1,960 TEU each, the SL-7's were the largest container ships in the world. With a 33-knot speed, they were also the fastest cargo ships ever built. For the names of Sea-Land's new ships, Malcom initially wanted them to be called #1 through #8 but relented over objections that this would be too far outside of maritime tradition. Malcom had little fondness for maritime tradition and as a trucker at heart viewed a ship as another power unit to move cargo. His new tractors were numbered and he thought the same framework should be used for ships.

Despite this straightforward approach when it came to naming ships, Malcom had a more flamboyant side when it came to marketing how his ships were different. A key differentiating factor of the SL-7's was their speed and Malcom would recount for me the plan he had developed to get customer attention as they were deployed in various services. As an SL-7 approached a port for the first time, Malcom envisioned surfers riding the wakes on each side. His research had confirmed that the size of the wave and its speed were sufficient for a professional surfer to continuously ride. Malcom was confident that such an event would get local news coverage that would favorably highlight the maiden entries of these large and fast ships. Concerns developed related to where the surfers would begin and what happened if they fell off their surfboards. In the end, the capabilities of the SL-7's were announced by press release in each port they first entered without this tangible example of one of those capabilities.

When the SL-7's were ordered, crude oil was selling for $3 per barrel and the residual fuel used in ships was at a slight discount to the price of crude. At those prices, the overall cost economics of the 33-knot SL-7's were competitive and the transit time advantages were attractive to Sea-Land's customers. However, with the formation of OPEC shortly after the SL-7's were delivered, oil prices quadrupled and the SL-7's suddenly had a meaningful cost disadvantage at their design speed. To mitigate this, they operated at slower speeds and the service they offered was more in line with that of competitors.

Malcom's other key initiative as a Reynolds board member was pushing for the acquisition of U.S. Lines, a shipping company that had transitioned to container vessels. The government, however, blocked this combination on the grounds that it would reduce competition.

During the period he was on the Reynolds board, Malcom founded a major real estate development company that began building houses in a number of communities in the Southeast. In one instance, he built modular sections of homes in a central location and moved them by barge to where they would be assembled. He also bought Pinehurst, the premiere golf retreat in his native North Carolina. After the spike up in oil prices in 1973, Malcom acquired 200,000 acres of land in North Carolina with large peat deposits where he explored using it as a fuel source for utilities. Among his other investments during this period was a life insurance company and various venture capital related situations brought to his attention by his investment bank.

These investments were funded from sales of his R.J. Reynolds stock as he was increasingly restless in the role of an individual board member. Malcom's hands on approach didn't sit well on a large corporate board. From his growing up in North Carolina and hauling tobacco products in the trucking industry, he knew the tobacco industry. Aware of a competitor initiative with a new cigarette with a distinctive colored filter, enroute to a board meeting he counted cigarette butts in large sand filled ash urns in the hotel he lived in.

Armed with data from his impromptu survey, Malcom indicated to the board that the initiative was much more successful than expected and R.J. Reynolds needed to move quickly to come out with a similar product. Management dismissed his observations as being inconsistent with their more detailed data. Six months later after the actual volume figures had been tabulated, the board would learn that Malcom's observations were almost exactly on point. Unfortunately, by that point the competitor had a big jump and R.J. Reynolds attempts to catch up with its own similar product failed. With the success of its new Malboro product, the title of largest cigarette producer in the world had passed to Phillip Morris.

In another example of Malcom's recognition that board service was not his highest and best calling, he recounted a board meeting where R.J. Reynolds management along with its investment bank outlined a potential acquisition that was being reviewed. Because of a confidentiality agreement, they said they weren't able to reveal the name of the company. Malcom asked, "If we guess who it is, will you tell us if we are right?" As the characteristics of the company were described, Malcom would in fact guess who it was. Around the same time, he came to a final determination that this board role just wasn't for him.

Malcom would observe to me more than once that "after someone has worked for himself, he is ruined to work for anyone else". While that's an accurate assessment for just about anybody, I believe it was particularly applicable to Malcom himself. He had effectively worked for himself since he was 21 and had grown accustomed to implementing decisions based upon his own rigorous analysis and judgment. R.J. Reynolds preferred passive directors who followed management's direction and this was chafing to Malcom.

In 1972, Malcom's investment bank arranged a luncheon meeting for him with a 26 year-old named Fred Smith who was seeking an anchor investor for a startup transportation company moving packages overnight by air. At that point in time, nobody offered such a service and the market for it was largely undefined. Malcom was very impressed with Smith but admitted that with his constant focus on the lowest cost method of moving any freight, he was a little out of his element on air transport, the highest cost mode. Nevertheless, he had studied Smith's business plan carefully and his biggest questions related to the pricing of this new premium service.

In his projections, Smith had used $1.50 per package for his revenue estimate. Malcom told Smith he thought that was too low, and that $3.00 per package made more sense to him. When Smith asked Malcom how he came up with that, Malcom said that the cab fare from where they were in midtown to downturn Manhattan was $3.00. Malcom said that was the closest comparable he could think of for quick delivery of important documents. He reasoned that Smith should get at least that for a package going overnight across the country.

Smith appreciated Malcom's insight. When he returned a couple of months later still seeking an anchor investor, the projections were based on revenue of $3.00 per package. Malcom enjoyed telling the story of his tangential role in the birth of Fedex. While it would have been an even better story had he agreed to invest a million dollars at the second meeting that would have been worth billions today, Malcom would remain friends with Fred Smith for decades.

By the late 1970's, Malcom had come off the board of R.J. Reynolds and was focused on getting directly back into a transportation business himself. He indicated to his investment bank what he wanted to spend and that he would like to know about any transportation business that they believed was available within that range. His bankers came back with two candidates they believed could be bought for something in his range.

Those transportation companies were American Airlines and U.S. Lines. While American Airlines intrigued him, its passenger focus and higher cost mode couldn't really compete with the other company that he knew well and that fit squarely into his area of expertise.

Malcom bought U.S. Lines in 1979 for $160 million. At the time, it was one of the larger container shipping companies with a network of transatlantic and transpacific services. Those included domestic services connecting the east and west coasts as well as Hawaii. However, it had an aging fleet and little that differentiated it from the rest of the industry. U.S. Lines was a U.S. flag carrier and a distant second in size to Sea-Land. Malcom would now be going head to head with his former company. In an article in Forbes magazine, the purchase was aptly described as "as if Henry Ford after leaving Ford decided to buy Chrysler."

It was at this point in time that I entered into Malcom's orbit. I was in my first year at Harvard Business School after having spent a few years in corporate banking with a large New York City bank. In March 1979, Business Week had Malcom on the cover with an accompanying article entitled "Malcom McLean's $500 Million Gamble". My managerial accounting professor started his class by holding up the magazine and saying it was a great read and an example of the sort of initiatives we hope to teach you about here. I read the article, which rotated around Malcom's idea to rebuild a moribund shipping company with new vessels, and was fascinated. I had heard stories about him growing up, as he had become a local legend in my hometown of Mobile when he bought Waterman Steamship to start the container revolution.

Ditching my plans to take a summer job at an investment bank, I sought and obtained a summer job at U.S. Lines. It seemed like a fairly low risk way to explore what looked like an exciting entrepreneurial situation. My summer job exposed me to an exciting, tangible industry and I was hooked, particularly after meeting Malcom. He was at a separate holding company where he worked with a small group of professionals. Presumably Malcom was curious about the interest of a young Harvard Business School student and agreed to a meeting. I spent an hour with him and heard firsthand his plans for reinvigorating U.S. Lines. When back at school, I stayed in contact with Malcom's office and upon graduating from business school, I went to work at the holding company.

Reporting to the chief financial officer of what was then called McLean Securities, I assisted in analysis and obtaining financing related to revitalizing U.S. Lines fleet and assets. The key element of that related to building twelve new vessels known as Econships. Tasking his naval architects with designing the biggest container ship that could transit the Panama Canal fully loaded, these ships would have 30% container capacity than any vessels afloat.

When delivered, the Econships would be deployed in a unique eastbound round-the-world deployment. In doing so, they would cover the strongest legs of U.S. Lines routes, such as the Far East to the U.S. and the U.S. to Europe, with more capacity. The round-the-world deployment would also open up major new routes to the Middle East and a multitude of smaller routes within the overall deployment. Smaller feeder vessels would augment the deployment at key hub ports. The Econships were also designed to operate at a relatively slow 18 knots to conserve fuel.

Malcom was focused on the Econships having the lowest cost per container mile, by a wide margin, compared to any ship in the world. With that in hand, and the core existing business from the 19 older vessels in transatlantic and transpacific services the Econships would replace, Malcom was confident that his latest ideas made sense.

Malcom had always been comfortable with debt and his confidence in the low cost economics of the Econships resulted in our seeking significant financing for the vessels and related containers. Over a course of a couple of years, we obtained various financing commitments for ships and related equipment of over $1 billion.

One sticking point with a key lender was not the new Econships themselves, but the round-the-world deployment. To address their specific concerns, I prepared a detailed analysis demonstrating that if the Econships were simply deployed in U.S. Lines current routes carrying only existing container volume, profits would increase. This allayed their concerns and they accepted the view that the best deployment of the significant capacity of the Econships was the eastbound round-the-world route.

In 1982, the trigger was pulled on contracts to build the twelve Econships along with all of the related container equipment. Daewoo Shipbuilding in Korea would build the ships under what was the largest shipbuilding contract in history. That contract was a key catalyst in moving Korea to displace Japan as the largest shipbuilding country in the world. To provide additional liquidity and financial flexibility, McLean Industries, the renamed parent company of U.S. Lines, went public and also issued several hundred million of public debentures.

When Malcom acquired U.S. Lines, it had annual revenue in the $600 million range. It operated on the largest routes in the world but an aging fleet near full capacity constrained its growth. Malcom's plans to revitalize its fleet and assets put the company on a strong growth curve. Additional vessels were chartered and acquisitions were made. Moore McCormack Lines, a large U.S. flag shipping line with services to South America and Africa, was purchased along with Delta Lines and Farrell Lines, two U.S. flag operators serving the South America and Europe markets, respectively.

As the Econships were being built, they were criticized by many in the shipping industry as being too big and not needed. One competitor derisively referred to them as "Malcom's canoes". There was even a rumor originating in the industry that the Econships were too wide and wouldn't be able to fit through the Panama Canal. Malcom took all of this in stride, quietly re-affirming his confidence in ships that would have a materially lower cost per container mile compared to any of the competitors. One of his favorite expressions was "you can't stop progress" and he clearly viewed these behemoths as the next step in the natural progression of container shipping.

Fundamentally a private man with no interest in generating press coverage, Malcom's latest efforts nevertheless had him more in the public light. He turned down all requests by business and industry publications for interviews. A voracious reader himself of newspapers and magazines where he gleaned useful information on competitors, Malcom had no interest in providing his competitors the same insight. When he wasn't reading or working through an analysis on his yellow pad at his midtown Manhattan office, he was likely to be doing the same thing a block away at his residence in the Pierre Hotel.

For relaxation, one of Malcom's favorite activities was to walk his dog, a small Shih Tzu named Lucky, in nearby Central Park. One of those walks in 1982 resulted in an encounter one summer evening that said much about Malcom. Sitting on a park bench and playing with his dog, Malcom noticed a young man at the other end of the long bench reading a magazine. Several minutes later, the young man noticed Malcom and his dog and a conversation ensued, rotating around the cute dog. The young man then said, holding up and pointing to his Forbes magazine, "I've been reading about all these rich people in the Forbes 400. None of them understand the joy of walking dogs. Don't ever get where you can't walk your dog". With that, the young man departed. In that issue, Malcom was listed among the top fifty in the Forbes 400 with an estimated net worth of $500 million. Because the young man had referred to the conglomerate he worked at as assistant treasurer, Malcom thought about reaching out to him to highlight the irony in his comments. Not surprisingly, he decided not to do something that would have been out of character for him.

The only public presentation Malcom would make during this period was in 1983 at the Merchant Marine Academy at Kings Point, New York. He acquiesced to repeated requests by alumni and friends of Kings Point who had worked with him in the early days of Sea-Land. They wanted him to share his insights on the shipping industry with students at the federally chartered college tasked with turning out trained mariners. Malcom did so by walking the students through a series of whimsical cartoons that he had produced, with the assistance of my sister as the artist. An auditorium packed with students and alumni listened to and enjoyed this rare public presentation by Malcom.

In 1984, Malcom was named the recipient of the Admiral of the Ocean Sea Award, the highest recognition given by the U.S. merchant marine sector. President Reagan sent a telegram to Malcom which read "America was built by men and women possessed of a dream for a better future and the courage and conviction to realize their vision. Your career has exemplified this spirit of determined optimism."

Around the same time, Walter Wriston, the junior banker who worked with Malcom three decades earlier on the purchase of Waterman, published his own autobiography. Wriston had risen to the top of Citibank and was widely recognized as the most influential and powerful banker in modern times. In the foreword of his autobiography, Wriston referred to only one other person and it was Malcom, who he called "the sort of entrepreneurial risk-taker that America could use more of".

Beginning in mid-1984, the Econships started to be delivered and were slotted into service. Volume and revenue at U.S. Lines stepped up to a new level. By late 1985, annualized revenue was running at more than $2 billion, some four times what it was when Malcom acquired the company. U.S. Lines was now the largest container shipping company in the world, with slightly more revenue than Sea-Land.

However, the operating results were poor and the company was losing money. Less than expected vessel utilization on the Econships and U.S. Lines network of other vessels resulted in debilitating rate reductions. In addition, a sharp reduction in oil prices reduced the cost advantages of the Econships. The 18-knot vessels also had a service disadvantage compared to other ships that increased speed due to lower fuel costs.

The Econships had been ordered when oil prices were at historical highs and projected by many leading economists to go even higher. With the collapse of oil prices, this turned out very differently. The Econship design wzs influenced by relatively high oil prices, just as the SL-7 was influenced by low oil prices. The impact of both of these then largest container ships in the world was mitigated by the unexpected price changes of energy. While Malcom was on the wrong side as it turned out, in both cases the speeds the vessels were optimized for was a logical decision based on the facts that existed at that time. As analytical and focused on the current facts as he always was, Malcom was not someone to spend much time on speculating about fundamentally unknowable things like the future direction of oil prices. He dealt squarely with the facts that were in front of him which for the most part served him very well.

Against this backdrop, competitors in the industry were also doing everything they could to make things difficult for U.S. Lines. Competitors would take turns having what was referred to in the industry as a "fighting ship" arrive in a port a few days ahead of an Econship and offer low one-time rates to divert cargo. In addition, U.S. Lines belonged to a rate setting conference that refused to allow lower rates for all-water Far East to East Coast service compared to faster service with double stack trains via the West Coast. This made it easy for shippers to select the faster service, as it had the same price as the slower service. Malcom was particularly frustrated by the illogic of setting equalized rates for a premium intermodal service compared to an all-water service with two weeks more transit time. His efforts to get conferences and regulators to intervene in this nonsensical policy were unsuccessful. While competitors had derided the Econships just a couple of years earlier, by their actions they feared them and there was a concerted effort to defeat them.

The poor operating results at U.S. Lines were stanched by cash injections from McLean Industries. The parent company had several hundred million in liquidity owing to its public equity and debt offerings that I was managing in short-term money market investments. However, lenders became increasingly concerned as losses continued and cash dwindled. Various discussions and negotiations with lenders failed to come up with any agreeable restructuring and by mid-1986 the situation was becoming tenuous.

Malcom's focus returned to his earlier idea of a combination between U.S. Lines and Sea-Land. This time, his idea was that both would be acquired by CSX, the large railroad. Malcom envisioned that U.S. Lines newer fleet, the services of the two biggest container carriers and largest eastern railroad would combine into a formidable transportation juggernaut. Starting in mid-1985, Malcom would travel to Richmond, Virginia, the headquarters of CSX, more than half a dozen times to promote his plan. At each of those meetings, CSX's receptivity increased and we further refined the deck highlighting the benefits of such a combination.

In the end, CSX implemented just part of Malcom's plan by acquiring Sea-Land for $700 million in mid-1986. We would learn that Sea-Land executives had convinced CSX that U.S. Lines was headed for bankruptcy and its key assets could be purchased for less at that time. As an aside, the financial advisor to CSX on its acquisition of Sea-Land was the newly formed Blackstone Group in what was their first major assignment. A young Steve Schwartzman came by Malcom's office as part of his due diligence. Blackstone received a large fee for that transaction, but Malcom was the real catalyst behind the deal. Today, Schwartzman heads up Blackstone Group, which is considered by many to be the most powerful financial institution in the world.

In November 1986, U.S. Lines filed for bankruptcy protection. Due to the intertwined corporate relationships, this also resulted in bankruptcy filings by McLean Industries and its real estate subsidiaries. It was the largest international bankruptcy filing in history. Because many overseas locations didn't recognize the jurisdiction of the U.S. bankruptcy court, the ability to continue various services was severely constrained as vessels and assets were subject to random seizure. The round-the-world service was discontinued and the twelve Econships were laid-up in friendly jurisdictions.

Concerned about having their cargo adversely affected, customers abandoned U.S. Lines for other carriers who were actively fanning the flames of those risks. Various attempts to reorganize as a smaller shipping company failed and the bankruptcy proceedings evolved into a process of auctioning off vessels and remaining services. Sea-Land purchased the Econships and the Hawaii service at bargain basement prices. At the end of the bankruptcy proceeding, the only thing that remained to reorganize around were large tax loss carryforwards of over $1 billion each at both U.S. Lines and its parent McLean Industries.

The bankruptcy filing and the process that ensued after the filing devastated Malcom. This went beyond the economic loss to him, even though no party was more economically harmed than Malcom. His stock in McLean Industries, once worth over $800 million, became worthless. He had never sold any of his stock, either at the initial public offering or as performance later declined, and maintained his holdings equal to 85% of McLean Industries total outstanding stock.

Furthermore, because the predecessor to McLean Industries was his personal holding company, many assets that were more personal in nature remained and were drawn into the bankruptcy. This included a 25,000 acre hunting preserve and $10 million of R.J. Reynolds stock, both at such a low cost basis that they were unknown to investors but that became a windfall for creditors. While Malcom recognized early on in the process that there would be no recovery on his stock holdings, he stayed involved. He had never known failure like this, but he was still committed to doing what he could to maximize the recovery to creditors. There is little doubt that he was also motivated to do what he could to restore his reputation.

Despite a number of ideas suggested by Malcom to operate a smaller shipping company, the creditors were ill disposed to give any of those ideas serious consideration. When it came down to selecting a strategy to monetize the net operating loss carryforwards, the creditors exhibited the same bias against Malcom.

By this point, I was working directly with Malcom on an idea I had developed to monetize the large tax loss carryforward. He was willing to provide the capital for a new company formed by McLean Industries that would issue adjustable rate preferred stock and invest the proceeds in the highest rated commercial paper. The dividend income on adjustable rate preferred is effectively tax free to the corporations that buy it and they are willing to accept lower rates than comparable taxable investments. Because the net operating loss carryforwards would shield all income taxes on the taxable commerical paper, this investment vehicle could capture the 1.5% historical spread between these securities. With the initial capital, the commercial paper securing the adjustable rate preferred and the quality of the securities, the rating agencies told us they would give their highest rating to an investment vehicle that could be leveraged twenty times.

This elegant financial arbitrage would therefore result in a 1.5% times 20, or 30%, annual return on whatever capital was invested. Rather than moving ahead and joining Malcom on this approach, however, the creditors elected to turn the net operating loss carryforwards over to private equity sponsors who convinced them that the carryforwards would make their returns even bigger. In exchange, the creditors got small minority positions in new leveraged buyout vehicles. Nothing came out of that ill-fated decision and the rejection of a tangible way to monetize the tax benefits for what was a speculative bet was extremely wrongheaded. However, the creditors blamed Malcom for all of their problems and didn't want to be associated in any way with him.

Malcom's legacy was certainly impacted by the U.S. Lines bankruptcy, but the reasons behind the failure are still much misunderstood. While most put the blame on the Econships and pointed to Malcom's hubris in pushing ahead on such an ambitious expansion and deployment, neither was the primary catalyst. The Econships in fact lived up to projections of having the lowest cost per container mile slot of any vessel afloat. It wasn't them, but it was other vessels that proceeded them.

Departing from the original plan, the acquisition of additional vessels and companies in the lead up to the delivery of the Econships collectively represented a financial commitment as large as the Econships. These acquisitions were championed by operating management at U.S. Lines. Anytime U.S. flag vessels or companies became available, they pushed to acquire, both to ramp up volume in anticipation of the Econships and to minimize potential competition. While that may have made for a smoother transition, when the Econships were delivered, the existence of that higher cost capacity was very problematic. The market for U.S. flag vessels is limited and there was no ability for U.S. Lines to rid itself of high cost, high debt burdened vessels that were no longer needed.

Management at U.S. Lines included a near family member as CEO, Malcom's son as president and his two son-in-laws in senior executive positions. Neither they nor other associates brought into senior positions had particularly relevant work experience. There were no material changes in management at U.S. Lines during a period when the company more than quadrupled in size. In my view, this operating management group was over their competence level from the beginning and the gap increased over time.

The involvement of family members also complicated the ability to remedy the situation. While all of this was still Malcom's responsibility in the end, he fulfilled his role as visionary with the introduction of the Econships. He was however poorly served by people around him in the implementation of the original plan. It is fair to say that he viewed the relative cost benefits of the Econships to be so pronounced that anybody could succeed so he minimized the role of operating management. Among other things, the failure at U.S. Lines is also a case study in the inherent dangers of nepotism.

With the wind down of the U.S. Lines and McLean Industries bankruptcies, Malcom asked me to stay with him and further develop some ideas he had. Our focus quickly moved to what we might be able to do with a new transportation venture focused on the domestic U.S. trade lanes. This came at a time that the truckload sector in the U.S. was quickly transitioning to larger equipment sizes. The container shipping industry has historically achieved less utilization on the inland segment of intermodal movements. In the continental U.S., much of that was due to the fundamental fact that the 40' container typically used was now much smaller than the equipment moving pure domestic freight.

The truckload industry had already transitioned to 48' equipment and was beginning a further shift to 53' equipment in some states. This equipment was not only longer, but higher and wider than typical containers and had up to 50% more inside cubic space. We were determined to address this directly by adapting our vessels to what works best on the highway rather than vice versa.

This resulted in our buying two large barges with almost 15,000 linear feet of lanes on three decks which could be adapted to accommodate any length equipment. A detailed and systematic review of each of the Jones Act markets lead to the conclusion that our relative competitive cost advantages would be most pronounced in the Puerto Rico market.

It was during these formative years of analyzing, discussing and implementing his next steps that Malcom would begin sharing with me firsthand accounts of his earlier days at McLean Trucking and Sea-Land. Over long lunches and dinners that would often go late into the night, Malcom gave me an oral history of all the key points in his extraordinary business life. More than once, I encouraged him to work with a biographical author to have his story put in a book so that the public and history would benefit from a firsthand account of his extraordinary life.

Malcom was fundamentally a very private man and almost everything written about him had been without his cooperation. When I gave him a copy of such a biography just written about J.B. Hunt, a pioneer in the truckload sector, he seemed to be warming up to the idea. At the time, we were in discussions with Mr. Hunt to participate with us in our new Puerto Rico service.

In the end, however, it went too much against the grain of who he was. Malcom remarked that long after he was gone, maybe I should write the book. My wanting to add to the historical record on Malcom's life was a large part of the inspiration in undertaking to write this book. History would have been better served if he had cooperated with a professional writer on his biography. However, my hope is that people and history will learn more about this extraordinary man from my attempt to be the James Boswell to his Samuel Johnson.

One prominent characteristic of Malcom was his ability to constantly absorb new information. He was consistently focused on taking in new inputs, both through direct observation and from a voracious appetite for reading relevant periodicals. Malcom was always learning. This extended to words and one of his favorite reference books was a large unabridged dictionary that was always open on its own rostrum in his study.

When he heard or came across a word that was used in a way that puzzled him, he looked it up in his dictionary. Perhaps because of this habit and his preference for precise language, one of his few pet peeves was the use of buzzwords by business people in general and transportation people in particular. In the latter category, few words raised his ire as much as "logistics".

That came up one day in his study when Malcom, looking at his dictionary, pointed that it is primarily defined as the military procurement of supplies. His view was that it was a broadly misused term often used by people who knew little about transportation. Indeed, on many occasions when someone had used that term in Malcom's presence, I would hear Malcom say "Logistics. What do you mean by that?"

In any case, what made that day in the study memorable was Malcom's observation of the word that came just after "logistics" in his dictionary which was "logjam". Malcom smiled, noting that transport folks who talk about logistics rather than just efficiently moving freight from one point to another will often find themselves in a logjam. He would share his observation with J.B. Hunt, another plainspoken transport pioneer who also began as a truck driver. That observation would be repeated often by Mr. Hunt at many of his own presentations.

Malcom's curious nature and his constant learning mode translated into very little confirmation bias in the business decisions he reached. Confirmation bias is the tendency to have past decisions channel and direct present decisions and it is typically present to one degree or another in almost all business people. But just as Malcom started with a clean sheet on his yellow pad for any detailed calculation, he tended to look at each business matter he focused on as a separate event requiring its own analysis.

This extended the decision time but almost always resulted in better decisions. Like expert carpenters say, measure twice and cut once. Malcom would look at things from many different angles prior to making a decision. Indeed, discussions with Malcom could sometimes be confounding because of his ability to see the merits in various sides of a given situation. Just when he seemed to be leaning in one direction, he would come up with the arguments against that approach before landing at a conclusion. In Malcom and other exceptionally gifted thinkers I've come across, I believe the ability to recognize contrasting arguments and the absence of any strong confirmation bias results in both insight and the best decisions.

The ability to look at and weigh both sides of a given situation didn't mean that Malcom was without core business principles from which he wouldn't vary. First and foremost was his overriding view that cost was everything when it came to moving freight. One of his favorite expressions was that "freight was something added to the cost of the product" and as such he always believed the focus of manufacturers has been and always will be minimizing that cost.

To succeed in the freight business, Malcom believed the prime focus had to be on minimizing your underlying cost to be in synch with the goals of your customers. When anybody would say that service or some other aspect was more important than cost, Malcom would gently probe those assertions. Invariably, the core of those assertions would turn out to be costs expressed in a different way.

One element of his focus on costs rooted in his days as a trucker was that using the largest available equipment size resulted in the most efficient system-wide costs. Among other things, this resulted in a strong disdain for 20' containers that even extended to using the term TEU for twenty-foot equivalent units to describe vessel capacity. Everyone who dealt with Malcom knew that the appropriate metric to use related to vessel capacity was the size in terms of forty-foot equivalent units. They also knew that if Malcom saw any twenty-foot containers in one of his terminals there better be a very good reason for it being there. While he recognized that equipment size worked for selected shipments, his overriding concern was it didn't work for the large majority of shipments. These smaller containers result in low utilization, which is never good for transport efficiency.

Malcom would recall a trip to Puerto Rico in the mid-1960's where he was walking the terminal with his local manager. Coming across a 20' container on a chassis at the edge of the terminal, it was surrounded on all sides by grass almost three feet high. Malcom expressed his displeasure in seeing that equipment and asked the manager how long it had not moved. His answer of a couple of days wasn't credible to Malcom who pointed to the grass. The manager said, "Mr. McLean, you have no idea how fast the grass grows down here in Puerto Rico". His point having been made, Malcom would never again see a 20' container in Puerto Rico or in any of Sea-Land's other terminals in future visits.

Given his edict against those small containers, I was flabbergasted when he came into the office one morning in 1989 and said "Maybe I've been wrong about 20' containers. There is a legitimate use for them." I must have been slack jawed, for it was as if Moses had said not to worry about the commandments. Recognizing my confusion, Malcom smiled and said from watching the news the previous night, he saw that Iran's Ayatollah Khomeini was buried in a twenty-foot container.

While Malcom spent most of his time thinking about his businesses and working through numbers on a yellow pad on how to improve them, he relaxed through his favorite pastimes of golf and quail hunting. Most of this occurred at Sehoy, his 25,000-acre hunting preserve in Hurtsboro, Alabama. The property included a large antebellum house, private nine-hole golf course, large lake, assorted outbuildings and a private runway for Malcom's Gulfstream II. His luxurious 12-passenger jet was used almost exclusively to fly Malcom and assorted guests from New York to Sehoy, which was named after a native-American princess. Sehoy was originally owned by the DuPont family and was one of the largest privately owned plantations in the south. Malcom was an extraordinary host and time spent at Sehoy was always a very enjoyable and memorable experience.

Malcom had taken up golf later than most people had but he embraced it and enjoyed the sport immensely. His private golf course at Sehoy was among the first in the country and it and the beautiful countryside that surrounded it was a central part of almost every day at Sehoy. Malcom's passion for the game had earlier become evident when a real estate company controlled by him purchased Pinehurst, the legendary golf resort in North Carolina, in 1971. At Sehoy, he could indulge in that with a close knit group of friends whose company he enjoyed. At a lunch we had with an investment banker who knew of Malcom's interest in golf, he volunteered that Malcom must have done lots of business and deals on golf courses over the decades. Reflecting for a moment, Malcom said "I don't think I've ever done any business while golfing. I just like to play golf with friends."

Sehoy was located in the eastern part of Alabama near the Georgia border in an area referred to as the plantation belt. That area contains some of the best natural quail hunting in the country. Sehoy was a venue allowing Malcom and his guests to engage in this sport at the highest level while enjoying five star accommodations. To ride on horseback through magnificent countryside, watching the dogs work the fields, come to a point when they sense a covey of quails and then see the covey being flushed is to commune with nature in the grandest manner.

Malcom's friend Sam Walton shared his passion for quail hunting and several times piloted his own small plane to Sehoy, accompanied only by his favorite hunting dogs. Walton reciprocated with invitations to his own quail-hunting place in West Texas that Malcom went to once. Quite different from Sehoy, it was more of a typical rustic hunting camp with sparce accomodations in trailers. Malcom would not return, recounting later that he "didn't like to travel somewhere to be uncomfortable".

In 1992, at the age of seventy-eight, Malcom launched Trailer Bridge, which provided weekly service between the mainland and Puerto Rico in the largest vans that moved on the highway. Malcom's simple analogy was that if there was an actual bridge to Puerto Rico, all of the full-load freight would move in the same efficient sizes that the same freight was moving in on the mainland. In effect, the vessels were floating highways, hence the name Trailer Bridge.

Rather than typical container vessels, the cargo Trailer Bridge handled was moved on two large roll-on, roll-off barges that were towed by 8,000 horsepower ocean-going tugs. Trailers and containers on chassis were moved on and off the vessels by driving them on via a ramp with no cranes used. That the inventor of container shipping would choose to use the roll-on, roll-off method underscores the fresh, driven by the analysis approach Malcom took to all major business decisions.

The value proposition Trailer Bridge offered was well received by customers and it consistently grew its business by a double-digit percentage in a flat market. Starting with two vessels, Trailer Bridge grew to seven vessels in 1998 when it began taking delivery of new vessels it built following its initial public offering of stock. They were the first vessels in the world designed to exclusively move 53' containers. To load and unload these vessels, we developed a new process was was patented with Malcom and I as co-inventors. Ironically, that is the only actual patent that lists Malcom as an inventor.

The naval architect we relied on as Trailer Bridge first mid-bodied existing vessels and then built new vessels was Charles Cushing who was an early employee at Sea-Land. A decade earlier his firm had designed the Econships.

Many of our meetings would start with Malcom asking "Charlie, how many of those too-big container ships are now operating around the world?" Over the years, the answer went from 20 to 50 to 100 to hundreds. Today, the number of container ships now operating equal to or larger than the Econships stands at 2,146 vessels. With an average capacity of 7,703 TEU's, the typical vessel in that gargantuan fleet is almost twice the size of an Econship. The largest vessels are more than five times the size of an Econship.

Malcom's vision of Econships and the economic benefits they would deliver was clearly ahead of its time. The Econships redeployed by a healthy Sea-Land in its key routes more than proved their cost efficiency. To compete with those vessels, competitors were required to build new vessels that size. Not content to just match sizes, it was predictable at some point that the Panamax barrier was broken. This cycle accelerated as China entered the World Trade Organization. Each step up in size would lead to another round of matching and exceeding to both stay competitive and gain an edge. This effectively became an arms race to get ever larger and more efficient container ships. While this resulted in excess capacity and poor results for the container shipping sector itself, world trade volume benefited immensely from the rates resulting from this arms race.

A strong case can be made that Malcom's leadership with the Econships and what flowed from that innovation was almost as ground breaking as his earlier invention in terms of the economic benefits it delivered to the world. Just as the sailing of the *Ideal X* in 1956 was the beginning of the container revolution, the deliver of the Econships in 1984 and the larger vessels they ushered in started a second container revolution that lowered shipping costs further and dramatically increased world trade. The first revolution was from specialization with similar sized vessels. The second revolution was from the geometric expansion in size of those specialized vessels. Malcom was the catalyst for both.

The advent of container shipping had pronounced effects on labor on the docks and even on the ships. Both the number of men needed to work a ship and the total time it took to work a ship went down geometrically, decimating the employment ranks of longshoremen. The manning level on a typical ship carrying merchandise cargo also came down as with containers there was little for the crew to do relative to cargo.

However, these were never primary goals of Malcom. He was focused solely on developing a new and better process. He was known to say "a ship earns money only when she's at sea" and his recognition of that truism certainly played a role in developing the groundbreaking process he invented. That this significantly faster process also required significantly fewer men was a causal effect.

From my direct experience with him, I never heard him make a single negative comment about labor. Quite the opposite, in all his analysis he assumed that prevailing manning and wages would apply. More that once, Malcom said that container shipping was the natural progression and someone else would have come up with it if he hadn't.

Malcom saw progress as inevitable. Everyone, however, did certainly not share his views. I vividly recall being at a shipping industry event with Malcom honoring a maritime labor leader. Also in attendance was Teddy Gleason, the 90-year-old former President of the International Longshoreman's Association during many of the early growth years of container shipping. When he passed our table, Mr. Gleason was heard to say, with a sneer, "There he is, Mr. Automation".

I suppose it's understandable that a leader of a union whose membership would drop by more than a factor of ten wouldn't like container shipping, but his animosity towards Malcom was misplaced. In an industry that is often viewed as anti-labor, Malcom embraced the dignity of labor and never went out of his way to hurt labor.

On the 40th anniversary of the sailing of the *Ideal X* in 1996, there was a large industry dinner featuring former Secretary of State Henry Kissinger as the speaker. In his speech, Dr. Kissinger extolled the role of trade in promoting peace worldwide. President Clinton sent a message which read as follows "Four decades ago, when the *Ideal X* sailed with the first shipment of containerized cargo, few could have foreseen the global impact of your innovative idea. Containerization has created international trading relationships that have fueled the world's economy and helped to keep its peace. You have helped to ensure a brighter, more secure future for us all."

Around the same time, Malcom was inducted in the Business Hall of Fame by Fortune Magazine and was named by American Heritage Magazine as one of ten outstanding innovators over the past 40 years. Forbes also described him as "one of the few men who changed the world".

Malcom's personal life was not without loss and drama. The death of his wife Margaret in 1992 after 55 years of marriage was a sharp blow. Malcom would spend much of the next couple of years at his hunting preserve in Alabama. Following his return to his apartment at the Pierre Hotel in New York, he would meet a woman who worked at the Pierre. They began spending time together and would eventually marry in 1995.

Because Irena McLean was significantly younger than Malcom, this relationship resulted in a fair amount of acrimony among various members of Malcom's family. Malcom went into the relationship with his eyes open and required that Irena agree to a pre-nuptial agreement, which would provide a relatively modest sum for Irena. She cared for Malcom and he cared for her over the course of their marriage. Over the years, Malcom would elect to make additional provisions that would provide for Irena beyond what was in the pre-nuptial agreement.

While less involved in his business interests following his marriage, Malcom took great satisfaction in the success of Trailer Bridge. Its initial public offering in 1997 represented the fifth IPO of a company Malcom had founded. Those companies were McLean Trucking, the first McLean Industries which owned Sea-Land, Diamondhead Corporation, a large real estate development company, the second McLean Industries which included U.S. Lines, and Trailer Bridge. From research by stock exchange officials at the time, that was a record as there was no other individual involved in founding five completely separate public companies.

In 2000 at a large ceremony held at the United Nations in New York, the International Maritime Hall of Fame recognized Malcom as the "Man of the Century". In his brief remarks, Malcom, as he always did when he was given such an award, referenced the contributions of others that were involved in the development of container shipping.

Following a brief illness, Malcom died at his home in New York on May 25, 2001 at the age of 87. Dozens of newspapers and magazines ran articles on this largely unknown individual and a summary of his innovative life. Previous quotes from presidents were referenced, such as Reagan's characterization of Malcom as having a "spirit of determined optimism" and Clinton's statement that Malcom helped to "fuel the worlds economy". The Baltimore Sun said "he ranks next to Robert Fulton as the greatest revolutionary in the history of maritime trade". Secretary of

Transportation Norman Mineta said "Malcom revolutionized the maritime industry in the 20th century. His idea for modernizing the loading and unloading of ships, which was previously conducted in much the same way the Phoenicians did 3,000 years ago, has resulted in much safer and less expensive transport of goods, faster delivery, and better service. We owe so much to a man of vision, 'the father of containerization', Malcom P. McLean".

A crowd that overflowed onto Fifth Avenue attended Malcom's memorial service at a large Manhattan church. Business leaders such as Walter Wriston, the banker who helped finance his purchase of what would become Sea-Land almost half a century earlier, were in attendance. The eloquent eulogies by Charles Cushing and Helen Bentley touched on the personal relationships they had developed over more than four decades of friendship with Malcom.

Midway through the service, container ships around the world sounded their horns in tribute to Malcom. What had started with our instructing Trailer Bridge vessels to sound their horns, and then making calls to people at Sea-Land to request they do the same, had quickly spread to dozens of shipping companies around the globe. At the appointed time, there were literally thousands of ships at sea that made three long blasts, a traditional maritime acknowledgement, in a final salute to Malcom. Given that one of his favorite expressions was "Don't honk your horn until you're ready to pass", I'm certain that Malcom would have smiled at that tribute.

As Malcom's executor, over the next few years I would take on the added responsibility of administering his estate and distributing his assets as he instructed in his will. That would prove to be a role with its own set of challenges given the dynamics at work. However, the estate was successfully settled and more than two hundred million in value was distributed collectively to the beneficiaries.

There are a multitude of thoughts and memories that come to mind when I think of Malcom. Over the last twenty years of his life, I had almost daily contact with him, either in person or by phone. First and foremost, he was a man of great insight and foresight. When you reflect on the arc of his life and what resulted from his innovations, its hard not to conclude as I have that he was the greatest transportation thinker in history. I think much of his extraordinary vision came from an insatiable curiosity that always seemed to be present in Malcom.

This repeatedly showed itself in matters big and small. Malcom prioritized the big business matters and always had a way of separating the wheat and chafe to circle in on the core issue. He liked to break things down into granular components as part of his analytical processing. Malcom also had a gift for reconstructing the pieces into easy to understand examples. In the case of a freight movement, that included the estimated cost per load at each node and how that compared to competitors.

Malcom saw everything in relative terms and one of his favorite expressions was "If you don't have a comparison, you don't have anything". His business decisions came from a bottom up analytical approach that he was constantly revisiting and refining. Numbers were the language he was most comfortable with when it came to talking about any business decision.

He took the same methodical and analytical approach to key personal decisions he made. While Malcom was a teetotaler who never drank alcohol the entire time I knew him, he did drink earlier in his life. He recounted to me an evening decades earlier when he found himself awake in the middle of the night after having had too much to drink earlier. He went to his study and on a yellow pad, proceeded to list those things he did better after drinking on one side and those things he did worse on the other side. After spending a fair amount of time thrashing out both lists, Malcom surveyed the results and determined then and there that he would never have another drink with alcohol. However, that was a quiet resolution and with his graciousness as a host many of his guests were never aware that he didn't drink. Malcom would later show the same direct and immediate approach when he went from a heavy smoker to a non-smoker overnight.

Malcom's curiosity about how things do and should work extended beyond his own business interests. Whether it was something he read about that morning or saw on television the night before, conversations over lunch would sometimes go into interesting tangents that would often result in a friendly wager. The number of cows in Florida, whether the U.S. treasury would accept a donation and the number of people migrating out of New York in a given year were among dozens of such discussions, often involving a $1 wager related to the outcome.

He took everything in like a sponge, whether walking around a freight yard, reading multiple newspapers and periodicals or listening to colleagues. Malcom took all the relevant information in, worked up his own numerical analysis and came to a decision driven by his own counsel. He was a man of action who was confident in his decisions without being arrogant.

The combination of a strong intellect and a sharp focus on the key cost factors had Malcom confident in and comfortable with the business decisions he made. Because he had usually broken the situation down, looked at it from every angle and put it back together on his yellow pad, his bottoms up approach gave him insight. Malcom was certainly smart, but he was also wise. There are many more smart people in business than there are wise people. I believe Malcom's higher level insight emanated from his detailed first-hand experience from the ground up in the freight business and the businessess in which it interected. Whether on a customer loading dock or driving to the destination with hours to reflect on the cargo and the business, he was absorbing the relevant information. Malcom would in effect utilize that same framework when he was at his desk analyzing a particular business situation. His analysis was smart and focused, but the judgment coming out of his process was usually wise.

Malcom had a genteel, unassuming manner in how he dealt with everyone. Like the young man in Central Park who said he should never quit walking his dog, if you didn't know who he was, a discussion with Malcom would be recalled as a talk with an unusually polite southern gentleman rather than a businessman whose thoughts and efforts changed the world. A shipping industry colleague who knew him well captured this characteristic when she referred to Malcom as a "gentle giant".

The consistent thread in everything Malcom did was about using superior assets. In the freight businesses that dominated his life that meant using better hard assets that by themselves resulted in a cost advantage. One of his favorite sayings was that freight was something that was added to the cost of the product. He thought freight decision-makers were similarly motivated and if you could show that your freight service resulted in lower costs, you would get their business.

Malcom's mission in life was developing and utilizing better hard assets that would give his companies a cost edge. He was always looking for how he could move freight from one point to another point for a lower cost. Malcom achieved that time and time again in both the trucking and shipping sectors. While his focus was on what those efforts could do for his companies, his greatest initiatives were copied and the benefits were spread throughout the economy and the world. To the extent that imitation is the greatest form of flattery, Malcom is probably the most flattered businessman in history based on the eventual economic impact of his genius.

There are dozens of stories that I could recount that highlight Malcom's insight into matters related to shipping, transportation and business. There are two stories, however, that come to mind that in my view underscore the curiosity and observation skills that under-girded his incredible insight. Both involved site visits, one of Malcom's favorite ways to absorb primary data about whatever he was working on.

The first story related to spending most of a Saturday morning watching a container ship being discharged in Port Newark. The company was in the process of being sold and after looking at the numbers we wanted to observe firsthand its unloading process. We were intrigued with the possibility of buying this company and transitioning its business to something more similar to the Trailer Bridge model. Coincidentally, the ship was being worked just a few hundred yards from where the *Ideal X* began its pivotal voyage more than four decades earlier.

Much of Malcom's observations related to that historic day and his vision that containers would be handled just as we could see them now being handled in front of us. At one point, after ten minutes of intently watching a series of containers being discharged, he turned and asked "So do you think this new system is going to work?" His big smile gave away that he was channeling the skepticism from decades earlier. He went on to note that, after seeing this operation, we would be better off to organically grow Trailer Bridge.

The second story involved inspecting an operating tanker that was for sale on the market. One of the paths to growing Trailer Bridge we were considering was to acquire a tanker and convert it to move 53' containers on its deck. No doubt Malcom was in part influenced by what he had done four decades earlier. We were met at the gangway by a young second mate who had recently graduated from one of the merchant marine academies. The ship's agent had alerted the captain that a potential purchaser wanted to inspect the ship and the captain assigned the second mate to accompany us.

As we toured the deck and engine room of the vessel, the second mate heard us talking about our potential conversion plans. Malcom responded to one of his questions by saying he had once converted a tanker to carry containers and he was thinking about doing it again. The second mate stopped in his tracks and pulled the pad out of his pocket, which had our names that he had written at the gangway. Looking at his pad, he said, "Are you THAT McLean?" Malcom smiled and nodded, to which the young man said, "I thought you died a long time ago!" Malcom, in his early 80's at the time, laughed and couldn't have been more tickled at the reaction of this young mariner.

That someone the second mate immediately recognized as an industry legend was still walking around a ship to see firsthand if it might fit an innovative idea he had says much about Malcom. Beyond that interchange which would make Malcom smile each time he recalled it, the visit re-affirmed our plan to build new vessels to move 53' containers. This was primarily because the unique cargo handling method we had devised for those new vessels would be more cost efficient than what could be accomplished with converted tankers.

Malcom was an extraordinary entrepreneur whose keen insight allowed him to see new innovative ways of moving things from one point to another. Just like any man, however, he had his weaknesses. One of those weaknesses was that he didn't put as much of a premium on the experience and competence of other managers as he should have. His innovations resulted in using different assets and processes that resulted in meaningfully lower costs, and once that was accomplished, he perhaps minimized the role of operating management in implementing a better system.

More than once, I observed to folks that Malcom didn't really like to compete. By that, I didn't at all mean that he didn't like to go head to head against other companies to secure customers business as he embraced the challenge of the marketplace. However, he didn't believe that challenge was won by just more work with the same hard assets. Malcom wanted to have a tangible edge in the hard assets his companies deployed to move freight from one point to another. He always wanted to have a built-in advantage in his business model.

It is in that sense that Malcom didn't like to compete, for his best innovations did in fact give him such an edge cost-wise that it really wasn't a real competition to gain customers and grow well above other freight providers. With that model top of mind, he didn't always pay appropriate attention to the effectiveness of management in implementing his vision.

That certainly was the case of the Econships and the failures at U.S. Lines where he was ill served by family members and others with which he had historical relationships. Like the proverbial frog in boiling water, by the time Malcom realized his colossal mistake in the managers he selected, the die had been cast and it was too late. While in later conversations with me it was clear that he recognized and took ownership of that mistake, he also learned from it. A core edict of Malcom's while we were building Trailer Bridge was that none of his family members would be involved in managing the company.

It was my great pleasure and distinct honor to work with Malcom. While I benefited from a great education at Harvard Business School, I learned about the freight and transportation business from a master and true giant. It was that constant state of learning that most comes to mind when I reflect on that period. You rarely came away from a meeting, lunch or dinner with Malcom without learning something.

What started as my high respect for Malcom only grew over the years. While he had no reason to view me as anything other than someone with potential when our relationship began, his respect for me also grew over the years. Through time spent together and perhaps something akin to osmosis, I believe I came to look at and process things the way Malcom did. I'd like to think that some of his insight and foresight on all matters related to transport rubbed off on me in our work over two decades. Among other things, that contributed to two patents in my name and a focus on innovative processes at Trailer Bridge. Customers embraced our differentiated transportation system and by 2005 Trailer Bridge had the highest profit margins of any container shipping operator in the world.

Malcom was not someone who gave out many compliments, but his highest compliment to me came over a lunch shortly after Trailer Bridge's IPO in 1997. Musing about where I was in his organization some fifteen years earlier, Malcom said he thought U.S. Lines would have turned out very different if we had the same relationship back then that we had now. I'd like to think he was right on that observation.

As we go to press, there was a recent recognition of Malcom that it many ways best sums up his contributions. The Cato Institute, a well regarded think tank based in Washington, D.C., recently initiated a project known as Human Progress. Their goal is to share data that shows dramatic improvement in human well being throughout the world. As part of this effort, they have published a series referred to as "Hero of Progress" where they profile individuals whose lives have tangibly improved human well being. People profiled include Johanness Gutenberg, the inventor of the printing press, and Jonas Salk, the discoverer of the polio vaccine.

The 17th Hero of Progress recognized by Human Progress was Malcom McLean. In its profile, they recognized that the lower cost from container shipping was the key to the growth in world trade that lifted hundreds of millions of people out of poverty. Malcom is the first and so far only businessman to be so recognized by the Cato Institute. That's an incredible legacy for anyone, but one that is entirely deserved when you understand what sprang forth for the world from the genius of this remarkable giant.

7. D.K. Ludwig

The Father of the Supertanker.

This secretive entrepreneur's pioneering use of innovative construction and financing techniques catapulted him to the top ahead of more colorful shipowners. As the first to cross the 100,000 DWT barrier, he ushered in the era of supersized ships. Forbes named Ludwig the richest man in the world in its inaugural Forbes 400 issue.

Daniel Keith Ludwig was born on June 24, 1897 in South Haven, Michigan, a port city on Lake Michigan. He was the son of Daniel F. and Flora Ludwig. His father was the captain of the *Mary Ludwig*, a two-masted 85' long cargo vessel that provided shipping service in the Great Lakes region. The *Mary Ludwig* was built in 1873 at a small shipyard operated by Charles Ludwig, D.K. Ludwig's grandfather. Charles Ludwig was a local entrepreneur who also operated several sawmills and constructed Ludwig's Pier that also housed several of his enterprises.

Like his future friend Malcom McLean, the first money Ludwig ever earned came from shining shoes. At the age of nine, with $75 he had saved from shining shoes and selling peanuts and popcorn, Ludwig with the assistance of his father bought a sunken 26' boat that was raised and then repaired at his grandfather's shipyard. Upon completion, the boat was chartered out. Despite it being a project involving several family members, Ludwig's father saw to it that all the profits went to his young son. Ludwig would spend the next several years working around the shipyard and the other business enterprises operated by his family.

In 1912, his parents divorced and 15-year-old Daniel Ludwig headed down the Mississippi with his father to Port Arthur, Texas. His father had a job in shipping and Ludwig became a runner for a ship chandler who sold marine equipment. Ludwig took a math course at night as he was focused on becoming a marine engineer.

A year later, they relocated to Michigan where Ludwig got a job at a Fairbanks Morse marine engine plant for twenty cents an hour. He proved to be extremely proficient and after a year was sent to the Pacific Northwest to install marine engines. By this time, he had completed all the requirements to get a marine engineer's license.

Shortly after arriving in the Pacific Northwest, Ludwig began moonlighting and installing engines on his own time. This work proved to be so profitable that he quit his company job and focused on working for himself. At the age of 19, he would never draw a check from someone else and was now working for himself.

Ludwig learned of an old sidewheel lake steamer that was idle and up for sale. Controlled by a Detroit bank that had foreclosed on it, the *Idlewylde* was available for $5,000. With a guarantee provided by his father, Ludwig was able to buy the *Idlewylde*. Using his knowledge of marine engines and seeking to reduce his risk, Ludwig recovered almost his entire purchase price by gutting the vessel and selling off the machinery and boilers. This effectively turned the vessel into an iron-hulled barge.

He then successfully chartered the barge along with a tug he bought to a distributor who moved molasses from New York to a distillery in Ontario via the Hudson River, Erie Canal and Great Lakes. Shortly after this charter began, the U.S. passed the 18th amendment prohibiting alcohol. This resulted in a sharp increase in demand for Canadian whiskey that would find its way back into the U.S. After a few years of profitable charter income, Ludwig sold the vessels to the distributor. His first overall experience as a vessel owner had been very lucrative.

In 1921, Ludwig became aware of a refinery in Massachusetts with a Navy contract to supply fuel oil. If he could find any available vessels, he reasoned he could charter them to the refinery in a low risk venture. Ludwig found a nearly complete tanker whose construction was abruptly stopped by the War Shipping board when World War I ended. His engineering skills allowed him to complete the vessel and get a Coast Guard seaworthiness certificate. With the 474 ton *Anahuac* leased from the War Shipping Board, Ludwig was now in the oil tanker business. However, the *Anahuac* was too small to fulfill the charter requirement he now had with the refinery.

Searching for any available vessels, from a scrap dealer he learned of the 35-year-old *Wico*, one of the first tankers ever built but now considered too old by Standard Oil. The asking price was $25,000 that he didn't have. Ludwig turned to a former customer, however, who provided the funds in exchange for a 51% interest in the venture, including the leased vessel and the refinery charter. The venture proved to be nicely profitable over the next couple of years, but Ludwig's partner was predatory and used his majority holding to squeeze out the young entrepreneur. Ludwig settled for $40,000 in cash, telling himself he would always be in control in any future business ventures.

Now with a solid knowledge of the oil tanker business, Ludwig used the settlement cash to establish American Tankers Corporation, which obtained a contract to provide gasoline to a chain of filling stations in Boston. He had a couple of partners who had an ownership interest in the filling stations, but they were passive. Ludwig saw to it that the documents put him in total control. His first move was to purchase the *Phoenix*, a 7,400-ton tanker owned by the War Shipping Board, for $57,000. Amtankers, as he called his company, put up just $14,000 with the rest of the purchase price borrowed from his bank.

Ludwig put the *Phoenix* into service and most of its time was spent fulfilling the contract to supply gasoline where it was earning a consistent profit. An incident in 1926, however, would forever affect Ludwig and also influence various aspects of his future career. Coming into Boston harbor with a load of gasoline, vapors started leaking through tank seams secured by rivets. Fumes overcame two crewmembers working on a pump. Ludwig was onboard and went down to investigate.

As Ludwig was going down the ladder in the hold, a spark ignited an explosion that blew him twenty-five feet up where he landed on another deck on his spine. It was painful, but it didn't seem that serious at the time. The next day, he had recovered enough to go back down the hold and recover the bodies of the two crewmembers who were overcome with fumes. Ludwig's back injury would cause him decades of pain. Years later he would find that three of his vertebrae had cracked in the accident and had fused back together as new bone tissue formed. Right away, however, he had determined that he was going to be a proponent of the new process of welding ship seams rather than the traditional riveting method.

By 1927, Ludwig was operating out of an office in lower Manhattan and had bought two more tankers. During the late 1920's, he was actually more involved in buying and selling ships than in operating ships, but he managed to make a profit in all of the transactions. In 1929, Ludwig purchased the *Ulysses*, a 14,000-ton coal collier that was laid-up in the Panama Canal Zone. With an adroit financing package underwritten by the U.S. government, Ludwig had the *Ulysses* converted at Baltimore's Bethlehem shipyard into the largest tanker in the world.

The *Ulysses* project marked the beginning of Ludwig's relationship with Robert Malone. A bureaucrat who knew his way around Washington, Malone would become Ludwig's long term Washington representative. The *Ulysses* was a profitable ship for Ludwig and it would figure in a series of successful restructurings Ludwig and Malone would engineer as the effects of the Great Depression were felt on Ludwig's business in the early 1930's. At this time, the government held most of his loans. Ludwig and Malone were particularly adroit at getting extensions and changes that benefited his financial interests. More than once, they were able to forestall threatened foreclosures on various vessels.

During the 1930's, Ludwig added to his fleet by purchasing additional tankers, each of which he elected to hold in a separate Delaware corporation. His growing prosperity was evident as he moved to a more impressive office in midtown Manhattan. In 1935, his flagship tanker *Ulysses* entered into a charter to move oil to Italy. That immediately got him embroiled in a diplomatic situation involving President Roosevelt and Secretary of State Cordell Hull. Neither wanted any perception of American support for the fascist government of Benito Mussolini. It typical fashion, Ludwig was able to extract concessions and expand his government connections from this episode.

In 1936, Ludwig established National Bulk Carriers, which would become the flagship corporation for his group of companies. The idea behind this, which apparently came in large part from a government suggestion, was to buy surplus government ships and convert them into vessels that could move liquid bulk cargo such as oil and dry bulk cargo such as coal. The flexibility to carry one type of cargo outbound and another type of cargo inbound was attractive and the government wanted to replace old, slower oil tankers and coal colliers with faster merchant ships. To put him in the best position for this expansion, Ludwig sold his prized *Ulysses* and that allowed him to payoff all of his government loans.

Ludwig then bought two surplus ships from the government for unusually low prices. This was in part due to his commitment to spend many times the purchase price to convert these vessels. It also probably had much more to do with the effectiveness of Malone and another former government shipping employee who now worked for him. By this time, Ludwig had an excellent understanding of how to leverage his government connections and influence to his personal economic advantage. The most important thing that happened in 1936, however, was Ludwig's development of a financing concept that would drive the extraordinary growth in the shipping empire that was to come.

His early experiences with partnerships had been costly and the continuous workouts he had found himself involved in with government loans had been frustrating. Ludwig wanted a way to get money quickly to expand without taking on partners or heavy mortgages. What he developed at the time may seem obvious now but it was pure genius then.

Ludwig referred to it as the "two-name paper" arrangement. It involved signing a long-term charter to ship oil with an oil company, then taking the charter to a bank and using it as collateral to build or renovate a ship to move the oil to fulfill the charter. The oil company would make charter payments directly to the bank which, after taking out the principal and interest due on the loan, would put the balance in Ludwig's account.

This simple arrangement was legal and logical and would benefit Ludwig immensely. It would also be copied in one version or another by other ship owners, some claiming it was their idea. For instance, Aristotle Onassis put together similar structures but it was at least three years after Ludwig first started using his structure.

Ludwig's brilliant financial engineering concept began a steady climb towards his becoming the largest tanker owner in the world. His climb was also aided by the fact that a new customer that had recently come onboard would become his dominant customer. Ludwig was now moving crude oil to refineries controlled by the Rockefeller Empire.

Colonel E.L. Drake drilled the first oil well in the world in 1859 near Titusville, Pennsylvania. While this discovery did little for Colonel Drake, it was the catalyst for a young accountant to begin a business venture that would be well known in history. In 1864, 25 year-old John D. Rockefeller ventured into the oil fields of western Pennsylvania with a goal of making money from this new commodity. Crude oil itself seemed to now exist in unlimited quantifies, but by itself was viewed as having little value. Ironically, one of the few uses of crude oil in an unaltered state was for relieving coughs as settlers had learned to drink small amounts of the viscous liquid to coat their throats to relieve coughs.

However, when refined, the products from crude oil could be used for lighting and heating homes and as raw materials in an array of manufactured products. Young Rockefeller quickly surmised that the most advantageous part of this new business to be involved in was refineries. Rockefeller began building what would eventually be a monopoly in the U.S. refinery sector. He was able to utilize products beyond the kerosene that other refineries focused on and this resulted in competitive advantages that he used to consolidate much of the industry.

The advent of automobiles and further industrial uses for refined oil products resulted in extraordinary growth in demand for Rockefeller's refineries. He built what became by 1911 the largest business enterprise, measured relative to the economy it operated in, that the world had ever seen and probably ever will see. In that year, the government broke it up into individual oil companies. Today's corporate descendents of the original Standard Oil include Exxon, Mobil, Chevron, Amoco, Sunoco, Marathon and most of the U.S. operations of British Petroleum. John D. Rockefeller's wealth in 1913 even after the breakup is estimated to be the equivalent of $392 billion in today's dollars.

For decades after the breakup, the oil companies controlled by Rockefeller's descendants would be the dominant forces in both the domestic and international oil businesses. By hooking up with what was effectively a cartel via long term vessel charters, their growth propelled increased demand for Ludwig's tankers. With his "two-name paper" structure, he could get the financing he needed to build the tankers to satisfy demand from the oil companies.

A charter with a major Rockefeller controlled oil company was obviously viewed favorably by most banks. What made this virtuous circle even better for Ludwig was that the bank he came to work with most related to his new financing structure was Chemical Bank, which itself was controlled by the Rockefeller family at the time.

Ludwig first used his financing structure to convert existing cargo ships into tankers that he then chartered out long term. Focused as he always was on costs, he established a shipyard in Virginia where he performed his own conversion work. With the expectation that the U.S. would be drawn into the war that was raging in Europe, the government notified Ludwig that he would need to relocate his shipyard. Ludwig found a new location in Norfolk, Virginia and named it Welding Shipyards based on the construction method that would be exclusively used by his shipyard. Ludwig wanted to focus on building new tankers that he saw as fitting even better with his financing structure.

The buildup to the U.S. entering World War II was good for shipping and for Ludwig's business. By 1941, he owned nine tankers which were all operating under long term charter. With the formal declaration of war, there was an immediate need for additional new tankers and Ludwig's Welding Shipyards was operating at full capacity. As new tankers were built, they were chartered to the government and their construction was financed using his innovative structure.

In addition to growth in his owned vessel fleet, Ludwig obtained a contract to manage dozens of government owned tankers. At the height of World War II, Ludwig owned almost twenty tankers and also managed forty tankers owned by the government. The years during World War II were prosperous for Ludwig with some owned tankers generating profits of up to $1 million annually. In addition, he was also getting steady and lucrative management fees from the government owned tankers.

Ludwig's Welding Shipyards constructed 21 tankers between 1941 and 1950. As the name indicated, his shipyard joined the steel plates and beams used to construct ships through welding them together rather than using rivets. This method had been developed and implemented by Henry J. Kaiser's West Coast shipyards to build Liberty ships. Ludwig was not too far behind in implementing this approach in the first completely commercial application. This fundamental difference in shipbuilding methods saved both costs and time.

The first tanker built at Welding was the *Virginia I,* an 18,900 DWT vessel named after Ludwig's wife. The *Virginia I* was sunk by a German submarine in the Gulf of Mexico in May 1942 but Ludwig was already building additional tankers of the same size. These tankers were some 2,000 tons bigger than the conventional T-2 tankers being built by other American shipyards. By this time, Ludwig had developed a strong conviction that bigger is better and that those larger vessels were the most cost efficient and economical to operate.

This simple conviction would drive almost everything he did in the shipping industry going forward. A couple of years after building the Virginia class tankers, Ludwig's Welding Shipyard began building a series of new 23,600 deadweight ton vessels. They were not only a third larger than the then largest tankers, but had some of the largest cargo vessel engines ever that would propel them at an 18 knot speed. In building these larger and faster tankers, Ludwig had an eye on the commercial markets and the extensive rebuilding that would be required after the end of the war. At the same time he was populating his fleet with new and larger tankers, Ludwig was adroitly selling some of his older tankers to the government.

With the end of World War II, Ludwig turned his attention to the new commercial markets that were developing. One of his companies, however, would continue to manage for several years government-owned tankers under a lucrative contract. He sought and succeeded in buying from the government T-2 tankers that he repaired and improved at Welding shipyard.

Ludwig was also successful in getting legislation passed which effectively pushed up the prices the government asked for smaller Liberty tankers and also precluded converting Liberty general cargo ships into tankers. While Ludwig had no interest in the former type vessels, that legislation served to increase the value of all U.S. flag tankers including his own. With regard to the latter type vessels, Ludwig wanted to cutoff to other ship owners the very path he used after World War I.

By early 1947, Welding Shipyard was busy employing almost 1,500 workers on numerous projects. Ludwig had just laid the keel on his latest "world's biggest tanker", a 28,000 deadweight ton tanker he was naming the *Ulysses* after his prized earlier ship of the same name. He was also repairing and converting surplus ships he had purchased as well as repairing tankers owned by the government and others. Welding Shipyard was humming with activity twenty-four hours per day. Sticking with his bigger is better philosophy, Ludwig moved ahead with designs and plans related to the construction of five new tankers that would be twice the size of a typical T-2 tanker.

The general manager in 1948 of Welding Shipyards was Elmer Hann, who previously was the production manager at Kaiser's Swan Island, Oregon shipyard. Hann had developed a welding method that could be taught to unskilled workers in 10 days. After the end of the war, Hann joined Welding Shipyards and it benefited from the experience of this innovative and efficient shipbuilder. All of the vessels Ludwig built at Welding Shipyards were operated as U.S. flag vessels. At the time, that did not confer a meaningful cost disadvantage compared to the other major merchant marine fleets.

Ludwig was now the largest independent tanker owner and operator of U.S. flag tankers. By building large new tankers and buying up surplus tankers, he had risen in the two years since the war ended from fifth to first among U.S. flag tanker owners. But increasingly, Ludwig was finding that he was losing out in many bids related to international oil movements. More often than not, the two ship owners he was losing out to were Aristotle Onassis and Stavros Niarchos, two Greek ship owners.

Both of these Greek ship owners were also active buyers of surplus tankers. When they won sales open to foreign bidders, they would typically re-flag under the Panamanian registry. This initial flag of convenience registry had effectively been setup by the Roosevelt administration to skirt a neutrality law in order to provide supplies to England and France prior to the U.S. officially entering the war. However, it took off after the war as ship owners realized it could lead to a meaningful reduction in crew costs.

In addition, Onassis and Niarchos established American companies with U.S. citizens as front men to bid in tanker sales not open to foreign bidders. Ludwig complained strongly to the government about the subterfuge he saw at work but it was ineffective. In all likelihood, what bothered Ludwig the most were that the Greeks were adroitly maneuvering and taking advantage of connections. In other words, they were doing what Ludwig had now been doing so well over the last decade.

Between the lower costs they achieved under the Panama flag and aggressive spot rates as opposed to the long-term charters Ludwig sought, Onassis and Niarchos virtually cornered the market for crude oil moving from the Mideast to Europe. Ludwig determined that the only real way to compete with Panamanian flag ships was to have his own Panamanian flag ships. But he realized this would be a tricky maneuver. Approval from the U.S. government was required to transfer any U.S. flag vessel built with government funds to a foreign registry. At the time, all of Ludwig's tankers were U.S. flag and he knew it would likely be impossible to get approval to transfer his best tankers outright.

Ludwig established a Panama company and proceeded to place smaller surplus tankers that he had bought into that company. Because they were older, smaller ships, this drew little attention and all the necessary approval was readily obtained. Within a couple of years, Ludwig had a dozen vessels under the Panamanian flag that were highly profitable. This also allowed him to learn firsthand about the cost savings from operating ships under flags of convenience.

Ludwig now wanted to move into larger tankers that benefited from this cost efficiency to compete better in the major international oil hauling lanes. The ideal candidates for this were the five large tankers he was now building at Welding Shipyard. Because they were being built with government funding, however, approval would be required.

Ludwig's solution to this was to leverage his connections with the Navy, which was expected to charter each of the tankers as they were delivered. Consistent with prior understandings, when the *Bulkpetrol*, which at 30.011 DWT was the largest tanker in the world, was launched in 1948 the Navy formally declined to charter it.

With no established government use for the vessel, this automatically paved the way for Ludwig to register the largest, fastest tanker in the world under the Panama flag. As each of the next four ships was delivered, the Navy declined to charter them also and Ludwig then registered each of them in Panama. By late 1949, Ludwig had all five vessels under charter to move oil from the Mideast to Europe. He had more than made up the distance between himself and Aristotle Onassis and Stavros Niachos.

The postwar period represented the peak in terms of the U.S. flag merchant marine representation. Thousands of Liberty and other types of vessels, which had all operated under the U.S. flag during World War II, were transitioning to commercial service. In 1950, U.S. flag cargo vessels represented 43% of total cargo ship tonnage in the world. From that peak, it declined, in part due to sales of surplus vessels to foreign ship owners who re-flagged the vessels.

In larger part, however, the decline in U.S. flag representation related to U.S. based ship owners like Ludwig electing to focus more on foreign registries in order to more effectively compete in the growing international trade lanes. Another factor that also played a role came out of a series of congressional hearings investigating wartime profits of various military contractors. These hearings resulted in what are now broadly referred to as the maritime scandals.

Senator Aiken of Vermont led a committee that was investigating possible wartime profiteering by contractors. Ship owners were looked at as they collectively received total wartime payments of $21 billion, or some 6% of the total estimated $350 billion that the U.S. spent during World War II. During hearings, it became clear that abuses had occurred and based on staff sifting through stacks of documents, Senator Aiken claimed that much of that amount represented taxpayers being plundered by ship owners. The U.S. General Accounting Office was dispatched to do a more complete investigation but encountered obstacles in locating government and shipping company records. Working with what the had, the General Accounting Office estimated that as much as $8 billion of the payments to ship owners were inaccurate or inappropriate, primarily due to inflated vessel values. How much of this related to collusion or corruption was widely debated, but there were enough cases of the latter to tarnish the merchant marine industry in the eyes of the government and the public.

These shipping cost figures, even after adjusted for the claimed inappropriate amounts, underscore the higher cost of shipping before the postwar period. Taking into account that only a relatively small amount of that total represented the value of material and supplies moved by ship, those numbers reaffirm that shipping costs were typically a moderate to medium two digit percentage of cargo value.

Neither Ludwig nor his Welding Shipyard was ever specifically charged with any wrongdoing, but it is fair to say that his net worth increased dramatically during World War II. As a consequence of the hearings, President Truman substantially reorganized the federal government entities dealing with the industry, disbanding the powerful Maritime Commission and establishing the Maritime Administration and the Federal Maritime Board to better police the industry.

Ludwig's successful and very profitable operation of the *Bulkpetrol* class of vessels re-confirmed his view that the scale economies of operating larger tankers were significant. He wanted to build even larger tankers, but he had already reached the limit in terms of what size tanker could be built at Welding Shipyards. In addition, the multitude of changes that resulted from the maritime scandals made shipbuilding in the U.S. less attractive to Ludwig. He was now on the lookout for a better shipbuilding platform to expand on his bigger is better thesis.

Scouting for available shipyards, Ludwig became aware of the former Japanese naval shipyard in Kure, Japan that was controlled by the U.S. government. The Kure shipyard had built the *Yamato*, the largest battleship ever built, and it had building ways large enough to build the mammoth tankers Ludwig envisioned.

Negotions ensued and Ludwig entered into a 10-year lease of the yard with an option to renew for another 5 years. It became known as National Bulk Carriers, Inc. Kure Shipyards division. Ludwig sent Elmer Hann to Japan in 1951 to manage the shipyard. Hann instituted the same type of training program that had worked well in his previous assignments. Japanese workers were taught the same construction methods that the U.S. had used to revolutionize the shipbuilding industry during the prior decade.

The first vessel built by Ludwig at the Kure shipyard was the *Petrokure*, a 38,021 DWT tanker that became the biggest tanker in the world when it was launched in 1952. Ludwig would build 43 ships for his various operating companies at the Kure shipyard between 1952 and 1962. Another 32 ships were built for other companies. Most were tankers, but he also built a number of ore carriers, most of which were the largest such vessels in the world when they were launched.

Noteworthy tankers the Ludwig built for his own operating company included the 85,515 DWT *Universe Leader* in 1956 and the 104,520 DWT *Universe Apollo* in 1958. Both vessels were the first in a class of vessels that were the largest tankers in the world when they were first launched. The delivery of the *Universe Apollo*, the first ship in the world to cross the 100,000 ton mark, was a tangible reminder that the age of large tankers was here to stay.

The epicenter of the international crude oil transport market was now centered on exports from the Middle East. The Suez Crisis of 1956 resulted in the temporary closure of the Suez Canal that proved to be a positive catalyst for the tanker sector by geometrically lengthening voyages on the largest routes. Both ship owners and oil companies began to more appreciate the superior economics that resulted from larger tankers.

Ludwig continued to follow a strategy of securing long term charters for the new tankers he was building. This reduced his risk and allowed him to grow faster as these charters effectively provided collateral to finance his newbuildings. He was now registering most of his ships in Liberia as that registry resulted in even lower operating costs than the Panama registry. Ludwig became the biggest tanker operator in key tanker trade lanes involved in moving crude oil from the Mideast.

By 1958, Japan had displaced Britain as the largest shipbuilding country in the world. This was achieved as a direct result of the introduction of innovative methods and techniques of welded and modular construction of large ships. Ludwig introduced these techniques to Japan at his Kure shipyard. Other shipyards in Japan would utilize those techniques as they hired workers away from the Kure shipyard. Shipbuilding was the first industry where Japan rose to the top in the postwar period. In many ways, the shipbuilding industry became a model for Japan's later success in other industries.

There is a direct link between Henry J. Kaiser, D.K. Ludwig, Elmer Hann and the development of Japan's large shipbuilding industry. It is ironic to realize that in a way the shipbuilding innovations that played a key role in the Allies World War II victory were recycled to become one of Japan's most important industries. The role of Elmer Hann in developing this industry was acknowledged by the Emperor of Japan who honored him with the prestigious Third Order of the Sacred Treasure award. Hann was only the second non-Japanese person in history to receive this award. The success of Ludwig's Kure shipyard was a prime catalyst in the rebuilding of Japan's industry after World War II.

In the late 1950's and early 1960's, the bragging rights for who owned the largest ship in the world would change frequently between Ludwig and his Greek rivals Onassis and Niarchos. It's fair to say, however, that Ludwig was consistently the thought leader. His constant focus was on how to deliver crude oil in the most cost efficient way in any given situation.

Among the close relationships Ludwig had developed with major oil companies was his friendship with Sidney Swensrud, the CEO of Gulf Oil responsible for broadly expanding the company's operations. In discussions with that oil company, Ludwig developed a plan that would make use of Gulf's terminal in Ireland that could accommodate unusually large ships. His plan was to build very large crude carriers which would sail from the Middle East to Ireland via the southern tip of Africa where they would offload their cargo into 85,000 DWT tankers owned by Ludwig for re-delivery to major ports in Europe. At 326,000 DWT, they were both too big to go through the Suez Canal loaded or to be discharged anywhere but at Gulf's unique Ireland terminal. However, the line-haul at sea economics of these behemoths more than compensated for the additional distance and re-handling costs.

Ludwig convinced Gulf of his plan and in 1966 entered into contracts to build six 326,000 DWT tankers that would be chartered to Gulf Oil. Officially he was no longer a builder as his lease on the Kure shipyard had expired and the yard had been taken over by IHI which was now the world's largest shipbuilder. However, Ludwig retained an equity interest in IHI and took an active interest in overseeing construction of the six vessels.

With a length of 1,100 feet and a capacity of 2.2 million barrels of crude oil, these were the largest ships in the world by a wide margin. They began being referred to by the acronym VLCC, for very large crude carrier, and their operation gave rise to the term lightering, involving transferring cargo to smaller vessels for the last leg of the voyage. While various lightering operations occur routinely today in dozens of ports and coastal areas, this was a new concept at the time and another pioneering example of Ludwig's genius as it related to moving oil by vessel.

With the construction of his VLCC's, Ludwig ushered in the era of super sized ships and it wasn't too long before others were building their own VLCC's. Temporary closures of the Suez Canal as well as the steady rise in the price of crude oil were also positive catalysts for these giant vessels.

The VLCC would become the default transporter of crude oil on the major long haul trade lanes. Eventually hundreds of VLCC's would be built and they would give rise to the construction of dozens of even larger tankers, which were referred to as ULCC's for ultra large crude carriers. These ULCC's, however, would prove to be too limited in where they could go and often ended up as the preferred vessels in which to store crude oil or to be converted to offshore production and storage platforms. Not surprisingly, Ludwig never built any ULCC's as, despite his leadership on the scale economy advantages of larger ships, he recognized that there were limits and the overriding metric was total end to end delivery costs.

At his peak, Ludwig owned a fleet of some 60 vessels that was comprised primarily of large tankers. The significant wealth he generated from shipping funded investments in other industries, including mining, agriculture, oil refining and financial services. A common thread in many of these investments was that they had a major real estate component or resulted in a product that was a key consumer of shipping services. These investments included a luxury hotel chain, a key role in developing real estate in the Bahamas and the Jari project in Brazil.

The Jari project related to Ludwig's purchase of 4 million acres in the Amazon basin with a plan to grow trees that could be converted into pulp. This was driven by Ludwig's projection that there would be a shortage of fiber in coming decades. He was also mindful that products coming out of

Jari could result in significant cargo for the purpose built fleet of ships he envisioned. Clearing the land, developing thousands of miles of roads and planting a variety of trees in a new settlement in the interior of Brazil eventually resulted in 30,000 inhabitants. To convert the trees into pulp, Ludwig had a large floating plant constructed in Japan which was then towed more than halfway around the world in another pioneering maritime related first.

Among the investments that Ludwig made was one that resulted in a meaningful minority position in Malcom McLean's Sea-Land operation. Ludwig had initially looked into expanding into the Jones Act liner business himself but ended up joining forces with McLean. That began a decades long business relationship between Ludwig and McLean that is discussed more in the chapter on McLean.

While I never met Ludwig, I heard many stories directly from McLean about their interactions that gave me a strong sense of who he was. Not surprisingly, I saw many similarities in terms of the business acumen of both men. It was clear from conversations that McLean respected Ludwig. It was equally clear from conversations I had with Palmer Baker, a close associate of Ludwig's who was also executor of his estate who I did know well, that Ludwig had a similar respect for McLean.

Following the sale of Sea-Land to R.J. Reynolds, a time that coincided with both men moving to broaden their investments beyond the respective shipping sectors they were most known for, the two men traveled around the world in McLean's private plane. Hop scotching from one operation to another either controlled or being looked at by one of them, they shared insights with each other. Suffice to say the conversations between these two business titans on that trip must have been fascinating. They were both insightful big picture thinkers traveling with the sole person whose business judgment they respected like their own.

When Forbes business magazine launched its inaugural Forbes 400 list in 1982 showing the four hundred richest people in the world, Ludwig was No. 1 with an estimated net worth of $2 billion. That listing had made Ludwig better known to the public, but he was still quite secretive and avoided the press. Prior to the Forbes listing, the only mainstream media article on Ludwig was a New York Times story a few years earlier surveying his business empire. That article had speculated that he was the first person in the world whose net worth had crossed the billion-dollar threshold.

An event in 1977 highlighted how much Ludwig appreciated his privacy. He was known for walking each morning from his midtown cooperative apartment on Fifth Avenue and 59th Street to his office half a dozen blocks away in a fifty-story office building he also owned. One day a photographer was perched in front of his office building to get a picture of the man the New York Times had just labeled as the richest person in the world. As the grey haired man that the photographer was fairly certain was Ludwig approached, he snapped a picture. Eighty-year-old Ludwig, still fit and trim from daily workouts in a private pool in the basement of his office building, spun and grabbed the photographer in a hold, wrestling him to the ground and taking his camera.

Ludwig died in 1992 at the age of 95 from heart failure following several years of poor health. He had no direct descendants and left the bulk of his estate to the Ludwig Cancer Institute, a foundation focused on cancer research that he had initially established in Switzerland in 1971. One of three trustees of the foundation was Malcom McLean. Under the terms of his will, research centers founded and funded by the foundation were established in 2006 at Johns Hopkins University, Harvard University, MIT, Memorial Sloan Kettering, Stanford University and University of Chicago. To date, the foundation has distributed billions of dollars around the world focused solely on cancer research.

8. Ole Skaarup

The Father of the Modern Bulk Carrier.

As a young shipbroker, Skaarup recognized the need for specialized ships to move dry-bulk cargoes. His visionary adaptation of general cargo ships led to the modern bulk carrier that is the most numerous type of vessel in the world today. Less known than others, the contributions of this extraordinary man rank him near the top in terms of impact.

Ole Skaarup was born on March 22, 1916 in Copenhagen, Denmark. Growing up in this port city, he was exposed early to the shipping industry by his stepfather who was a sea captain. He liked his early apprentice jobs and Skaarup's love of the sea that he got from his stepfather would stay with him throughout his life.

In 1940, Skaarup left Denmark at the age of 24 shortly after the German invasion. He went to New York where he landed an entry-level job with A.P. Moller, a large Danish shipping company. Skaarup continued his training in the shipping business by going to work at the 80 Broad Street, New York City office of Blidberg Rothchild, a ship brokerage firm with Swedish ties, where he gained his initial direct exposure to cargo movements by ship.

When the U.S. became formally involved in World War II in 1941, Skaarup volunteered to enter the U.S. Army. After a succession of postings in various logistics roles, Skaarup eventually rose in rank to where he served as superintendent of the Army's Water Division at his posting in Belfast, Northern Ireland.

In his role with the U.S. army, Skaarup designed the loading plan for 50 Liberty ships and 12 landing craft for the June 1944 Normandy invasion. He also developed a loading plan to move aircraft across the Atlantic Ocean on the decks of Liberty ships. Skaarup had a detailed knowledge of the cargo capabilities of Liberty ships and how best to adapt them to what he was planning to move.

I remember the first time I met Skaarup and his description of the steps he took to maximize the military cargo that could be loaded in Liberty ships. It was clear that he had a detailed knowledge of the layout of those vessels and this allowed him to efficiently construct loading plans. It was equally clear that he had a passion for implementing his plans.

After being discharged from the U.S. Army in 1945, Skaarup returned to Blidberg Rothschild in New York. He prospered in that ship brokerage organization. Confident that he could do better on his own, in 1951 he left that firm and established Skaarup Shipping on a shoestring budget. By 1954, his small ship brokerage firm was increasingly involved in fixing ships for owners and shippers of bulk cargoes.

At that time, almost all ocean cargo moved in Liberty ships and other general-purpose cargo vessels. From his first hand experience, Skaarup believed they were too narrow and awkward for most bulk cargoes, particularly grain. The only specialized vessels were a relatively small number of oil-ore carriers that moved the limited amount of those cargoes moving internationally at the time. To put that into perspective, total international vessel shipments of iron ore were less than 25 million tons in 1954.

Sitting in his office at 21 West Street in New York City in January of 1954, Skaarup found himself focusing on the vessels that shippers of dry bulk cargoes he was familiar with had available to them. Neither Liberty ships or oil-ore carriers worked well. The former was difficult to discharge and the latter lacked the cubic capacity to efficiently carry grain and many other dry bulk cargoes. Dry-bulk needed wide, clear cargo holds with all the machinery out of the way and in the aft section of the vessel. From his initial design on a napkin, Skaarup continued to work on and refine what he thought the ideal cargo hold for dry-bulk products should look like.

The key design feature that Skaarup came up with was that the large holds should also be inward slanting at the top. This acted to minimize any empty space in the hold as dry-bulk cargoes were being loaded, typically by a conveyor belt or gravity chute resulting in pyramid-like accumulations in the hold.

By having the cargo hold mirror the natural flow of dry-bulk cargoes, Skaarup theorized that he could eliminate most of the dangerous situations that could develop at sea from cargo shifting. When there are void spaces in a hold carrying dry-bulk cargoes, a ship encountering rough seas could experience cargo shifting into those void spaces. This can radically change the stability of the ship, and with each roll the ship could be listing more to one side or the other. In the worst cases, shifting dry-bulk cargoes can lead to a vessel capsizing and then sinking.

Skaarup's straightforward design innovation largely addressed this major safety situation. There is no doubt that he was inspired by his work years earlier in developing load plans for Liberty vessels. If and when dry-bulk cargoes moved in part of a hold in those vessels, elaborate chambers and bulkheads had to be built by carpenters to prevent cargo shifting. It was costly to erect and dismantle these temporary barriers and it was also an inefficient use of space.

Skaarup came up with a permanent and efficient solution to the issue of shifting dry bulk cargoes by developing a specialized vessel with cargo holds configured to work with how dry-bulk cargoes flowed. The inward sloping at the top of the hold was accentuated and extended by the addition of raised hatch covers. On the other side of the hold would be sloping wing tanks that could carry ballast water and also fill this void. All the machinery would be aft, providing ready access to wide holds whose raised covers could also better accomodate on dock grain feeders. Dry-bulk cargoes could now be quickly loaded from the center of the hold with confidence that the cargo would naturally flow throughout the space with no dangerous voids remaining.

Skaarup put all of his ideas into the design of a new vessel and then worked with a naval architect to develop detailed plans. When these architectural plans were completed, Skaarup began searching for capital to underwrite his idea. With extensive contacts in the shipping industry, he was introduced by Swedish shipowners to Marcus Wallenburg, Sweden's most prominent businessman.

The two men began what was to become a lifelong friendship. Skaarup would recall years later a test Wallenburg put him through to access his credibility. Having heard from one of his advisers that Skaarup had indicated he was the saxophone player in a band he had put together in his native Copenhagen, one night at dinner somebody brought in a saxophone. "Fortunately, I was a pretty good sax player at the time. I blew them a few tunes and that established my credibility" said Skaarup.

Upon hearing Skaarup explain his concept of how ships should be built to carry bulk cargoes, Wallenburg was sold and agreed to collaborate. A contract was entered into on March 22, 1954 with the Kockums shipyard in Malmo, Sweden to build what was then referred to as the OS type design. The OS refers to Ole Skaarup's initials.

Building what was such a unique ship at the time encountered all sorts of objections from the engineers at the shipyard. To counter the claim that that you can't steer from aft, Skaarup said put an auxiliary navigation bridge up front. When they complained that such large hatches would need a stronger deck, Skaarup authorized additional structure to strengthen the deck. They suggested putting a bulkhead in the middle of the holds, but Skaarup saw that as redundant and crossed it out on the building drawings. As issues came up, Skaarup was there to come up with solutions. By mid-1955, he had his new ship.

The *Cassiopeia* was the name given to Kockums hull No. 407 which was launched in 1955 and cost a total of $2.5 million. With a 19,000-ton deadweight capacity, it could carry roughly twice as much cargo as a Liberty ship and was one of the largest vessels afloat at the time. It immediately went into service carrying grain and other dry-bulk cargoes.

The economic advantages of the *Cassiopeia* in moving bulk cargoes compared to Liberty ships quickly became apparent. For instance, the cost of loading and trimming in a U.S. port was 50 cents per ton less compared to a Liberty ship and the savings on the discharge port was similar. Skaarup calculated that just the savings in stevedoring costs alone would pay for his ship in ten years. In addition, the scale economies from the relatively large size of the *Cassiopeia* added to the economic benefits it offered shipowners. In short order after word spread about its actual performance, Kockums sold five sister ships. Stavros Niarchos, the Greek shipowner, bought three of those ships.

The building and subsequent operation of the *Cassiopeia* was well covered by the trade press. Almost immediately, naval architects and shipyards around the world adopted the inward sloping holds and raised hatch cover design aspects developed by Skaarup. These vessels began to constitute a separate segment by themselves and shippers began to demand this type of vessel for moving the whole array of dry-bulk cargoes. While ship owners didn't have the flexibility they had enjoyed with general cargo vessels, the improved efficiency of these vessels more than made up for that constraint.

It wasn't too long before shipyards around the world were building similar vessels for shipowners anxious to move bulk cargoes more efficiently. Around the same time container shipping was being invented, modern bulk carriers were also being invented around Skaarup's basic OS design. That basic design has held up well and the thousands of bulk carriers that exist today are nearly identical in their key aspects to Skaarup's OS design.

The efficiency of these new specialized ships also played a role in increasing the volume of dry-bulk cargoes. This virtuous circle of more volume leading to larger, more efficient ships resulting in additional volume first played out in the dry-bulk sector. The sector would also experience significant volume growth in the not too distant future due to the sharp growth in steel production in Japan and Korea as well as other countries without the natural resources that go into producing steel. Iron ore and coal, the key ingredients in steel, would become the two largest commodities moved in dry-bulk ships.

Ole Skaarup was also a catalyst for the development of a specialized ocean going bulk carrier known as the self-unloading bulk carrier. This technology has been used for decades on the Great Lakes where pelletized iron ore was a key shipment in short voyages across the lakes. These ships had tunnels running the length of vessel with a conveyor belt system deployed in the tunnel and connected to a moveable boom on the vessel. When the ship arrived at a terminal, it positioned the boom where the cargo was to be discharged and then turned on the gravity fed conveyor belt system.

Skaarup thought such self-unloading bulk carriers made particular sense for the movement of dense bulk cargoes such as gypsum rock. He targeted the National Gypsum Company as a potential customer for a vessel he had designed because they moved substantial amounts of gypsum up and down the East Coast of the U.S. and Canada. Skaarup convinced National Gysum that with one ship they could move the same amount of gypsum as three Liberty ships, which typically took one week to discharge. The company agreed and construction began on a new vessel that was named after the founder of National Gypsum, Melvin H. Baker.

Built in 1956 by the Ag Weser shipyard in Bremen, Germany, the *Melvin H. Baker* had a deadweight capacity of 17,940 tons. In actual service, the vessel would achieve all of the impressive economics that Skaarup had predicted. The self-unloading system would discharge 2,000 tons of gypsum per hour with only three men working at the discharge port. The *Melvin H. Baker* had an unusually long life that began with 1,900 voyages for National Gypsum over 36 years. It was then sold to a Taiwanese company that used it to move gypsum rock in Asia. Finally, in 2009, the *Melvin H. Baker* was sold for scrap to a demolition yard in China for $2.1 million.

With the other individual giants profiled herein, they generally had at least a first mover advantage related to their insights and innovations. Their companies benefited economically before their insights and innovations could be completely copied.

In the case of Ole Skaarup and his straightforward development of the modern bulk carrier, however, this was not the case as the copying really occurred too fast. In addition to being simple to incorporate design aspects, the absence of the intermediate decks and shipboard gear made these the easiest type of vessels to build. As new shipyards were established, they focused on building dry-bulk carriers and this further expanded the supply of this new type of vessel.

Skaarup's inventions, along with those by McLean in the container sector, clearly involved unique intellectual property that would qualify as patentable ideas or processes if they had occurred today. However, the collective view of what was or should be patentable was narrower in the 1950's, particularly related to processes. We don't really know what the outcome would have been had patents actually been pursued back then.

In Skaarup's case, he even asked the head of Kockums shipyard if he thought he could patent his OS design and was told no, its only another way to make a ship. "That misleading advice is the saddest thing that ever happened to me" said Skaarup. With regard to patents, a case could also be made that if Ludwig's innovative financing mechanism was something that had first occurred today, he might have even been able to obtain a patent on that unique process.

Despite the success of the *Melvin H. Baker* in the movement of gypsum, that proved to be an isolated niche and inroads weren't made with self-unloaders in other ocean markets. In the 1980's, Skaarup became involved in initiatives to expand where they are utilized. As the growth of containerization was accelerating in the 1980's largely due to the cargo handling efficiencies it offered, Skaarup envisioned self-unloading technology as offering some of the same benefits to the dry-bulk sector.

Working with a large Canadian shipping company, Skaarup oversaw the development of a series of such vessels that were generally deployed in routes between Canada and the Caribbean. Improved cost economics were achieved with certain cargoes, but the self-unloading technology did not lend itself to all cargoes nor fit with existing terminal layouts.

Skaarup's company would operate six self-unloading dry-bulk ships in various short sea routes between the U.S. and Mexico and Canada. Gypsum, the same cargo he built his first self-unloader for, remained an important cargo for his Liberian and Panamanian flag ships. He also operated six traditional bulkers in the spot market that he controlled under long-term charters. In addition to his role as an operator, Skaarup remained active in running what was one of the largest ship chartering operations in the country.

With his hands-on approach and granular operating knowledge, it's hardly surprising that his company was consistently profitable. "We're in the lucky position that we have been profitable both when the market is good and when its bad" he said in an interview. His explanation for this showed the same straightforward common sense exhibited in his OS design "We usually do better when times are tough because we know our business". Skaarup also believed that when times are good, people tend to make bad decisions.

Following the *Exxon Valdez* oil spill in 1989, Skaarup championed the development of double hulls on tankers, which made spills less likely. In 1993, he was awarded an honorary degree from the Webb Institute of Naval Architecture, the leading such institution in the U.S. If there was ever anyone whose life's work had proven his innate naval architecture skills, it was Ole Skaarup. Throughout the 1990's, Skaarup lobbied government officials in Washington with a myriad of ideas related to revitalizing shipbuilding as well as coastal shipping aimed at getting trucks off the highways and moving cargo by water.

Skaarup was for decades the leading spokesperson for ship owners based in the U.S. who operated foreign flag ships. He was also one of the first shipping industry firms in the U.S. to migrate out of the traditional office area in lower Manhattan to offices in and around Stamford, Connecticut. Following his lead, dozens of other shipping related firms migrated out to what is now the largest concentration of shipping professionals anywhere in the world outside of London.

The Connecticut Maritime Association now includes thousands of members that gather annually for a three-day event that is typically the largest meeting of shipping professionals in the world. Each year at the dinner at that event, an individual is honored with the Commodore

Award, which is considered the most prestigious award someone in the international shipping industry can receive.

In 1990 at the first Connecticut Maritime Association event, Ole Skaarup was the unanimous choice to receive the first Commodore Award. He had a gracious acceptance speech noting the many people on whose behalf he was accepting the award. Skaarup then pulled out his saxaphone and regaled the audience with a few tunes, just as he did almost four decades ago when seeking the financing for the first modern bulk carrier.

As Skaarup reached 75, he began to wind down his day to day involvement in his operating businessess. He sold a major interest in most of his maritime businesses to Mitsui OSK Lines, the second largest Japanesse shipping company that is involved in all of the shipping sectors. Skaarup had a longstanding ship brokerage relationship with Mitsui OSK Lines that went back decades.

I had the pleasure of meeting Ole Skaarup a number of times. He was an absolutely delightful gentleman with a quick wit and a warm smile. I vividly remember a lunch Malcom McLean and I had with Skaarup where he was outlining the load plans he developed for the Liberty ships involved in the Normandy invasion. In an animated fashion, he went over in granular detail how he was able to maximize usage of the available vessel space. That granular knowledge of the cargo subject he was focused on was a trait Ole shared with Malcom. After studying the other individuals profiled herein, I'm quite certain that was a shared characteristic among all of them.

Ole Skaarup died in 2010 at the age of 94 in Greenwich, CT. The Ole Skaarup Foundation continues to this day, supporting educational and cultural initiatives that were important to Skaarup. His legacy as one of the most important individuals in the development of the modern shipping industry, along with also being one of its most popular participants ever, will live on.

9. Stavros Niarchos

The More Successful Greek & Archrival of Onassis.

While lesser known than his Greek archrival Aristotle Onassis, Niarchos in 1951 built what was then the largest tanker in the world. By 1956 he was the largest shipowner in the world and on the cover of Time. He too was a colorful man with an interesting personal life.

Stavros Spyros Niarchos was born on July 3, 1909 in Athens, Greece. It is helpful to first go back a couple of generations, as there were specific aspects of his family history that would play a significant role in the man Niarchos would become.

His grandparents, Stavros Niarchos and Maria Adamantioschoupas, lived in Banbakou, Greece, a small town not far from Sparta. They, like almost everyone in the town, were poor, hard-working religious people. It was towns like theirs that were the source of the large mass of immigrants to America in the 1880's and 1890's. The family had two sons, Spyros and his younger brother Paraskevas. As these boys grew up, stories of immigrants who had gone to America and made their fortunes were well known to them and all the villagers. Seeing firsthand some of these immigrants returning to Greece for a visit, wearing fine suits and displaying gold watches with chains, just reinforced to the boys their growing desire to leave Banbakou and go to America.

In 1893, with just a few drachmas in their coats, the brothers joined the wave of immigrants going to America. Spyros knew that their family name in ancient Greek (Nearchos) meant shipmaster. It came from the name of the naval chief of staff for Alexander the Great. But he and his brother knew nothing of the sea. Banbakou was nowhere near the sea and they had never even seen it before the voyage across the Atlantic to America.

Arriving in America through Ellis Island, Spyros and Paraskevas traveled to Philadelphia where a series of odd jobs allowed them to accumulate some savings. Partnering with another Greek immigrant who preceded them, they opened a Greek restaurant that met with limited success. Hearing that Buffalo was a faster growing area, the brothers sold out their interest and moved to Buffalo where they opened a restaurant at 317 Main Street.

With a location in the heart of the downtown Buffalo area, Niarchos's, as their restaurant was called, prospered. The brothers soon enlarged it by adding an ice cream parlor. Spyros, the senior partner, made homemade candy in the back on a large black stove that proved to be increasingly popular with their patrons. They became more known when they hoisted a lighted sign that jutted into the street from the second floor and spelled the Niarchos name in flowing script. By this time, their most popular products were the candy, baklava and fudge they sold.

The Niarchos brothers emerged as leaders among a large Greek community in Buffalo and helped organize a building committee for the first Greek Orthodox church. With a successful business and a secure social and religious position, Spyros began to think more about marriage. A typical pattern at the time was for a young man to become engaged to someone in Greece through correspondence who would then be sent to America. Spryos Niarchos, however, had enough money to go back to Greece where he wanted to pick his own wife.

Upon returning to Greece, he became aware of the Coumandaros family from Sparta. The family's four brothers ran a grain and feed business that was moderately successful and highly respected. Their one sister, Eugenia, was educated and beautiful. Niarchos, dressed in a well-tailored suit complete with a gold watch and chain across the vest, came to call on the Coumandaros family. The couple liked each other immediately. In 1903, Niarchos married Eugenia and took her back to Buffalo.

The Niarchos candy store business continued to thrive. Eugenia gave birth to a girl they named Maria after Spyros's mother. While Spyros liked Buffalo and the Greek community, his wife was not happy there. When she became pregnant again in 1908, she pleaded with her husband to return to Greece. She missed her family and the more gracious lifestyle she had in her home country. They had accumulated enough money where he didn't need to work if he didn't want to. Eugenia said that Spyros, if he wanted to stay in business, could work with her brothers who were doing very well in the family's growing grain business. With Eugenia four months pregnant, Niarchos finally agreed and the family sailed for Greece in March 1909. A few months later, Stavros Niarchos was born.

With Niarchos's investment in return for half of the profits, the Coumandaros brothers built a modern flourmill in Piraeus, the port for Athens. By locating directly at the port, they saved transportation costs. They bought grain from Argentina and Russia and milled it into their Evrotas brand flour, which became well known throughout Greece. The brothers focused on the business of milling grain into flour while Spyros focused on the intricacies of grain futures and the difference between Argentine and Russian grain.

During World War I the business prospered with some of the brothers now representing family interests in New York and Argentina. There was, however, constant disagreement and bickering among the brothers. Spyros and his family remained in Athens and were enjoying life at the top rungs of the social ladder. Young Stavros was a handsome boy now in private school. Growing up next to the sea in Piraeus, he was swimming almost as soon as he was walking. He loved the sea and was a proficient sailor by the age of nine.

Stavros was 14 in 1923 when his father lost all his money. While the Coumandaros brothers had done very well speculating on grain futures, his father had been speculating on the stock market. He had initially done well, but in the postwar depression and on the Athens Stock Exchange where there were few regulations, he lost everything. To pay his debts, he was forced to sell his interest in the flourmill. Even with that, debts from his stock speculation remained and he was effectively bankrupt.

Stavros had to leave private school and enroll in a local public high school. His mother Eugenia was embittered and never forgave her husband. A proud woman, she attempted to hide the effect the changed circumstances were having on her, but young Stavros would frequently see his mother crying alone. The Coumandaros brothers gave his father a distributorship for some of the products of what had recently been half his own mill. While he never made a lot of money with the distributorship, over a period of years he managed to completely payoff all his debts.

Stavros Niarchos persevered and got excellent grades in school and enrolled at the University of Athens. He passed the examination to enter the law school but never studied law and spent only a relatively short time at the University of Athens. Due to his family's limited financial circumstances, his father couldn't afford to send him to the university. He adjusted to the transition from living with the advantages of his family's prior wealth to having less. This period was, however, a significant turning point in his life. It was the catalyst for a drive to achieve wealth and the possessions that came with it that would stay with him for the rest of his life.

In 1928, at the age of 19, Niarchos went to work for his uncles at the flourmill as an office assistant. In that role, he became aware that transportation costs related to raw materials and products were a major expense. As he became more involved in this area, he pointed out to his uncles that it would be cheaper to charter a fleet of trucks to move their products than to rely on other trucking companies.

When Niarchos found a company that would provide that fleet of trucks, they moved ahead and were pleased that they achieved the savings that he forecast. The uncles would later find that Niarchos himself had setup that company with borrowed money and he was personally profiting from the transaction. Instead of being angry, the uncles were impressed with their nephew's business ability.

Using his new income, Niarchos rented an apartment and outfitted it in the opulent style that he preferred. The handsome young man had an active social life. In 1930, he eloped and married Helen Sporides, the daughter of a Greek admiral. When the admiral found out, he made his displeasure known and the marriage lasted only a month. Niarchos returned to the dating scene and was a frequent visitor to all of the most popular nightspots in Athens.

Niarchos was persistent in his views that significant cost savings would result from getting directly involved in shipping. He based this on his analysis of what would result from their buying their own ships to transport the grain that the flourmill was buying in Argentina. He had spent time at a local shipping agency in Piraeus where he had learned everything he could about the expenses as well as the risks and opportunities in shipping.

Niarchos had his eye out for the right opportunity and saw what he was looking for in 1935. Six twenty-nine year old 9,000-ton capacity British freighters were on the market. These ships were 50% larger than the 6,000-ton vessels they typically chartered. While larger, Niarchos also knew these vessels could be loaded in smaller ports upriver from Buenos Aires that his research had indicated would result in lower loading fees due to non-union workers. Between the savings from direct ownership, larger vessels and changing load ports, Stavros presented this to his uncles as an irresistible opportunity. He convinced them and they bought the ships for $20,000 each. On the first voyage, they made a profit of $10,000, or half of the purchase price of the ship.

The savings resulting from Niarchos's recommendation to buy the ships reduced the total cost of importing grain by 35%. The family expanded their business by buying more flourmills. Three of the purchased freighters were exclusively used for the family's flourmill business. Niarchos was put in charge of the new shipping department, including employing the ships in the spot market when they weren't being used to move the family's grain. This had him traveling throughout

Europe, including Russia. From what he saw and heard from his extensive traveling, Niarchos concluded that war was likely and that it would be good for shipping.

Niarchos tried without success to get his uncles to buy even more ships, but this time they had no interest. By 1938 with war looking more likely, ship values had increased. Niarchos noted that the ship *Maleas* was the least profitable vessel in their fleet but could still probably be sold for over $60,000. Not surprisingly, the uncles were anxious to sell. Niarchos pooled some of his money with additional funds he raised from a distant cousin and traveled to London where, through a shipbroker, he purchased a 60% interest in the *Maleas,* which gave him control. Stavros Niarchos was now an actual shipowner.

Niarchos moved to London where he was focused on buying more ships. It was difficult to find anything suitable as prices had skyrocketed following Hitler's invasion of Poland in 1939. To protect his investment in the *Maleas,* he insured it for almost $1 million. Niarchos maintained an active social life and in 1940 he married for the second time. His new wife was Melpomene Alexandropoulos, a beautiful 20-year-old Greek widow.

The newlyweds were at the London Ritz Hotel when Niarchos received word that the *Maleas,* while unloading its sugar cargo in Antwerp, had sunk as a result of a major strike by the German Luftwaffe targeting the port. The ship was determined to be a total constructive loss and the owners applied for and received almost $1 million, or sixteen times the purchase price.

Flush with the proceeds from his insurance, Niarchos bought the *Bayou*, a 7,000 ton Great Lakes ore carrier, and the *Olympic*, a freighter that had been converted into a tanker. In late 1941, a German submarine sank the *Olympic* as it was carrying a cargo of gasoline to England. Niarchos had insured it for $900,000, or three times his purchase price of $300,000. Still looking for ships to buy, Niarchos bought the *Atlantic,* a 9,000-ton tanker he purchased for $312,000.

The war had resulted in a spike in shipping rates just as Niarchos had forecast. On one of the first voyages of the *Atlantic* following his purchase of the vessel, the profit was $100,000, or one-third of the purchase price. Not soon after, a German submarine sank the *Bayou* while it was carrying a cargo of bauxite in the Caribbean. By this time, the American marine insurance companies were more suspicious of the tendency of Greek shipowners to over-insure vessels and Niarchos's policy on the *Bayou* was limited to $500,000. However, that was still almost 50% higher than the $350,000 that Niarchos had paid for the ship a year earlier.

With war raging in Europe, Niarchos decided that the best place from which to manage his growing shipping business was New York City. He did that from a one-room office at 17 Battery Place in lower Manhattan. At that time, almost every office in that building was directly involved in the shipping industry. Niarchos was also known to conduct business at the bar of the St. Regis hotel. Meetings at the St. Moritz and the Plaza, both hotels where major Greek shippers lived and gathered, were also frequent. As a successful, attractive 31 year old Greek in New York, Niarchos quickly became a member of what was then known as café society. Most evenings he could be seen at El Morroco, which was the preeminent café society nightclub.

In 1942, Niarchos volunteered for the Greek navy. He saw service on a tank-landing vessel and was attached to the headquarters staff of the Greek navy in Alexandria, Egypt, where the Greek government in exile was located. Niarchos finished his service as the assistant to the naval attaché at the Greek embassy in Washington.

Throughout the war Niarchos's vessel *Atlantic* was chartered to the U.S. government. The $40,000 payment per month resulted in a profit of at least $15,000 per month. Looking for additional ships to buy, in 1942 Niarchos became aware of the *Phoenix,* an older tanker that was being sold by Daniel K. Ludwig. Niarchos learned that another Greek, Aristotle Onassis, was also negotiating to buy the vessel. The vessel was eventually sold to a partnership where Niarchos and Onassis each owned 40% with the balance from other Greek investors. This vessel was also chartered to the U.S. government where it produced a profit of $15,000 per month. Between the insurance proceeds he received and the profits from his two remaining vessels, Niarchos was estimated to have a net worth of $2 million as World War II ended.

As the war ended, the expectation among many ship owners was that there would be a slump, similar to the prolonged shipping slump that came after World War I. That earlier postwar slump was certainly top of mind to Stavros Livanos, the dean of Greek ship owners with the largest shipping fleet in the world. Livanos lived in a suite at the Plaza hotel in New York. His suite was a gathering place for other ship owners and all were interested in his views.

Livanos played his cards very close to his vest, but he was quietly optimistic about the future. He reasoned that much of Europe and Asia would require food and other products from the U.S. and this would support shipping demand. However, Livanos proceeded cautiously, selectively buying used ships and entering into contracts for new ships only after he had negotiated what he thought was a reasonable price. As was his custom, he always paid for his ship purchases with cash and didn't believe in taking out loans to buy ships.

There were, however, two smaller and younger Greek ship owners who were much more optimistic and who went full stream ahead with expansion. They were Stavros Niachos and Aristotle Onassis. Onassis had operated tankers throughout the war. His newest ships had been interned in occupied Europe for most of the war and were only recently released to him. Onassis was bullish about the postwar prospects of his now formidable tanker fleet.

Niarchos, however, was even more bullish than Onassis and was convinced that the postwar period would be an economic boon that would be great for ship owners. At that point, he had only two tankers, including one partially owned with Onassis. But he had his $2 million and a willingness to leverage that with loans to expand his fleet.

To accomplish this expansion, Niarchos put in orders with brokers in both London and New York to buy ships that were on the market. He also put the word out that he was interested in ships regardless of their condition. His one condition was that he was able to finance a significant portion of the purchase price of these vessels with mortgages.

In short order, Niarchos had accumulated a small fleet of older cargo ships of all types, all mortgaged to the hilt. He avoided new ships that would require too much cash and continued to be the largest purchaser of older ships. Niachos aggressive purchasing was getting much attention in the shipping community. Stavros Livanos, when he heard of what Niarhos was doing, viewed it as the reckless actions of a novice, both in terms of expansion and the significant use of credit.

Niachos next turned his attention to the significant number of Liberty ships that were coming on the market. These ships were being offered to U.S. shipping companies as well as allies. The Greek government sounded out owners on their interest and got the strongest responses from Onassis and Niarchos, both of whom urged the Greek government to seek the maximum amount of Liberty ships which were being offered at $550,000 each.

With the Greek government involved, these ships could be bought for just $125,000 down, with the balance financed by the U.S. government over 20 years at a relatively low interest rate. In the end, the Greeks were allocated 100 Liberty ships that were parceled out among many owners who were now more optimistic. Niarchos got to buy eight of the Liberty ships, while Onassis didn't get a single ship. Onassis was bitter and this incident exacerbated a growing antagonism and competitiveness between Onassis and Niarchos. This would show itself in both significant and petty ways for the rest of their lives.

Despite their competitiveness, they frequently viewed situations in a similar manner. For instance, they both saw tankers as the most profitable ships to own. Onassis had one of the most modern tanker fleets. Niarchos had a smaller, older tanker fleet and wasn't interested in building new vessels. He established North American Shipping and Trading Company in order to purchase eight T-2 tankers from the U.S. government.

Hundreds of T-2's were built during the war as the tanker equivalent of the Liberty ships. The vessels weren't offered to the allied governments and any sale had to comply with the requirement to be owned by corporations where at least Americans held 75% of the stock. To meet the citizenship requirement, 75% of the stock was held by Niarchos's sister and three American business associates with Niarchos owning the remaining 25%. His sister was a U.S. citizen by virtue of being born in Buffalo.

Overnight, Niarchos had built a more modern, respectable tanker fleet. To finance this, he sold many of his old Liberty and Victory ships at a profit. Niarchos had the eight T-2 tankers chartered at a breakeven rate to a Panamanian company owned entirely by him. This structure allowed him to comply with the citizenship requirements while retaining all the economics and paying little or no income taxes. The latter was important as the vessels were generating considerable profits. Niarchos then bought another five T-2 tankers through a second similar structure where the owners included a former Secretary of State and a former congressman, both social friends of Niarchos. His growing tanker fleet and bulging profits made Niarchos a young man whose actions were increasingly admired and watched.

In 1947, after the divorce from his second wife was granted, Niarchos married Eugenia Livanos, the oldest daughter of Stavros Livanos. Presumably having such a close link to the then largest shipowner in the world was part of the appeal to Niarchos. They were married in the same Greek Orthodox cathedral in New York where his archrival Aristotle Onassis had wed Tina Livanos, Eugenia's younger sister, less than a year before.

Stavros Livanos was rumored to have provided his daughter Eugenia with a larger dowry than he provided Tina. This supposedly was the reason Aristotle Onassis was not present at the wedding. While the expectation of many was that these new family relationships would lead to some consolidation among the three shipping groups, that was not the case at all. Each of the three Greek shipowners fought to get as large an allocation as possible from the Greek government to purchase surplus Liberty ships.

Niarchos, still with a smaller and older tanker fleet than Onassis, now began focusing for the first time on building new tankers. His hiring as a fulltime employee an advisor to Metropolitan Insurance Company helped those efforts. Metropolitan Insurance was one of the first financial firms to finance new vessels based on long term charters. With much of the construction price financed, Niarchos built the 18,000-ton *World Peace* at Bethlehem Steel's Sparrows Point yard in Baltimore and the 30,000-ton *World Liberty* at Bethlehem Steel's Quincy yard in Boston.

In addition to building new vessels with credit, he entered into long-term contracts to charter vessels when they were available under reasonable terms. His intuition proved right, and growing oil consumption and rapidly rising charter rates resulted in significant profits, all of which Niarchos reinvested into new shipbuilding contracts where he used as much financing as he could obtain.

One cost advantage of Niarchos's growing fleet was that most of his vessels were registered in Panama or under other flags of convenience. Prior to World War II, ships typically carried the flag of where they were built and there was little difference in operating costs among the major merchant marines. The catalyst for change was actually the U.S. government. American shipping companies were encouraged to register some vessels under the Panama flag so that the U.S. could moves supplies to England on those vessels without violating U.S. neutrality. Companies became aware that such flags of convenience could lower costs through less regulations and taxes.

The Greeks, in particular, were adroit at minimizing income taxes and the flag of convenience structure provided further assistance. Niarchos himself embraced the concept of mobility and in 1949 moved his center of operations to London from New York. He was the first Greek shipowner to relocate to London and he would be followed by many in the decades to come.

Niarchos's move to London coincided with British shipyards growing thirst for business that he was happy to oblige. Tied with Onassis for the largest tanker in the world, Niarchos moved ahead with the launching of the 31,745-ton *World Unity* in 1951. Losing the title to Onassis the next year by a few hundred tons, it was Niarchos's again in 1953 with the delivery of the 33,000-ton *World Enterprise*. He beat his own record by a wide margin the next year with the 45,000-ton *World Glory*. Onassis regained the title in 1955, but it came back to Niarchos with the 1956 launching of the *Spryos Niarchos*, named after his father.

As the heavyweight title went back and forth, Niarchos was adding many additional tankers to his fleet. Even Onassis obtaining a significant charter contract for the Arabian oil fields played to his advantage. When that happened, many oil companies moved away from Onassis. Niarchos was there to sign them all up to long term charters, which further fueled his newbuilding efforts.

By 1956, Niarchos had passed his archrival Onassis in total tanker fleet size and both were now well ahead of their father-in-law, Stavros Livanos. Livanos had eschewed tankers and stayed primarily with dry-bulk vessels, which were yet to see the growth curve that tankers had followed. Tankers were the first vessel types to see the sort of extraordinary growth in typical vessel size. This wouldn't be seen until many years later by bulkers and container ships, which were actually just being invented in the pivotal shipping year of 1956.

The event that changed the shipping world and exponentially expanded the already considerable fortunes of Niarchos and Onassis was the closing of the Suez Canal by Egypt's President Nasser in 1956. At that time almost all of the oil from the large Middle East fields was moving to Europe or the U.S. via the Suez Canal. With the closure of the canal, now tankers would have to go around the tip of Africa, increasing voyage distances by three and four times. That sharp increase automatically soaked up all the excess tanker supply, but was still far short of what was needed.

Shipping rates are always set at the intersection of supply and demand, and the closing of the Suez Canal was such a sharp change in that dynamic that tanker rates went up by three and four times overnight. Niarchos had many of his tankers on long term charters. However, buttressed with a large staff of British and U.S. lawyers, he argued that the canal closing triggered the force majeure clause in the charters that allowed them to be cancelled. He then made his tankers available to the highest bidders. There would be lawsuits and settlements for relatively small amounts many years later. The amounts that Niarchos made as a result of the six-month closure of the Suez Canal may have been more than any single individual had ever made over such a short period.

Niarchos's rise to the top of the shipping world was underscored with his picture on the cover of Time magazine in August 1956 under the caption "Shipping Tycoon". The article traced the boom in shipping that was occurring then and Niarchos was acknowledged as the largest shipowner in the world. That was to prove the highwater mark in his competition for supremacy in the tanker market with Onassis.

The Suez crisis was a boon for the tanker market and Niarchos's fleet would grow to a peak of some 80 tankers. However, by 1960 the market had moved into a slump with many tankers laid-up. Niarchos, however, was able to avoid the brunt of this downturn with a deftly timed contract to move large quantities of Russian crude oil from the Black Sea. He even agreed to build some tankers in Russian shipyards.

By the early 1960's the 100,000-deadweight ton barrier was being breeched by many owners with their new vessels. In 1962, Niarchos built a series of 106,500 deadweight tankers at the Fore River Shipyard in Quincy, Massachusetts. One of those tankers in 1969 would make history as the first vessel to transit the fabled Northwest Passage across the Artic Ocean. The *Manhattan*, the largest U.S. flag vessel at the time, had been modified to be an ice breaking tanker. The vessel started on the East Coast of North America and plowed through the permanent polar ice in the Artic Ocean to reach the West Coast of North America.

The catalyst for this voyage was the discovery of a massive oil field in Prudhoe Bay, Alaska and the view that moving that oil entirely by ship would be more efficient than a proposed pipeline to the all weather port of Valdez. While the *Manhattan* proved it was possible, the voyage time, the cost of the ice-breaker escorts to get through heavy sea ice and the multiple jurisdictional issues that arose with Canada resulted in the pipeline being built.

Greece turned Niarchos into a local hero after he started a Greek shipyard. This was the first commercial shipyard in Greece in modern times and fit with Niarchos's growing desire to make investments that clearly benefited his home country. The Skaramanga shipyard, seven miles west of Athens, was on the Bay of Eleusis, which was the site of the famous battle of Salamis in 480 B.C. In that battle, the Greeks defeated the massive invasion fleet of the Persian leader Xerxes.

Niarchos must have appreciated this symbolism as indicative of the conquests he was achieving in the shipping industry.

While Niarchos and Onassis had been among the first to recognize the scale economies in operating larger tankers, they weren't the only owners to do so. Not long after the 100,000-deadweight ton barrier was breeched in 1958, the 250,000-deadweight ton barrier was breeched in 1966, in both cases by the American Daniel K. Ludwig. More owners were now copying what had initially been a niche dominated by Niarchos, Onassis and Ludwig. As more of these supertankers were built, the competitive advantages that the three gentlemen had were reduced. The golden age of tanker profitability for them was the 1950's and 1960's.

As other owners became aware of the immense profits they were achieving and emulated their vessel size choices, the market began to experience long periods of systematic over-capacity. There is no industry whose results are so closely correlated with supply versus demand as shipping. When either the former or the latter is on top, financial performance is dramatically affected.

Niarchos's excellent sense of timing continued to work for him as he elected to sell off the majority of his fleet before the large downturn in the tanker market in the 1970's. While he continued to have some presence in the sector, he chose to get more involved in real estate and other industries. Coincidentally, an uncle of mine who spent his career in shipping industry worked for a Niarchos controlled company in the 1970's.

Much of Niarchos's investments outside of shipping were focused on Greece. While he was now living in palatial homes in London and Paris, he would always view Greece as his home. Among those investments was a joint venture in 1970 with Onassis to build an oil refinery in Greece. Their love of country resulted in a rare truce in the highly competitive relationship that would constantly be at the forefront.

His intense rivalry with Onassis extended well beyond the shipping industry and expanded into the yachts and Greek Islands they owned and even the women they married. Both men developed opulent lifestyles and what effectively became a quest for supremacy in conspicuous consumption was well chronicled by the media.

Niarchos had owned luxury yachts since the late 1930's, but with the delivery of the *Creole* in the early 1950's, he became the undisputed king in this area. A black-hulled, three masted schooner, the 190' long *Creole* was not only the world's biggest privately owned yacht, it was also viewed by many as the most beautiful yacht in the world. It included murals in the main salon painted by Salvador Dali. With its graceful lines and elegant styling, it was a breathtaking experience for its many guests.

Even years later when Onassis would build the much larger motor yacht *Christina*, many believed that Niarchos was still the king in terms of luxury yachts. In 1973, Niarchos put any questions to rest when he took delivery of his own motor yacht, the *Atlantis*, which was thirty feet longer than the *Christina*.

In 1962, Niarchos bought Spetsopoula, a 500 acre island in the Aegean Sea that was located approximately 50 miles from Athens. Niarchos would travel frequently by helicopter with guests to this private getaway. Stocked with rare plants and game, it was also a hunting preserve where

Niarhcos entertained royalty and members of the jet set. Perhaps jealous of glowing magazine reports on Niarchos's opulent lifestyle, his rival Onassis bought a Greek island of his own, Skorios, six years later.

However, it was the rivalry in terms of who they took to the altar that would become what both men were most known for outside of shipping. The dean of the Greek shipping community prior to the accession of Niarchos and Onassis was Stavros Livanos. While he came to admire both gentlemen, he was conservative and initially thought their approach to the shipping industry was way too risky. Importantly, Livanos also had two daughters.

In 1946, Onassis married Tina Livanos, the 17 old daughter of Stavros Livanos. Niarchos would marry the other daughter, Eugenie, less than a year later. In 1965, Niarchos divorced Eugenie to marry Charlotte Ford, the 24 year old daughter of automobile tycoon Henry Ford 2nd. She gave birth to a child shortly thereafter and they were divorced in 1967. Because the Greek Church had not recognized his divorce in Mexico from Eugenie, Niarchos simply resumed his marriage with Eugenie. In 1970, she died from an overdose of sleeping pills.

Meanwhile, his archrival Onassis had divorced Tina and married Jacqueline Kennedy in 1968, forever trumping Niarchos in the matrimonial competition between them. But there was another move that Niarchos would make that would get attention and at least presumably give him a consolation prize in this particular contest. In 1971, Niarchos married Tina, Onassis's former wife and his former wife's sister. She died three years later from an apparent drug overdose. When you chart out this marital history, it can probably best be described as part Greek tragedy and part Greek comedy.

In 1996, Niarchos died at the age of 86. At that time, he was down to some ten tankers, a tenth of the fleet size compared to his peak. His fortune was estimated to be as much as $4 billion and resided mostly outside of shipping and in his foundation.

The Stavros Niarchos Foundation has remained active and is among the largest philanthropic organizations in the world today. In 2017, the foundation committed $150 million to a joint effort with Johns Hopkins University to forge new ways to address the deterioration of civic engagement worldwide and facilitate open and inclusive discourse that is the cornerstone of democracy. The foundation of someone whose life was marked by hyper-competitiveness has exemplified its Greek roots by supporting core principals related to democracy.

I was reminded of the the far reaching impact of the Niarchos Foundation when I was recently in a wing of a New York City hospital named in his honor. In another coincidence that links me with this shipping giant, my daughter recently graduated from Johns Hopkins University.

Niarchos epitomized the risk-taking shipping magnate who was all-in in support of his convictions. He didn't hedge and he stood to loose almost everything if things didn't go the way he expected. But in his meteoric rise from the end of the war through the closing of the Suez Canal, everything generally went as he expected. His use of credit and leverage made the financial returns to him over that period extraordinary. The secret of his success could be reduced down to buy cheap and buy big. Through his foundation, the world continues to benefit immensely from his vision and success.

10. Aristotle Onassis

The Colorful Enterpreneur Most Identified With Shipping.

The most well known shipowner in history, Onassis was a colorful Greek who, along with D.K. Ludwig and Stavros Niarchos, dominated the tanker sector for decades. His epic struggle for dominance in the movement of oil across the globe is as intriguing as his more highly chronicled personal life.

Aristotle Socrates Onassis was born on January 20, 1906, in Karatas, a suburb of Izmir, Turkey. His father, Socrates Onassis, had settled in this area of Turkey, like thousands of other Greeks, after Greece had become part of the Turkish Empire. With their excellent business skills, the Greeks had become the administrators and businessmen throughout the region.

Socrates Onassis was in the tobacco trading business and as it grew he employed many members of his large family. In 1904, he married Penelope Dologlu. His thriving business allowed them to move into a suburban house overlooking the sea. His wife first gave birth to a girl who was christened Artemis and a year later his son Aristotle was born.

While they weren't technically in Greece, Greeks surrounded the family. In an area of Turkey known as Smyrna, there were actually five times as many Greeks as in Athens. Like all Greeks in Smyrna, the Onassis family was quietly dedicated to the Greek cause even though they were technically Turkish subjects.

Young Aristotle went by the nickname of Aristo with his family. He was bright and playful and his distinguishing feature as a child was his large dark eyes. He was, in particular, very close to his gentle mother. When Onassis was six, his mother went to the hospital and never came back. She had a kidney operation that initially went well, but it later resulted in a fatal infection.

Onassis didn't understand all the details but did know that his mother was gone forever. However, his grandmother Gethsemane had come to live with the family long before and almost immediately she became his surrogate mother. Onassis would always say in later years that his grandmother raised him.

Gethsemane watched over everything Onassis and his sister did. From passing inspection as they left for school each day to talking about what they learned at school when they arrived home, she was a constant presence in their life. She was also an extremely religious person and this would play an important part in young Aristo's life. He attended church regularly with his grandmother and sang in the choir every Sunday. Choir practice at church was a frequent event. He studied Greek catechism at home under his grandmother's watchful eye and was drilled in theology for two hours each week by the local priest. Onassis would later claim that he spent so much time in church as a boy that he should be granted special dispensation as an adult.

In 1915, Onassis's father remarried and soon he and his sister had two half-sisters, Merope and Callirrhoe. Onassis was a good student in school and very popular with his classmates. He also became a good athlete despite his relatively short statue. During his childhood he developed an early love of the sea. From where he slept, it was the first thing he saw each morning and the last thing he saw each night.

The region the Onassis family lived in began to be more affected by World War I in 1917 when Greece abandoned its neutrality and sided with the Allies. As a result, the Turks who sided with the Germans looked at Greeks in the area with suspicion. This resulted in much uneasiness, but most Greeks kept their support of their homeland quiet and avoided any confrontations.

Young Aristo didn't possess a fanatical bent. The family's business had prospered and by the end of World War I in 1918, his father Socrates was one of three leading merchants in Smyrna. In addition to tobacco, he was dealing in grain and hides and had expanded to provide storage and loans to his customers.

Smyrna was occupied by Greek troops in 1919 and for the next three years it was part of Greece. Onassis was now a student at Evangelical High School where he joined a sporting club and became outstanding at water polo. If it was a sport that had anything to do with water, Onassis was involved. He was a strong swimmer and if he wasn't swimming, he was often sailing or rowing in Smyrna's harbor.

The Greek occupation of Smyrna brought about halcyon days for Socrates Onassis and his family. However, it also sowed the seeds for what would become a disruptive period for all. While the Turks had retreated inland, they grew increasingly restive at what the Greeks had done. This simmering unrest found an avenue of expression when Turkish nationalist forces coalesced and began attacking the occupying army. By 1922, those forces had driven the Greek forces to the sea and Turkey retook control of Smyrna. With that, the Turks turned their attention to seeking revenge against the Greeks that remained in Smyrna.

Socrates Onassis was arrested and put in a Turkish prison. His wife and three daughters were sent to an evacuation center to await transportation to Greece. Only sixteen year old Aristo and his grandmother were left in the family home. They were told that would end shortly as a Turkish general had requisitioned the home for his personal quarters.

But a polite Aristo, speaking perfect Turkish, impressed upon the general that he could be a useful resource related to finding liquor and other goods and was asked to stay. Similarly, he ingratiated himself with a U.S. vice consul who lived nearby. As a reward for something he had done for the U.S. vice consul, he was given a fine bottle of French brandy. He immediately re-gifted this to the Turkish general. The young Onassis had just engaged in his first business transaction and he now had two important friends in high places.

Onassis obtained passes from both the Turkish general and the U.S. vice consul that allowed him to access much of the city. He immediately turned his attention to what he could do to help his family. Through the intercession of the U.S. consul, he got his stepmother and sisters put on an American ship bound for the island of Lesbos.

Upon learning where his father was being held prisoner, Onassis began visiting him twice a day. His father's situation was desperate and everyday quick military trials were being held with scores of Greeks then being sentenced to death by hanging. Onassis organized a march of fifty leading Turkish businessmen from Smyrna who, flourishing a banner protesting the arrest of Socrates Onassis, called for his release. That didn't occur, but it did remove his father from the process that would have resulted in execution.

From his daily visits, Onassis was told where his father kept cash and other valuables. Using his passes, he was able to go to the old office and open and empty the safe. Onassis visited his father, leaving some cash with him. They developed a plan for him to go to Athens with much of the family's money along with important messages for friends in Athens. A new law had also just been passed requiring the deportation of any military age Greek, so it was known that Onassis wouldn't be able to stay in Smyrna. As he was leaving, he was stopped by guards and led to the prison commandant's office to be questioned. Before that started, the commandant was summoned away but said he would be back shortly.

Onassis was fearful that questioning and a search, finding secret messages and a large amount of money, would exacerbate the situation for both his father and himself. He managed to distract the guard and slip out of the commandant's office. Once on the street, he ran as fast as he could to the U.S. marine compound where he told the Vice Consul of his situation. Within an hour, he was outfitted in a sailor's uniform and on an American destroyer headed to Lesbos. Onassis believed that he owed his life to this quick action by the Americans.

Reunited with much of his family on Lesbos, Onassis shepherded everyone on to Athens. A family meeting was held on how to secure Socrates Onassis release from prison. It was decided the best approach was for young Onassis to travel to Constantinople and attempt to bribe officials. He travelled to Turkey and, while it was expensive, he succeeded and orders were sent to the prison. Upon returning to Athens, he was astounded that some uncles and other relatives thought he had spent too much money. His father was released and made his way to Athens. After the initial jubilation of rejoining his family, Socrates Onassis too joined the chorus and expressed to his son his own view that he could have been released without spending so much cash.

Onassis was dumbfounded at the reaction by his family and his father and this quickly turned to resentment and anger. He decided that if they didn't have faith in his judgment, he certainly did. He didn't need them and made a decision that he would separate and make it on his own.

With just a small amount of cash, in August 1922 Onassis waived goodbye to his family from the deck of an Italian steamship departing from Piraeus and bound for Buenos Aires, Argentina. He was booked in steerage class, but with a $5 bribe was able to move from those wretched conditions at night to a machinery area on deck where he slept on a cage that held ropes used to secure the ship to the dock.

In September 1922, Onassis arrived in Buenos Aires, knowing no one and with only $40 in his pocket. He found a cheap rooming house to stay at and immediately found a job rowing dockworkers between various areas of the dock. He was then able to make a little more at a series of construction and restaurant jobs. Onassis liked living near the waterfront, as there was a constant procession of seaman from Greek ships that were involved in moving Argentine grain and beef to Europe.

After over a year of taking any job he could get, in late 1924 Onassis landed a salaried job at the local telephone company. He went from fastening wires together to being a night operator where he was collecting overtime. Nineteen-year-old Onassis moved to better quarters and started enjoying some of the nightlife that Buenos Aires offered. He joined a rowing club and reconnected via correspondence with his father who had reestablished his tobacco business in Athens.

When his father asked him to look into the market for Turkish tobacco in Argentina, Onassis jumped at the opportunity and asked his father to send him samples. Initially hawking cigarettes on the streets of Buenos Aires, Onassis then began focusing on the large cigarette factories. Identifying one of the largest manufacturers, for fourteen straight days he went to the office of the president until he was able to get a meeting. This lead to a large order and then orders from other manufacturers started coming in.

Onassis left his job at the telephone company to focus fulltime on his growing tobacco business. He started his own small factory to make hand rolled cigarettes. The bulk of his business, however, was selling tobacco to larger manufacturers. In addition to the imported Turkish tobacco, he began buying local tobacco from farmers to offer a broader product range to his customers. Onassis expanded into being a wholesaler of hides based on the relationships he had developed with local farmers. Despite his growing wealth, he made a point of using credit to fund his business.

By 1929, Onassis was a millionaire. He had a desire to see his family and also had business he thought could best be done in person. Trouble in the Balkans had resulted in Greece announcing its intention to levy a 1000 per cent tariff on imported goods from countries where no trade agreement existed. Argentina had no trade agreement and Onassis was sure that this would quickly lead to a corresponding tariff by Argentina on goods imported from Greece, severely impacting his tobacco business.

Onassis prepared a memorandum on this while crossing the Atlantic in first class in a dramatic change from his westward crossing six years earlier. His family greeted him, many of which he was now supporting, like a conquering hero. With memorandum in hand, he sought and obtained a meeting with the premier of Greece. The next day, Argentina was exempted from the provisions of the decree. Furthermore, Onassis was appointed special envoy and tasked with a mission of undertaking negotiations with Argentina to improve Greece's commercial relations with that country.

Upon his return to Argentina, Onassis succeeded brilliantly in his mission and smoothed away any friction so that a trade treaty between Greece and Argentina could be affected. Shortly thereafter, Onassis was appointed as the Greek consul in Buenos Aires. In that capacity, he became involved in clearing and assisting the hundreds of Greek merchant vessels that called on Buenos Aires each year.

The stock market crash of 1929 came and went with little effect on Argentina. Much of its economy was tied to providing beef and grain to Europe and that market was generally unaffected. Onassis's tobacco and hide business continued to grow and he expanded into the grain exporting business.

As consul, Onassis now had an enormous amount of power related to both shipping and import-export in general. Every door in those areas, along with every door to the banks that financed such transactions, was open to Onassis. He exploited all of his contacts and the overlap between his official role and his private businesses worked to his advantage. Onassis's tobacco business and his trading in hides and grains all prospered during this period.

Onassis was now making frequent business trips to Europe to expand his business. Most were via luxury liner but he made one eastbound trip in 1931 via the dirigible *Graf Zeppelin*. In his role as consul he had become very familiar with shipping. His knowledge was extended through his now frequent chartering of ships to export grain from Argentina. As he became more knowledgeable about shipping as it related to his various businesses, he pondered the pros and cons of becoming more directly involved in the industry. His instincts on the direction of commodity prices had generally proved accurate.

Shipping remained in the doldrums due to the depression. However, Onassis sensed that if secondhand ships that were laid up could be bought for bargain prices, the tide would turn and this would prove to be an attractive investment. On a trip around Europe, Onassis visited shipyards, ship owners and agents from Antwerp to Goteborg. Armed with a growing understanding of shipping, six months later he made a trip to London, the center of the shipping world.

Onassis outlined to agents and brokers the ideal ships he was seeking. Instead of the typical 5,000-ton freighter, he was focused on larger ships. He had long ago come to appreciate the economics of larger ships and knew that while a 10,000 ton ship would generate twice the revenue of a typical ship, it didn't cost nearly twice as much to operate. This simple concept would guide much of what Onassis did in shipping and it would prove to serve him well.

The London trip proved fruitful and Onassis became aware of ten 10,000 ton general cargo ships owned by Canadian National Steamship that were laid up in Montreal. He immediately booked passage to Montreal to inspect the vessels. Climbing over the snow-covered ships with an engineer he had brought along, Onassis determined that these vessels were just what he was looking for. He returned to London and negotiated a transaction to buy six of the vessels for $20,000 each. Onassis felt good about the transaction as he estimated that price was about 5% of what it would cost to build new vessels that size.

Within a year, things started to look up and Onassis began taking his bargain-basement ships out of lay-up one at a time. His ships were showing more profits than competitors who had been shipping for generations. While he was new as an operator, his years as consul had exposed him to various business strategies and he had been an excellent student.

Onassis first registered his ships in Greece and Argentina but as he studied regulations more, he switched his ships to the Panama registry. Onassis was a pioneer in registering his ships under Panama's flag of convenience and this resulted in lower costs than most of his competitors. His attention to costs, an uncanny knack for getting good charter rates and his decision to operate only very large vessels resulted in solid and growing profits for this new ship owner.

Onassis now wanted more ships. Seeing coal being increasingly displaced by oil, he thought the best opportunity was in tankers. He believed the best way to capitalize on some original ideas he had was to build the largest tankers in the world.

In 1934 during a trip to Europe, Onassis met Ingeborg Dedichen, a recently divorced Norwegian. That began a long-term relationship with her. He began spending more time in Europe, particularly in Paris where he purchased a nice home. Dedichen introduced him to the Scandinavian shipping world and Onassis began intense negotiations with Swedish shipyards to build his new tankers.

The Greek who had actually not spent much time in Greece now began to spend his summers in Greece with Dedichen. It was there in Athens in 1934 that he first met Stavros Niarchos who wasn't yet nearly as far along as Onassis was in shipping.

This would begin a decades long competition between these men with regard to both their business and personal lives. Unbeknownst to both men at the time, these outsiders in the Greek shipping community had shared views both in terms of a more optimistic view of shipping and a belief that the real money would come from building very large tankers.

In 1936, Onassis signed contracts with a shipyard in Goteborg, Sweden to build three new tankers designed by his naval architects based on his specificications. The tankers would have a capacity of 15,000 tons, making them the largest tankers in the world.

Onassis was optimistic about the expansion of the oil transport business. He also liked the fact that tankers were the most automated ships and didn't rely on dozens of dockworkers and cargo winches. They simply had to be hooked up to hoses and could be fully loaded in a fraction of the time it took to pack the hold of a general cargo ship. Unloading simply involved reversing this process and didn't require much labor at all. In this sense, the tanker segment was more pure shipping than any other shipping segment. Those segments invariably involved significant time and costs in loading and unloading cargoes. Onassis liked this distinction.

The new tankers that Onassis was building cost $700,000 each, but only one-quarter of that was due during construction and he was able to finance most of that. He had ten years to pay off the balance and that entire amount was financed. Onassis had developed excellent credit with his banks and this allowed him to maximize the vessel financing he received, a core principle that would guide all of his shipping activities.

His new vessels were not only the largest and most modern tankers afloat, but by putting them under the Panama flag they had relatively low operating costs. Onassis anticipated that they would be the most profitable vessels in the world and with the delivery of the *Ariston* in June 1938 followed shortly thereafter by her sisterships *Aristophanes* and *Buenos Aires*, their actual operation proved him correct.

By now, Onassis had excellent relationships with his banks by virtue of his financial performance and improved financial condition. He utilized the credit he was getting from banks to aggressively grow his fleet, which was now exclusively focused on the tanker segment. Onassis preferred tankers because of his faith in the expansion of the oil business. He also liked the fact that tankers were the most automated. Time in port was a fraction of the time spent by a general cargo ship. This not only resulted in less port time, but made that time more predictable and consistent.

The skies were darkening over Europe in the late 1930's as the specter of war became more apparent. This did not, however, dampen Onassis's optimism with regard to tankers. That had been a growing view of his since the end of the depression and it had served him well. In addition to benefiting from rebounding economies, he had also experienced firsthand that wars and rumors of wars had been good for the tanker business. For instance, the Spanish civil war was a positive catalyst for the sector as Greek shipowners including Onassis had moved oil for both sides.

The established Greek shipowners had initially looked at Onassis as an outsider who shared little of their heritage. He hadn't sailed before the mast like their fathers and grandfathers and hadn't been raised on the tradition of the sea. Onassis wasn't a Greek islander and wasn't even a London Greek. However, this man that they had initially scoffed at as just an Argentine tobacco merchant who was almost a Turk had become a force to be reckoned with in the shipping world.

Now just over thirty, Onassis was busily shuttling back and forth between Europe and both North and South America to manage his growing fleet. He became well known to the staffs on luxury liners and at the best hotels as he began to take on the glamorous lifestyle he would become known for.

This even extended to the owner's suite he had installed in the *Ariston*, the largest tanker in the world when it was delivered. The two bedroom suite in that ship, designed by Onassis himself, included a grand piano and was outfitted like the best suite in a top Paris hotel. Onassis made the maiden journey of the *Ariston* from Sweden to San Francisco, during which he hosted his three sisters and some of their friends.

As grand as the *Ariston* was as a personal cruiser on its voyage from the shipyard to its first load port, it would prove to be even much better as a money making cargo ship. Onassis had arranged for a charter to move oil to Japan for its first year of operation. In that first year, the flagship of his fleet earned a net profit of over $600,000. That was almost equal to the entire cost to build the ship and many times the down payment made by Onassis as his banks had financed most of the construction cost.

More so than almost anything else, the actual performance of the *Ariston* in her first year of operation reinforced Onassis's belief in large tankers financed with lots of credit. As its two sister ships were delivered, they were also employed under profitable charters moving oil.

Resulting from his negotiations with the shipyard, Onassis had agreed to register the *Ariston* under the Swedish flag. The sister ship *Aristophanes* was registered under the Greek flag while the *Buenos Aires* was registered under the Argentine flag. While Onassis was by that time generally flagging most of his tankers under the Panama flag, it is believed that he had some silent partners for these new vessels that originated from Greece and Argentina. Including those registries presumably assisted in recruiting some of those investors.

No details are known on the ownership interest or role such silent partners had with these vessels. While they no doubt further reduced the initial equity Onassis needed to build the ships, they typically contained provisions that would have allowed him to buyback such interests. They also usually contained various fees that would accrue prior to any profit split. Indeed, many Greek shipowners became known for structuring complex agreements that had the effect of substantially reducing their own downside without materially limiting their own upside. Onassis was one of the pioneers of such arrangements.

With a growing fleet operating in the booming international tanker market due to the threat of war, Onassis was becoming very rich and it showed up in his increasingly glamorous lifestyle. When in New York, he now always stayed in a suite at the St. Moritz Hotel on Central Park South. This had become the unofficial headquarters for Greek shipowners when they were in New York. In London, he would stay in a suite at the Savoy Hotel.

By this time, Ingeborg Dedichen, the beautiful Norwegian that he had met on a cruise always accompanied him. He was smitten when he first saw her and paid a steward to move him to the room next to hers. Onassis made his move and by the end of the cruise it was agreed that he would set her up in a sumptuous apartment in Paris. He also had a permanent suite in the nicest hotel in Buenos Aires and was building a new house in Montevideo, Argentina. Wherever Onassis traveled, he now went in style both in terms of the journey and the destination. The actual results of his growing fleet were more than capable of supporting such a lifestyle.

Most Greek shipowners including Onassis didn't think Hitler would actually go to war, but thought they would continue to benefit from the threat of war. This would prove to be one of the few major miscalculations by Onassis. In 1939, Hitler invaded Poland and much of Europe quickly became engulfed in war. When this happened, all three of his new tankers were in neutral Scandinavian ports and they were flagged with countries that were all neutral also.

The ships were all immobilized by the Scandinavian governments, which were neutral and wanted to avoid any involvement with the warring countries. Onassis was frantic as he knew how much his ships, still the largest tankers in the world, had been earning moving oil to Britain and other countries building up supplies in anticipation of war. He went to Sweden immediately and attempted without success to secure the release of his new ships. He would learn to his dismay that Sweden had agreed to keep all neutral ships tied up for the duration of the war.

Onassis, however, still had six tankers under Panama flag that were profitable and benefiting from the war tensions. He also had several million in cash accumulated over the last few years. He determined that he would use those funds to rebuild his fleet and that the best place to do that from would be New York rather than London where he now spent much of his time.

Onassis booked passage on the first available cruise liner and was crossing the Atlantic when the Germans were invading France. He wasn't the only one who had that idea. Onassis would beat his soon to be archrival Niarchos to New York by just a few weeks.

It was during this period that Onassis became well known with the café society of New York. He was frequently seen at popular nightclubs such as El Morocco and Monte Carlo. Onassis also became a regular visitor to the suite at the Plaza Hotel where Stavros Livanos, still the dean of the Greek shipping community, lived. With two of his tankers now moving oil from Los Angeles to Canada, he was often on the West Coast and became ensconced in the social scene in Hollywood.

He was assisted in this regard by his good friend Spyros Skouras, the respected head of Twentieth Century Fox. Coincidentally, Skouras's grandson by the same name is a friend and classmate of mine from business school. His family had subsequently also gone into the shipping business. As it would turn out, young Skouras and I were the only two people out of a graduating class of some 800 at Harvard Business School that chose to go into the shipping industry.

With the invasion of Pearl Harbor, the U.S. became directly involved in the war. This proved to be a boon for all shipowners. As the war progressed, all of Onassis's tankers were steadily employed at good rates hauling cargoes for the U.S. war effort. It was impossible for a non-U.S. citizen like Onassis to buy new ships in the U.S. However, this didn't stop him from incrementally adding to his fleet by purchasing existing vessels.

Onassis was on the prowl for any ship that became available. In one transaction, he actually partnered with Stavros Niarchos to purchase a old tanker from D.K. Ludwig, the American who was the largest tanker operator in the world. As he bought other older tankers, he chartered them directly to the U.S. government.

When the war ended, Onassis had a large fleet and a fortune estimated at $30 million, a considerable sum in those days. The war had decimated the Greek merchant marine fleet, with 360 ships lost out of the 450 ships that had participated. However, Onassis was alone among major Greek shipowners in not having lost a single ship during the war. In addition, the three modern tankers and the pride of his fleet, which were still the largest tankers in the world, remained unscathed in Scandinavian ports. Not surprisingly, Onassis was brimming with optimism for the future as the war concluded.

Many shipowners, recalling the downturn that followed World War I, took steps to reduce their risk and exposure. Onassis, however, was very confident that rebuilding efforts and increasing trade as the global economy grew would make for a robust market and was determined to expand his fleet.

It would be years before shipyards outside of the U.S. could be rebuilt and he thought U.S. shipyard prices were too high at that time. He set his sights on the hundreds of surplus Liberty ships and tankers that he expected the U.S. government would shortly be selling.

Meanwhile, as Onassis was approaching forty, he was thinking more about settling down and ending his bachelor days. His relationship with Ingeberg wasn't what it used to be and he had never seriously considered marrying her. Onassis was frequently seen in nightclubs with different young actresses, but none of them seemed to fit what he was looking for. As with everything, Onassis took a strategic approach to this and concluded that the ideal wife would be Greek. If she happened to be from a leading Greek ship owning family, that would even be better.

In 1943 on one of his visits to the suite at the Plaza Hotel where Stavros Livanos lived, Onassis first met his two daughters Eugenia and Tina, then 16 and 14 years old. For three years on his frequent visits, he had watched them grow into lovely young ladies. Eugenia was a dark haired well-educated beauty who spoke several languages and had a slight British accent. Her blonde sister Tina was more outgoing and a bit of a tomboy at that time. Onassis began to think more about Eugenia and how she might be the ideal wife for him.

Both girls had been introduced to social life among Greeks in New York by 1946. Onassis began squiring them together to movies and his favorite spots in New York. As this was going on, he quietly phased Ingeberg out of his life. After months of frequent companionship, Onassis decided he wanted to marry Eugenia. He knew he would need her father's permission, but believed after thinking it over he would agree despite the two decades age difference. Onassis asked Eugenia and to his great shock, she refused while saying she wanted to remain friends.

Onassis threw himself back into expanding his fleet. However, consistent with her promise to remain friends, Eugenia seemed to be more anxious than ever for him to take her to movies and plays where she always brought her younger sister Tina. Unbeknown to Onassis, Tina had already determined that if her sister Eugenia wasn't going to marry him, she would. Six months later in late 1946, Onassis and Tina Livanos were married when he was 40 years old and she was 17 years old.

Surplus ships were beginning to pile up as they were taken out of service and the U.S. government developed a program to sell them. The axis occupation had decimated Greece's merchant marine fleet and countries like it were allowed to buy ships under generous terms, which included long term financing. The structure that was in place was that the U.S. would negotiate a block sale of ships to the country. Those countries in turn would distribute the ships and the favorable credit terms to individual shipowners.

As the first sale negotiation approached, the Greek mission arrived in the U.S. with a plan to buy 100 ships. After discussions with mostly unenthusiastic Greek shipowners, they decided to cut the number of ships they wanted to 60. Onassis was the only major Greek shipowner to urge that Greece take all the ships it could get and the still much smaller Niarchos seconded him.

Presumably swayed, the Greek government upped its request back to the original 100 ships and was awarded the same number. However, when it was announced how those ships would be allocated to each owner who had applied to be part of the Greek quota, Onassis was left out and didn't get a single ship. He knew this went back to the misgivings within the shipping fraternity of just how Greek Onassis was. To make matters even worse, his smaller growing rival Niarchos was allocated eight ships.

Upset but undeterred, Onassis wouldn't allow this slight to undermine his growth plans. He knew that an individual could also negotiate to buy surplus ships, although such purchases came without the favorable credit terms reserved for governments.

A confident Onassis applied to the U.S. government to personally buy 16 surplus ships, offering to pay cash, and an $8.8 million agreement was quickly reached. The Argentine-Greek was no doubt pleased that he would now be getting twice as many ships as Niarchos. While Onassis could have readily paid for the ships himself, he wanted to take advantage of financial leverage by getting partners or financing.

When it came to financing the purchase of existing ships, partnerships were a typical structure. However, none of the Greek owners Onassis knew would be interested in a transaction that was less favorable than they could get through just participating in the overall Greek quota which brought with it in place favorable credit terms.

Bank financing was primarily available for new vessels but they were uncomfortable with used vessels. American banks had been very leery of shipping in general and didn't participate at all in that lending sector. Onassis would make breakthroughs in both areas that would benefit him well beyond this particular transaction.

Now ensconced in a luxury four-story Manhattan townhouse, the Onassis's quickly found themselves in elite social circles. The house was a wedding gift to Tina from her father Stavros Livanos. Her dowry also included a promise to transfer two surplus Liberty ships that Livanos had acquired as part of his allocation of the Greek quota. Onassis was reportedly far from overjoyed with this negligible portion of the Livanos fleet, but it assisted with his own growth plans. Those plans were very ably assisted by the growing social connections among bankers, oil company executives and government officials that the witty Onassis and his vibrant young wife were making.

Whether at night clubs, the theater or at their townhouse hosting dinner parties, almost every night they had some event where they intersected with people who might be helpful to Onassis's business interests. One of those people turned out to be the head of a major New York bank and Onassis's persuaded him to lend half the money to buy the 16 surplus ships.

At the same time he was putting together this financing, he was lining up cargoes for these ships. Onassis had persuaded government officials he knew that he was the right person to move coal to war-torn France and Germany under the Marshall Plan. This latest venture became immediately profitable. More importantly, it became a model that he would copy many times going forward.

Onassis was now ready to implement a plan he had long been refining in his mind. At parties they held and other social events where he interacted with oil executives, he preached the efficacy of long term fixed price contracts to transport oil. After winning over executives on this principle, he went to work negotiating with Bethlehem Steel to build the largest tankers ever at its Sparrows Point shipyard in Baltimore.

He first got Mobil Oil to agree to a five-year charter of one of these large 28,000-ton deadweight tankers. A few months later, Texaco signed a long-term charter for four such ships. More oil companies came around to commit to charters and Onassis would move ahead on a newbuilding program involving 20 new tankers costing $40 million in total.

With these charter commitments from major American oil companies as collateral, Onassis had little trouble getting almost the entire construction cost of these ships financed by American banks. While they were built in the U.S., all of these ships would serve international trade routes and be registered in Panama to minimize operating costs and taxes.

When surplus T-2 tankers were put up for sale by the U.S. government, they were offered only to U.S. citizens or U.S. citizen corporations. Onassis got around this by setting up a U.S. corporation with prominent American friends as minority shareholders and bought a handful of surplus tankers. These were added to his growing tanker fleet except for one, which was converted in Germany to be the flagship of a whaling fleet he had also established.

By 1950, Onassis's fleet had grown to 37 ships. The onset of the Korean War was another positive catalyst for tanker demand and charter rates. Onassis responded by aggressively adding to his fleet. He was now primarily using German shipyards, but also placed new orders with French and American shipyards.

In 1953, he took delivery in Germany of the *Tina Onassis*, which at 42,000 deadweight tons, was now the largest tanker in the world. With a cost of $6 million, it was also the most expensive cargo ship ever built. As he had in the past, Onassis continued to finance much of the construction cost of his new vessels, with charter contracts from major oil companies the primary collateral.

Onassis reached the peak of his tanker capacity in the mid-1950's when he controlled almost one hundred ships with a total capacity of 1.5 million deadweight tons. At that time he was the undisputed owner of the largest tanker fleet in the world which represented almost 10% of total tanker capacity. His growth benefited from a contract he personally negotiated with King Saud that made his fleet the preferred hauler of Saudi Arabian crude oil.

While this was a great deal for Onassis by itself, it so alarmed the major oil companies who feared he could get a monopoly on certain key routes that they purposefully began moving away from him when their own charters expired. A key benefactor of this switching by oil companies was his rival Niarchos who became the second largest tanker operator and who was now his brother-in-law following his own marriage to Eugenia Livanos. Their rivalry, however, was now only beginning to enter a higher more intense phase.

As soon as the *Tina Onassis* was launched, Niarchos announced that he was beginning construction on the *World Glory*, which at 45,000 tons would be the largest tanker in the world. Niarchos contracted to build that tanker at Bethlehem Steel's shipyard in Baltimore. Already with 39 ships totaling some one million deadweight tons, Niarchos also had ships being built in Germany, Sweden, Britain and Japan. Like Onassis, he was optimistic on the tanker market outlook. As he took delivery of his new tankers, Niarchos's fleet would grow to 80 ships within a few years.

Onassis was now an extraordinarily wealthy man and he had no issue with consuming a portion of that wealth for his own enjoyment and pleasure. He bought control of much of the small principality of Monte Carlo and became even more of a celebrity whose every move was followed by the press. He converted a 325' long Canadian Navy corvette into a luxurious yacht that he named *Christina* after his daughter. He would buy Skorpios, his own Greek island in the Ionian Sea, and transform it into a bustling private kingdom.

Just as they actively competed on ship and fleet size, Onassis and his brother-in-law competed on their personal expenditures. Whether it was a yacht, a private island or another palatial home, when one bought something of note, the other would often follow with something even more noteworthy.

The *Christina* was a floating paradise on which Onassis entertained world leaders and celebrities. Over the years his guests included Winston Churchill, Richard Burton, Eva Peron, Frank Sinatra, King Farouk and Greta Garbo, among others. Even the Rothchilds and Rockefellers who cruised on her were swept up in the opulence and splendor of everything onboard, from the onyx and silver staircase to the Renoirs and other paintings in the salon.

Onassis delighted in giving guests a tour of his magnificent yacht, which often ended at the bar on the fantail. More often than not, guests would note that the leather covering the barstools was unusually soft and supple. This allowed Onassis to indulge regularly in one of his favorite observations that the stools were upholstered with the foreskin of a minke whale. For female guests sitting on the barstools, the never subtle Onassis delighted in saying that they were in effect sitting on the largest penis in the world. Presumably this choice of barstool covering resulted in part from his previous involvement in the whaling business.

The closure of the Suez Canal by Egypt's President Nasser in 1956 had an immediate and pronounced effect on the tanker market. Because almost all of the oil from the Middle East was moving to Europe or the U.S. via the Suez Canal, it now would have to go around the tip of Africa. This increased voyage distances by three and four times, immediately soaking up all the excess tanker supply, but capacity was still well short of what was needed.

Shipping rates quadrupled overnight and would eventually go up more than ten times what they were prior to the closure. Onassis benefited immensely but his rival Niarchos benefited even more as he had been more aggressively building his fleet and he had fewer tankers committed to long term charters. By 1956, Onassis had relinquished his title of the world's largest tanker operator to his brother-in-law Niarchos.

Onassis continued to earn significant profits from his tanker fleet but increasingly those profits were being directed to other investments and interests of his. In 1957, he bought the Greek national airline and renamed it Olympic Airways. Onassis began to invest in stocks of oil companies as well as real estate and office buildings, most notably what would become the Olympic Tower, an iconic 52 story building in midtown Manhattan. He launched an investment initiative to build industrial activity in Greece, which included infrastructure investments in an oil refinery and an aluminum smelter.

All the while, he continued to build new tankers, but not at the pace and the relative sizes that had marked his career through the mid-1950's. There was a downturn in the tanker market in the late-1950's and while it remained profitable, it wasn't showing the extraordinary profits he had experienced most of his career. It wouldn't be until 1967 and the closure of the Suez Canal due to the Arab-Israeli conflict that significant profitability would return to the tanker market. Onassis, however, now seemed to be primarily focused on the personal part of his life for which he is most known.

In 1960, Onassis and his wife Tina divorced. Their 14-year marriage had produced his son Alexander and his daughter Christina. The end of the marriage came when Tina found him in bed with a friend of hers at one of their many homes. His brother-in-law Niarchos would buy that house for his wife, Eugenia, who was Tina's older sister. Ironically, Tina herself would marry Niarchos in 1971 several years after the death of her sister Eugenia.

Onassis had a multi-year relationship with Maria Callas, an opera singer who, after Onassis, was probably the most famous Greek alive at the time. Their relationship and the events they hosted, often involving either his yacht *Christina* or his private island Skorpios, were legendary and frequent subjects of media attention. They would never marry, however, and their relationship ended with the event that Onassis is most famously known.

In 1968, Onassis married Jacqueline Kennedy, the widow of President John F. Kennedy. They had known each other for some ten years going back to when the Kennedy's had been guests aboard the *Christina*. The marriage took place on the island of Skorpios and the couple would reside in luxurious accommodations in six different residences in the U.S. and Europe. Onassis and his life had been well covered by the media prior to his marriage to Ms. Kennedy. However, it now ramped up geometrically as they became one of the most photographed and written about couples in history.

Much has been written and speculated about this relationship and the marital contract that supposedly accompanied it. In some respects, Onassis likely viewed it as another business transaction to achieve his goal. It is also easy to think that he saw this as winning any wife related competition with his former brother-in-law. On the other hand, it also might have been the catalyst for Niarchos to respond three years later by marrying Onassis's first wife Tina.

Onassis died in 1975 of respiratory failure at age 69. He is buried on his island of Skorpios in Greece. Half of his estate went to the Alexander S. Onassis Foundation, which he had established in memory of his son who died in an airplane crash in 1973. The other half of his estate went to his daughter Christina. The foundation remains active to this day and is now one of the largest foundations in Europe.

The foundation consists of two parts, an operating division that runs various businesses including shipping and real estate, and a public benefit foundation that distributes funds from the businesses. The foundation actively supports Greek cultural, health and educational causes. Among other activities, it awards 250 scholarships annually to Greek postgraduates studying abroad. Each year the foundation awards Onassis International Prizes for academic research and publications in the categories of Finance, Trade and Shipping. These awards and the recognition that comes with them are now among the most coveted awards in those fields.

Aristotle Onassis lived life large at all times. He was an outsider who clawed his way to the top largely by virtue of keeping his own counsel. He was viewed as arrogant and opinionated by many, but he also had an outsized personality that endeared him to almost all of the people he met. Onassis had an ever-present drive to prove himself and to others that he was the best at whatever he was doing. This was clearly the catalyst behind his epic competitiveness.

In pushing against the outside edge of the envelope, Onassis pushed the tanker industry to develop bigger, more efficient tankers. He was one of the pioneers who first recognized the scale economies in larger ships and significant financing available from long-term charters with major oil companies. In implementing this, he paved the way for other shipowners to follow, first in the tanker sector but eventually in the other sectors that would follow the lead of tankers and go bigger for cost efficiencies. Onassis did all of this in a very colorful manner that gave rise to his becoming the quintessential image of a shipping magnate.

11. Y.K. Pao

The Lord of the Sea & Owner of World's Largest Fleet.

This Hong Kong shipowner built up a tanker fleet that made him the largest shipowner in world history in the mid-1970's. An unofficial ambassador for his native China who played key role in its transition to capitalism, Deng Xiaoping referred to Pao as "Lord of the Sea".

Yue-Kong Pao was born on November 10, 1918 in Ningbo, China, a port city to the south of Shanghai separated by a large bay. He was the third of seven children of a prosperous upper middle-class family.

In 1931 when he was 13, Pao went to Hankou, a city on the Yangtze River, to work in his father's shoe manufacturing business. Working during the day, he continued his education at night. Pao was a diligent student and he performed well in school. This was particularly the case in math where he was always at the top of his class.

Upon finishing school, Pao decided that his family's shoe business wasn't for him. Around the same time, Hankou came under attack in 1937 by the Japanese. Young Pao moved to Shanghai where his math skills landed him a trainee position in the insurance division of the Central Trust of China, a large bank. A year later at the age of twenty, he was established in his position and married a girl selected by his parents. Pao's father was a key sounding board and adviser on this decision, just as he would be for many important business decisions throughout his career.

In 1940 when the Japanese occupied Shanghai, Pao and his wife moved to Chongqing where he was transferred to the banking division. Chongqing served as the provisional capital of China during most of World War II. Pao's banking skills were noticed and he was quickly promoted to branch manager of the Bank of Industry and Mining. He remained in that post until the end of the war in August 1945.

With the end of the war, the capital returned to Shanghai and the Chinese government wanted to re-establish it as the financial center of the country. One tactic to accomplish this goal was to select ten young bankers recognized as rising stars and to relocate them to Shanghai. Pao was one of the ten bankers selected. As an indication of his elevated status, he and his wife were flown to Shanghai on a military plane.

In Shanghai, Pao was assigned to work as the deputy manager in charge of credit for the Bank of Shanghai. That was a very prestigious position for a 27-year-old young man. Pao welcomed the birth of his first daughter shortly after they relocated to Shanghai. The family lived in a large and attractive house in the French section of Shanghai. The three story European styled house had a pitched red roof and a small garden.

Pao thrived at the Bank of Shanghai where he became recognized for solid financial judgment and particularly fast mental arithmetic. He also became known as someone who was excellent in dealing with the customers of the bank. Known as a dapper dresser, Pao was a good-looking young man who had a presence about him. His looks resulted in Pao being nicknamed the "Mei Lanfang of the Shanghai Banking World". Mei Lanfang was a famous opera artist and considered the quintessential elegant and handsome Chinese man.

As his professional life in Shanghai flourished, Pao's family grew with the arrival of his second daughter in 1948. Pao and his wife would eventually have four daughters. By numerous accounts, Pao was a wonderful, engaged father, instilling in all his children his core values of integrity, hard work, thrift and compassion.

Pao developed his values as a child growing up in his beloved hometown of Ningbo. He grew up in a town where the word thrift in Ningbo dialect literally translated into "manage the household". Among Chinese cities, Ningbo was well known for its disdain for waste. This philosophy resulted in the Ningbo diet being particularly salty compared to other parts of China, as the salt would preserve vegetables and food longer. The core values that Pao developed as a child would constantly reappear and beneficially affect business decisions he would make for the rest of his life.

The business climate in Shanghai was deteriorating by autumn of 1948. Inflation was rampant due to anxiety regarding the civil war between the nationalists under Chiang Kaishek and the communists. It was increasingly looking like the communists would win and the impact of this on Shanghai was uncertain. Pao was apolitical, but took some comfort in his view that the communists would want to build up Shanghai and this could benefit his bank.

His wife's first cousin ran a successful trading company and was one of Pao's closest friends. When he announced that he was moving his trading company to Hong Kong, Pao became more concerned about Shanghai's prospects.

In a subsequent meeting, his friend strongly advised Pao to leave Shanghai for Hong Kong. His primary point was that Hong Kong and its unfettered capitalism offered much more to a smart young man like Pao. After giving the issue much thought, Pao concluded at the end of 1948 that he would move his family to Hong Kong and tendered his resignation to his ultimate boss, the mayor of Shanghai.

By October 1949, the communists had achieved full victory and formed the Peoples Republic of China with its capital in Beijing. The nationalist government moved from Shanghai to Taiwan. The combined effect of these changes was negative for Shanghai, re-affirming that Pao had made the right decision.

In Hong Kong, Pao started an export-import business due in large part to the familiarity he had with trade from his banking days in Shanghai. He leased a small office with two desks, which allowed him and three other people to sit by using each side of the desk. Pao and his co-workers would take turns going out of the office on business calls. Pao's father was also a frequent visitor to the office and would act as a constant and effective sounding board for his son.

Pao's export-import business benefited from the extensive contacts he had developed as a banker. It was also helped by the embargo the U.S. and other countries had put on trade with Mainland China after the communist victory. Hong Kong became the back door way to trade with

China, a position it would benefit from and retain for decades. Much of Pao's business involved trade with China. For instance, he bought soybeans and other grains from South America and then engaged in transactions to sell them to Mainland China.

His business grew and prospered. Pao and his family enjoyed spending time with a widening circle of immigrants from Shanghai who moved to Hong Kong in 1949 and the early 1950's. Like his business, most of these immigrants were involved in Hong Kong businesses that were tied directly to Mainland China. Pao was a relentless worker during the week but he generally reserved the weekends for time with his family and friends. He would grow restless, however, after a couple of days out of the office.

Pao sought to consistently utilize his time as efficiently as possible. He continued to teach himself how to speak English, something he had begun in Shanghai. His time after dinner was utilized by listening to tapes. Pao believed that learning English would help him professionally. Along with language, he taught himself about western manners, food and culture. To all around him, Pao exhibited a zest for life and learning.

Pao was aware of the limits of the expatriate trading business in Hong Kong and foresaw the eventual opening up of China, which would then directly purchase goods from other countries. He had a growing desire to apply his strong analytical skills in another area without any clear limits. From his trading business, he had become more acquainted with shipping and the business of moving products from one place to another.

Starting in 1954, he began collecting information and studying the shipping sector in detail and concluded that it had a number of attractive attributes. Ships were moveable assets, allowing you to redeploy them if geo-political factors like the ones that had recently buffeted Asia occurred.

Pao recognized that there was a need throughout the world for transporting goods and he envisioned sharp growth in trade between countries. Pao also liked the global nature of the shipping business and knew that widespread travel would be satisfying to his innate curiosity. Within a year of starting his detailed analysis of the sector, Pao was ready to turn his business focus exclusively to shipping.

In 1955, Pao set up World Wide Shipping Company in Hong Kong to operate vessels and purchased his first ship, a 25-year old 8.201 DWT coal carrier. He bought the ship, which was built in Glascow, Scotland, for approximately $200,000 and renamed it the *Golden Alpha*. Taking the risk averse approach that he had developed as a banker, Pao immediately chartered the ship for a year to a Japanese company he had developed a relationship with from his export-import business. The usual practice among ship owners at the time was to charter their vessels for a single voyage. Industry veterans viewed Pao's relatively long charter as a conservative approach by a novice ship owner.

His initial charter, however, was profitable and resulted in some immediate return on his initial investment. The name he chose for his first vessel turned out to be prophetic as around the time the initial charter ended, Egyptian President Nasser closed the Suez Canal. This forced ships moving between Europe and Asia, the largest trade route in the world, to take the much longer route around the Cape of Good Hope.

Rates moved up geometrically and Pao re-chartered the *Golden Alpha* at four times the rate he obtained with his initial charter. With the profits he made, he bought his second ship and a short time later he bought his third ship. With both of these additional ships, he entered into four and five-year charters with Japanese companies he had relationships with.

Pao's initial experiences with his first three ships would begin a pattern in his approach to shipping that would repeat itself throughout his career. First, he adopted a low-risk strategy that was likely grounded in his experience as a banker. He saw the ups and downs of international shipping and wanted to have the steady income that came with longer-term charters. Pao also recognized that even though the daily rates for voyage charters were often higher, putting his banker hat on he intuitively knew that such short term charters weren't the best approach if you wanted to get bankers to fund expansion projects. It was better to have a lower rate and a much longer term if you wanted to be attractive to bankers.

While this seems fairly obvious now, in the early days of the cargo shipping revolution when banks weren't actively involved in the sector, there was not much focus on this approach. Pao would benefit immensely by following this approach. Importantly, Pao aligned himself with many Japanese companies that were just beginning to grow at what would be globe-leading rates for decades.

In her book on her father, Anna Pao Sohmen highlighted what he told her about the factors that resulted in his admiration for the Japanese. Pao believed there was much to learn from the Japanese, both individually and as a country. In particular, he admired their strong sense of loyalty, great discipline and strong desire to improve. Pao viewed the Japanese as selfless with a strong devotion to company and country. While he acknowledged that Japan was only starting to rebuild, he strongly believed that it was only a matter of time before Japan became a very strong economic force in the world.

In many respects, early in his shipping career Pao hitched his shipping business to Japan and that turned out to be a prescient decision. Pao's foresight into long term trends would work to his benefit throughout his life. The qualities of loyalty and unity that he admired about the Japanese also reflected factors he believed could make his beloved China a much stronger country.

Pao's fleet continued to grow as he purchased existing vessels that he was able to buy and partially finance from the profits and stability of his long term charter model. By the early 1960's, he had some twenty ships that were owned by World-Wide Shipping Company, primarily operating in bulk and breakbulk sectors. These older ships, however, brought with them various technical challenges. By this time, he had developed a strong reputation with bankers and he started to focus more on building new vessels that wouldn't have the same technical challenges and that he believed he could obtain more favorable financing terms on.

After reviews of and discussions with many shipyards, Pao entered into a contract in the early 1960's to build his first new vessel. In late 1962, Pao took delivery of the 16,372 DWT bulk log carrier at the Hakodate shipyard in Hokkaido, Japan. He named this vessel *Eastern Sakura*, with sakura being the Japanese word for cherry blossom. He had the vessel christened by his daughter Anna in a memorable ceremony.

With much of his family in attendance along with bankers who financed the ship and the charterer who had already entered into a long term charter for the ship, the young girl smashed the champagne bottle against the bow of the ship and it broke into many pieces. At the same time, the huge silk ball that hung from the bow of the ship opened and a dozen doves flew from it as it also released colorful paper steamers and helium balloons.

It was a very proud moment for Pao and marked his transition from a buyer of used vessels to a buyer of new vessels. With the lower risk model that had worked well for him, he would repeat it over and over again but this time with a focus on building new vessels.

Pao's relationship with Japanese shipyards and the development of a pivotal financial relationship would pave the way for the meteoric growth World-Wide Shipping was about to experience. He began building new ships just as the Japanese shipbuilding industry was starting to make its mark in the world.

In no small part, the ascendancy of the Japanese shipbuilding industry is tied to the previous efforts of two other individual giants, Henry J. Kaiser and D.K. Ludwig, discussed elsewhere. Kaiser laid the groundwork for modern shipbuilding and Ludwig's Japanese shipyard introduced those processes to Japan.

The Japanese shipbuilding industry embraced the best technology as it developed and focused primarily on export orders, which resulted in preferential treatment for foreigners. Labor was disciplined and loyal and the prevailing wages were less than Europe which was the largest commercial shipbuilder at the time. All these factors came together to result in extraordinary growth in the Japanese shipbuilding industry throughout the 1960's and 1970's.

Pao would build his new vessels exclusively in Japan as he believed the quality was better, the prices were one-third less and the delivery was faster. Pao's embrace of Japanesse shipbuilders at that time would prove to be brilliant. He also valued the after sale service and the down payment and progress payment terms. Those related to what percent of the contract is paid at signing and various other milestones and were more attractive with Japanesse shipbuilders. These terms and the contract priced in U.S. dollars would also make it easier to finance these new vessels.

In 1962, Pao had a meeting with a banker that would result in a long-term mutually beneficial business relationship. While he had success with a number of smaller banks, Pao reasoned that a larger bank with a broader presence in Asia and throughout the world would enhance his flexibility. There was no bank in Hong Kong larger than Hongkong and Shanghai Banking Corporation and Pao decided to approach them. Seeking a meeting with John Saunders, the British chief accountant for the bank, he waited outside his office every morning for a week. Finally, he agreed to a meeting.

Pao explained how the Japanese shipyards had better quality and pricing and that he entered into long term contracts to charter his ships to Japanese companies. He said that these ships were needed to supply the large amounts of imported raw materials Japan required for its growing economy.

When Mr. Saunders asked why those companies didn't just build their own ships rather than chartering them, Pao explained that Japan needs foreign currency and the shipyards are an export industry pricing its product in U.S. dollars. The domestic fleet doesn't bring in foreign currency so the government works to give foreign shipowners better terms. Pao had gone a long way towards relieving the credit concerns of Mr. Saunders. His bank had never done business with shipping companies because they viewed the industry as simply too high risk.

However, a bit of a political problem remained and that was the centrality of Japan in Pao's business dealings. Tensions from the war remained and Mr. Saunders thought that would have others in the bank seeing the business as too risky. Seeking an explanation of what terms the bank would need to do business with him, Pao was told any loan would have to be guaranteed in a manner that effectively eliminated most of the credit risk. Pao asked if a letter of credit from a Japanese bank would be a sufficient guarantee. Saunders readily agreed, but thought it was not likely attainable.

Pao left the meeting and quickly proceeded to Japan where he met with bankers that were impressed with his track record and business plan. Obviously the centrality of his dealings with Japan was a plus and not a minus, and after many meetings where he diligently laid out his plans, he obtained his letter of credit. With that guaranty, he was able to borrow the money he needed from Hongkong and Shanghai Banking Corporation to implement his new ship building plans.

This relationship with Asia's largest bank would endure for the rest of Pao's career and play a key role in his business success. That relationship would also accrue to the benefit of the bank, as it became a leader related to ship financing. Indeed, in large part because of its relationship with Pao and the shipping industry, Hongkong and Shanghai Banking Corporation became the first truly global bank.

With a solid business plan built around long term charters typically before a ship was launched and a reliable source of financing for new vessels, the growth in World-Wide Shipping's fleet kicked into high gear. By 1970, the owned fleet had grown to some 50 vessels totaling 3 million deadweight tons. Pao initial involvement in shipping had been exclusively with dry-bulk carriers, but as he grew he diversified into tankers and that was to become the segment he increasingly focused on.

Pao leveraged on his relationship with the Japanese shipyards and his ready financing ability to enter into large orders for many vessels at a time. This bulk ordering put him in an even stronger position to negotiate the best discounts with shipyards and he took advantage of this. He entered into many new contracts and was the largest customer of multiple Japanese shipyards.

The relationship between Pao, the Japanese shipbuilders and the Japanese banks was a symbiotic one that benefited all parties, particularly Pao. In 1973 when the Suez Canal was closed and the demand for large tankers skyrocketed, Pao was able to place new orders at several Japanese shipyards and was given the first available building slot rather than going to the end of a long queue like other ship owners.

By the mid-1970's, World-Wide Shipping's fleet had more than quadrupled to 13 million deadweight tons. It stood out as the largest ship owner in the world by a very large margin with more than twice the tonnage of any other shipping company. Below is a ranking from what was then the leading shipbroker in London of the ten largest ship owners in the world based on total deadweight tonnage. Pao was well ahead in terms of fleet size at the time of four other individual giants profiled elsewhere.

World-Wide Shipping	13,474,737
Sanko-Kisen	5,940,302
A.P. Moller	5,238,800
Japan Line	5,065,656
D.K. Ludwig	4,868,546
Nippon Yusen Kasen	4,658,379
C.Y. Tung	4,522,276
Aristotle Onassis	4,483,463
Salen	4,191,830
Bergesen	4,091,830

At its peak in 1979, World-Wide Shipping owned 220 ships totaling 20.5 million deadweight tons. That likely represented something more than 4% of the total vessel tonnage in the world at the time, making Pao by far the largest shipowner. World-Wide Shipping also operated hundreds of other ships through charters. No individual or company had ever controlled a medium to high single digit percentage of the world's merchant marine fleet and it's doubtful that this feat will be repeated.

Not surprisingly, that same year Pao was named "Lord of the Sea" with his picture on the cover of Newsweek magazine. In its cover article, Newsweek said that Pao didn't resemble a real shipping tycoon, as the public had associated more colorful ship owners like Onassis with yachts, private jets and glamorous parties.

Pao was content with his methodical, banker-like approach to his shipping business and if others thought it colorless, it certainly didn't bother him. He told his daughter more than once that holding big parties to promote yourself is superficial and it is more useful to take concrete action.

Pao accurately anticipated the prolonged nature of the depression in the tanker market beginning in the early 1980's. The reduction in the demand for oil had a pronounced effect on the demand for his large tankers deployed in long Middle East voyages. Recognizing that this oversupply would last longer than typical shipping cycles, Pao reduced his fleet from 220 ships to 70 ships by 1983. He was able to raise cash to diversify into other areas, most notably real estate through the purchases of Hongkong and Kowloon Wharf as well as Wheelock Marden. These moves were all timely, as the downturn in the tanker market would last for more than ten years and his investments in real estate increased exponentially in value over that same period.

As his business grew, so did Pao's reputation for solid judgment that was increasingly sought after by business and political leaders. Now a board member at Hongkong and Shangai Banking Corporation, he was among the business elite of Hong Kong. His international travels and his enjoyment of golf resulted in introductions to various political leaders. Pao became a confidant of British Prime Minister Edward Heath who sought his advice on matters relating to both shipping and banking. As a result of his services to Britain, both directly and presumably indirectly though Hong Kong, Queen Elizabeth II knighted Pao in 1978.

In the mid-1980's, Pao turned over control of his shipping and real estate businesses to family members. He immersed himself totally in efforts to benefit his beloved China. By this time, he had close relationships with the leaders of China and many of the leaders in other countries. He counted Deng Xiaopong, Margaret Thatcher, Ronald Reagan and Henry Kissinger as friends.

There was something about this extraordinarily successful but humble and plain speaking man that drew him into the confidence of world leaders as a treasured adviser. In particular, he played a significant role during Hong Kong's return to China, acting as a communication link by utilizing his special relationship with both sides. Pao was known for his unmatched access to a broad array of leaders in both the commercial and political arenas. He was equally at ease with Western political leaders and the Chinese leadership.

Pao became instrumental in the development of his hometown Ningbo into a busy, world-class port and was involved in a series of activities that promoted growth at his beloved birthplace. Among other initiatives, this included a $20 million donation that was the catalyst for the founding of Ningbo University where today 20,000 college students study. Today, Ningbo is the fourth largest port in the world in terms of total container volume.

Pao was referred to by Chinese leaders as someone who made many selfless contributions to China's modernization, especially in the education sector. More than once he was referred to as "the Unofficial Ambassador" between China and the United Kingdom. Pao was broadly acknowledged as the most important person outside of China that Deng Xiaopong listened to and bonded with. From Deng's perspective, what made Pao such a valued adviser was his extraordinary success in dealing with practical issues, his contacts with world leaders and knowledge of world affairs, his grasp of long term trends and his readiness to speak the truth as he saw it.

Pao died in 1991 at the age of 72. His descendants continue to operate what are now large and separate shipping and real estate businesses, both of which are valued in the billions. The shipping businesses operate under the banner of privately owned BW Group and are primarily focused on crude oil tankers, LNG tankers, LPG tankers and floating storage and production platforms, or FSPO's. Today Andreas Sohmen-Pao, a Harvard MBA and the grandson of Sir Y.K. Pao, runs that business.

I've had the pleasure of meeting Andreas Sohmen-Pao when the hedge fund I worked at elected to invest in the initial public offering of its LPG unit. Andreas is among the brightist and most articulate leaders in the shipping industry today. In reviewing and analyzing his company, I saw that the attributes and policies that made his grandfather so successful were still in place. Strong analytical focus, professional management and a focus on the long term are just as much a framework for success today as it was fifty years ago. Sir Y.K. Pao would I'm certain be very proud of what his grandson has done with his legacy.

12. C.Y. Tung

The Innovator across Segments & Builder of World's Largest Ship.

This Hong Kong shipowner was at the forefront of the post-war expansion of the shipping industry with significant involvement in the container, tanker and cruise sectors. A tanker built and owned by one of Tung's companies remains the biggest ship ever built.

C.Y. Tung was born on August 18, 1912 in Shanghai. He was the third of five children, three boys and two girls, of parents from Ningbo, a Chinese port city near Shanghai. His given name was Chao-Yung, which meant, "heralding fame and prosperity". Eventually he would come to be known solely by his initials C.Y.

Tung's father was a modest businessman who first ran a print shop and then a hardware store. His father was a disciplinarian and C.Y. was said to inherit the quick temper that was often displayed by his father. As a boy, Tung was an excellent student and a voracious reader, although his formal school was often disrupted by poor health. Much of what he learned was self-taught. He became well versed in classical Chinese literature and also taught himself English. Tung was particularly facile with numbers and early on he displayed a memory that constantly amazed those around him.

His first job at age 17 was as a trainee in the Shanghai office of Kokusai Transport, a Japanese shipping company. One year later, he left to join Tientsin Navigation, a Chinese shipping company. Tung's commitment to and preoccupation with shipping was evident in the entries in the diary he kept and would continue to keep for the rest of his life.

He progressed rapidly at Tientsin Navigation where he was known as a hard worker. In particular, he developed a reputation of someone who always seemed to come up with new ideas to improve the performance of the company. While Tung was reserved and even shy as a young man, his boundless energy and strong work ethic overpowered any obstacles that the former traits may have erected.

Tung's marriage in 1933 to 18 year old Koo Lee-ching was arranged in the traditional Chinese way and they had never met before their actual engagement. The bride's father was a former customs broker who was also involved in the shipping industry. He was very pleased with the match as he viewed Tung as an ambitious man with a bright future. The bride was from Shanghai, but she moved to Tientsin after the marriage. In time, they would have two sons and three daughters.

Shortly after his marriage, Tung took a three-month sabbatical at a Buddhist temple in Hangchow, China to learn more about mediation from the masters. This would prove to be a life-changing sabbatical for Tung. His health improved during this interlude, but the experience affected him even more profoundly in other ways.

Tumg came away from his sabbatical with an even more enhanced ability to focus his efforts in a determined way and to exercise extraordinary personal discipline. Mediation became a constant habit that supported him throughout his career. In addition to increasing his focus, it also served to keep at bay the stresses that would accompany his life as an entrepreneur.

In 1934, Tung noted in his diary the backward condition of China's transport system and his determination to play a role in improving that situation. He wrote about it like it was a mission that he was destined to carry out. His private thoughts would have not surprised his colleagues at Tientsin Navigation at all. Many of them had often heard him speaking out against the privileges conferred by extraterritorial rights that were enjoyed by the foreign shipping community.

Tung's diplomatic skill, however, was evident early on when he was instrumental in arranging an agreement to settle differences between foreign shipping companies and Chinese tugboat and lighter operators. He also successfully negotiated the move of the Tientsin Navigation Company's office, a move fraught with difficulties in those days.

His accomplishments also weren't going unrecognized in the broader shipping community. In 1935 at the young age of 23, he was appointed Vice President of the Tientsin Shipowners Association. The next year Tung played a leading part in a government rescue mission related to icebound ships in northern China. Tientsin Navigation ships were used alongside small airplanes dispatched by the government to airlift needed supplies to the trapped vessels.

With Tung's transfer in 1937 to Tung Cheng Shipping, an affiliate of Teintsin Navigation, the family moved from Teintsin to Shanghai. Based upon the reputation he had built in the sector and his successful interaction with the government during the rescue mission, Tung was commissioned by the Chinese Ministry of Transportation to submit a master plan for rehabilitating the Chinese shipping industry. The industry had suffered badly from the worldwide depression in the early 1930's. This request was well received by him and likely seemed fateful, as it was just a few years earlier that he was recording in his diary the shortfalls of the industry and his views on how to improve conditions.

Tung worked long and hard on his plan. In the submission he made to the Ministry of Transportation, he urged a national policy built around a system of subsidies to shipping companies. It was aimed at both strenghtening Chinese coastal shipping and establishing a presence in international shipping. At the time, most of the Chinese owned and manned vessels were involved primarily in coastal and river voyages along with voyages to nearby countries. There was no presence by Chinese ships in long distance intercontinental voyages. Tung's plan became a framework for a number of initiatives by the government to strengthen Chinese shipping.

Tung's entrepreneurial spirit had him constantly on the lookout for the right time and opportunity to establish his own company. His experience in both Tientsin and Shanghai had given him solid insight into the shipping industry and was a source of ideas that were noted in his diary. Frequent business and personal travel throughout China augmented his experience and provided more ideas.

In 1941 at the age of 29, Tung established his first company, Chinese Maritime Trust (1941) Ltd in Hong Kong. This company was focused on ships' agency business for British and Panamanian flag vessels calling on Chinese ports as well as servicing the China coastal trade. With this business, he knew he would benefit from all the various privileges enjoyed by foreign shipping firms that he had learned about earlier in his shipping career. With the capture of Hong Kong by the Japanese, the office was moved to Chongking, China's inland wartime capital.

Towards the end of World War II, Tung was at the forefront of talks related to rehabilitating the Chinese shipping industry. Those discussions included after the end of the war the disposition of Liberty ships that the U.S. government had agreed to sell the Chinese government. He was part of a small delegation that traveled to the U.S. to finalize the terms of how these vessels would be acquired.

More so than others in China, Tung saw a very bright future for shipping in the postwar period. He envisioned that the demand for raw materials for resurgent industrial plants and more goods for consumers would drive strong growth in trade that would be good for shipping. In addition to that, he was confident that Chinese shipping companies, which at the time represented a very small part of the world's merchant marine, were capable of obtaining a larger share.

Part of Tung's confidence in the future of Chinese shipping came from his knowledge of and pride in the precedent set in China's distant marine past. Ancient records have been interpreted to show that Chinese ships may have sailed as far as the Pacific Coast of North America more than one thousand years before Columbus reached America.

Tung was particularly inspired by the seven documented expeditionary voyages of Admiral Cheng Ho from 1405 onwards. With up to 300 ships manned by some 27,500 men, those voyages from Nanking and Shanghai traversed most of Asia. On one of those voyages, Admiral Cheng Ho sailed southwest to the Strait of Malacca and then on to the Indian Ocean, Persian Gulf and Red Sea.

No doubt inspired by his knowledge of China's proud maritime heritage, Tung's determination to be at the forefront in developing a strong Chinese shipping industry was stronger than ever as World War II ended and attention returned to the challenges of rebuilding.

Tung's confidence in what he could accomplish in shipping was driven by his direct experience and the consistent process he had developed by then to systematically analyze all the factors before committing capital to a project. His combination of hard work, determination and perseverance also acted to inspire his colleagues and get the most out of them in accomplishing his goals.

With confidence in his capabilities and his vision of the future of Chinese shipping, after the end of the war in 1945, Tung established China Maritime Trust Ltd in Shanghai. It had the same name as his Hong Kong agency business except that the year 1941 had been deleted. The purpose of the new company was no less than to revive Chinese maritime greatness with ships owned, manned and operated on international routes entirely by Chinese.

Tung initially bought existing general cargo vessels and deployed them in international trade. His first vessel was the 10,471 deadweight ton *Tien Loong*, which sailed from Shanghai on September 8, 1947 and arrived in Le Havre, France on October 29, 1947 for an average speed at sea of 10 knots per hour. That was the first Chinese cargo ship to ever reach the Atlantic and arrive in Europe. The *Tien Loong* then crossed the Atlantic and arrived in Norfolk, Virginia to become the first Chinese cargo ship to reach the East Coast of the U.S. Tung's company had signed a contract to move 100,000 tons of coal and charcoal from Europe to the U.S. so that would take up to ten voyages for the *Tien Loong*.

Several months after the initial voyage of his first ship, Tung's second vessel, the slightly larger *Tung Ping*, sailed from Shanghai and arrived in San Francisco in July 1948. That was the first Chinese cargo ship to cross the Pacific and the first to reach the West Coast of the U.S. It then went to call on several ports in South America where it discharged cargo loaded in Asia. The *Tung Ping* then sailed for New Orleans, becoming the first Chinese vessel to call on that U.S. Gulf Coast port, where it loaded cargo bound for China.

Tung's pioneering initial voyages were well covered in the Chinese and maritime press and given warm welcomes at the various overseas ports. He quickly added another seven existing general cargo ships, most of which were Liberty vessels, to his owned vessel fleet. His agency business where he managed ships for other Chinese owners almost doubled the number of vessels he controlled. While collectively this represented only 15/100ths of one percent of world tonnage of 70 million deadweight tons, this substantial expansion of Chinese shipping now had it involved in major international routes.

In 1949, with the communist takeover of China, Tung relocated his headquarters to Hong Kong and made that port and Kaoshiung, Taiwan his base of operations. Tung was the first international ship owner to be based in Hong Kong. That relocation was a catalyst for what would eventually turn the strategically located Hong Kong into the largest ship-owning center and busiest port in the world, in no small part due to ships owned by Tung companies.

The development of shipping played a direct role in the growth and prosperity of Hong Kong. More so than any industry, it was shipping that would drive the transformation for a place that was once denounced as a "barren rock" when the British first occupied the island of Hong Kong in 1841.

The size and scope of Tung's shipping operations continued to grow as additional ships were added. Regular services involving general cargo ships were added and a company named Orient Overseas Line was formed to operate these services. The logo that was put on the funnels of all of its steamships, an artistic rendering of the red Chinese plum blossom on a yellow background, was increasingly seen in ports around the world.

By the mid-1950's, with growth continuing and the supply of existing ships including surplus Liberty vessels shrinking, Tung turned to shipyards to get additional tonnage. He entered into contracts related to both conversion projects and new vessel construction projects. Unlike the other individual giants discussed elsewhere who focused on one segment, Tung's diverse shipping interests were to include significant involvement in all the major segments.

Tung's first major shipyard project was in 1955 when he purchased a T-2 tanker. Hundreds of T-2's were built in America during the war as the tanker equivalent of the Liberty ships. He then had this ship converted to a bulk carrier to move iron ore from Venezuela under a long-term contract he had entered into with the U.S. Steel Corporation. This vessel, renamed *Atlantic Pride*, was followed in 1956 by another T-2 tanker converted in Japan and renamed *Atlantic Triumph* which was also used to move iron ore from Venezuela for U.S. Steel. These projects would mark the beginning of long-term relationships he would have with U.S. Steel, various Japanese shipyards and the Louis Dreyfus organization, which acted as an intermediary.

That relationship with the Paris based Louis Dreyfus organization had much to do with the 1956 delivery in France of the *Oriental Star*, a 13,900 deadweight ton general cargo ship and the first new ship built by Tung.

In 1958, Tung built his first ship in Japan, the 22,100 deadweight ton *Atlantic Faith*, a combination ore/oil carrier. This was the first vessel of its type to be built in Japan. The concept behind such combination vessels, often referred to as OBO's for Ore/Bulk/Oil, was to increase flexibility and utilization. Traditionally, a dedicated ore carrier or crude tanker would be loaded only half the time and would be empty on its return leg. OBO's had the possibility of increasing their loaded utilization percentage by matching an iron ore voyage leg with a crude oil voyage leg. In addition, such vessels offered the flexibility of switching between segments for an extended period when the supply and demand dynamics were more attractive. As we shall discuss in another section, the merits of the OBO concept were overtaken by various factors as the progression towards specialized ships continued.

Next came the 70,000 deadweight ton *Oriental Giant*, a pure tanker that Tung took delivery of in 1959. This was the largest ship ever built in Asia at the time. This milestone and the accompanying coverage, including its being featured in the 1960 Britannica Book of the Year, was a point of pride for Tung. For the ceremony related to the christening of this new ship, Tung arranged for special music to be composed.

Tung continued a tradition of colorful and elaborate ceremonies at the launching of his new vessels with celebrities such as Princess Grace of Monaco breaking the champagne bottle on the new hull in front of elite business and government guests. Tung would then personally conduct a tour of the new ship for his guests, who would often see that he knew most of the crew by name. His pride in the new ships he was building was evident in the numerous pictures he himself took and that he would later send to his guests. Tung's meticulously planned christening ceremonies were well remembered by all attendees.

The 1960's would see Tung build a total of 19 new ships in shipyards in Japan. By this time, Japan had surpassed Great Britain as the largest shipbuilder in the world, in no small part due to the innovations introduced by D.K. Ludwig's Kure shipyard. Tung was a major customer of shipyards operated by both Mitsubishi Heavy Industries and Sasebo Heavy Industries. In 1965, Tung took delivery of the 120,000 deadweight ton tanker *Oriental Dragon*, his first ship to cross the 100,000-ton barrier. Starting in 1968 with the 250,000 deadweight ton *Energy Transport*, he took delivery of a series of ten such supertankers, or VLCC's for Very Large Crude Carriers as they were then being called. Tung wasn't the first to build such large tankers, but he wasn't too far behind Ludwig and the Greeks.

Tung's fleet remained diverse across almost all of the shipping segments. These interests along with growing investments in the real estate sector were held by the parent company called Orient Overseas (International) Limited. He was the first Asian shipowner to recognize the benefits of containerization and those services were now being operated by Orient Overseas Container Line. Tung first converted general cargo ship to accommodate containers and began building new container vessels. By 1969, his Far East to U.S. West Coast regular liner service was fully containerized.

During the 1970's, Tung would build a total of 65 new ships in Japan, Germany and Portugal. The peak building activity was in 1975 when he launched a dozen new ships. Key among the vessels was the 386,620 deadweight ton *Brazilian Hope* built in Germany and its three sister vessels built in Portugal. These tankers, so large that they were called ULCC's for Ultra Large Crude Carriers, were built to operate under long-term charters with Petrobras, Brazil's national oil company. Tung also continued to build smaller tankers and product carriers, dry-bulk carriers, container ships, vehicle carriers and even passenger cruise ships. His Island Navigation was one of the largest bulk shipping companies in Asia. Tung's American Hawaii Cruises operated U.S. flag cruise ships. He remained intrigued with the potential for improved economics with combination ore/bulk/oil carriers, and built the 150,000 deadweight ton *Energy Transmission*, one of the largest OBO's ever built.

Tung was one the largest shipowners in the world towards the end of the 1970's. He was a major player in most of the segments and the leader within the growing Chinese shipping community. While he had come close several times, he had never been the owner of the world's largest ship. Tung remained interested in reaching that goal. An opportunity to achieve that presented itself when a Greek shipowner building a ULCC in Japan ran into financial problems. Tung bought the 418,611 deadweight ton tanker and contracted to enlarge the vessel by cutting it in two and inserting a 268' midbody which increased its capacity by 146,152 tons.

In 1980, Tung launched the 564,763 deadweight ton tanker *Seawise Giant*, the largest and longest ship ever built. With a length of 1,504', a width of 226' and a draft when fully loaded of 81', everything about the *Seawise Giant* was a superlative. This more than five-football-fields long vessel remains to this day the largest ship ever built. When fully loaded it would carry 4.1 million barrels or 174 million gallons of crude oil. The derivation of the "Giant" portion of the name was clear and obvious. Less obvious, but indicative of the owner's pride in this ship, is the derivation of "Seawise" which came from a phonetic spelling of the initials in his own name.

Tung's personal philosophy involved a consistent drive for knowledge and facts and this flowed over to his interest in educating others. He was an active supporter of education throughout his life and established the Seawise Foundation to support various endeavors in that area.

His interest in both education and shipping intersected in a dramatic and tangible way when he bought the *Queen Elizabeth II*, the famous passenger liner, with a plan to convert her into a floating university. This plan, however, was pre-empted shortly thereafter when a relentless fire in Hong Kong destroyed the passenger liner. Undeterred, Tung converted another one of his cruise ships, the liner *Atlantic*, into the cruising university he envisioned and renamed her *Universe Campus*.

In cooperation with several U.S. colleges, 500 undergraduates in their second or third year were selected to spend a semester at sea as the *Universe Campus* cruised around the world. Each year, there were two such cruises. Successor vessels provided by the Seawise Foundation continue to operate semester at sea programs and a total of more than 55,000 students from 1,500 colleges worldwide have benefited from Tung's educational legacy.

More so than any of the other individuals profiled herein, Tung's experience as an owner and operator of ships bridged the period from small conventional general cargo ships to the giant specialized cargo ships of the modern era. He saw much of this change firsthand. Many of the initiatives that Tung was involved in were disruptive to his own general cargo ships, which made his decisions to proceed more courageous. This, however, was consistent with his discipline and perseverance after he had analyzed all the factors.

Tung systematically looked at and analyzed any shipping project and his decision was always determined by wherever the facts led him. His dispassionate focus was presumably helped by his practice of daily meditation for at least two hours. Tung also neither smoked nor drank any alcohol. Tung's simple and even austere lifestyle extended to not drinking either tea or coffee, with water the only beverage he consumed. His singular focus was shipping and he was driven by a passion to extend the reach of the Chinese merchant marine, a goal that he readily achieved.

C.Y. Tung died suddenly of a heart attack on April 15, 1982 at the age of 70. This occurred as he was waiting to greet Prince Rainier and Princess Grace of Monaco on their arrival in Hong Kong. Tung was Monaco's honorary counsel.

At the time of his death, through various companies Tung owned a diversified fleet of 150 vessels. His funeral service in Hong Kong was similar to that of a head of state with thousands of people attending Buddhist ceremonies that extended over three days. Tung's pallbearers included a dozen of Hong Kong's most prominent business and government leaders. Similar memorial services were held in Taiwan and New York. Following the services, Tung's ashes were simultaneously scattered in the Pacific, Indian and Atlantic Oceans by the captains of three of his vessels.

His family continued to manage Tung's diverse shipping interests. His oldest son, C.H., went on to become in 1997 the first chief executive of Hong Kong when it ceased to be controlled by the British. Today, Orient Overseas Container Line, a publicly held container operator that the Tung family still has a substantial financial interest in, is the best performing container shipping company in the world. While it is not the largest liner company, its operating income as a percent of revenue is consistently five percentage points higher than most other companies. It just recently built a series of container ships with a capacity of 21,100 TEU's each. When delivered they were the largest container vessels in the world and the cost economics that come with them should support continued superior performance at the company. One of those extraordinary vessels, the OOCL Hong Kong, is on the cover of this book.

The superior financial performance of Orient Overseas Container Line is in my view a direct result of the disciplined culture and analytical approach to shipping that was instilled by C.Y. Tung. A family member has continually managed it and the current CEO, Andy Tung, is the grandson of C.Y. Tung. In late 2018, COSCO, the large shipping group in China and the third largest container operator in the world, acquired a majority stake in Orient Overseas Container Line. Only time will tell if it is able to maintain this exceptional performance in the future.

As it turns out, my daughter would be a catalyst in my learning more about this remarkable man and his family. Years ago, we hosted a birthday dinner party for my daughter where she invited her closest friends from the boarding school she was attending. As one of the girls was talking about her family in Hong Kong, I connected the dots and realized that she was the great-granddaughter of C.Y. Tung. She was and remains one of my daughter's closest friends from boarding school and participated years later in my daughter's debutante ball in New York. Through our daughters' friendship, I've met and gotten to know Andy Tung. Malcom McLean always had the highest respect for C.Y. Tung and the company he and his family built and it was a pleasant coincidence that I would develop my own connection with this remarkable family.

13. Maersk McKinney Moller

The Creator of the World's Largest Shipping Company.

This secretive Dane took the reins of his family's small shipping company and over many decades turned it into the largest shipping enterprise the world has ever seen. It includes the largest container shipping company and the largest container terminal company.

Maersk McKinney Moller was born on July 13, 1913 in Copenhagen, Denmark. He was the son of Arnold Peter Moller and Christine McKinney. His father was Danish and himself the son of a Danish sea captain. His mother was an American born in Kentucky who resettled in Denmark after marrying his father. Because of his mother's heritage, Moller would always think of himself as half-American.

Moller's grandfather Peter Maersk Moller had always told his son that he would assist him in becoming a shipowner some day. In 1904, this long held goal was achieved when he helped his son form a shipping company whose assets consisted of one secondhand steamship. The company was called A.P. Moller. Peter Moller was 28 at the time. By 1912, he was operating three general cargo ships. The company continued to grow and by the late 1920's had diversified into tankers that handled much of Denmark's oil needs.

Following his father into the family business, Maersk Moller became a full partner in 1940 at the age of 27. Around the same time, he married Emma Rasmussen, his high school sweetheart. In April 1940 with World War II looming and Moller's father concerned the Nazis would occupy Denmark, he dispatched his son to New York. His ships were told not to follow any instructions received from Denmark.

Maersk Moller would operate the fleet, which had grown to 46 tankers and general cargo ships, from New York throughout the war. Two of his three daughters were born in New York in 1941 and 1944.

More than half of Maersk's fleet was sunk during World War II. At the end of the war, it was operating just seven ships for its own account. It was managing another 14 ships owned by the U.S. government until 1946. To rebuild his fleet, Moller took several steps simultaneously. First, Maersk bought several Liberty ships that were being offered to allies by the U.S. government. In 1947, Moller had the company begin a large shipbuilding program with new vessels ordered at yards in Denmark, Sweden, Germany, Italy, Belgium and the Netherlands.

Moller surmised that between the good prices he was getting as one of the first customers at rebuilt European shipyards and his view that shipping markets would remain strong, this newbuilding program made good business sense. In addition, he was mindful that his orders would play a constructive role in rebuilding the economies of Europe. This was an early sign of the benevolence Moller's stewardship would consistently show in his dealing with Denmark and other allied countries.

Moller returned to Denmark in 1947 with his young family. In 1948, his third daughter was born in Denmark. By this time, Moller's father was 72 years old and he was 35 years old. While his father would formally retain the title of CEO and Chairman until his death in 1965 when he was 89, Moller was making all the key decisions. Given his success in running the business during the war from New York, he obviously had the full confidence of his father.

In 1953, Moller spearheaded another newbuilding program, this time involving 13 of a new class of faster cargo ships. The *Chastine Maersk*, the first vessel in the class, was diesel powered rather than steam powered based largely on Moller's detailed analysis of relative costs. These ships were among the first in the world to transition from steam power. From that point on, all new vessels built by Maersk would be diesel powered.

The 1950's and 1960's were periods of consistent growth for Maersk. The post war boom in trade that Moller had foreseen resulted in a sharp increase in demand for vessel capacity. The company established and operated a large modern shipyard in Odense, Denmark that would play a key role in its growth going forward. While the parent company retained the A.P. Moller name, by this time most of the shipping units were operating under the Maersk brand name. Tankers and general cargo ships dominated the company's fleet. Moller was, however, paying particular attention to what was occurring first in America with the advent of container shipping. Maersk began to adapt some of its general cargo ships to handle containers on deck and was among the first European shipping companies to do this.

The company logo was a seven pointed white star on a light blue background that dated back to a banner Moller's grandfather flew when his wife recovered from a serious illness. A deeply religious Christian, he told his wife he had prayed for her one night and asked for a sign, in the form of a star in the gray and cloudy sky, that his prayers were being heard. Later that night, a single star appeared and his depiction of that star became the logo.

Another catalyst for growth was the discovery of offshore oil in the North Sea in the early 1960's. With that discovery, Moller's company was given the Danish concession to produce that oil. This resulted in an expansion into the offshore drilling business, not only in the North Sea but also around the world. as these large offshore drilling units were mobile. The discovery of North Sea oil also resulted in Maersk increasing its tanker fleet to move crude oil and expanding into specialized tankers such as those carrying LNG. The Odense shipyard was building VLCC tankers for the Maersk tanker unit as well as bulk carriers and roll-on, roll-off vessels.

As its general cargo operations expanded, Moller got his shipyard to focus on building fast vessels. For instance, in 1967 he began taking delivery of seven 26-knot ships that were deployed in a weekly Europe to Far East service. Moller was also experimenting with different ways to stow as well as load and unload general cargo ships and this resulted in adapting vessels to better accommodate pallets.

Pallet ships in particular were something that intrigued Moller as they offered a way to reduce cargo-handling costs. Pallet ships had side or stern ramps that allowed a forklift to drive into a ship carrying pallets that would then be placed on decks configured to maximize pallet storage. For uniform cargoes moving to or from dockside warehouses, this method resulted in reduced cargo handling costs compared to traditional ways of handling general cargo. Maersk converted some of its general cargo ships into full pallet ships.

However, watching what was developing as Malcom McLean's containerization initiative expanded outside of coastal U.S. routes, Moller realized that no other innovation offered the same level of cargo handling efficiency. In addition, unlike pallet ships, with containers the cargo could be moved to and from inland points without rehandling. With his Odense shipyard busy building large tankers, he turned to a Japanesse yard to build his first full containership.

The 1,800 TEU *Svenborg Maersk* was delivered in 1973, making it one of the largest container ships at the time. Moller then began converting his general cargo ships, first into semi-containerships and then into full containerships. He was not unique in doing this as the early 1970's saw many shipping companies converting general cargo ships to accommodate containers in some manner.

By this time, the benefits from containerization were abundantely clear and irrefutable. It was a relatively simple job to convert general cargo ships to accommodate containers on deck and only a little more difficult to carry containers below deck in holds. Because of the large supply of such ships in good hull and machinery condition, much of the early growth in container shipping was handled by converting general cargo vessels.

Maersk was quicker to embrace containerization than most of the other European shipping companies. By 1983, it was the fifth largest container operator with a vessel fleet having a total capacity of 51,250 TEU's. It was also a significant participant in the tanker sector as well as other niches related to offshore oil production.

By this time, Moller's reputation as an astute businessman was well known. In evidence of this, he became the first non-American member of IBM's board of directors. Perhaps Moller had much to do with promoting and expanding the "World Peace Through World Trade" slogan IBM had developed earlier.

Moller continued to expand Maersk's container services, opening up new routes and vertically integrating to build its own containers and operate container terminals for its own operation as well as for others. In the late 1980's, it introduced larger 45' containers and its Odense shipyard built what were then the largest container ships in the world. Moller had a systematic approach focused on building up a cost efficient overall system. In addition to methodically growing his business organically, Moller selectively acquired other container shipping companies such as P&O and Safmarine.

By 1998, Maersk had become the largest container shipping operator in the world but several other carriers were close to it in total fleet capacity. That changed dramatically in 1999 when Maersk acquired the international operations of Sea-Land, the second largest container operator in the world and the company originally founded by Malcom McLean. That acquisition catapulted Maersk to the top of the sector in terms of total fleet capacity with a large gap between it and the other large carriers. Moller had stepped down as CEO in 1993 but he remained actively involved in the business as Chairman.

As Sea-Land's operation was integrated into Maersk, a series of new vessels were ordered that further expanded on Maersk's absolute and relative size. The E-class vessels that were delivered beginning in 2006 were the largest container ships in the world. They would be eclipsed by the one-third larger Triple E-class vessels that it began taking delivery of in 2013. Further growth resulted from the acquisition of Hamburg-Sud, a large container operator primarily focused on routes involving South America. Today, Maersk is by far the largest container operator with a fleet of over 600 vessels representing some 15% of worldwide container ship capacity.

Under Moller's leadership, Maersk also developed an extensive network of container terminals in ports around the world. Initially these terminals serviced just Maersk vessels, but as the business and their expertise grew, they began servicing vessels operated by other companies. In 2001, the terminal business was established as a separate entity within the larger Maersk Group known as APM Terminals. Today, APM Terminals operates 76 terminals in 59 countries. In addition to providing terminal services to Maersk, APM provides such services to more than 60 other shipping lines.

In addition to its broad involvement in the shipping and energy sectors, Maersk also expanded into banking, supermarkets and trucking and logistics. In total, today the company employs some 88,000 people across operations in 130 countries. It is the largest Danish company by a variety of measures and represents approximately 11% of the country's total annual GDP.

Moller, who was known as MMM to his staff, was a very private man. In a rare interview in 1998, he told a writer "I hope you understand our peculiar inclination that we perhaps have the most to gain by being unobserved". His reputation in business circles, however, was well known and continued to grow. In addition to his role in advising IBM as a board member over 14 years, business leaders throughout the world sought his counsel. At home, he was extremely well regarded and was made a knight of the Order of the Elephant, one of the few Danes to be so honored who was not a member of royalty or head of state.

Even after he resigned as Chairman in 2003 at the age of 90, Moller continued to come to the office each day. He packed his lunch at home and each day walked up six flights of stairs to his office. He also continued a ritual that he had started decades ago that became a much-appreciated tradition by employees around the world. On each July 13 when he would become one year older, every one of the tens of thousands of Maersk employees worldwide would receive a personal gift from Moller of a fresh Danish pastry.

Moller died on April 16, 2012 at the age of 98. The stock that he and his family control, which is now worth approximately $23 billion, remains mostly in a foundation that he established long ago dedicated to a host of philanthropic activities in Denmark.

The reputation of Moller and his company for actions that took into account Denmark's national interests was consistent and significant. The two became so intertwined that many Danes came to view the company as a national asset rather than a profit-making corporation. Moller delivered for both his shareholders and his country, and in that sense should be viewed as one of the most successful and benevolent CEO's of our time.

I never had the pleasure of meeting Moller, but from colleagues, who worked with and knew him, I know he was a gentleman with a temperament similar to my mentor Malcom McLean. Both were gentle giants who let their accomplishments speak for them.

There was a coincidence in my life that also drew me to the company he built. Denmark had a large three masted sailing ship known as the *Danmark* that was used to train cadets. When Denmark was invaded and occupied by Germany at the start of World War II, the *Danmark* was in the U.S. following its participation in the 1939 World's Fair. It was confiscated by the U.S. and moved to New London, CT where it was used to train cadets at the Coast Guard Academy. That training would grow to include patrols up and down the coast of New England in search of German submarines. The captain and some of the crew were Danish, but the Coast Guard assigned a young lieutenant to serve as second mate on the *Danmark*. That young lieutenant was my father and he served aboard the *Danmark* for some six months.

In 1976, the first parade of tall ships from around the world occurred in New York harbor when the U.S. was celebrating its bi-centennial. The *Danmark* was second in line after the *Eagle*, the official Coast Guard sailing ship, owing to the *Danmark* once being a U.S. flag ship when my father served on it.

I had just started my first job in New York and my father came up for the bi-centennial. Following the parade, we managed to make our way to where the *Danmark* was docked and my father explained his connection to the young Danish sailor manning the gangplank. He retreated and returned minutes later with the captain. He was well aware of the *Danmark's* history, in no small part because his own father was the captain when my father served as second mate years ago. The captain graciously gave us a tour of the *Danmark*, which was virtually the same as my father remembered from more than three decades earlier.

It was the Coast Guard's successful operation of the *Danmark* as a training vessel for approximately 5,000 cadets from 1940 to 1945 when it was returned to Denmark that motivated it to obtain its own sailing ship to continue training cadets. The *Eagle* was built as a training ship in Germany in 1936 and was taken by the U.S. as war reparations in 1946. The 295' long three masted barque is one of only two active commissioned sailing vessels in the U.S. today, with the other one being the *USS Constitution* which is posted in Boston harbor.

The provenance of the Eagle, officially known as the *USCGC Eagle (WIX-327)*, with USCGC standing for United States Coast Guard Cutter, is somewhat surprising. Originally called the *Horst Wessel*, when it was launched in 1936 the christening speech was given by Rudolph Hess with Adolph Hitler present. The mother of Horst Wessel broke the champagne bottle on the ship. Horst Wessel was a stormtrooper leader who wrote the lyrics of what became the Nazi national anthem and whose death became a major propaganda symbol for the Nazi Party.

I've seen the *Danmark* in several subsequent parades of tall ships and each time feel a special kinship at several levels. Today, the *Danmark* is operated as a training ship for young sailors, not by the Danish government but by Maersk itself. I even promoted the idea of looking into whether to arrange for my son Jack to spend a summer between college years aboard the *Danmark*. He was after all named after my father and I thought it would be an educational experience in many ways for my son. However, when I raised the subject for discussion with my wife, she did not enthusiastically embrace the idea. She noted that our 18-year-old had no business spending time on a sailing ship halfway around the world when he had no interest or experience in what sounded like hard and potentially dangerous work. Her point, of course, had much merit.

By any measure, Maersk is now the largest shipping enterprise in the world. While primarily focused on container shipping after diversifying away from tankers, it is also a large operator of marine terminals and specialized oil service vessels. Its more than 600 container ships move the equivalent of 22 million TEU's of containers annually in a network that connects some 59 countries. Today, there is no single company in the world that does more to make trade possible than Maersk. That fact fits nicely with the benevolent leadership of Maersk McKinnsey Moller and the "World Peace Through World Trade" motto of the IBM board on which he served.

14. Container Ships

Container ships collectively moved $7.0 trillion worth of goods in 2017. On a per capita basis, that was equivalent to $933 for each person on Earth. Those goods represented 60% of the total value of world trade that moves by vessel. This category of ships didn't even exist until after World War II. Today, if you equate what moves on container ships to world gross product excluding services, you realize that one-quarter of the value of all tangible products produced globally move on container ships at some point. That is an amazing statistic for a mode largely invisible to the public. It is hard to overstate the world trade empowering ability of container ships. They literally are delivering benefits to almost every one of the 7.5 billion inhabitants on the planet.

There are currently 3,048 container ships 600' or longer. Lined up end to end, those ships would stretch out to 533 miles. If you include the container ships between 300' and 600' in length, the worldwide container fleet swells to 4,932 ships and the resulting ribbon of steel would be 693 miles long. A complete breakdown of those vessels based on their broad deadweight ton size categories is shown in the following table.

Container Category (DWT)	Vessels	Total DWT	DWT/Vessel
Handy Feeder 300-600' (<20,000)	1,884	27,750,809	14,730
Feeder (20-45,000)	902	30,541,923	33,830
Panamax (45-60,000)	660	35,776,805	54,207
Post Panamax (60-120,00)	1,088	98,260,059	90,313
New Panamax (120-160,000)	282	39,717,211	140,841
Ultra Large Container (+160,000)	116	21,439,995	184,828
Total All Above	4,932	253,486,802	51,396
Subtotal > 600'	3,048	225,735,993	74,060

And what exactly do these container ships contain, as my future wife asked me upon our first meeting? My tongue-tied response was in part because that question is actually easier to answer in terms of what does not move on those ships, but even that is a shrinking list. Crude oil, iron ore and coal and other major wet and dry bulk commodities generally don't move on container ships. Almost every other product you can imagine can and does move within the ubiquitous containers on those vessels. Some of the larger categories are retail merchandise, clothes, auto parts, televisions, wine, tires, chemicals, construction materials, paper, food, bicycles, toys and an array of industrial components and products. The list could go on and on. Anything that can be put in a truck or a railcar can also be put in a container.

There also continues to be a transition of goods that historically moved in special purpose vessels into special containers. Refrigerated containers have encroached on meat and vegetable products that historically moved on refrigerated general cargo ships. Tank containers continue to encroach on chemical shipments that historically moved on parcel tankers. Bananas in containers have replaced banana boats. Coffee beans, cocao beans and minor grains now move in containers with reusable plastic liners and modified to accommodate required ventilation. There are many other examples of product transitioning to container transit. As container ships get bigger and ever more efficient, the cost of moving various commodities in smaller increments becomes manageable and the utility and flexibility of such movements is significant. The overriding point is that, except for relatively low value commodities that will likely move in large full shipload quantities, almost anything can and does move in containers.

In 2017, these container ships moved in total 161,683,580 twenty-foot equivalent units, or TEU's, of cargo worldwide. The enormity of that amount of tangible products is hard to comprehend. Strung end to end, that number of containers would extend to over 3.2 billion feet, or 612,438 miles. Imagine a ribbon of steel containers, 8' wide and 8' high, stretching for 612,438 miles, with its 207 billion cubic feet filled with almost any product you can imagine. That ribbon of steel would circle the equator 25 times. To put that ribbon of steel into even more perspective, it is 2.56 times the distance between the earth and the moon. In other words, the volume of goods moved in containers annually is more than enough to duplicate the route that Apollo 11 took to and from the moon in 1969.

There is no industry that involves as much volumetric capacity as the container shipping industry. The 207 billion cubic feet of tangible products moved each year, if stacked together in one symmetrical cube, would be 5,915' on each side. If a cube over one mile on each side doesn't sound that big to you, take out a calculator and estimate the hypothetical cube of any other industry. For instance, certainly one of the larger industries in terms of the size of their products is the vehicle manufacturing industry. Each year some 90 million cars and trucks are produced worldwide. If you were able to put a frame around all those cars that aligned with their length, width and height and then stacked them in a cube, that cube would contain 41 billion cubic feet. That is less than one quarter of the cubic feet moved each year by the container industry.

The only industries that come close to the container shipping industry in terms of volumetric output are actually other sectors in shipping. Crude oil and iron ore shipments each year equate to 68 billion and 25 billion cubic feet, respectively. The hypothetical cube of all the cars made worldwide is between those, but the cubic feet of the container sector is two and one half times crude oil and seven times iron ore. On this cubic foot metric, there is simply no industry in the world bigger than the container shipping industry. Those millions of physical packets loaded with tangible goods are constantly moving in an endless conveyance system that delivers economic benefits to every individual in the world.

Container freight runs the gamut in terms of what is weight cargo and what is measurement cargo. The former leaves unused space in the container while the later uses all the space. The large majority of cargo moving in containers tends to be measurement cargo. On an overall basis, container cargo can be thought of as measurement cargo. Because of this, unlike tankers and dry-bulk carriers whose cargo is entirely in holds or tanks below deck, a container ship doesn't weigh out from the cargo in its hold. Container ships also stack containers on its deck. In fact, on a typical fully loaded container vessel, the cargo carried in containers on deck will equal 48% of total cargo. Container vessels carry almost as much on deck, an area not utilized by either tankers or dry-bulk carriers, as it carries below deck. On the largest vessels, those containers are stacked on deck up to ten high. In terms of vessel stability, this is made possible by the fact that container cargo is lighter. Even loading containers on deck as much as ten high, the vessel still isn't at its maximum weight limit.

This distinction results in container ships having a unique look relative to other vessels. The containers stacked on deck are an ever-changing kaleidoscope of patterns and colors. With their lighter cargo weight the vessels ride higher in the water than the other vessel types. This characteristic and the generally finer hull shape of container ships results in faster speeds, a differentiation consistent with the higher valued cargoes that move on container ships. Container ships typically operate at speeds 33% higher than tankers and 39% higher than bulk carriers.

Deadweight capacity is not a particularly relevant metric for a container vessel because they are generally not fully loaded from a weight standpoint. Naval architects determine the load line of each vessel based on calculations related to the stability of the vessel and how it performs in various sea conditions. The statutory load line is then painted on the hull of the vessel as a visual reminder to never load so much cargo that you immerse the load line. The deadweight capacity of a vessel is equal to the actual weight that brings a vessel down to its load line. The whole purpose of the load line is to establish the minimum freeboard, which is the distance the vessel hull is above the waterline.

The best metric to describe the capacity of a container ship is its TEU, or twenty-foot equivalent unit, capacity. That measure was established by the International Organization for Standardization, or ISO, which is a standard setting society composed of representatives from various national standards organizations. TEU is a measure of how many standard ISO containers 20' long, 8' wide and 8' high can be loaded on a ship. While only a relatively small number of containers today are actually just 20' long, the TEU has remained the primary measuring unit. Almost all container cargo actually moves in 40' and 45' containers, which are usually 9'6" high. The table below shows the approximate TEU range that corresponds to the size breakdown by deadweight shown in the preceding table.

Container Category	DWT Range	TEU Range	Vessels
Handy Feeder 300-600'	<20,000	< 1,500	1,884
Feeder	20-45,000	1,500-3,000	902
Panamax	45-60,000	3,000-5,000	660
Post Panamax	60-120,000	5,000-10,000	1,088
New Panamax	120-160,000	10,000-14,000	282
Ultra Large Container Vessel	> 160,000	> 14,000	116
Average All Above	51,396	4,229	4,932
Average > 600'	74.060	6,161	3,048

In aggregate, the 4,932 container vessels in the table have a capacity of 20,855,006 TEU's, or an average capacity of 4,229 TEU's per vessel. Excluding vessels that are less than 600' in length, the aggregate capacity of the 3,048 vessels is 18,779,058 TEU's for an average capacity per vessel of 6,161 TEU's. Much more so than any other shipping sector, the container sector has experienced a pronounced increase in average vessel size over the last thirty years. The table at the top of the next page shows a detailed breakdown of container ships by size category with the actual aggregate TEU capacity and average TEU capacity in each category.

Container Category	Vessels	Total TEU	TEU/Vessel
Handy Feeder 300-600'	1,884	2,075,948	1,102
Feeder	902	2,248,177	2,492
Panamax	660	2,853,739	4,324
Post Panamax	1,088	8,059,239	7,407
New Panamax	282	3,599,661	12,765
Ultra Large Container Vessel	116	2,018,242	17,399
Total All Above	4,932	20,855,006	4,229
Subtotal > 600'	3,048	18,779,058	6,161

There are dozens of large trade lanes where strings of same-sized container vessels are deployed in regular, typically weekly, service. The largest vessels are generally deployed in the largest trade lanes. The two biggest container trade lanes in the world are Asia to North America and Asia to Europe. The intra Asia market is the name used for what is really many different lanes. It is extraordinarily large as components and semi-finished goods are moved around to achieve the best manufacturing cost efficiencies. The transatlantic trade lane connecting the U.S. with Europe was once the biggest and remains a large route today. While east-west trade lanes have traditionally been the largest, north-south trade lanes connecting with emerging markets in South America and Africa are growing in importance.

As larger container vessels are deployed, there has been a consistent shift to consolidating the number of port calls these large vessels make. In addition, these large vessels have resulted in greater use of feeder vessels. An Asia to the U.S. deployment that may have involved 15 port calls in the early 1980's may have less than half as many port calls today, with feeder vessels often utilized to serve the smaller ports. This hub and spoke approach results in cost and service efficiencies with the largest vessels as well as in terminals that more than offset the cost of the feeder vessels.

Container carriers increasingly put their largest ships in long deployments, some even round-the-world, where they can serve multiple trade lanes and augment the containers they pickup with extensive feeder vessel networks at each port. The challenges in obtaining good utilization of today's largest container vessels require a different approach to deployments and the greater use of feeder vessels. A striking examples of the change in container shipping even in the last 30 years is that what would have been one of the largest vessels in the world back then is the size used as a feeder vessel in certain trade lanes today.

In terms of the historical development of container shipping, it is helpful to remember that it would be ten years after the end of World War II before the first container ship voyage. On April 26, 1956, a tanker named *Ideal X* that had been converted to carry 33' containers on its deck sailed from New York bound for Houston. With a cargo of 58 33' containers, this experiment was the brainchild of trucker Malcom McLean. What led to his invention along with the early halcyon growth days is covered in more detail in the chapter on Malcom McLean.

Prior to the advent of containerization, most ocean freight moved on breakbulk ships where large numbers of dockworkers could accommodate almost any cargo through a laborious process that occurred at both the load port and the discharge port. The thousands of smaller vessels that were engaged in this business were operated by hundreds of companies. One way to segment the companies operating these general cargo ships was between those with a set port rotation, known as liners, and those that went wherever their cargo was destined, known as tramp operators. The distinction between the two, however, was not always clear and the vagaries resulting from the significant time in port would often lead to schedule adjustments. The changes that would come about, first for the shipping industry and then for the entire world economy, in the decades following the catalytic sailing of the *Ideal X* would be astonishing.

Just as Vasco da Gama's circumnavigation of Africa became known as the beginning of the Age of Discovery, the sailing of the *Ideal X* can be looked at as the prime catalyst for what is now referred to as globalization. From that first container sailing in 1956, McLean's company, which became known as Sea-Land Service, grew quickly as it moved domestic cargo in containers from one part of the U.S. to another by water. McLean, who had previously operated one of the largest trucking companies in the country, had devised Sea-Land Service as a more cost-efficient way to move cargo he was already familiar with than relying just on trucks.

Sea-Land's main initial routes involved New York to Texas and Florida and vice versa. Additional coastwise routes on the Gulf and West Coasts were added. These routes were served typically with tankers and general cargo ships that had been converted to handle containers on deck. In 1958, Sea-Land started service to Puerto Rico, which represented the first container route involving an offshore destination. In 1963, an intercoastal service connecting the East Coast and West Coast was started by Sea-Land. Around the same time, Sea-Land and other U.S. flag shipping companies introduced container service to Alaska and Hawaii. Despite its obvious success in the domestic U.S. market, container services had not developed in any of the large international routes and skeptics had developed a number of rationales on why that wouldn't happen.

In 1966, Sea-Land was awarded a contract to move military shipments in containers from the U.S. to Vietnam. The military was experiencing logistical bottlenecks in unloading and storing cargo and they were hopeful that this new system would ease some of the problems. The success was well beyond even what Sea-Land had expected. In short order, three container ships operated by Sea-Land would replace a dozen general cargo ships. Because those ships initially were returning from Asia with mostly empty containers, Malcom McLean reasoned that they should approach Asian manufacturers to solicit their interest in shipping products in containers.

In a whirlwind business trip to Japan in 1967, Malcom McLean received commitments from Mitsubishi and other large shippers. As these manufacturers compared the actual total costs and time of moving products in containers versus in general cargo ships, they completely embraced the new system and quickly changed to moving all of their products by container. Containerization was an under recognized catalyst for the export boom from Asia that would ensue. Sea-Land started a transatlantic container service and it and their transpacific service was quickly copied by other companies as word on the effectiveness of this new system spread. Some dozen years after the advent of container shipping as a domestic conveyance system, it was rapidly morphing into the international conveyance system that has shown extraordinary growth ever since.

160

For those first dozen years, all the ships that moved containers were conversions of one type or another of general cargo ships or tankers. That would remain a key source as rapid international demand for container services now had dozens of traditional shipping companies converting vessels. As this occurred, a trend towards consolidation began as smaller operators joined forces in large part to better address the significant capital requirements they anticipated going forward. In addition, for the first time new vessels designed specifically to carry containers were being built. The late 1960's and all of the 1970's were periods of extraordinary growth for container shipping. Just the conversion of existing cargo from general cargo ships to containers would make it so. Added to that, however, was the beginning of additional cargo and new routes that effectively were only made possible by containerization.

The establishment of the International Council of Containership Operators in 1974 played a key role in developing a worldwide framework for the nascent industry as it was just beginning to be embraced globally. The new technology had brought rapid upheaval to an old industry, but the path forward wasn't entirely clear. Shipping companies realized that the way they had previously operated would disappear forever. With the major changes related to containerization, they were in some respects starting from scratch. The council, with a long name and an ungainly acronym, quickly began to be referred to as the Box Club. Its charter members included eleven of the then largest container operators, including McLean's Sea-Land, four European operators, four Asian operators and two other American operators.

The ever-changing membership roster of the Box Club and where those members ranked in terms of size is a testimony to the dynamic nature of the container shipping industry. Of the original eleven charter members, only four exist today in the same form. In terms of the others, four succumbed to bankruptcies or other major business failures. Other companies purchased three, although that was typically when it was apparent that their continued existence as independent companies was in serious jeopardy.

The Box Club obtained regulatory approval and became an open forum where members could talk about issues confronting the industry but take no collective action. Specifically, they could not discuss rates, capacity or quotas and minutes of their CEO level meetings were filed with regulators. However, they were able to deliberate on regulatory, legislative and political trends affecting the industry. In doing that, the Box Club became an important clearinghouse of information that played a beneficial role in harmonizing regulations and laws affecting the new industry. Given the worldwide nature of shipping with the laws of multiple countries effecting any container shipment, having divergent laws would have hurt the new container shipping industry.

When reflecting on the growth of international container shipping, it is useful to break it down into two fundamental periods. In the first period, from 1966 to 1982, the sharp growth was more mechanical and driven by the conversion from breakbulk and general cargo ships to container ships. Consolidation had dramatically reduced the number of operators and they adhered to precise, regular schedules. Unlike the tanker or bulk sectors where someone could become involved in the segment with a single vessel, the container segment required at a minimum a string of vessels along with large investments in container equipment and terminal facilities. These capital requirements drove consolidation and created barriers to entry that transitioned the container segment to be quite different from the tanker and bulk segments in terms of number of participants.

While this initial period from 1966 to 1982 involved bigger ships, most of the improved economics came from a better system. By 1982, most of the conversion had occurred but the sharp growth continued, driven by the cost efficiencies resulting from scale economics as container ships started to get geometrically bigger. This later period of capacity growth from 1982 on was driven exclusively by new vessel construction. From doubling to quadrupling to quintupling in size, each successive generation of new container ships resulted in lower underlying per unit costs. In terms of this exponential increase in average size, the container segment was following the path that the tanker segment had gone down earlier. These improved cost economics were a catalyst in actually generating significant container volume. That trend continues to this very day. In hindsight, it turns out that container volume is much more elastic to shipping rates than economists would have ever thought.

The Panama Canal plays a prominent role in terms used to describe the different container ship sizes. The Panama Canal locks restrict the size of a vessel across all three dimensions, and until 2016 that meant a maximum length of 950', a maximum width of 106' and a maximum water draft of 39.5'. Panamax vessels are so-named because they approach the limits in terms of the size of a vessel that can go through the Panama Canal. While all types of vessels utilize the Panama Canal, it is particularly important for container ships. The Far East to U.S. East Coast lane is one of the largest container routes and the Panama Canal results in less than half the distance compared to going around the tip of South America. A situation I was directly involved in highlights both the effects of the Panama Canal and the geometric change that has occurred in the container sector even in the recent past.

In 1982, Malcom McLean, in an initiative almost three decades after he invented container shipping, tasked his naval architect Charles Cushing with designing the largest container ship that could move loaded through the Panama Canal. Cushing expanded on the design of a ship he had recently developed that he referred to as an Econship as it maximized the containers that could be carried within a given set of dimensions. What came out of that was a design for what Cushing called a Jumbo Econship, a ship with the largest number of loaded container that could transit the Panama Canal. McLean's focus was that the economies of scale from such a large ship would result in the lowest possible cost per container mile at sea. I was involved in obtaining the financing for a 12-vessel order in what was the largest commerical shipbuilding order in history at the time. When delivery of these large ships started in 1984, the Econships, with a capacity of 4,482 TEU's each, were the largest container ships in the world with a 30% larger container capacity than anything afloat.

At the time, the Econships were viewed by many in the container shipping industry as way too large. McLean, however, was undaunted by this criticism and was focused on the cost per container mile at sea economics these ships would produce. So as not to focus their large capacity on any single market, McLean also elected to deploy them in an innovative round-the-world deployment. By going eastbound, he tied into the heavier volume transpacific and transatlantic markets while simultaneously spreading capacity around to numerous smaller markets.

McLean's Econships did in fact deliver superior cost economics and in order to compete with those ships, other carriers built similar size and even larger vessels. The movement to significantly larger vessels beginning in 1982 marked the beginning of a period of even more significant growth in containerization. These larger container ships were both cause and effect in the extraordinary growth that would follow in world trade. Indeed, there was and is a symbiotic relationship between the two. Bigger ships mean lower freight costs which itself result in more trade. As it turns out, in the age of globalization, container trade volume is elastic and in part a function of freight costs.

Data supporting the synergistic relationship between the cost efficiency of container ships and the growth in world trade comes in the form of the shifting mix of trade. In 1960, before containerization became a real factor in international trade, manufactured products accounted for 50% of the value of world trade in goods. By 1990, manufactured products represented 70% of the value of world trade in goods. A decade later by 2000, 75% of the value of world trade in goods was in manufactured products. Today, manufactured products are estimated to account for approximately 80% of the value of world trade in goods. Manufactured products now move primarily in containers. The shift over the last fifty years from representing 50% to 80% of the value of world trade in goods underscores the catalytic role of container shipping.

McLean's Econships changed the dynamics of the major east-west trade routes by lowering cost per container mile at sea costs to the point that the only way they could be competed with was to build similar large ships. The broad reduction in costs across many trade routes occurred at the same time that the U.S. and the world were experiencing strong growth. The establishment of various free trade associations and the fall of the Soviet Union and its conversion more to a capitalist model added to the demand for additional container shipping capacity.

The greatest catalyst for the growth in container shipping, however, occurred in 2001 when China became a full member of the World Ttrade Organization. Now with the ability to more readily export products throughout the world, this quickly ramped up China's already large and growing economy to become a major exporter. This in turn improved economic prosperity across China, increasing the massive shift from rural to urban areas. New housing was needed for hundreds of millions of Chinese. The combination of sharply growing exports and a fast growing domestic economy required massive amounts of raw materials imports, benefiting both dry-bulk and tanker shipping. Almost all of China's exports went out in containers. There was also growth in imports in containers, both in the form of components for further manufacturing as well as finished products for a growing domestic economy.

Total container ship capacity has increased more than twenty-fold since 1982 when McLean ordered his Econships. That is a staggering increase for what was already a large industry in 1982. Some carriers grew even faster as containerization resulted in some established carriers being displaced by more aggressive operators and new companies that started only after the container revolution began. For instance, Maersk Line, the largest container operator in the world today, has grown twice as fast as the sector with more than a forty-fold increase in capacity since 1982. MSC, or Mediterranean Shipping Company, is the second largest operator today and was launched in 1970.

Data from the Box Club on the ten largest carriers in 1983, 1998 and 2013 highlights both the growth of the sector and the changing mix of the largest carriers. The data also underscores the energetic changes in carrier rankings over these relatively short fifteen-year periods. The table at the top of the next page shows the top ten carriers in 1983 ranked by the total TEU capacity of their vessel fleet.

Company	1983 Vessel TEU Capacity
U.S. Lines	88,028
Evergreen	69,728
Sea-Land	61,002
Hapag-Lloyd	53,636
Maersk	51,250
Nedlloyd	51,186
OCL	43,986
MOL	33,349
OOCL	32,717
NYK	30,954
Total Top 10	515,836

In the fifteen years from 1983 to 1998, capacity among the largest carriers grew at an 8.6% compounded annual rate and five of the companies above were displaced in the rankings of the top ten carriers. Maersk grew faster at an 11.9% rate over that period and emerged as the largest carrier in 1998. The table below shows the top ten carriers in 1998 ranked by the total TEU capacity of their vessel fleet.

Company	1998 Vessel TEU Capacity
Maersk	232,257
Evergreen	228,248
P&O Nedlloyd	221,531
Sea-Land	215,114
COSCO	201,593
Hanjin	174,526
MSC	154,185
NYK	128,154
MOL	115,763
Hyundai	112,958
Total Top 10	1,784,329

Over the next fifteen-year period from 1998 to 2013, capacity growth among the largest carriers accelerated to an 11.9% annual rate. Another four carriers were displaced from the top ten as the sector continued to show the dynamic nature of the business. Growth at Maersk, still the largest carrier, was well above average at a 16.0% annual rate. MSC, now the second largest container shipping company, grew even faster at an 18.9% annual rate over the fifteen-year period. The table at the top of the next page shows the top ten carriers in 2013 ranked by the total TEU capacity of their vessel fleet.

Company	2013 Vessel TEU Capacity
Maersk	2,159,524
MSC	2,064,118
CMA CGM	1,153,088
COSCO	715,219
Evergreen	709,702
Hapag-Lloyd	639,148
APL	570,497
CSCL	564,151
Hanjin	555,279
MOL	507,894
Total Top 10	9,638,620

Since 2013, capacity at the largest carriers has grown at a 10.0% annual rate. Four carriers being displaced from the top ten in 2017 compared to 2013 underscored the vigorous nature of the sector. Growth at Maersk was above average at 10.5% and growth at COSCO and CMA CGM was well above average at a 23.2% and 16.9%, respectively. The total capacity of the top ten carriers in 2017 was 27.4 times higher than the total capacity of the top ten carriers in 1983. That translates into a growth rate of 10.2% annually over the 34-year period. It would be difficult to find any large industry whose capacity has grown at a double-digit rate over an extended multi-decade period. The table below shows the top ten carriers in 2017 ranked by the total TEU capacity of their vessel fleet.

Company	2017 Vessel TEU Capacity
Maersk	3,217,889
MSC	2,872,067
CMA CGM	2,151,284
COSCO	1,648,582
Evergreen	992,905
Hapag-Lloyd	983,335
Hamburg Sud	589,634
Yang Ming	575,240
OOCL	559,955
United Arab	517,824
Total Top 10	14,108,715

As noted, the twelve Econships ordered by McLean in 1982 that were 30% larger than any existing container vessel at the time ushered in the era of the mega container ships. They were the first genuine Panamax container ships and were simply designed to get the maximum number of containers through the Panama Canal. Today, there are 2,146 container ships in operation that are equal to or larger than those Econships. That includes 660 Panamax vessels that are effectively the same size as the Econships. With the opening of the new locks at the Panama Canal in 2016, the rational for container ships in this size category has diminished. Not surprisingly, in just the last two years, the number of container ships in this size category has declined 18% over that period. They have, however, been replaced by even larger container ships.

There are 1,486 container ships larger than those initial twelve Econships that were decried as being way too big in the early 1980's. Those vessels are not just slightly larger than the Econships. With an average capacity of 9,204 TEU's each, those 1,486 behemoths are more than twice the size of the Econships on average.

The largest container ships operating in the world today are a group of vessels launched by OOCL with a capacity of 21,413 TEU's, or 4.8 times the capacity of the Econships. The title of world's largest container ship is, however, a rapidly evolving one and vessels with a capacity of over 23,000 TEU's each are now being built and will soon be deployed.

When container operators began building ships too large to go through the Panama Canal, they went well beyond the earlier sizes and the new size category of Post Panamax was developed. These vessels were typically deployed in trade routes such as Asia to Europe and Asia to the U.S. West Coast where the Panama Canal wasn't an issue. Much more so than any of the other vessel types, container ships are the largest users of the Panama Canal as it dramatically shortens the distance for numerous container trade routes.

As container ships grew in size, the government of Panama became concerned vessel operators would increasingly focus on deployments that didn't require a canal transit. For instance, some container operators were opting to move Asia to the U.S. East Coast containers via the Suez Canal. Even with a slightly longer voyage, the larger container ships that could transit the Suez Canal made this an attractive option.

In order to counter this, a few years ago Panama embarked on a $7 billion project to add a larger set of locks to the canal. Completed in 2016, the new locks can accommodate vessels up to 1,401' in length, 180' in width and with a draft up to 60'. This has the effect of allowing a container ship with a capacity of up to 14,000 TEU's to transit the canal. Operators ordered even more vessels of that size and the new size category New Panamax is now used to describe the 282 container ships with capacity between 10,000 and 14,000 TEU's. The number of vessels in that size category has increased 32% in the last two years. Vessels in that category are up to approximately three times the capacity of a current Panamax container ship.

While the Panama Canal results in shorter voyages for many container ships, the canal authorities have calculators and an awareness of vessel costs and much of the cost benefit is mitigated by canal tolls. The roundtrip Panama Canal tolls for a Panamax container ship is $711,000. With the New Panamax container ships now using the larger lock, the roundtrip canal tolls for them is often over $1.5 million.

The Asia to Europe trade lane, the biggest container route in the world, goes via the larger Suez Canal. The Suez Canal has no locks and can accommodate vessels with a width of up to 254' and a draft of up to 66'. With hardly any constraints, container ships in those trade routes continue to get larger. The new category name that is used to describe the largest container ships that are too big to transit even the expanded Panama Canal is Ultra Large Container Vessels or ULCV's as they are also called. There are presently 116 of these giant container ships, a category that has tripled in the last three years and increased 59% in the last two years. However, this category can be expected to continue to grow significantly in the years to come based on the extraordinary economies of scale that result with those vessels.

The sharp progression in the size of the largest container ships parallels the increase in container volume in all of the major trade lanes. Over the last few decades, overall container volume has been increasing at a double-digit annual percentage growth rate. Certainly Asia has been a noteworthy part of this extraordinary growth. In 2017, Asia represented 56.5% of worldwide container exports and 39.4% of worldwide container imports. The table below shows a breakdown of actual worldwide loaded container volume between exports and imports by continent or major region.

Total Loaded TEU's	Exports	Imports
Asia	91,393,628	63,766,494
Australia	3,042,448	4,091,060
Europe	28,126,465	31,433,116
Middle East/India	12,011,267	17,611,483
North America	15,486,438	27,541,091
South America	8,639,789	10,311,477
Africa	2,983,546	6,928,857
Total	161,683,580	161,683,580

The following table shows a breakdown of the volume data above based on the respective percentages of total exports and imports.

% Of Total Loaded TEU's	Exports	Imports
Asia	56.5%	39.4%
Australia	1.9%	2.5%
Europe	17.4%	19.4%
Middle East/India	7.4%	10.9%
North America	9.6%	17.0%
South America	5.3%	6.4%
Africa	1.8%	4.3%
Total	100.0%	100.0%

Asia is the only region where exports exceeded imports, with all other regions being net importers. Asia exports to those regions and is now the manufacturing center of the world, with much of that manufacturing in China. The largest individual trade lane in the world in terms of container volume is Asia to North America. The second largest is Asia to Europe. Both of those, however, are eclipsed in terms of total volume by a collection of numerous lanes between China,

Japan, Korea and Southeast Asia broadly referred to as the intra Asia trade. Most of the major manufacturing cities in Asia are either on or near the coast. Many products in Asia are manufactured in one country using components made in another Asian country. Container ships act as the primary delivery system, ferrying products between countries in Asia. Beyond these largest trade lanes, there are dozens of major east-west and north-south trade lanes that crisscross the world.

The table below lists the largest container trade lanes in the world in terms of how they ranked in overall loaded TEU volume in a recent period. The respective trade lanes are shown both in terms of percent of total volume in both directions and percent of total volume miles after including average shipment distance. The latter figure is a more relevant measure of trade lane size. While the intra Asia trade collectively has the most volume, with an average shipment distance of 1,230 nautical miles, its volume miles pales compared to either the Asia to North America or Asia to Europe trade lanes. With their significant volume and respective average shipment distances of 8,366 and 9,043 nautical miles, those two trade lanes collectively represent over half the total volume miles in the container shipping industry. The fourteen largest identifiable trade lanes comprising 93% of volume and 92% of volume miles are shown with their respective measures and the relationship between those two measures.

Trade Lane	% TEU's	% TEU Miles	Relationship
Intra Asia	23.79%	5.43%	4.378
Asia – North America	15.83%	24.58%	.644
Asia – Europe	15.23%	25.57%	.594
Asia – Middle East	5.41%	5.46%	.990
Intra Europe	5.35%	1.45%	3.690
Europe – North America	5.16%	5.93%	.870
Europe – Middle East	4.28%	3.42%	1.251
Asia – South America	3.58%	6.43%	.556
Asia – Africa	2.77%	3.37%	.822
N. America – S. America	2.67%	1.82%	1.467
Asia – Australia	2.62%	2.27%	1.154
Europe – South America	2.47%	2.58%	.957
Intra Middle East	2.08%	0.91%	2.278
N. America – Middle East	1.92%	3.10%	.618
All Other Trade Lanes	6.83%	7.66%	.893
Total	100.00%	100.00%	1.000

From the table above, some 70% of container shipments touch Asia at one point or another. Invariably, the part of Asia they touch more than all others combined is China.

China and its extraordinary growth has been the largest catalyst across all of the shipping segments the last 20 years. The basic framework is that bulk products move in and manufactured goods in containers move out. There is also lots of movement of components from and to other points in China and Asia that move via container. The growth in China's container volume has been breathtaking in a relatively short period. When starting in the industry in 1980, China simply wasn't a relevant factor. A portion of the volume that went through Hong Kong was related to China. However, Japan, Korea and Taiwan geometrically overshadowed that volume. Today, China's container volume is 3 times the collective volume of those three countries.

In 2017, seven of the ten largest ports in the world in term of container volume were in China. The table below shows the ten largest container ports and their respective total TEU volume along with the collective volume of groups of ten ports through the largest 100 ports. The collective volume of ports outside of the largest 100 container ports is then included. Also shown is what those respective volumes represent in terms of total worldwide container volume in 2017. Note that this port data includes both loaded and empty containers in both directions.

Port	2017 TEU's	% World Volume
Shanghai, China	40,233,000	5.54%
Singapore, Singapore	33,666,600	4.63%
Shenzhen, China	25,208,700	3.47%
Ningbo, China	24,607,000	3.39%
Hong Kong, China	20,770,000	2.86%
Busan, South Korea	20,493,475	2.82%
Guangzhou, China	20,370,000	2.80%
Qingdao, China	18,262,000	2.51%
Dubai, UAE	15,368,000	2.11%
Tianjin, China	15,040,000	2.07%
Ports #11 thru #20	100,655,517	13.85%
Ports #21 thru #30	58,945,652	8.11%
Ports #31 thru #40	42,552,664	5.86%
Ports #41 thru #50	31,785,661	4.37%
Ports #51 thru #60	30,096,626	4.14%
Ports #61 thru #70	27,426,524	3.77%
Ports #71 thru #80	23,337,778	3.35%
Ports #81 thru #90	20,473,363	2.82%
Ports #91 thru #100	16,143,775	2.22%
Subtotal Top 100 Ports	586,436,335	80.70%
All Other Ports	140,234,834	19.30%
Total All Ports	726,671,169	100.00%

This table underscores both the central role of China in container shipping as well as the broad worldwide reach and impact of the container shipping sector. Within the top 100 ports are 22 ports in China that represented 38% of total volume in the top 100 ports. To put that into more perspective, just the average volume of those 22 ports was larger than the volume at Los Angeles, the largest U.S. port, but only the 17th largest ports worldwide. The table on the next page breaks down volume at the top 100 ports by broad geographic area along with the number of ports and average volume per port for each area.

Geographic Area	2017 TEU's	% TEU's	Ports	TEU's/Port
China	224,707,703	38.22%	22	10,213,987
Asia Ex China	148,165,424	25.27%	20	7,408,271
Europe	79,414,077	13.54%	18	4,411,893
Middle East/India	59,704,544	10.18%	18	3,316,919
North America	48,972,868	8.35%	13	3,767,144
South America	17,435,183	2.97%	6	2,905,864
Australia	5,336,558	0.91%	2	2,668,279
Africa	2,699,978	0.46%	1	2,699,978
100 Port Total	586,436,335	100.00%	100	5,864,363

Outside of the top 100 ports, there are literally hundreds of other ports worldwide that handle containers in smaller volumes than at the larger ports above. Collectively, those ports handled more than 140 million TEU's in 2017. While certain areas like Africa are unrepresented among the larger ports today, they are well represented among the smaller ports. For instance, there are dozens of ports throughout Africa that currently handle containers. Just as the scale of the container shipping sector is largely under recognized, its breadth worldwide is also less known. The container revolution that Malcom McLean started has literally now touched every corner of the planet.

In terms of its relative affect, a case can be made that the relative impact of container shipping has been most pronounced in the areas served by these smaller ports. Those are after all the areas that have seen the largest growth in per capita income. A recent recognition of this occurred when Human Progress, a joint project by the Cato Institute and the John Templeton Foundation to chart humanity's major milestones, named Malcom McLean as their 17th Hero of Progress. Prior individuals recognized included Johannes Gutenberg and Jonas Salk, with Malcom McLean the first businessman recognized by the project. Human Progress cited McLean because they saw a direct link between his invention of containerization, the world trade it made possible and the lifting of hundreds of millions of people from poverty levels. That is an accurate analysis and an amazing legacy for a man whose efforts literally changed the world for the better in a material way.

China's growth rate in container volume has significantly exceeded that of all the countries involved in the container shipping sector. Using the latest fully comparable data that is available, China alone represented 27% of total container volume worldwide in 2014, up sharply from 15% ten years earlier. China's container volume was four times the U.S., the second largest country. The annual growth rate in container volume in and out of China is over 14% over those ten years, almost three times the growth rate rest of the world excluding China.

The table at the beginning of the next page shows the top 10 countries in terms of percent of total 2014 container volume, how that compares to 2004 and the compound annual growth rate (CAGR) over the last 10 years. That is the most recent ten-year period for which comparable data was available.

Country	2004 % Total	2014 % Total	10Y CAGR
China	15.0%	26.7%	14.2%
U.S.	9.9%	6.8%	2.7%
Singopore	6.1%	5.1%	5.1%
Korea	4.1%	3.5%	5.2%
Hong Kong	6.3%	3.4%	0.2%
Japan	4.7%	3.3%	3.0%
Malaysia	3.3%	3.3%	7.1%
United Arab Emirates	2.5%	3.0%	9.4%
Germany	3.6%	2.8%	4.2%
Taiwan	3.7%	2.4%	1.9%
Subtotal Top 10	59.7%	60.6%	7.3%
All Other Countries	40.3%	39.4%	6.8%
World Total	100.0%	100.0%	7.1%
World Excluding China	85.0%	73.3%	5.4%

The list is dominated by countries in Asia which represent seven of the top ten countries. Just in that ten year period, however, the transition in the relative importance of China is obvious as it went from being equivalent to half the volume of the rest of Asia to being 1.3 times the volume of the rest of Asia. Since 2014, China has continued to experience well above average growth in its container volume. The transition to it being an ever-larger portion of Asia volume has continued. The more timely data indicating that China volume was 38% of top 100 port volume in 2017 suggests that it is now at least 31% of total worldwide container volume.

A fundamental difference between container shipping and all other shipping sectors relates to vessel utilization. In most of the other sectors, cargoes move in full shipload quantities from where the product is sourced to where it is consumed. Crude oil moves from the Arabian Gulf to Japan and iron ore moves from Brazil to China are examples. Ships involved with such moves typically operate at 50% overall utilization as they are loaded in one direction and empty in the other backhaul direction. While these ships don't move back and forth between the same points and occasionally may get cargoes that effectively cover a portion of the backhaul, for the most part they aren't loaded much more than half of their time at sea.

Container ships, on the other hand, always have loaded containers onboard. These ships have loads from hundreds of customers, each moving between different points along a scheduled route. Due to the diversity in the types of cargoes moved, there will be loads even on the backhaul direction. This two way traffic results in higher overall utilization at container ships compared to other shipping sectors. Across all trade lanes, container ships typically experience utilization rates in excess of 75%.

Container ships operate as part of a larger network providing regularly scheduled service between a consistent group of ports. Unlike tankers or bulk-carriers which operate as individual units going to random ports based on the particular cargo, container ships operate as part of a larger string of vessels, each following the other at regular intervals. For instance, six container ships are typically needed to provide weekly service between the Far East and the U.S. West Coast while eleven container ships are typically needed to provide weekly service between the Far East and Northern Europe.

The multiple ships required along with the container equipment and terminal facilities needed to operate a container shipping service translates into it requiring significantly larger investments than those related to either tanker or dry-bulk shipping. In the latter, almost all the expenses are related to the ship itself. In container shipping, the carrier operates an integrated service that provides the container, trucks the loaded container from the inland point to the terminal where loads it on the vessel and then reverses that process on the other side.

The genius behind container shipping relates to both cargo-handling efficiency and movements beyond the ship. A prime driver is that allows cargo to be moved from the initial origin point to the final destination point in the same container. To move inland, the container is placed on a chassis where it is easily secured via corner castings on the container. A tractor can then pull this container/chassis unit, just as it would pull a standard highway trailer. On the road, the former can typically be differentiated from the latter by their box-like design. For longer movement inland, containers will be stacked two-high on specially designed rail cars.

The efficient handoff of the same container from one transport mode to the other gave rise to the term intermodal. This intermodal transport system dramatically reduces handling costs at each handoff point. It is much less expensive to move a container once than to move all of the cargo within it at each handoff point. This is particularly important for the manufactured goods typically moving in containers as they always have an inland movement, even if it is just a local delivery. While tanker and dry-bulk cargoes are often delivered directly by ships to seaside refineries, mills and power plants where they are used, container shipping cargoes all typically go inland some distance. Whether its 20 miles or 2,000 miles, the efficiency gain resulting from just transferring the container rather than unloading the cargo from the ship into a shed or warehouse and then later reloading it into a truck as it was done before containerization, is extraordinary.

Containers are predominately made of steel and are always 8' wide to fit in cell guides within the holds of container ships. The typical lengths are 20', 40' and 45' with the holds apportioned into cell guides of those respective lengths. The 20' containers represent less than 5% of the total number of containers and are primarily used to move exceptionally heavy cargoes. If moved in larger containers, such cargoes wouldn't be in compliance with highway weight restrictions and therefore would loose much of their intermodal ability. The most popular containers are 40' in length and after that are containers 45' in length. Most containers now are 9.5' in height as containers of any height can be placed in cell guides and a higher container adds to its cubic feet volume. Almost all container cargo is cubic rather than weight freight, with the across the board average of 131 cubic feet of container cargo per weight ton. When a weight ton of cargo takes up more than 40 cubic feet, it is known as cubic or measurement freight.

The number of containers an operator needs is substantially above the number of equivalent container slots on their vessels to take into account the containers at terminals and inland points. The ratio will vary depending on the service. One rule of thumb for large trade lanes involving significant inland movements is that total containers needed are six times the weekly capacity of the service plus the total capacity of the vessels in the service. For instance, in a weekly service involving six ships, the total containers needed are equivalent to twice the capacity of all six ships. The investment in container and chassis equipment will often approach the total amount invested in container ships. Chassis are only needed for containers that are not onboard vessels and therefore are typically no more than half the number of containers.

In aggregate, an estimated 38.4 million TEU's of actual container equipment are currently utilized to operate the present worldwide fleet of container vessels. If lined up end to end, those physical containers would stretch out 146,537 miles, an 8' x 8' chain of steel that would circle the equator almost six times. If stacked six high, you would have a globe circling 48' high wall that was more than ten times longer than the Great Wall of China.

With a total container ship fleet with capacity equivalent to 20.9 million TEU's, slightly more than half of those containers are typically onboard ships at sea. The remaining 17.5 million TEU's on land are equivalent to 5.6 weeks based on average weekly worldwide container volume of 3.1 million TEU's in 2017. Note that this calculation is based on the capacity of full container ships only and excludes the container carrying capacity on general cargo ships. While such vessels typically have limited container capacity, the thousands of general cargo ships can add up to an additional 10 to 20% in container carrying capacity. Taking this into account would skew the split between physical containers at sea and on land more towards the former. The chassis equipment that is required never exceeds the containers on land, as chassis are not required at sea. In addition, it is increasingly less than the quantities on land as most terminals now stack containers prior to placing them on chassis. Many containers also move on rail flatcars without chassis. Therefore, the quantity of physical chassis worldwide is something less than the equivalent of 17.5 million TEU's.

Containership operators have large terminals at most of the ports in which they call. Port authorities and independent terminal operators also provide such terminals to containership operators under various arrangements. These terminals, which can range in size to over 100 acres, are generally leased and are used as a staging area to receive incoming containers and dispatch outgoing containers. The labor needed to manage this full time terminal, as well as the labor utilized to load and unload the ships, is contracted for and paid by the container operator. This is another fundamental difference with tanker or dry-bulk shipping where the smaller cargo handling expenses are almost always paid directly by the cargo owner. The most noteworthy feature of any container terminal is the massive gantry cranes used to actually move the containers on and off the ships and the mobile handling equipment for movements within the terminal.

The specialized gantry cranes that have been developed to load and unload containers are often 15 stories high. They are set on rails so they can move alongside the vessel to align precisely with the cell on which they are working. The cranes have spreaders that can be quickly adjusted to the different length containers. A tractor pulling a container/chassis unit will drive under the crane and the spreader will engage the outbound container top. Each corner of the spreader has guides that are deployed to align exactly with the container, at which time twist locks on the spreader turn and lock into each of the four corner castings on the container. With this secure grip, the gantry crane lifts the container up and moves it out on the stationary boom that goes out at a right angle to the dock across the entire vessel. Once over the selected cell, the container is lowered until it rests on the container below it, at which time the crane disengages from the container. The entire process from start to finish takes less than two minutes. The crane then moves to another cell and the inbound container it retrieves is placed on the waiting empty chassis under the crane ashore. At that rate, a gantry crane can load 30 containers per hour. A typical 40' container has cargo weighing 19.8 tons, so that translates into 594 tons loaded per crane per hour. Large container ships are typically worked with six or more gantry cranes at the same time. The productivity and cost efficiency of these cranes relative to how cargo was handled prior to containerization is extraordinary.

Large container terminals involve hundreds of acres of flat paved land where containers are stacked up to six high either waiting to be loaded on a ship or to be dispatched to an inland point. A wide variety of specialized equipment has been developed to move containers between the shore-side gantry cranes and where they are stacked in the terminal. The technology exists to make this process fully automated with driver-less equipment guided by GPS transporting containers within the terminal. While only a few terminals are taking full advantage of this technology, expectations are that it will be increasingly utilized going forward.

Port authorities around the world track the volume of containers moving in and out of their ports. Analysts and economists frequently point to this data as a real time measure of the regional economic activity. In 2017 the imports and exports of containers worldwide totaled 726,671,169 TEU's. Note that because that number includes both imports and exports, each actual load is counted twice. For instance, a shipment from Shanghai to Long Beach would count as an export for Shanghai and an import for Long Beach. In addition, that number includes movements of empty containers as well as loaded containers. For example, if a container moved loaded from one point to another and then returned empty, that one actual load would result in four movements at the two ports.

If you divide that worldwide port activity figure by four, you arrive at 181,667,792 TEU's, which would be the actual loads if the return leg were always empty. That figure is equal to 112.4% of the actual 2017 container volume of 161,683,580 as reported by the carriers. Those figures broadly reconcile when another factor is considered. The carriers actual load count doesn't show a movement which involves a feeder vessel as a separate actual load as that is not how it contracts with customers who pay a single price for the entire end to end movement. Particularly in Asia and Europe, many movements start or end with a short voyage on a small feeder ship that links with a large container ship for the longer voyage. Such containers only count as one load in the carrier provided volume data both will show up as if it were two separate loads in the port activity data. When that factor is considered the actual volume data from the carriers and the overall import and export data from the ports reconcile.

Inland transportation of containers is typically contracted out by container operators to trucking companies who connect with the container/chassis unit at large terminals alongside where the vessel docks. Trucking is typically the preferred method for inland movements of less than 500 miles. For longer inland movements, rail is the preferred method due to its lower cost per mile. Many container operators have such a large volume moving by rail that they contract for dedicated regular service where locomotives are pulling a double-stacked trainload exclusively filled with that operator's containers. These dedicated trains are sometimes loaded directly from the ship with the train moving under the gantry cranes. This on-dock loading pre-empts the need to store the container at the terminal. Typically at the end of the rail movement there will be a further local trucking movement to get the container to the final destination point. It isn't unusual for the same container to move by ship then by rail and then by truck, with the same process occurring in reverse on the return leg.

174

The equipment, terminal, trucking and rail activities of container shipping companies represent significant investments and expenses that only that sector has compared to the other shipping sectors. In fact, collectively those expenses overshadow the direct expenses of the container ship itself, which are typically just 25% of your total costs. In tanker and dry-bulk shipping, expenses related to the ship itself are typically more than 90% of the total costs. They are fundamentally just in the shipping business, whereas container shipping companies are in a broader integrated transportation business.

Container ships are the racehorses of the shipping industry, both in terms of their speed and beauty. At sea in the busier head haul direction they typically average 18.5 knots. A knot is an old mariner's term derived from nautical mile. The nautical mile is based on the circumference of the earth and is equal to one minute of latitude. With 60 minutes per degree and 360 degrees of total latitude, the earth is 21,600 nautical miles around. Because the same measure in statute miles is 24,901, speed in knots can be converted into miles per hour by multiplying knots by 115%. In other words, a container ship going 18.5 knots is actually moving at 21.3 miles per hour.

Following the financial crisis of 2008, a phenomenon developed related to vessel speed across all shipping sectors. It particularly affected container vessels. This phenomenon related to a slowing down of vessel speed driven by two factors. The first and main factor related to the reduction in demand and demand growth and slower speeds in effect reduced the supply of vessels. The second factor was higher oil prices and the lower vessel fuel costs that came with less fuel consumption per mile at sea with slower speeds. In the case of container vessels, this was largely achieved by reducing the speed of vessels mainly on the less important, or backhaul, leg of a particularly trade lane. For instance, in the Asia to Europe trade lane, the string of vessels may travel at 18.5 knots in the higher container volume westbound direction and slow down to 11.5 knots on the backhaul return leg to Asia that has less container volume. This would result in an average speed at sea of 15 knots with much of the reduction focused on the backhaul leg to minimize the service effect on customers. Since fuel consumption increases exponentially with increased speed, the fuel cost savings from slow steaming were and continue to be significant.

Precise data exists for actual speeds based on the transponders now mandated for all ocean going vessels and this data is accessible from various sources. The same type of data on an historical basis allows for a precise comparison of how vessel speeds have changed over time. Since the financial crisis began in 2008, average container vessel speeds have declined consistently and are now approximately 25% below what they were then. Most other vessel types have shown a similar reduction in average speeds in order to both reduce vessel supply and lower fuel costs.

The data shows that container vessels currently collectively have an average speed of 10.06 knots including all time spent in port. The data is constructed based on the average speed from multiple readings each hour whether or not the vessel is moving. Generally container vessels as an overall group will spend 75% or more of their time at sea, with the balance represented by port time, piloting time, canal time and slack time. Given the importance of maintaining published schedules, most container deployments will have up to 5% slack built into the schedule so that weather and other unexpected delays don't ripple ahead for weeks. An overall average of 10.06 knots and 75% time at sea equates to an average speed at sea of 13.4 knots.

However, actual time in port isn't available and we will stay focused on the most precise data which translates into container vessels presently averaging 88,126 nautical miles per year. That data indicates that container vessels now move 18% faster than all vessels as a group and 37% faster than vessels comprising the general type outside of the three main vessel types as shown in the table below.

Vessel Type	Miles/Year	Speed	Container Vs
Container	88,126	10.06	0.0%
Dry-bulk	76,738	8.76	+14.8%
Tanker	69,554	7.94	+26.7%
Other/General	64,474	7.36	+36.7%
Total	74,745	8.53	+17.9%

The annual cargo carried on container vessels is worth $7.0 trillion and has a weight of 1.759 billion tons, resulting in a value per ton of $3,996. That cargo value per ton is 23.7 times the average value per ton of cargo moved on dry-bulk vessels and 7.4 times the average value per ton of cargo moved on tankers. The relationship between cargo value and vessel value and shipping cost plays a role in the overall economics of each shipping sector and its respective volatility. In terms of value per capita, each year container vessels carry $933 worth of cargo for each person on the planet. That per capita figure is comprised of 523 pounds of cargo with a value per pound of $1.78.

The high value cargo in container ships has always justified a higher speed than in the other shipping sectors. To achieve that speed in the most fuel-efficient manner, container ships have finer hull shapes that allow them to move through the water faster. Container ships are also typically longer and usually have a higher ratio of length to width, an attribution that supports greater fuel efficiency. The reason for this is simple. Additional vessel length doesn't increase fuel consumption, which is more a function of the width and draft of a vessel. The latter two measures, augmented by the shape of the hull, determine how much water needs to be moved out of the way when a vessel is moving at sea. Once that metaphorical hole has been punched in the water, additional length with the same width and draft does not necessitate proportionately more power or fuel.

In fact, up to a certain point additional length can actually improve fuel efficiency if it reduces vessel motions resulting from waves. A countervailing factor that prevents vessels from being lengthened ad infinitum relates to longitudinal stress, as the longer a vessel is the more structural strength is needed to prevent it from bending and failing due to wave action. The stresses that a vessel at sea is exposed to are dynamic and complex. The heavier the cargo weight in a ship, the higher the structural stress it is exposed to when it pitches lengthwise and sideways at sea. For this reason, at some point it becomes cost prohibitive and technically infeasible to make certain types of vessels longer.

Charles Cushing, a naval architect who played a pivotal role in the conversion of many general cargo ships into some of the early containerships and was the designer of the first Panamax container ships referred to earlier, has a wonderful gift for explaining technical concepts. I've learned from him that length doesn't change the hole the vessel needs to punch in the water. He also had an elegant explanation of the theoretically perfect ship design that has always stayed with me. That perfect ship would be hinged. This would allow maximum length without requiring the incremental structural strength, as the vessel would bend with the waves. This perfect ship would need to have sections in synch with the size and direction of the waves. However, waves are not symmetrical either in terms of size or direction. There is also no reasonable hinge that could be developed to withstand the multi-dimensional forces and stresses that a vessel is exposed to at sea.

Almost all of the longest cargo ships in the world are container ships. Of the 296 cargo ships longer than 1,200' feet, 294 are container ships. The reason for this is clear. Unlike the typical heavy cargoes moved by bulk carriers and tankers, the cargoes moved by container ships are much lighter. This allows them to be designed to be longer than other types of vessels because the lighter weight results in less structural stress to the midsection of the ship. To put that length into context, each of those 294 container ships are longer than the largest aircraft carriers in the world.

Pricing and pricing indices within the container shipping sector are based on rates per actual container shipped. Each voyage of a container ship includes dozens, hundreds or even thousands of different customers who have contracted to move containers between various points served by that container shipping company. Typically, a customer will outline their anticipated shipments for the next year in terms of container volume and both origin and destination points with several container operators, inviting them to submit bids. The container operators will analyze their costs in handling those loads and submit proposals. Discussions ensue and the customers make decisions based primarily on pricing but with consideration also for service factors such as on-time departures and arrivals.

The agreed upon pricing will be included in a contract which details all the potential origin and destination points and shows the per container rate for all anticipated container sizes. These rates are typically fixed for one-year terms and the customer is only charged when an actual container shipment is made. While the rates are initially all-inclusive, there is generally a fuel surcharge mechanism that is meant to adjust the overall price as fuel costs move up or down subsequent to the initial contract.

Historically, contracts in the container shipping industry have tended to benefit the customer more than the container operator as there is little or no penalty for not meeting expected container volume. This has the effect of binding the container operator in a rising rate environment while allowing the customer to re-bid its business in a declining rate environment. There have been various initiatives to address the inequities both sides see in the present pricing framework, including linking contract pricing to various container pricing indices, but little has changed so far. The continuing growth in credible container pricing indices, all of which are expressed in overall cost per TEU among various trade lanes including any surcharges such as fuel surcharge, is providing additional benchmarks to compare both historical pricing trends and pricing across trade lanes.

The longest and largest container ships in the world currently are a group of six 1,312' long vessels delivered beginning in the second half of 2017 and owned by Hong Kong based Orient Overseas Container Line. To put that into perspective, that is 220' or 20% longer than the largest U.S. aircraft carrier. OOCL has consistently been among the best operating container lines and the average vessel size of its fleet has been at the top among all container operators. These behemoths are also 194' wide and have a maximum draft of 52.5'. At that draft, the vessels have a deadweight capacity of 191,688 tons. The vessels' 107,200 horsepower engine propels it at speeds up to 24 knots while at sea. Samsung Heavy Industries built these vessels for $159 million per ship at their Geoje, South Korea shipyard. All of the vessels, known as the G Class, have been registered under the Hong Kong flag. In terms of container capacity, each of the OOCL vessels can carry 21,413 TEU's. Fully loaded, every ship is carrying $931 million worth of hundreds of different types of cargoes loaded in the containers it carries. That cargo value per vessel is 11.2 times the cargo value of a VLCC tanker and 88 times the cargo value of the largest bulk carriers when they move an iron ore cargo.

The OOCL G class container ships are 62' longer than the Empire State Building is high. In addition to being 20% longer than today's largest aircraft carrier, they are more than 52% longer than the Iowa class battleships, the heaviest warship ever built by the U.S.

At full capacity, each G class vessel will move 312,558 TEU's of containers each year. If connected end to end, that would result in a line of containers stretching 1,104 miles. The value of the products inside those containers would be equal to $13.6 billion. OOCL refers to these vessels as ambassadors of world trade and that is in fact an apt description.

As incredibly large as the G class vessels and the statistics related to the cargo they carry are, even larger vessels are now being built. That is consistent with the past as the size of what constitutes the largest container ship has expanded by more than a factor of five over the past thirty years.

Fittingly, the company founded by C.Y. Tung, one of the individual giants discussed elsewhere, ordered the building of these six ULCV's. OOCL continued to be controlled by descendants of C.Y. Tung and is generally regarded as the most efficient, well-managed company in the container sector. As we go to press, control of OOCL has just been acquired by China's COSCO and the combined operation will be the third largest container operator in the world.

15. Tankers

In 2017 tankers collectively moved 3.5 billion tons of crude oil and refined products, the equivalent of 26 billion barrels worth $1.9 trillion. That works out to 145 gallons for every one of the people on earth. Petroleum that moves by tanker represents 73.4% of total 2017 worldwide consumption of some 97 million barrels per day. In other words, almost three-quarters of the oil used by everyone moves at some point in tankers.

There are currently 4,810 tankers 600' or longer. If lined up end to end, those tankers would stretch out for 760 miles. If you include the tankers between 300' and 600' in length, the worldwide tanker fleet swells to 9,766 ships and the line of ships extends to 1,183 miles. A complete breakdown of tankers of all types based on how they fit within broad size categories is shown in the following table. The categories use the industry terms for tankers and the related deadweight ton range typically defining that category.

All Tankers Category (DWT)	Vessels	Total DWT	DWT/Vessel
Handy 300-600' (< 20,000)	4,956	81,447,552	16,434
Handysize/MR (20-50,000)	1,102	50,173,310	45,529
Panamax/LR1 (50-80,000)	1,147	72,833,286	63,499
Aframax/LR2 (80-120,000)	1,246	130,361,356	104,624
Suezmax (120-200,000)	597	92,231,534	154,492
VLCC (200-325,000)	716	220,066,598	307,356
ULCC (> 325,000)	2	883,146	441,573
Total All Above	9,766	647,996,782	66,352
Subtotal > 600'	4,810	566,549,230	117,786

Tankers are the behemoths of the shipping industry as they are, on average, the largest in terms of average deadweight capacity of all the different types of vessels. The 4,810 tankers over 600' in length have an average deadweight of 117,786 tons, 28% and 59% more deadweight capacity than dry-bulk vessels and container ships, respectively. The large number of very large crude carriers, or VLCC's drives this. The 716 VLCC's represent over 34% of the total deadweight capacity of all tankers and have an average deadweight capacity of 307,356 tons each.

VLCC's are at the top of the pecking order in terms of deadweight capacity and were referred to as super tankers and superships when they initially came into service. Crude oil tankers were the first category of vessels whose typical size expanded exponentially in the postwar period. As the benefits of scale economies became apparent, these vesssels were an inspiration to increase the typical size of other tankers as well as other vessel types.

Traditionally, the primary unit of measurement in the oil business has been the barrel. This goes back to the early logistics of the industry when oil was transported in metal barrels. These barrels could be rolled and stacked and this made transporting oil, first on trucks and then on railroads and general cargo ships, as part of an overall load of mixed cargo possible. While barrels are no longer used in the transport of oil, they have remained the primary unit of measurement. Therefore, it is useful to understand how they relate to other units of measurement.

A barrel contains 42 gallons of liquid when completely full. A typical barrel of crude oil weighs 306 pounds, with slight variations based on where the crude oil comes from. That results in 7.33 barrels in a metric ton of crude oil. As you move into lighter petroleum liquids such as gasoline or heavier liquids such as residual fuel, the weight relationships will change slightly. Because crude oil is the primary liquid moved in tankers, however, those ratios can be broadly used to convert tanker capacity measures into more broadly understood units.

Vessel capacity for both tankers and dry-bulk vessels are most commonly expressed in terms of tons of deadweight capacity as both sectors predominately move weight cargoes that will take the vessel down to its loadline marks, or maximum draft. For instance, the average deadweight capacity of the 716 VLCC's is 307,356 tons. That is the equivalent of 2.3 million barrels and 95 million gallons. To put the latter measure into context, a VLCC's worth of gasoline would be enough fuel to propel 165,709 cars for a year based on the average car in the U.S. going 13,476 miles per year and the average car in the U.S. getting 23.6 miles per gallon. Extending that out to the entire fleet of VLCC's, at any given time if fully loaded they have enough fuel to propel 118 million cars for a year. When you consider that the VLCC's perform multiple annual voyages and that they are only one group of tankers, you realize how directly and significantly shipping is tied into the energy industry. The majority of the fuel in the car you last drove traveled thousands of miles in a tanker.

More than two-thirds of what is now moved in tankers is crude oil moving from oil producing regions to areas where it is refined into various products. Different from container ships where there are hundreds of customers on each vessel who pay an amount per container, tankers typically have one customer for each voyage who pays either a lump sum amount under a voyage charter or time charters the tanker at a rate per day. The term of a voyage charter is self-explanatory. Time charters can be for any stated period. Under a time charter, the customer directs the tanker's movements. The port costs and any terminal costs of loading and unloading the cargo are paid directly by the customer. However, unlike the labor, equipment and land intensive activity of loading and unloading container ships that results in high cargo handling costs, loading and unloading a tanker is more straightforward and less costly.

Tankers carry their liquid cargoes within their hulls in various compartments or holds referred to as tanks. The deck of a tanker is laced with pipes that are utilized to both load and discharge these liquid cargoes. The terminal operations for tankers involve little more than docking the vessel and connecting with shore based pipelines. The liquid is pumped, with the direction depending on whether the tanker is being loaded or discharged, and the liquid flows to designated tanks. The oil is pumped either by pumps on the ship or shoreside pumps in the tank farm. After the initial connection to the shore based pipelines is made, there is little additional effort that is required and the process is monitored, with minor adjustments, until it is completed.

Crude oil cargoes are generally discharged either directly into or near large refineries on the coast. The crude oil will typically be stored in large tank farms until processed by the refinery. If the crude oil is destined for points beyond where it is discharged, it will almost always be moved by pipeline, which is the most cost efficient method for inland movements. In contrast, petroleum product cargoes are generally loaded at those same refineries, with the cargo being the end product of what the refinery made from the crude oil. These refined products are also generally stored in tank farms until they are loaded and will be discharged at facilities in close proximity to the where the product is consumed. For instance, gasoline is a large inbound product for the ports in and around New York City. Lots of refined products are usually moved in barges for final local delivery.

The income statement for a tanker owner revolves almost exclusively around revenue and costs directly related to the ship. The tanker owner is rarely responsible for any loading or unloading costs or costs that go beyond the operating, fuel and capital costs of the vessel itself. In that sense, the income statement of a tanker owner, similar to a dry-bulk ship owner, is almost totally related to the shipping business. This is quite different from the income statement of a container ship owner and operator where only some 25% of costs are directly related to its vessels, with the balance comprised of significant cargo handling, equipment, inland transportation and marketing costs.

Tanker pricing and pricing indices are expressed in terms of a daily rate that covers crew, maintenance, stores, supplies and insurance as well as capital cost and profit but which excludes fuel cost. Customers contract for tankers either on at a lump sum to move a full load cargo from one point to another or based on a daily time charter rate where the customer pays the fuel and port costs. If on the former basis where the tanker owner paid for the fuel and port costs, these can be backed out and the resulting net revenue can be divided by the relevant days to determine the time charter equivalent, or TCE, daily rate.

These TCE rates are the primary pricing benchmarks in the tanker sector and allow historical comparisons as well as comparisons across trade lanes among the various types of tankers. The TCE rates for tankers are determined at the intersection of vessel supply and demand and are quite volatile when either factor changes even by a small amount.

The Worldscale Association maintains another widely used tanker pricing benchmark. Worldscale is a unified system for establishing payment of a freight rate per ton given the origin and destination of the tanker's cargo. It was established in 1952 by a consortium of brokers and is based on the average total cost of shipping oil from one port to another. It involves a large matrix table resulting from 320,000 voyages, which include almost all permutations from single and multiple loading and discharge ports. When negotiating a price, the table is referred to as WS100 or 100% of Worldscale. The actual price the parties agree will be expressed as a percent of Worldscale. This results in pricing indices that can not only be compared to similar historical shipments but also to shipments across the many different origin and destinations points.

Crude tankers comprise 68% of the total deadweight capacity of tankers while representing just 27% of the number of tankers afloat. An even larger group in terms of number of tankers, however, is product tankers and tankers that can accommodate either products or chemicals, which comprise 22% of total deadweight capacity and 57% of the number of tankers. Products refer to anything that is an output from a refinery where the input was crude oil. Gasoline, diesel, kerosene, naphtha and heating oil are all products that move in product tankers.

The remaining types of tankers are even more specialized and collectively represent 10% of total deadweight capacity and 16% of the number of tankers afloat. Chemical only tankers have stainless steel holds designed to accommodate an array of very specialized chemicals. Liquefied natural gas, or LNG, and liquefied petroleum gas, or LPG, are petroleum-based outputs that move at cryogenic or very low temperatures on sophisticated tankers specifically designed to accommodate only those products. Finally, there is a small group of tankers specifically designed to carry special single cargoes such as orange juice, molten sulfur and asphalt that are fairly unique and outside of the earlier types.

A complete breakdown of the 9,766 tankers over 300' in length by type of tanker is shown in the table below.

Tanker Type	Vessels	% Category
Crude	2,658	27.2%
Product	1,625	16.6%
Product/Chemical	3,896	39.9%
Chemical	121	1.2%
LNG	485	5.0%
LPG	837	8.6%
Other	144	1.4%
Total	9,766	100.0%

Focusing solely on crude tankers, of the 2,658 total in the table above, 2,549 or 96% are more than 600' long. This is understandable as crude oil moves long distances while short voyages are the main deployment of smaller vessels. The 2,549 crude oil tankers over 600' in length have an average deadweight of 170,314 tons. Crude oil typically works out to an average of 7.33 barrels per ton, with some variation depending on the grade of crude oil. That means that just the average crude oil tanker can carry over one million barrels of crude oil. The table below is a breakdown of all of the crude tankers in the world including the relatively small number between 300' and 600' in length. The categories are broken down using the common names that are usually used to describe them, with the deadweight range that equates to that name also shown. In addition to the number of vessels and total deadweight capacity of each category, the average deadweight capacity per vessel of each category is shown.

Crude Tankers Category (DWT)	Vessels	Total DWT	DWT/Vessel
Handy 300-600' (< 20,000)	109	3,184,152	29,212
Handysize (20-50,000)	38	1,760,043	46,317
Panamax (50-80,000)	272	19,176,728	70,503
Aframax (80-120,000)	954	103,860,813	108,869
Suezmax (120-200,000)	567	88,383,939	155,880
VLCC (200-325,000)	716	220,066,598	307,356
ULCC (> 325,000)	2	883,146	441,573
Total All Above	2,658	437,315,419	164,528
Subtotal > 600'	2,549	434,131,267	170,314

The majority of crude tanker tonnage is represented by the size class known as VLCC's, an acronym that stands for Very Large Crude Carrier. The VLCC's, sometimes referred to by the shortened acronym of VL's, were the first giant cargo ships and began appearing in earnest in the 1960's. The initial catalyst was the closing of the Suez Canal during the 1956 Mideast crisis. Tanker owners were forced to move crude oil around the tip of Africa in much longer voyages and quickly began to recognize the economies of scale and greater cost efficiency per unit mile at sea that would result from larger vessels. Tankers were the first segment to embrace this reality and the term superships initially only applied to tankers. Eventually, the dry-bulk segment would follow the lead of tankers and, many years later, the container sector would take the same approach.

In 1958, American Daniel K. Ludwig built the first super tanker and vessel that broke the 100,000-ton deadweight barrier. Larger tankers followed with the record alternating frequently between Ludwig and Greek shipowners Stavros Niarchos and Aristotle Onassis. Fuel costs are a significant expense for all ships, particularly for large VLCC's, and the sharp increase in oil prices in the early 1970's further supported the case for the economies of scale that VLCC's produced. In the late 1970's, a number of vessels were built that were even larger than VLCC's. A new category name emerged and they were called ULCC's, for Ultra Large Crude Carrier. Within this category is the largest tanker and vessel ever built. The *Seawise Giant*, delivered in 1980 to shipowner C.Y. Tung, had a deadweight capacity of 564,763 tons. It was 1,504' in length and 226' wide and when fully loaded had a draft of 81'. Like an iceberg, a fully loaded tanker has much more of itself under the water than above the water.

Currently there are 716 VLCC's and 2 ULCC's that collectively represent 51% of the total capacity of crude oil tankers. Each of these vessels can move some 2.3 million barrels of crude oil. At a crude oil price of $59 per barrel, that cargo is worth $135 million. However, that is after the decline in oil prices. A few years ago at a crude oil price of $100 per barrel, the cargo value of a VLCC full of crude oil was $230 million. The current VLCC cargo value is just 15% of the cargo value on the largest container ships, but it is still several times the cargo value on the largest dry-bulk vessels moving iron ore. Comparing the cargo value on a VLCC to the current cost of building a new VLCC, the crude oil cargo is worth 129% of the ship.

In terms of the historical development of tankers, they can be traced back to 1892 when the predecessor of Royal Dutch Shell moved Russian crude oil in 5,010 deadweight tankers from the Black Sea to the Far East via the Suez Canal. While small by today's standards, they were giants at the time. However, the international trade in crude oil and related products was relatively modest then and much of it moved in wooden barrels or cans on general cargo ships. Prior to the invention and widespread use of automobiles, the underlying demand for petroleum and related products was a very small fraction of what it would become.

As trade in oil expanded with the automobile, the cost of moving much larger quantities in barrels and cans quickly resulted in companies refining methods for the bulk transport of oil. By the early part of the twentieth century, most of the seaborne crude oil trade was moving on tankers. With that development, tankers were the first category of special purpose ships.

However, in the U.S. and various other countries with growth in automobiles, the large majority of crude oil demand was being sourced domestically. The fleets of the two largest oil companies in the world highlight one example of the relative smallness of the early tanker sector in 1907. Royal Dutch Shell had 24 steam driven oil tankers and Standard Oil, the forerunner of Exxon Mobil among others, had 20 tankers, but 16 were sail powered. Most of these early tankers were small and involved mainly in coastal trade. The international oil trade would remain fairly insignificant until World War II. From there, it would grow exponentially and demand would be satisfied with tankers, which would consistentaly grew in both number and average size.

The tanker sector was the first to realize the scale economic benefits of giant cargo ships. It was also the first sector to operate ships that were so big that other considerations outweighed those benefits. This is evident by the shrinking number of ULCC's. The largest ULCC and the largest vessel ever built, the *Seawise Giant*, was scrapped in 2010. From what once were dozens of operating ULCC's, only two exist today. Many were first converted to floating storage units as these behemoths proved to be too limited in the ports and facilities they could utilize.

The largest existing ULCC today is the *Overseas Laura Lynn*, a 441,573 deadweight ton tanker built in 2003. With a length of 1,246', a width of 233' and a loaded draft of 81', this giant surpasses all ships on all dimensions except for the biggest container ships that are longer. Fully loaded, the *Overseas Laura Lynn* is moving 129 million gallons of crude oil. When converted to gasoline, that amount is enough to propel 226,174 cars for a year based on a typical car going 13,476 miles annually and an average fuel consumption of 23.6 miles per gallon. In my role as an investor at a large hedge fund, I recommended and implemented a nine-figure investment as a key part of a more than billion-dollar re-capitalization of the company that owned the *Overseas Laura Lynn*.

The places where VLCC's can readily go are constrained by port facilities and canals. In the case of canals, the length, width and draft limitation of the locks are the primary constraints. All of those dimensions play a role in the ports VLCC's can access, but in most cases the most frequent constraint is draft, or how deep in the water the hull goes. This is particularly the case with VLCC's. When loaded with the maximum amount of crude oil they can safely carry, VLCC's have a draft of 76'. At that draft, a VLCC has a freeboard, which is a measure of how far the hull extends above the water line, of 24' when fully loaded. In other words, VLCC's have 3 times as much of their hulls underwater as they do above water when they are fully loaded. The draft of these giant tankers limits the port facilities VLCC's can access. The largest routes for VLCC's include the Arabian Gulf to Asia and the Arabian Gulf to the Louisiana Offshore Oil Port, or LOOP, via Africa's Cape of Good Hope.

As you move down in size classes from VLCC's, the next size class is Suezmax tankers. As the name implies, they represent the largest tankers that can transit the Suez Canal fully loaded. They have approximately half the crude oil capacity of VLCC's. Suezmax tankers generally carry 1 million barrels of crude oil. There are 567 Suezmax tankers with an average deadweight capacity of 155,880 tons and collectively they represent 20% of the total capacity of crude oil tankers. The largest routes for Suezmaxes are from the Arabian Gulf to Europe and West Africa to Europe.

The next crude oil tanker size class is Aframax. The name is derived from Average Freight Rate Assessment (AFRA), a tanker rate system developed in 1954 by Shell Oil to standardize shipping contract terms. Aframax tankers range in deadweight from 80,000 to 120,000 tons and typically carry one-third the amount of crude oil as a VLCC. Aframax tankers can serve most of the ports in the world and the 954 vessels in this size class make them the largest category of crude oil tankers in terms of number of vessels. With an average deadweight capacity of 108,869 tons,

Aframax tankers collectively represent 24% of the total capacity of crude oil tankers. These workhorses are most used in medium range trade lanes and are particularly prevalent in voyages involving the Caribbean Sea, Black Sea, North Sea, South China Sea and Mediterranean Sea.

On a combined basis, the VLCC, Suezmax and Aframax crude segments account for 94% of total deadweight capacity among the tankers that move crude oil. Together these groups of tankers efficiently move crude oil from where it is produced to where it is refined in hundreds of port pairs spanning the globe.

The smaller tanker sizes, Panamax and Handysize, are used in a very limited way in short sea and coastal trade lanes. These sizes are inefficient to move crude oil in any of the larger trade lanes and as such they are very underrepresented in the crude oil sector. As you will see, however, this size range is more actively used and relevant in the product tanker and dry-bulk sectors.

After crude oil, the most significant cargo moved in tankers is the range of refined petroleum products. These products include clean products such as gasoline, kerosene, naphtha and jet fuel and dirty products such as heating oil and diesel oil. In the refinery, the top of the distillation process are the light aromatic products such as naphtha. The bottom is asphalt and bunker oil typically used as ship fuel. If a product tanker has been used to move dirty products, it will require a particularly thorough cleaning if it then wants to move clean products. Crude oil is moved inbound to refineries and all the various products are moved outbound from refineries.

Traditionally the product tanker trade was inverted by direction compared to the crude oil trade. It wasn't unusual to even see a product tanker return and discharge products at the same place where the crude oil was initially loaded. However, this has changed as traditional areas where crude oil is produced are now building refineries. As and where this displacement occurs, what previously moved outbound in crude oil tankers will now move outbound in product tankers. In addition to the effect this trend will have on the mix of tanker types, it will also result in increases in the typical size of product tankers to move towards the scale economies of the large crude oil tankers.

Product tankers are much smaller than crude oil tankers and on average typically carry one-third the amount of total cargo. In addition to the size difference, product tankers have more cargo tanks than crude oil tankers and those tanks need to have special coatings to hold up to the more corrosive nature of refined products. Product tankers often carry several lots of different products for various customers. Size, cleanliness, compartment and coating differences limit the switching between the crude oil and products trades and there are no examples of a tanker discharging a crude oil cargo and then loading a product cargo from the same refinery.

Many product tankers can also readily move various petroleum-based chemicals that are further down the distillation chain. Until you get to very specialized chemicals that require stainless steel tanks or heated tanks, most petro-chemicals can move in the same cargo tanks on product tankers. Regulators categorize chemicals based on the degree of hazard they represent. Only the most toxic or corrosive chemicals require tanks coated with stainless steel or zinc. Many less hazardous chemicals can also move in product tankers.

The distinction between product tankers and chemical tankers is not easy and many are referred to as combination product/chemical tankers. For this reason, we will look at both tankers that are categorized as product tankers and tankers categorized as combined product/chemical tankers. That overall group is comprised of a total of 5,521 ships, of which 1,491 are more than 600' in length.

Of that overall group, 1,625 are categorized as just product tankers. The breakdown of those vessels is shown in the following table.

Product Tankers Category (DWT)	Vessels	Total DWT	DWT/Vessel
Handy 300-600' (< 20,000)	1,367	20,984,891	15,351
MR (20-50,000)	53	2,244,810	44,242
LR1 (50-80,000)	172	12,530,237	72,850
LR2 (80-120,000)	33	3,540,465	107,287
Total All Above	1,625	39,400,403	24,246
Subtotal > 600'	258	18,415,512	71,378

More than two-thirds of that larger overall group, or 3,896 ships in total, are categorized as combination product/chemical tankers. The breakdown of those vessels is shown in the following table.

Product/Chemical Tankers (DWT)	Vessels	Total DWT	DWT/Vessel
Handy 300-600' (< 20,000)	2,663	46,783,140	17,568
MR (20-50,000)	918	41,980,407	45,730
LR1 (50-80,000)	308	16,182,757	52,541
LR2 (80-120,000)	7	646,130	92,304
Total All Above	3,896	105,592,434	27,103
Subtotal > 600'	1,233	58,809,294	47,696

Product tankers have a unique nomenclature with vessels over 600' long referred to as MR's, LR1's and LR2's. Crude tankers of the same size are referred to as Handysize, Panamax and Aframax, respectively, but with coated tanks they are described by acronyms that stand for Medium Range, Long Range 1 and Long Range 2. The MR's are typically involved in short, often coastal voyages while the LR's are typically involved in longer voyages. The main distinction between LR1's and LR2's is vessel size, with the latter deployed in the largest product tanker trade lanes.

The primary physical difference between crude tankers and product tankers is the tank coating. Product tankers can therefore also move crude oil and are sometimes used for this purpose. Sour crude, defined as crude with a sulfur content of more than one-half of one percent, can be corrosive and often moves in tankers with coated tanks. In addition, product tankers are often segmented into more compartments in order to carry various grades of petroleum products. In order to increase the flexibility of a tanker, a recent trend has developed where vessels destined for the crude oil segment are also built with coated tanks which is much more cost efficient than having tanks coated at some later date. Such vessels can rotate between the crude oil and petroleum products segments, although a thorough cleaning will be needed prior to moving from crude to product. This recent trend has been particularly evident with Aframax tankers and those with coated tanks can transition and deploy on LR2 trade lanes.

The next group of specialized tankers is pure chemical tankers that have stainless steel tanks to move very corrosive chemicals such as sulfuric acid. Cargoes in this group also include vegetable oil and other consumable liquids. Often called parcel tankers as they move many different chemicals in various tanks for different customers, these vessels are among the smallest type of tankers. These chemical tankers with stainless steel tanks are typically much smaller than the combination product-chemical tankers which can also move less corrosive petro-chemicals. This group of pure chemical tankers is comprised of a total of 118 ships, of which only 10 are more than 600' in length. The breakdown of these vessels is shown in the following table.

Chemical Tankers Category (DWT)	Vessels	Total DWT	DWT/Vessel
Handy 300-600' (< 20,000)	118	1,679,998	14,237
MR (20-50,000)	3	108,673	36,224
Total All Above	121	1,788,671	14,782
Subtotal > 600'	3	108,673	36,224

LNG tankers are the most sophisticated and expensive specialized tankers afloat and are vessels designed to move liquefied natural gas, or LNG. To transport natural gas by vessel, it must be liquefied through a process that reduces it to a liquid state with a temperature of minus 260 degrees Fahrenheit. These tankers move the LNG in cryogenic cargo containment systems with sophisticated insulation and refrigeration plants that result in maintaining that low cargo temperature throughout the voyage. As a result, LNG tankers cost two and three times the amount of a similar sized crude oil tanker and are the most costly cargo ships in the world.

LNG movements involve large vessels and long voyages. Overall the worldwide LNG tanker fleet is comprised of a total of 485 ships, of which 460 are more than 600' in length. The largest trade lanes for LNG currently originate in Qatar and Australia but the U.S. is now a large exporter of LNG due to shale production. The breakdown of these vessels is shown in the following table.

LNG Tankers Category (DWT)	Vessels	Total DWT	DWT/Vessel
Handy 300-600' (< 20,000)	25	333,439	13,338
Handysize (20-50,000)	8	299,439	37,430
Panamax (50-80,000)	170	12,605,006	74,147
Aframax (80-120,000)	252	22,313,948	88,547
Suezmax (120-200,000)	30	3,847,595	128,253
Total All Above	485	39,399,427	81,236
Subtotal > 600'	460	39,065,988	84,926

LPG tankers are a somewhat similar but less sophisticated group of tankers specially designed to move liquefied petroleum gas, or LPG. Propane is by far the largest category of LPG, accounting for some three-quarters of all LPG, followed by butane. Propane is used for cooking and heating and is most familiar to retail consumers in the form of the five gallon cylinders connected to barbeque grills. These products are natural gas liquids that are by-products of gas and oil production. They typically move in vessels with pressurized compartments that do not require refrigeration. Smaller LPG vessels utilize refrigeration and the cargo is moved at atmospheric pressure.

LPG movements often involve smaller vessels and short coastal voyages. Overall the worldwide LPG tanker fleet is comprised of a total of 837 ships, of which 300 are more than 600' in length. These larger vessels are primarily involved in the U.S. to Asia and Qatar to Asia trade lanes. The U.S. just recently became the largest exporter of propane in the world. The growth in U.S. exports due to shale production is the reason this largest LPG tanker segment has grown by more than one-third in just the last couple of years. These vessels can move the equivalent of more than six million five-gallon cylinders of propane each. A complete breakdown of these vessels is shown in the following table.

LPG Tankers Category (DWT)	Vessels	Total DWT	DWT/Vessel
Handy 300-600' (< 20,000)	537	7,173,159	13,358
Handysize (20-50,000)	75	3,409,993	45,467
Panamax (50-80,000)	225	12,338,558	54,838
Total All Above	837	22,921,710	27,386
Subtotal > 600'	300	15,748,551	52,495

The last type of tankers are a small group of tankers with heated holds to move cargoes such as hot asphalt, molten sulfur and hot molasses and refrigerated holds to move orange juice, wine, beer, stout and various fruit juices. These are niche trades that are dominated by small tankers that tend to move in recurring voyages. The largest vessels in this segment move orange juice from Brazil to both the U.S. and Europe. The cargo owners that move orange juice and wine in small tanker loads do not go out of their way to discuss these logistics as moving food products through the pipeline system is not appetizing. Overall, this segment has 144 tankers, only 7 of which are more than 600' long, involved in moving a dozen or so specialized cargoes that aren't normally associated with tankers. A complete breakdown of these vessels is shown in the following table.

Other Tankers Category (DWT)	Vessels	Total DWT	DWT/Vessel
Handy 300-600' (< 20,000)	137	1,308,773	9,553
Handysize (20-50,000)	7	269,945	38,564
Total All Above	144	1,578,718	10,963
Subtotal > 600'	7	269,945	38,564

16. Bulk Carriers

In 2017 bulk carriers moved 4.5 billion tons of dry-bulk products. That is the equivalent of 1,352 pounds for each person in the world. While a wide array of products move, the largest dry-bulk commodities are iron ore, coal, wheat and corn that represent three-quarters of the total cargo moved. An estimated 36.4% of combined annual worldwide production of those commodities move on bulk carriers.

If you exclude China's large production of those same commodities, as all are consumed domestically and therefore do not move on bulk carriers, the products that move by vessel represents 62.6% of the remaining total. In other words, excluding those key domestic commodities, effectively almost two-thirds of the world's major dry-bulk commodities are transported on bulk carriers.

In terms of cargo weight, the products that move in bulk carriers represent 42.9% of total marine shipments. These products are characterized by their relatively low value compared to the other segments. Only 6.5% of the total cargo value shipped by water moves on bulk carriers. Not surprisingly, dry-bulk vessels are relatively slow moving. They perform only 6.4 voyages per year resulting in an overall average speed of 8.76 knots including time spent in port.

There are currently 7,849 bulk carriers 600' or longer. Stretched out end to end, those vessels would be a 1,203-mile long line of ships. If you include the bulk carriers between 300' and 600' in length, the bulker fleet worldwide swells to 9,420 ships that would stretch 1,336 miles. There are more bulk carriers than any other ship type in the world. A complete breakdown of those vessels based on size categories is shown in the following table.

All Bulk Carriers Catergory (DWT)	Vessels	Total DWT	DWT/Vessel
Handy 300-600' (< 25,000)	1,571	30,520,656	19,428
Handysize (25-35,000)	63	1,668,189	26,479
Handymax (35-50,000)	863	36,806,561	42,650
Panamax (50-80,000)	3,887	244,101,745	62,800
Capesize (80-200,000)	2,562	322,147,147	125,740
VLOC (+200,000)	424	116,548,383	245,883
Total All Above	9,420	751,792,681	79,808
Subtotal > 600'	7,849	721,272025	91,893

Bulk carriers are the workhorses of the shipping industry and move an array of generally heavy dry-bulk commodities. The largest of these is iron ore, which represents 30% of the total shipments on dry-bulk vessels. This is followed by coal at 26%, both steam coal used in power plants to produce electricity and coking or metallurgical coal used in the production of steel. Steam coal shipments equal to 20% of the total are more than three times the quantity of coking coal shipments equal to 6% of the total. Next in size are the main food products, corn and wheat, at 10% and 8%. Together these commodities are referred to as the major bulks and represent 75%

of the cargo that moves on bulk carriers. The remaining 25% is represented by what are referred to as the minor bulks. The minor bulks include an array of dozens of smaller bulk products, including nickel ore, steel, sugar, bauxite, forest products, wood chips, paper rolls, scrap metal, fertilizers and cement.

Collectively bulk carriers move 27.4 trillion ton-miles of bulk cargo annually. On a per capita basis, this works out to 3,630 ton-miles of cargo annually for every man, women and child in the world. To put that into more vivid context, a man pushing a wheelbarrow loaded with 100 pounds of material 24 hours per day, 365 days per year results in 1,212 ton-miles of freight activity. That is just one-third of the per capita activity of the world's dry-bulk fleet.

The dry-bulk sector is most directly tied to worldwide steel production as 36% of the cargo tons moved are raw materials used to produce steel. To produce a ton of steel in a modern blast furnace requires, as a rule of thumb, 1.5 tons of iron ore and 0.8 tons of coking coal as the primary inputs. Total annual steel production worldwide is now running at 1.6 billion tons. More than 800 million tons, or just over half of total worldwide production, is now being produced in China. Twenty years ago China was barely producing one-tenth as much steel as it is producing today.

The incredible growth in China's steel production, almost all of which is consumed domestically, is primarily related to the commercial and residential real estate and the roads and infrastructure needed for the urbanization of hundreds of millions of people. The growth that resulted from this was truly a super cycle for the shipping industry. As sharp as the growth in steel production in China was, the growth in seaborne iron ore imports was even higher. The reason for this is that China's domestic iron ore quality is poor and its production growth couldn't keep up with the growth in steel production.

In the recent past China has been the predominant catalyst for the shipping industry and the driver of much of the demand growth. If China is the dominant force in container shipping where it accounts for more than 35% of world volume, it is even more important in dry-bulk shipping. Today China accounts for two-thirds of global seaborne iron ore demand and over one-third of seaborne coal demand. In the dry-bulk sector, almost every vessel will typically have two voyages per year to China. That concentration is directly related to the ascendency of China as the world's major steel producer. This has fueled an average growth rate of iron ore imports into China since 2001 equal to a staggering 21% per year. The impact of China's so-called super cycle on the shipping markets is covered more in detail in a later chapter.

The loading and unloading of bulk carriers is more costly and complicated than liquid bulk tankers. Access to the cargo holds is through large hatches that are either temporarily lifted off or opened hydraulically by sliding to each side. Prior to loading, the holds are inspected to assure that they are clean of any prior cargo. This is particularly important if any grain or food cargoes are to be loaded.

The primary means of loading most bulk carriers is via a cargo gravity chute or conveyor belt where gravity does much of the work. Because dry commodities are dropping into the hold at a high rate, the loading activity of a dry-bulk vessel is often a dusty experience. The labor needed to load a bulk carrier is fairly minimal and mostly involved with regulating the flow of commodities going into the cargo hold and directing the positioning of the cargo gravity chute or conveyor belt.

The crew of the vessel is also involved in planning the sequence of loading the various holds as well as supervising vessel draft and condition during loading.

It is more difficult to unload a bulk carrier than load it because you don't have gravity working with you. The unloading process primarily involves clamshell buckets that scoop up several tons at a time or suction devices that continuously vacuum up lighter cargo such as grain. The unloading process takes longer than the longer process and involves more labor and a higher overall cost. It also involves a broad range in terms of efficiencies by discharge port where bucket size, number of cranes, crane speed and labor cost will all effect the time involved in unloading.

A vivid example of how these factors can come together to result in a surprising outcome occurred with me in 1981. I was port captain for the discharge of a vessel with 12,000 tons of bulk wheat in Port Said, Egypt. Driven by limited mechanization and low labor cost, the vessel was literally discharged by hand where dozens of three man teams worked together. One scooped the wheat into a burlap bag held by another, while the third man sewed the bag. The loaded bags were then fed to an endless line of men who put them on their shoulders, walked a wooden plank to shore and then loaded the bags on trucks. Fortunately, that was and is an exception. In most ports in the world today, the discharge of bulk carriers is highly mechanized and efficient.

Self-unloading bulk carriers were originally developed on the Great Lakes to more efficiently move pellitized iron ore in short voyage between ports in the Great Lakes. They discharge their cargo from hopper shaped cargo holds that feed a recessed conveyor that brings the bulk product up on to the deck and out onto a boom over the side of the ship. While still extensively used in shipments within the Great Lakes, this discharging system has had only limited success in other markets. The lost cargo space and cost of the discharging system, along with the limited number of dry-bulk commodities and discharge ports where it is viewed as acceptable, have prevented it from expanding into other markets.

Prior to the advent of the modern bulk carrier, dry-bulk cargoes were moved in general cargo ships. While the multiple decks on these vessels gave them maximum flexibility, they were not very well suited for loading dry-bulk cargoes. The layout required additional labor to move cargo that was in a conical pile in the middle of the hold by shifting the cargo into the wings. In addition, if often involved fitting cargoes with shifting boards and constructing temporary bulkheads to ensure there were no void spaces where dry-bulk cargo could flow while the ship was at sea.

A cardinal safety rule is that any area where a dry-bulk cargo is stowed should be full with no open space where the commodity can shift as the vessel pitches and rolls at sea. Shifting cargo produces a situation where the vessel isn't riding on an even keel. With each movement, this makes a ship more unstable and in the worst case results in the vessel capsizing. The time and expense in handling dry-bulk cargoes and preventing cargo shifting, whether as full or partial ship loads, in general cargo ships bore no relation to the fast and efficient processes used with modern bulk carriers today.

The revolution in cargo handling related to the largest vessel segment today goes back to 1954 and a shipbroker named Ole Skaarup. Skaarup was actively involved in brokering charters for vessels moving full dry-bulk loads. He was keenly aware of the inefficiencies at the same time he was seeing sharp growth in the demand to move full dry-bulk loads. Focusing solely on what would be the best design for a ship exclusively moving dry-bulk, he came up with a design which had several straightforward innovations. The vessel would have large holds with no internal decks and wide hatches to maximize loading and unloading efficiency. The top deck would be free of any derricks or rigging as the vessel would rely on cranes and other mechanized means at the discharge port to unload the ship.

The key design feature that Skaarup came up with was that the large holds should also be inward slanting at the top. This acted to minimize any empty space in the hold as dry-bulk cargoes were being loaded. The hold would mirror the natural flow of dry-bulk cargoes. This would automatically avoid dangerous situations that could develop at sea from cargo shifting. Skaarup also designed similar inward slanting at the bottom of the holds to have the natural flow of dry-bulk cargoes to also assist with the discharge process.

Skaarup had come up with a permanent and efficient solution by developing a specialized vessel with cargo holds configured to work with how dry-bulk cargoes flowed. Instead of fitting the cargo with the vessel, he fit the vessel with the cargo. Skaarup took his idea to a large shipper and obtained a commitment that gave him confidence to build a vessel based on his design. In 1956, he took delivery of the *Melvin H. Baker,* a 17,940-deadweight ton dry-bulk carrier. The loading and unloading efficiencies from the operation of the *Melvin H. Baker* exceeded all expectations. From that point forward, all full load movements of dry-bulk commodities would move on this new segment of specialized vessels.

As purpose built bulk carriers took hold, they began ramping up in size to achieve the scale economies and per unit mile at sea cost efficiencies pioneered by the tanker segment. The growth in steel production in Japan and other areas without sufficient natural resources in particular fueled the demand for larger dry-bulk carriers. In addition, the increase in electricity production around the world resulted in growing coal exports. Dry-bulk trade moved first towards Panamax size bulk carriers, typically around 55,000 deadweight tons.

It wasn't too long before the demand for iron ore, the key raw material for steel, made larger bulk carriers that couldn't transit either the Panama or Suez canals the preferred size for moving iron ore. Known as Capesize vessels because they had to sail around the tips of South America and Africa, they became to shipments of iron ore what VLCC's were to shipments of crude oil. Despite longer voyages because they couldn't use the canals, the extraordinary scale economics these vessels offered translated into their being the most cost efficient way to move mostly iron ore and occasionally coal cargoes.

Similar to tankers, the income statement of bulk carrier companies is driven by revenue and expenses directly related to the ship and the cost of loading and unloading cargo is generally paid by the cargo owner. The dry-bulk vessel owner is focused on the operating, fuel and capital costs of the vessel itself. In that sense, the income statement of a dry-bulk owner, similar to a tanker owner, is almost totally related to the shipping business. This is quite different from the income statement of a container ship owner and operator where only 25% of costs are directly related to its vessels, with the balance comprised of significant cargo handling, equipment, inland transportation and marketing costs.

Dry-bulk pricing and pricing indices for voyage and time chartered vessels are expressed in terms of a daily rate that covers crew and other operating costs as well as capital cost and profit but which excludes fuel cost. Customers contract for dry-bulk vessels either on a lump sum to move a full load cargo from one point to another or based on a daily time charter rate where the fuel and port costs are paid directly by the customer. If on the former basis where the dry-bulk owner paid for the fuel and port costs, these can be backed out and the resulting net revenue can be divided by the relevant days to determine the time charter equivalent, or TCE, daily rate.

These TCE rates are the primary pricing benchmarks in the dry-bulk sector and allow historical comparisons as well as comparisons across trade lanes among the various types of dry-bulk ships. The TCE rates for dry-bulk ships are determined at the intersection of vessel supply and demand and are volatile when either factor changes even by a small amount.

The most widely used pricing index in the dry-bulk sector is the Baltic Dry Index, or BDI. The BDI is a daily freight index issued by the Baltic Exchange in London and is a composite taking into account 23 major shipping routes for moving dry-bulk commodities in the four main sizes of dry-bulk vessels. Those sizes, starting with the smallest and going to the largest, are Handysize, Handymax, Panamax and Capesize. The routes used in the BDI primarily cover the movement of iron ore, coal and grains. While the historical origins of the Baltic Exchange go back to 1744 in a coffee house in London where merchants met to discuss their business interests, the daily BDI has only been published since 1985. In addition to the composite BDI, the Baltic Exchange publishes indices for each size category expressed in terms of the timecharter equivalent rate per day.

The BDI has become a familiar index to many people outside of shipping as some view it as a leading economic indicator and it is often reported on by the financial press, particular when it moves sharply. A misnomer of the BDI is that it is a measure of all shipping. The BDI is solely related to dry-bulk shipping and it does not measure anything in either the container or tanker sector. However, there are times when various sectors will move in similar directions.

Some indication of the extraordinary volatility of the dry-bulk sector comes from reviewing the recent history of the BDI. On May 20, 2008, the BDI hit an all-time high of 11,793. That period was consistent with the peak of a shipping super cycle, driven in large part by China. A little more than six months later, as the effect of the financial crisis took hold on shipping, the BDI had collapsed 94% to 663. As we go to press, the BDI is at 2,131. While that is well above the all time low of 290 four years ago, it is 82% below its 2008 peak. The volatility and economics of the dry-bulk and all the shipping sectors is reviewed in other chapters.

Within the bulk carrier category, there is very limited specialization in terms of vessel characteristics and unloading mechanisms. For the most part, however, bulk carriers can move almost any dry commodity. The table below breaks down the overall bulk carrier category into various types of bulk carriers.

Bulk Carrier Type	Vessels	% Category
General Bulk Carrier	8,537	90.6%
Ore Carrier	226	2.4%
Self-Unloading Bulker	133	1.4%
Ore/Bulk/Oil	1	0.0%

Other Specialized	523	5.6%
Total	9,420	100.0%

There are 8,537 general bulk carriers over 300' in length, with the large majority of those, or 7,361, over 600' in length. The average capacity in terms of deadweight of the entire group is 78,361 tons while the average deadweight for bulk carriers over 600' in length is 87,268 tons. The table below breaks down the general bulk carrier group by size range using the category name they are most frequently referred to and the general deadweight ton range for that category.

General Bulk Carriers (DWT)	Vessels	Total DWT	DWT/Vessel
Handy 300-600' (< 25,000)	1,176	26,588,606	22,609
Handysize (25-35,000)	36	1,013,908	28,016
Handymax (35-50,000)	761	32,273,469	42,409
Panamax (50-80,000)	3,773	236,913,924	62,792
Capesize (80-200,000)	2,535	319,161,025	125,902
VLOC (> 200,000)	256	53,018,112	207,102
Total All Above	8,537	668,969,044	78,361
Subtotal > 600'	7,361	642,380,438	87,268

Capesize vessels are the largest category of dry-bulk vessels, making up 56% of total deadweight capacity. In order to traverse between the largest oceans, these vessels must pass either the Cape of Good Hope around Africa or Cape Horn around South America, which is how they got their name. Capesize vessels are almost exclusively involved in the movement of iron ore and coal. A subset of Capesize vessels are the largest dry-bulk vessels in the world and are now referred to as Very Large Ore Carriers, or VLOC's. These vessels are entirely involved in the movement of iron ore and on almost all voyages are destined to China.

Panamax vessels are the next largest category of bulk carriers and are so named because they are able to transit the Panama Canal fully loaded. As all of the constraints related to the Suez Canal are more generous, any ship that can go through the Panama Canal can readily go through the Suez Canal. The limitations in moving through a typical canal are related to the dimensions of the locks that are used to raise and lower ships, as the water levels in the bodies of water canals connect are different. In the case of the Panama Canal, those lock dimensions prior to the recent expansion meant that vessels could be no longer than 950', no wider than 106' and no deeper in terms of draft than 39.5'. Panamax vessels are primarily involved in the movement of coal and the major bulk grains of corn and wheat.

Just thirty years ago, almost all ships except for the biggest tankers could actually go through the Panama Canal. The continuing growth in vessel dimensions across sectors has changed that dramatically. Driven by this change and desiring to re-capture business, Panama launched a multi-billion expansion and enlargement of the Panama Canal locks. Fully completed in 2017, the new locks allow vessels with a length up to 1,201', a width up to 161' and a draft up to 50' to transit the Panama Canal.

The completion of the new Panama Canal has had a pronounced effect on all shipping sectors, particularly the container sector. Less important, but of note, it has also thrown into disarray the terms historically used to describe different vessel size categories. No consensus has yet developed in the dry-bulk segment on what those terms will be and the historical terms continue to be utilized.

Handymax is the next size category after Panamax. Unlike Capesize and Panamax, which are categories defined by maximum routes, the ports they utilize broadly define Handymax. Larger Handymax vessels are also often referred to as Supramax vessels. While smaller than Panamax, these vessels are still longer than 600'. The characteristic that is shared by most Handymax vessels is that they have onboard cranes or other methods of unloading bulk cargo. Because they are often involved in voyages to ports with limited infrastructure, it is necessary for these vessels to be self-sufficient. Handymax vessels are primarily involved in movements of grain and lesser bulk commodities.

Handysize is the smallest category of bulk carrier and they are very similar to Handymax except they are generally one-third smaller. Handysize vessels move a broad array of products including minor grains, steel products, phosphate, logs, cement, woodchips, paper rolls and assorted other break bulk cargoes. It is not unusual for a Handysize bulk carrier to move different cargoes in different holds. Handysize vessels are almost always geared with onboard cranes and hydraulically operated hatch covers to result in efficient cargo operations in almost all ports. As their name implies, Handysize vessels can flexibly adapt to various situations. These vessels tend to be concentrated on ports and terminals with draft and length limitations and most are primarily involved in regional trade routes.

The vessel dimension that is, in general, the most constraining is draft due to depth of water at the berth and at harbor entrances. Tidal conditions also often play a key role in some situations. Vessel length, when it is a constraint, is typically related to a specific terminal within a port which may have been developed when vessels were generally shorter. Vessel width is typically the least constraining dimension in port and it primarily concerns the container sector as you need to have gantry cranes that can reach the outboard row of containers. The depth alongside at the port and terminal and how that compares to the fully loaded draft of the vessel is the key determinant of the vessel size that calls at that port.

Because dry-bulk commodities are typically weight cargoes that result in deep draft vessels, and those cargoes generally move to and from a much wider range of ports than tankers, port drafts are most constraining for the dry-bulk sector. The draft at a given port is a key factor in the determination of the size category of dry-bulk vessels that will serve that port. This is generally more important at the wider range of discharge ports as the loading ports for most dry-bulk commodities tend to be more concentrated and to have deeper port depths. The importance of this factor has become increasingly recognized and there are more cases of ports expending significant sums to deepen their berths and channels. These type of infrastructure investments allow larger vessels with greater economics to serve the local community.

Capesize ships and VLOC's, while comprising 32% of the total number of bulk carriers as shown in the table above, move 58% of total dry bulk cargo. Panamax sizes comprise 41% of the number of bulk carriers and move 32% of total dry bulk cargo. The smaller Handymax and

Handysize vessels taken together comprise 27% of the total number of bulk carriers but move only 9% of total dry bulk cargo.

The largest number of general bulk carriers, and the biggest single group comprising more than one-fifth of all vessels afloat that are at least 600' long, are Panamax bulk carriers. Panamax bulk carriers are primarily used to move coal and the major grains, corn and wheat. Among the major trade lanes for these vessels are grain shipments from Brazil and the U.S. Gulf Coast to Asia and coal shipments from both the U.S. Gulf Coast and U.S. West Coast to Asia as well as coal shipments from the U.S. Gulf to Northern Europe.

Before reviewing the census on the other sizes and types of bulk carriers, it's worth noting the historical movement of dry-bulk commodities and how and why the transition to the modern bulk carrier that exists today occurred. As is fairly clear, a key factor in the transition from general cargo ships to container ships was the significant reduction in cargo handling costs. While that linkage in the transition from general cargo ships to bulk carriers is less evident, it also played a key role in the dry-bulk category.

When dry-bulk commodities moved in general cargo ships it was impossible to have the efficiency you have today with cargo operations, whether the cargo moved as a partial load or even if it moved as a full load. After World War II, some grain cargoes began to move in surplus T-2 tankers where it was discharged with suction hoses. While this had some minor advantages compared to a typical general cargo ship, it worked only in limited situations. While loading a dry-bulk commodity into a general cargo ship wouldn't be significantly more difficult, unloading it certainly would be. The internal decks and the configuration of the holds that gave general cargo ships their flexibility simply didn't allow anything close to the efficient unloading of dry-bulk vessels that exists today.

The reason for this goes back to the ingenious insight and design of Ole Skaarup. The large open holds that conformed to how dry-bulk commodities flowed are also readily accessible to large clamshell buckets and other methods of discharging cargo. The hatch openings and shape of the holds allow easy access and tend to concentrate the cargo in the most accessible center. The large holds in specialized dry-bulk vessels resulted in the use of larger clamshell buckets. As the vessels got larger, the discharge equipment also got bigger and more efficient. While the sharp growth in dry-bulk vessel size drove lower costs per ton-mile at sea, much more efficient cargo handling also contributed to the low delivered cost of most dry-bulk commodities today.

Grain cargoes were the first to generally be moved in bulk in general cargo ships. Whether it was wheat, corn or some other grain, it typically moved as one of many cargoes on that vessel. It was often stowed in what was known as a tween deck of the vessel. The term tween deck goes back to the early 1800's when they first started appearing on sailing ships. The term literally means the space between two decks. Bulk commodities in general cargo ships were usually stowed in the lower holds or deep tanks. Tween decks were developed as one way of segregating space on a vessel. They continued to be used as cargo transitioned from sailing ships to steam powered general cargo ships that would have multiple decks in each hold.

If the bulk cargo moving on a general cargo ship weren't enough to fill the entire tween deck space, carpenters would install temporary bulkheads to wall off an area for the bulk cargo. If bulk cargos moved as a full shipload, the decks or hatchways might be kept open but care would have to be taken during loading to make sure all void spaces were filled. On the discharge side, even when the internal decks were kept open, bulk cargo would need to be pushed or swept from many locations, as the design didn't lend itself to flowing naturally. At best, moving dry-bulk commodities in general cargo ships was a difficult, time consuming and costly endeavor compared to those same commodities moving on a modern bulk carrier.

In terms of shipping cost as a percent of total delivered cost, the dry-bulk sector is quite different than either the tanker or the container sector. A relatively large part of the delivered cost of iron ore and coal as well as other bulk commodities is represented by ocean shipping cost involving bulk carriers. That is less so in the tanker sector and much less so in the container sector. Another chapter compares shipping costs to cargo value across sectors and discusses the ramifications this has on the economics of the different sectors.

Because the dry-bulk shipping sector handles dozens of commodities that are produced and consumed in a wide variety of countries, it has a wider dispersion of trade routes compared to either the tanker and container sectors. In contrast, where crude oil is produced along with where goods moving in containers are manufactured is more concentrated. Both also tend to flow to the larger developed economies and all these factors come together to result in less dispersion in tanker and container trade routes compared to dry-bulk trade routes.

This diversity leads to hundreds of meaningful individual trade routes for dry-bulk commodities. While it is difficult to come up with an exhaustive list of all of those routes, a few of them stand out in terms of total cargo volume. The largest dry-bulk trade routes today include movements of iron ore from Australia and Brazil to China, movements of coal from the U.S. to the Far East and movements of grain from the U.S. and Brazil to the Far East.

Fine metal ores such as nickle ore have posed major problems for operators of bulk carriers. If the moisture content of the ore is too high, the vibration resulting from the vessels motion and machinery can cause the ore to liquify and slurry, causing a dangerous situation that can result in a ship capsizing. In the past twenty years, this has caused many bulk carriers to be lost.

Iron ore is more than three times as heavy as coal, as a ton of iron ore occupies 11 cubic feet of vessel space while a ton of coal occupies 37 cubic feet of vessel space. The increased density of iron ore has resulted in a specialized subset of bulk carriers that are designed to solely carry iron ore. This category of vessels is almost entirely comprised of what are the largest bulk carriers in the world. The 217 vessels in this category have an average deadweight capacity of 291,292 tons. The difference between these vessels and general bulk carriers is that the holds are designed to carry the heavier cargo and the longitudinal structure is reinforced to accommodate the significant hull stresses a vessel fully loaded with iron ore experiences while at sea.

Ore carriers are optimized for the carriage of iron ore and would generally not be an effective way to carry coal. They are therefore called ore carriers, but the ore is always iron ore. This category of vessels has grown in response to several casualties at sea where general bulk carriers loaded with iron ore literally split in two from the dynamic stress on the hull during a storm. The table on the next page breaks down the ore carrier group by size range using the terms they are most frequently referred to.

Ore Carriers Category (DWT)	Vessels	Total DWT	DWT/Vessel
Handymax (35-50,000)	2	94,162	47,081
Panamax (50-80,000)	0	0	na
Capesize (80-200,000)	7	1,030,630	147,240
VLOC (> 200,000)	217	63,210,402	291,292
Total All Above	226	64,335,247	284,669
Subtotal > 600'	226	64,335,247	284,669

The main trade route for these ore carriers is from Brazil to China and from Australia to China. In the case of Very Large Ore Carriers, or VLOC's it is fair to say that almost all loaded voyages lead to China.

The largest dry-bulk vessels in the world are a class of almost three dozen VLOC's built by Vale S.A., a major iron ore mining company based in Brazil. These vessels are more than twice as large as a typical Capesize vessel and were built by Vale to make the delivered cost of its iron ore in China more competitive with iron ore produced in Australia. These huge vessels have come to be referred to as Valemax ships. The *Vale Brazil* was the first Valemax vessel delivered in 2011. It has a length of 1,188' and a width of 213'. When fully loaded, the 400,000-deadweight ton *Vale Brazil* has a draft of 75'.

The Valemax vessels were built solely to compensate for the distance disadvantage Brazil had with Australia in terms of providing iron ore to China. Because a voyage to China from Brazil was more than three times as long as the voyage from Australia, Brazil sought a way to minimize what would otherwise be a large freight cost disadvantage for its iron ore. With the Valemax vessels having a capacity more than twice that of a typical large Capesize vessel, they developed a conveyance system that they viewed as achieving their goal.

Built at a cost averaging $130 million each, the initial voyage of a Valemax vessel occurred when the *Vale Brazil* sailed in May 2011 from Brazil to Dalian, China with 391,000 tons of iron ore aboard. That was the largest dry-bulk cargo in history and 23 times as much cargo that could be put in Ole Skaarup's pioneering vessel that was the first modern bulk carrier. To put the *Vale Brazil's* first cargo into perspective, that amount of iron ore results in enough steel to produce 289,630 cars.

The improved cost per unit economies of the Valemax vessels were a threat to hundreds of Capesize vessels that were involved in the Brazil to China trade route. Many of those vessels were Chinese owned. Both of those factors were behind a saga that began to play out, as the *Vale Brazil* was enroute to China on its first voyage. Before it arrived, a Chinese regulatory agency announced that dry-bulk vessels larger than 300,000 deadweight tons would not be allowed in Chinese ports as they were deemed unsafe for unspecified reasons. Despite the fact that almost half the Valemax vessels were built in China, these vessels were barred from entering China for several years. Vale made arrangements to transship the iron ore in the Philippines from the Valemax vessels to smaller Capesize vessels, which reduced the beneficial impact of the Valemax vessels. Years later after much protest and discussion, Vale entered into a transaction to sell many of the Valemax vessels to a Chinese shipping company. Around the same time this transaction was disclosed, China lifted its ban and the Valemax vessels were allowed in Chinese ports.

A highly specialized type of bulk carrier developed in the Great Lakes is self-unloading vessels. They have been operating on the Great Lakes before the turn of the last century. Because they operate in fresh water only when the Great Lakes are ice-free, they have an exceptionally long lifespans, with some approaching one hundred years of service. These vessels have conveyor belt mechanisms built into the bottom of their holds which feed the cargo on to a conveyor on a large boom that can positioned to automatically discharge the cargo. The large majority of cargo moved on the Great Lakes self-unloaders is iron ore for numerous steel mills on the Great Lakes. The voyages of these vessels on the Great Lakes are short and often just a couple of days as they shuttle back and forth. The self-unloading system gives the most flexibility and regardless of what time the vessel arrives, it can swing its boom out and begin discharging. Terminal managers are known as they leave to place a stake where they want the iron ore pile centered. When they come in the next morning, a 10,000-ton pile of iron ore is centered on the stake.

Self-unloaders were operated solely in the Great Lakes until the 1980's. Those vessels are not suited for deployment in salt water. A shipping company involved in the Great Lakes built a deepsea self-unloading ship that it deployed in the Caribbean. In certain niche trades, this technology worked well and there was further growth in self-unloaders utilized outside of the Great Lakes. Some proponents saw an analogy between this and containerization, in that this technology would sharply reduce dry-bulk cargo handling costs just as containerization reduced cargo-handling costs.

Ole Skaarup became involved in this, both in terms of refining the design of deepsea self-unloaders and as an owner of such vessels. However, self-unloaders did not spread beyond a few niche trade routes. The self-unloading mechanism reduced vessel carrying capacity while adding to the construction cost of the vessel. Unlike the Great Lakes where the bulk cargo was discharged into a pile, most discharge ports were not setup for this. If the boom is tied into how the port normally received cargo, that usually constrained the self-unloading system. In those cases, more typical clamshell bucket discharging would be faster and more efficient.

The table below breaks down the self-unloading bulk carriers by size range using the terms they are most frequently referred to.

Self-Unloading Bulkers (DWT)	Vessels	Total DWT	DWT/Vessel
Handy 300-600' (< 25,000)	24	366,844	15,285
Handysize (25-35,000)	26	625,867	24,072
Handymax (35-50,000)	38	1,466,592	38,595
Panamax (50-80,000)	36	2,453,581	68,155
Capesize (80-200,000)	9	814,607	90,512
Total All Above	133	5,727,491	43,064
Subtotal > 600'	109	5,360,647	49,180

Another type of bulk carrier that came on the scene with much promise that was also never achieved was the Ore/Bulk/Oil, or OBO vessel. In that sense, OBO's are similar to self-unloaders and the promises of both were effectively overtaken by the extraordinary efficiency of plain vanilla modern bulk carriers.

The concept behind OBO's was that they could achieve higher loaded mile utilization through participating in both the dry bulk and wet bulk markets. D.K. Ludwig, the individual giant responsible for the development of supertankers more than anyone else, was also an early proponent of OBO's. Typical dry-bulk vessels in the major iron ore and coal trades, just like typical crude tankers, were loaded no more than 50% of their miles at sea as they shuttled between where the commodity was loaded to where it was consumed, returning without a backhaul cargo. Smaller bulk carriers are often able to exceed 50% loaded miles through participation in various dry-bulk commodities and triangulating those different routes.

The idea with OBO's is that they could do something similar in the larger bulk trades primarily by switching between iron ore and crude oil. For instance, an OBO could move iron ore from Brazil to the Far East. Rather than returning the entire way empty, it could stop in the Persian Gulf and load crude oil destined for the Americas. Despite the compelling logic, the realities of the cleaning involved in switching between such divergent cargoes as well as customer reluctance resulted in OBO's having only modest success. It has been over twenty years since any OBO's have been built and 28 OBO's have been scrapped in the last few years. Today, there is just one OBO in operation, a 319,869 ton VLOC category vessel.

Certain specialized dry-bulk cargoes have unique characteristics that have resulted in the development of bulk carriers designed to just move that commodity. Two of the more prominent examples are wood chips and bulk cement, but there are also other specialized subcategories. There are 523 vessels in total in the other dry-bulk category, 152 of which are over 600' in length. The table below breaks down the other dry-bulk category by size using the terms they are most frequently referred to.

Other Dry-Bulk Category (DWT)	Vessels	Total DWT	DWT/Vessel
Handy 300-600' (< 25,000)	371	3,565,206	9,610
Handysize (25-35,000)	1	28,414	28,414
Handymax (35-50,000)	62	2,972,338	47,941
Panamax (50-80,000)	78	4,734,240	60,695
Capesize (80-200,000)	11	1,140,832	103,712
Total All Above	523	12,441,030	23,788
Subtotal > 600'	152	8,875,824	58,394

17. Other Types Of Cargo Ships

Other cargo ships outside of the container, tanker and dry-bulk types collectively moved $2.0 trillion worth of various products in 2017. That is the equivalent of $265 annually for each person worldwide. In total, some 17.0% of the total cargo value shipped by water moved on these ships. Even though they are smaller in number and average size than other ships, this total cargo value shipped is well ahead of the dry-bulk sector, which is at 6.5% of the total moved by water, and slightly ahead of the tanker sector which is 16.4%.

The cargo value characteristics per ton of this sector are similar to those of the container sector. That is because the products moved include high value manufactured goods such as vehicles and cargo moving in roll-on, roll-off vessels as well as refrigerated cargo and other specialized cargo. This translates into the cargo value moving on these vessels being a multiple of the cargo weight moving on these vessels. In terms of cargo weight, these vessels moved 748 million tons of products in 2017 representing 7.1% of the total marine shipments based on weight. That works out to some 223 pounds per person in 2017.

The ships in this sector are smaller than the ships operating in the other sectors. They perform 5.3 voyages per year resulting in an overall average speed of 7.36 knots including time spent in port.

There are currently 1,839 vessels in this category that are 600' or longer. Linked end to end, those vessels would stretch out 270 miles. If the ships between 300' and 600' in length are included, the other vessel fleet swells to 7,127 ships that would stretch out 721 miles. The large number of smaller vessels is consistent with the short sea deployment of many of these general cargo ships. A complete breakdown of those vessels based on how they fit within the broad size categories along with the related deadweight range is shown in the following table.

All Other Vessels Category (DWT)	Vessels	Total DWT	DWT/Vessel
Handy 300-600' (< 15,000)	5,288	54,679,198	10,340
Handysize (15-45,000)	1.257	23,279,817	18,520
Panamax (45-60,000)	281	15,225,175	54,182
Post Panamax (60-120,000)	123	10,886,443	88,508
New Panamax (120-160,000)	50	6,848,736	136,975
VLCC (> 160,000)	128	36,465,848	284,889
Total All Above	7,127	147,385,217	20,680
Subtotal > 600'	1,839	92,706,019	50,411

As the table indicates, only 1,839 of the total 7,127 ships in this sector, or just 26%, are longer than 600'. Most of the smaller ships were primarily involved is regional or coastal deployments. For instance, that smaller category would include short sea ferry services.

The vessels in this other category are comprised of an array of different types, including heavy-lift ships, car carriers, roll-on, roll-off vessels, barge carriers and vessels used in offshore oil exploration and production. The majority, however, are comprised of the general multipurpose vessels that dominated shipping prior to the modern era of more specialized vessels. A complete breakdown of the 7.127 ships over 300' in length by type is shown in the table below.

Other Vessels Type	Vessels	% Category
General Multipurpose	4,276	60.0%
Offshore Vessels	534	7.5%
Vehicle Carriers	743	10.4%
Roll-on, Roll-off Vessels	701	9.8%
Refrigerated Vessels	397	5.6%
Passenger Vessels	219	3.1%
Other Vessels	257	3.6%
Total	7,127	100.0%

The general multipurpose vessels trade primarily on smaller routes where large specialized vessels cannot be economically justified. They are similar to the prewar vessels that moved a wide array of different cargoes at the same time. However, they are more modern versions of those vessels and have hydraulically controlled decks and tween decks as well as efficient shipboard cranes. They have the same flexibility as the prewar vessels but are much more efficient in terms of cargo handling than those vessels. Some 93% of the general multipurpose ships are less than 600' in length and they are typically deployed in regional trade routes. There are a limited number of ships longer than 600' and they are generally deployed on longer voyages where their cargo often involves particularly heavy or oversized cargo and various types of project freight. A complete breakdown of the 4,276 general multipurpose ships over 300' in length is shown in the table below.

General Multipurpose (DWT)	Vessels	Total DWT	DWT/Vessel
Handy 300-600' (< 15,000)	3,973	42,393,967	10,671
Handysize (15-45,000)	140	4,963,735	35,455
Panamax (45-60,000)	152	7,993,541	52,589
Post Panamax (60-120,000)	11	784,862	71,351
Total All Above	4,276	56,136,105	13,128
Subtotal > 600'	303	13,742,138	45,354

After general multipurpose vessels, the largest category among other vessel types from a deadweight standpoint is vessels involved in the offshore oil exploration industry. These vessels run the gamut from smaller service vessels between 300' and 600' to drilling ships to complex oil storage and LNG degasification units. One way or another, these highly specialized vessels are directly related to the exploration and production of petroleum offshore. They aren't cargo vessels in the purest sense and the cargo they handle is generally limited to something being stored or products and equipment used in the offshore exploration process. A complete breakdown of the 818 vessels longer than 300' that operate in the offshore industry is shown in the table below.

Offshore Vessels Category (DWT)	Vessels	Total DWT	DWT/Vessel
Handy 300-600' (< 15,000)	120	1,211,803	10,098
Handysize (15-45,000)	45	1,419,941	31,554
Panamax (45-60,000)	86	5,052,183	58,746
Post Panamax (60-120,000)	105	9,514,860	90,618
New Panamax (120-160,000)	50	6,848,736	136,975
VLCC (> 160,000)	128	36,465,848	284,889
Total All Above	534	60,513,371	113,321
Subtotal > 600'	414	59,301,568	143,241

The next largest category is vehicle carriers, which are vessels exclusively designed to move new cars. Vehicle carriers are like giant floating garages where cars are driven onboard and stowed on highly adjustable car decking. These are among the most easily recognizable cargo vessel as they have an exceptionally high freeboard, which is the distance from the waterline to the top deck of the vessel. Compared to other cargo, new vehicles are relatively light. As such, they are much more of a cubic space cargo than a weight cargo and the vessels are designed to maximize their cubic space. The primary trade routes for vehicle carriers are intra Asia, Asia to the U.S. and Europe and Europe to the U.S. A complete breakdown of the 743 vehicle carriers is shown in the table below.

Vehicle Carriers Category (DWT)	Vessels	Total DWT	DWT/Vessel
Handy 300-600' (< 15,000)	244	2,789,443	11,432
Handysize (15-45,000)	498	10,175,726	20,433
Panamax (45-60,000)	1	48,988	48,988
Total All Above	743	13,014,157	17,516
Subtotal > 600'	499	10,224,714	20,490

Collectively the 743 vehicle carriers can hold an estimated 3.2 million cars within their car decks at any one time. Based on typical 10.7 voyages per vessel per year, they can transport 33.7 million cars annually from where they are produced to countries where they are purchased. With worldwide car production now at 95 million units per year, that means that 36% of new cars make their way to consumers at least part of the way via voyages on vehicle carriers. Note that an increasing amount of cars are also now moved as complete knocked down kits in containers. These subassemblies are produced in one place with final assembly in another place to qualify as a domestically produced vehicle. This is yet another example of container shipping encroaching on cargo movements previously handled by other types of vessels. Millions of car equivalents move in boxes on container ships each year in numerous trade lanes, with Korea to the U.S. among the more prominent.

The largest vehicle carrier today, and the largest vehicle carrier ever built, is the *Hoegh Target* which can move 8,500 cars. Its 14 decks contain 768,550 square feet of parking space. If lined up end to end, the cars onboard at any one time would stretch out 23 miles. In terms of value, the cars onboard are worth $285 million and the total value of the cars typically moved by just that vessel in one year is $2.6 billion.

A hybrid type of vessel that combines elements of a vehicle carrier and a container ship is known as a roll-on, roll-off vessel. Sometimes called a Ro-Ro, as the name implies these are vessels where all the cargo moves on and off the vessel on wheels. Roll-on, roll-off vessels do not move cars but move trailers, containers on chassis, construction equipment and other heavy cargo items on wheels or secured to wheeled dollies. These vessels in effect move much of the same cargo in trailers or container chassis combinations that moves just in containers on full container ships. The difference is that the wheels go with the former, which results in a less efficient use of space on the vessel. On the other hand, roll-on, roll-off vessels involve a relatively simple process for loading and unloading. These ships have very large shipboard ramps mounted on their stern that are lowered when in port. Drivers using yard tractors pull the loads to and from the vessel.

The larger roll-on, roll-off vessels are employed in trade routes where considerable or much heavy construction equipment is moving. The buildup of the Middle East, particularly in the late 1970's and early 1980's, was one such market. Because this system is a less efficient use of vessel space while offering cargo operations that are simple and straightforward, most of the vessels today tend to be utilized in shorter trade routes. For instance, it is popular on various U.S. to the Caribbean trade routes. The company that I co-founded operated what was primarily a roll-on, roll-off service to Puerto Rico. A complete breakdown of the 701 roll-on, roll-off vessels is shown in the table below.

Roll-on, Roll-off Vessels (DWT)	Vessels	Total DWT	DWT/Vessel
Handy 300-600' (< 10,000)	360	2,672,591	7,424
Handysize (10-45,000)	335	3,901,892	11,647
Panamax (45-60,000)	6	278,523	46,421
Total All Above	701	6,853,006	9,776
Subtotal > 600'	341	4,180,415	12,259

Refrigerated vessels, also known as reefer vessels, are smaller vessels that have entire holds maintained at selected temperatures. These vessels can be broadly divided into two types. One type moves frozen meat, seafood and other food at below freezing temperatures. The other type moves perishables such as fruit and produce at cold temperatures that are above freezing. For instance, bananas are carried in reefer ships with temparatures in the 55-degree Fahrenheit range. These reefer ships typically move their cargo in equal sized pre-assembled pallets to assist with the loading and unloading operation.

From an energy used standpoint, it is more cost efficient to have centralized refrigeration rather than the individual units on refrigerated containers. However, for it to be more efficient you need to achieve a reasonable utilization and the high value of various frozen meats and seafood makes that a challenge. An average reefer vessel if it were fully loaded with frozen shrimp would be carrying a cargo with a $197 million value. Among the larger refrigerated vessel trade routes are meat from Australia and seafood from South America. A breakdown of the 422 refrigerated vessels is shown in the table below.

Refrigerated Vessels (DWT)	Vessels	Total DWT	DWT/Vessel
Handy 300-600' (< 10,000)	387	3,460,272	8,941
Handysize (10-45,000)	10	157,060	15,706
Total All Above	397	3,617,332	9,112
Subtotal > 600'	10	157,060	15,706

The reefer vessel category continues to shrink as cargo moves to refrigerated containers moving on container ships. The flexibility of these smaller increments of capacity and the ability to move inland without reloading often mitigates the cost efficiencies from centralized refrigeration. The significantly larger size of container ships also results in distributable at sea cost advantages compared to the small reefer ships. In fact, the largest reefer vessel in the world is actually a container ship. The *Cap San Lorenzo* is a Post Panamax container ship with a total capacity of 9,600 TEU, including 2,100 TEU that are dedicated solely to refrigerated containers. While that is only 22% of the capacity of the entire ship, just that portion can carry one-third more reefer cargo than the largest dedicated refrigerated vessel in the world.

Passenger and cruise vessels are among the smallest category of ships afloat. While the focus is of course passengers, most of them also handle a relatively small amount of priority freight. Because these are among the fastest ships and are concentrated in just a few places, in selected markets such as the Bahamas they often do play a meaningful role in moving cargo. However, as the deadweight figures on all passenger ships will attest, no matter how long or pretty they may be, they couldn't ever be a descent cargo ship even if they wanted to be. A breakdown of the 219 passenger ships is shown in the table below.

Passenger Vessels (DWT)	Vessels	Total DWT	DWT/Vessel
Handy 300-600' (<7,000)	18	91,869	5,104
Handysize (7-45,000)	201	1,844,924	9,179
Total All Above	219	1,936,793	8,844
Subtotal > 600'	201	1,844,924	9,179

The final category within the other vessel sector is a catch all that covers whatever doesn't fit in anything else. This double other category is a hodgepodge of extremely specialized vessels like cable layers, submersibles, dredges and other even more exotic craft. The table below shows a breakdown of the 257 other ships comprising this category.

All Other Vessels (DWT)	Vessels	Total DWT	DWT/Vessel
Handy 300-600' (< 15,000)	186	2,059,253	11,071
Handysize (15-45,000)	28	816,539	29,162
Panamax (45-60,000)	36	1,851,940	51,443
Post Panamax (60-120,000)	7	586,721	83,817
Total All Above	257	5,314,453	20,679
Subtotal > 600'	71	3,255,200	45,848

18. The Men Who Go To Sea

The nine pioneers we profile are the men most responsible for modern cargo shipping. However, without the millions of crewmembers that man the vessels they envisioned, all of their insight would have been for naught. Ships require crews of men to get them from where the voyage originates to where the voyage is destined. While the crews aren't as big as in the past, nor the work as dangerous and uncomfortable as it once was, millions of men still go to sea. They are unmistakably brave, as the sea remains a very challenging environment.

The crew size on modern cargo vessels varies based on the type of ship and under what flag country the ship is registered. All the registries and union agreements typically mandate a required minimum number of crewmembers to be on duty at any given time. When at sea, ships are operating around the clock with multiple shifts of crew needed. Shipping companies will often have more than the minimum required number to better distribute the workload and for maintenance and training purposes.

Crews are generally divided into members belonging to the deck department, the engine department and the stewards department. The deck department, typically comprised of a master, chief officer and other deck officers, is charged with navigating the ship and with oversight on cargo operations to ensure that vessel safety isn't compromised. The engine department, typically comprised of a chief engineer, a second engineer and other engineering officers, is charged with operating the ship's engine plant and machinery. Each department has additional seamen to assist with watches and various maintenance functions. The stewards department is responsible for feeding the crew and performing various hotel-like functions.

Vessels operate 24 hours per day at sea and crews are generally split into three shifts per day. At all times, there will be a deck officer on the bridge with at least one assistant. Likewise, there is always an engine officer on duty. Up until recently, he was always in the engine room with one or more assistants. However, with the transition to diesel engines, automation and the continuous improvement in the operation and maintenance of those engines, many engine rooms are now automated and unmanned for at least part of the day.

Largely gone is the extremely tough working environment faced by engine department workers when cargo ships were steam powered. I've been in such engine rooms while a vessel is at sea and the conditions were uncomfortable. The noise coming from machinery and the boilers requires yelling to be heard even when you are standing next to someone. The radiant heat emanating from almost everything is sauna-like and results in lots of perspiration. Even with the transition to diesel, engine rooms remain a noisy and industrial space. The smell of petroleum permeates the air. In testimony to this, one of the engine department positions is known as a wiper. His job is to wipe down any extraneous oil that would find its way into the engine room. It was in those conditions that engine room personnel would find themselves standing and working for eight to twelve hours per day.

The master of the ship has the ultimate responsibility and is the decision-maker on all matters related to the vessel and the safety of the crew. Particularly when the vessel is at sea, the master is in total control. In evidence of that, crewmembers still sign articles of employment when they join a vessel that documents their contract with the master. Up until recently, in a nod to tradition, those articles would also outline the equivalent daily and weekly amounts of food and drink that each crew member would be allocated while on board. These rations can be traced back to documents the British Navy established more than four hundred years ago. Among other things, those documents called for one pound of biscuits and one gallon of beer each day. In addition, they stipulated weekly rations of four pounds of beef, two pounds of salted pork, three-eights of a twenty four inch cod fish, two pints of peas, six ounces of butter and twelve ounces of cheese each week.

In terms of food at sea, the biscuits referred to in the articles were a staple for centuries. A simple mixture of crude flour, water and salt, they were purposely baked as hard as possible as they would soften and become more palatable over time due to exposure to humidity and other elements. Because they were so hard and dry, sailors called them hardtack and tack became a slang word for food. This basic sustenance ration was also known by other names such as sea biscuits, dog biscuits, molar breakers, tooth dullers and worm castles.

Reading the entire text of one of those articles of employment for an old cargo sailing ship not only highlights the absolute power of the master, but also the difficult living conditions of crew members on those vessels while at sea. The work aboard old cargo sailing ships was fraught with danger and discomfort. For example, in 1885 a report by the British Royal Commission on life at sea stated that every year one in 73 seafarers would die. In effect, that meant if you chose to make going to sea your career occupation in what was then the world's largest merchant marine, you had a 50/50 chance of being killed by that occupation.

Despite these challenges, men have elected to go to sea for centuries. For much of that period, it was really the only job that would take men away from the town they were born and raised in. Perhaps this desire to broaden their horizons has always been a key catalyst that had men going to sea. The sense of adventure and curiosity about the world are traits that most mariners have always shared. It is hard not to embrace the exhilaration these men must have felt on a clipper ship running before the wind under a full sail.

On sailing ships, however, those moments of exhilaration were punctuated by long periods of very hard work climbing the rigging, adjusting the sails and pulling and tying down lines. This work occurred round the clock in all types of weather conditions. The potential for all types of minor and serious accidents was ever present while at sea. Beyond that, the living conditions and the basic discomfort that seafarers experienced even when they weren't working would have been difficult by any of today's standards.

The transition from sail to steam brought with it many changes to the risks and conditions mariners experienced at sea. It became less labor intensive, but it still involved a great deal of manual labor. No longer did seaman need to worry about falling to their death from rigging or from having their hands go raw from pulling lines. However, the advent of steam power initially fueled by coal brought with it a new class of workers whose job was to constantly move and shovel coal into furnaces to keep the steam power plant operating. The constant heat, dust and noise that these mariners experienced in cramped quarters deep into the hold of a ship resulted in a miserable environment.

Coal was eventually displaced by heavy residual fuel to fire the steam power plants. Because the fuel was stored in tanks placed in the same area where coal bunkers previously existed, it became known as bunker fuel, which is a term still used today. The change from coal to oil resulted in the dust from coal being replaced by a fine mist from the oil. Most engine rooms had several wipers who paid constant attention to this new problem. Wipers were charged with wiping off this mist to avoid what would otherwise develop into very dangerous conditions. With numerous moving mechanical parts and piping through which super heated steam moved under pressure, cramped and noisy engine rooms offered a host of opportunities where missteps or malfunctions could and often did result in serious or even fatal accidents.

An additional risk for merchant seaman that started in World War I and increased significantly in World War II entailed cargo ships being sunk by submarines. In addition to the effectiveness of submarines in sinking enemy naval ships, they were particularly effective in sinking cargo ships and thereby disrupting supply chains. For instance, during World War II German U-boats sank thousands of Allied cargo vessels. Each sinking was fraught with danger for the lives for the lives of the crewmembers.

This was particularly the case during the early part of World War II when large amounts of supplies were being sent from the U.S. to Europe without the benefit of the better-protected convoys that would follow later in the war. Many of these ships were U.S. flag. In striking testimony to the dangers Amercian merchant marines were exposed to, their mortality rate was twice as high as the sailors on actual naval war ships. In total, 9,497 American merchant marines were killed when 733 cargo ships were sunk during World War II. As 243,000 mariners served during the war, that translates into a 1 in 26 mortality rate that was actually the highest rate of casualties of any military service.

While shipping is much safer for crewmembers today, it remains an occupation not for the faint of heart. The only occupation that is riskier than being a seafarer today is being a commercial fisherman. Compared to a typical job ashore, a recent Danish study concluded that seafarers have an eleven times higher mortality risk. The force of nature that is the sea can explain almost all of those differences.

Someone only has to experience a storm at sea to have a greater appreciation of the risk and the extraordinary ability of the waves and wind to move a large cargo ship around as if it were a toy. Thirty-foot waves and winds so loud it was very difficult to be heard reinforce the power and majesty of nature at sea. I experienced one such storm in the Pacific during the 1980's. Between the motion sickness from the constant movement and the sheer terror that the ship was moving too much, it effectively turned me into a landlubber as far as cargo ships were concerned.

Looking over the last ten years, on average of 127 ships of all sizes are lost at sea annually. Due to modern communications and life saving systems, however, even the loss of a ship at sea is not the same calamity it usually was in the past. Comprehensive data on crewmember loss of life at sea isn't readily available. The figures maintained by the International Maritime Organization, which is a division of the United Nations tasked with establishing international shipping standards, include fishing vessels, passengers on ferries and even overcrowded small vessels carrying refugees. It therefore goes well beyond the giant cargo vessels that are our focus. With that caveat, total loss of life at sea in recent years has been 1,200 annually. Something on the order to 10% to 20% of that number likely represents the loss of seafarers on cargo ships each year.

A comprehensive long-term study of mortality experience of British merchant marine crewmembers resulted in a determination of 12 deaths per year per 100.000 seafarers. For a variety of reasons related to ship type, size and age, it would be fair to characterize that as a minimum. As discussed later, the total seafarer employment related to our 17,546 giant cargo vessels is approximately 1,000,000. Combining that with the mortality experience of the recent study, we can estimate that 120 seafarers die each year as a direct result of their occupation of keeping this massive worldwide conveyance system moving.

The transition to steam and then diesel brought with it dramatic improvement in both working and living conditions for crewmembers. If you were to go onboard a new, just built cargo ship today, you would find spacious accommodations for sleeping, eating and recreation. Most typically have internet service and an array of entertainment devices to occupy the crew when they are off duty. The food is typically high quality and available in abundance.

Navigation and communications technology and an array of systems to highlight any unsafe situations have made shipping geometrically safer for crewmembers. However, there are exceptions, with unscrupulous vessel owners and lax regulatory bodies, but there numbers continue to decline with concerted efforts by regulators and insurance companies to raise minimum standards.

Gone for the most part are previous situations where crewmembers were actively involved in cargo, cleaning or heavy maintenance operations, which all raised safety issues. Now a ship's crew in primarily involved in navigation and engineering issues related to the vessel itself. Relative to what it was in the past, being a crewmember is a more conventional and safer job today. You can count on safely getting back home and while you are on the vessel, all of your needs are well taken care of. Most would say that the sleeping and eating situation on a modern cargo ship is comfortable.

One thing, however, that has been a significant change for the worse for crewmembers on modern cargo vessels is time in port. Just after World War II, it wasn't unusual for a ship to spend a third to a half of its total time in port being loaded or discharged. Prior to specialization that vastly improved cargo-handling techniques for all segments, particularly general cargo, it wasn't unusual for a ship to spend a week or more in any given port. For the crew, this translated into little or almost no work requirements and they were free to explore the port or region they happened to be in. At that time, it was also more typical for ships to call on numerous and ever changing ports. This shifting pattern presented crewmembers with a constantly changing tableau of opportunities to explore. It was a nice side benefit to a job that had its challenges, not the least of which is that you are away from your home, family and friends for extended periods of time. Those days of extended time in port, however, are no more.

A container ship is typically in port for less than a day and often in port for only a handful of hours. Improvements in cargo handling equipment for both dry and liquid bulk cargoes have those vessels with much faster port turn times than in the past. Most terminals across segments attempt to maintain rigid schedules to maximize capacity and work with more labor around the clock to get ships in and out quick. In addition, with larger, more specialized vessels, the number of ports called is less. Those that are called are often called repeatedly. Instead of a large number of constantly changing ports, ships are more likely to be constantly shuttling between the same small number of ports.

All of these changes come together to be a dramatic difference for the crew in terms of the time they have to explore. It is very hard to explore a new city if a vessel will only be in port for eight hours. And even if you find a way to explore it in that time, if it is one of just a few recurring ports the ship stops at, after a couple of port calls there is little new to see. This change in both the amount of time in any given port and the array of ports visited are striking changes from the past and both negative developments in terms of crewmember satisfaction and retention.

Today, a modern cargo ship will typically have a crew of 20 to 25 men. That is less than half the crew typically seen on much smaller cargo vessels just after World War II. The reductions resulted from the transition from steam to diesel, improvements in navigation and engine technology and the automation of an array of processes. As the number of required deck and engine personnel declined, the number of people needed to feed and house those crewmembers also declined.

Extending that typical crew size to the 17,546 cargo ships over 600' in length results in some 400,000 people on them at any given point in time. Almost no crewmember stays on a ship year round. Even though they may only be working eight hours each day, they are onboard the vessel 24 hours per day. Unlike other workers, they can't go just home and their free time comes with the major constraint that it is not really their time to do as they wish. My mentor Malcom McLean highlighting this for me early in my career by noting that vessel crew members are effectively working 24 hours per day and their compensation should reflect that fact. In any case, today it largely does and crews tend to be rotated two to three times per year. The net effect is that while 400,000 people are onboard at any given time, the full time employment of some one million people is required to man the 17,546 giant cargo ships over 600' in length. In terms of the larger group of 31,245 cargo ships over 300' in length, the total full time employment almost doubles to just under two million people in total.

While the cost of employing the full crew on a modern cargo vessel is large in an absolute sense, from the standpoint of relative costs, it typically pales in comparison to the other costs entailed in operating a vessel, most particularly fuel and capital costs. To put this into perspective, from my review of the income statements and cost detail of many publicly owned shipping companies, the total wage and benefit costs can be estimated at $250 to $300 per crew member per day. That is an average figure and officers would be higher while unlicensed crew would be lower. By extension to a ship with 20 to 25 crewmembers, those numbers translate into a total crew cost of $5,000 to $7,500 per day. The midpoint of $6,250 per day is a reasonable estimate of the labor cost related to a modern cargo ship. If you add crew food cost, other miscellaneous consumable and vessel insurance, they typically collectively represent another $2,500 per day.

So a ballpark total operating cost of a modern cargo ship is $7,500 to $10,000 per day. But if that ship burns 150 tons per day of fuel at sea at a cost of around $400 per ton, that adds $60,000 for most days. Furthermore, with the new cleaner fuel regulations that are being phased-in worldwide, the cost of vessel fuel could almost double. And if that vessel was just built for $50 million, you're going to need almost another $20,000 per day just to amortize investment costs over a fifteen year life before factoring in any real economic profit. In other words, today the wages and benefits paid to crewmembers are typically a single digit percentage of total vessel costs. That percentage will go down more when the new cleaner fuel regulations are fully implemented.

The reality of crew costs being a relatively small part of the total underlying cost of a ship has ramifications both now and in the future. Because shipping is not a labor-intensive industry, companies seek to employ competent crewmembers, which results in higher wages than you see in low-skilled, labor-intensive industries. It's not a race to the bottom because a less competent crew can result in navigational, engineering and management mistakes whose cost readily eclipses any small savings in crew costs.

As vessels have gotten bigger, with attendant increases in fuel consumption and capital investment, this truism has become even more important today. In terms of the future, this reality means that while the technology for autonomous cargo ships largely exists, that technology will need to be almost perfect as the labor costs it can save are relatively small and the costs of any imperfection are significant and potentially astronomical.

Today, the men who go to sea are an extraordinary melting pot of national origins. Where a ship is registered will often affect the crew origin, as some flag registries require part or all of the crew to be citizens of their country. However, many of the flag of convenience countries such as Panama or Liberia do not have such requirements and owners have total flexibility in sourcing their crew. For instance, some 42% of cargo ships worldwide are flagged in Panama, Liberia or the Marshall Islands and they are just the largest of many flags of convenience registries. They are typically crewed with individuals coming from a small group of countries. Today, the largest numbers of crewmembers come from the Philippines, eastern European countries, Greece, the Scandinavian countries and England.

There is often a bifurcation in terms of national origin between deck and engine officers and the remaining crew. The officers are the highest skilled positions and require more certification and specialized education. They will more often come from developed countries. While not as specialized, the remaining positions also require skilled workers who typically have specialized training. The call to the sea is still heard across the globe and almost every country in the world is the home of some crewmembers. By definition, shipping is a global industry and the crewmembers on these giant cargo vessels represent diversity in terms of national origin that is really not replicated in any other industry.

Each ship is a melting pot of different nationalities, cultures, foods and points of view. Despite these differences, each ship's crew comes together to safely maneuver thousands of giant vessels in and out of ports across the world each day. By definition, in terms of the people that work in the shipping industry, it is perhaps the most diverse industry in the world.

I will always remember being in El Salvador in the early 1980's, acting as port captain to manage the discharge of a cargo of bulk grain from a U.S. flag vessel. We were docked near a Russian flag vessel also discharging grain. Walking past that ship, I began talking to one of its crew and before long was invited onboard to visit the captain. Between his broken English and hand gestures, I accepted both his vodka shots and his invitation to a game of chess. Over that game we settled most of the problems between our respective countries and I even came close to winning the chess game as the gap between our respective consumption of vodka expanded. I imagine there are thousands of similar new exchanges each day as cargo ships are at dock and cultures that are new to each other interact and learn something from those interactions.

My view is that the 17,546 giant merchant marine vessels are in many respects also a type of civilian navy that has promoted peace in the world by linking countries in trade. Similarly, the million crewmembers that keep those ships moving have often acted as goodwill ambassadors. Today, English is the language of global shipping and that is a facillitator. In their day to day interactions across the globe, crewmembers dispel myths and highlight the common values shared by all people. In doing so, they have played a constructive role in maintaining world peace in addition to their primary role of keeping the ships that underpin the world economy moving.

19. Cost Economics of the Shipping Industry

The total cost of deploying a ship can be divided into three main areas: operating costs, fuel costs and capital costs. Operating costs are primarily composed of crew wages but also include food, supplies, maintenance and insurance. Fuel relates to the cost of propelling the vessel and, except for container ships, is usually paid directly by the shipping company's customer. Capital costs include amortizing the building or acquisition cost of the vessel and any related interest charges over the life or ownership term of the vessel. All of these costs and how they compare to revenue and related cargo value, along with how they are accounted for and managed against, vary by individual company and shipping industry sector. When combined with the revenue that is actually achieved, these cost economics determine the overall financial performance of the industry.

In my view, the very importance of the shipping industry has become a limiting factor today in the economic performance of the industry for its owners or shareholders. This is a function of the increasing governmental involvement in the shipping industry as a means to another end. The result is a focus on many objectives that come ahead of the profit performance economics of the shipping industry and the achievement of appropriate returns on capital invested in shipping. Prior to addressing what is a prime factor in the performance of the industry, we will outline various important characteristics related to the underlying cost economics of the shipping industry.

Over the years, observers have noted similarities between the shipping and commercial real estate industries. In testimony to that, many of the individual giants also became involved in real estate. Both industries involve large capital investments that are committed to years in advance of when the asset will be available to earn revenue. As such, both require a long-term view of what the economic environment will be both when the asset starts earning revenue and throughout the life of the asset. Those environments are often different than the environment when the decision is made. The large upfront capital investments are also effectively the majority of total costs. This results in a high degree of operating leverage, meaning that additional revenue does not result in large amounts of additional variable costs. How total costs are viewed has much to due with the economic performance of both shipping companies individually and the sectors and industry as a whole. Indeed, no single decision attribute has as much consequence on the collective results of the industry.

While both shipping and real estate are extraordinarily capital intensive, an important distinction relates to both asset life and depreciation. Ships are made of steel and when deployed on salt water they are the very definition of a wasting asset that, absent any change in macro factors, goes down in real value each year. While it varies based on a number of factors, the maximum physical life of a ship is generally 25 years. At that time it will be scrapped for what is generally a single digit percentage of its initial construction cost based upon steel value. Today many owners do not keep a new ship more than 15 years. As a ship ages, its maintenance cost, particularly the regulatory drydockings required every five years, increase sharply. At some point, the expected maintenance and drydocking cost make the vessel uneconomical to continue operating. The decision to scrap is usually made just before one of these required drydockings. In cases where technological advancements result in a vessel becoming obsolete, it will be scrapped before it reaches the end of its physical life.

Whatever the life assumption is, ship owners must recover their initial investment over that finite period. On the other hand, capital investment in real estate has an exponentially longer life expectancy. Furthermore, with reasonable maintenance practices, most real estate investments hold their value or actually appreciate. Many office buildings have an indefinite life with no replacement anticipated. In terms of real economic depreciation of the initial capital investment, real estate typically has none, while shipping has lots that move in line with the physical decline of the asset. That is a major difference between these two very capital-intensive industries. Shipowners who fail to recognize this fundamental difference do so at their own significant peril.

The ownership structure of shipping companies often includes equity holders that may have additional agendas other than just maximizing their equity interests in the shipping company. For instance, shipping companies often have large ownership stakes by customers or vendors. In those cases, they could be more interested in lowering their cost as a customer, or increasing their revenue as a vendor, than in maximizing the profit of the shipping company. Those situations are widespread and collectively have a deleterious affect on the financial performance of the shipping industry. As bad as they are, however, they pail in comparison to the affect government ownership and control have on the economic performance of shipping companies.

Although this has been present in some form for centuries, the degree to which government ownership and control plays a role is a fairly recent postwar phenomenon. It became more pronounced a few decades ago and has continued to grow since then. In economies that are focused on exports and where the government has played a key role in outlining priorities, the importance of shipping services quickly became apparent. That often resulted in the government becoming directly involved in promoting and providing capital to shipping companies serving its markets. In many of those cases, the government made a strategic decision to accept a suboptimal return on its shipping company investment if that is seen as being supportive of its agenda related to the larger economy.

For example, it is rational for a government controlled shipping company to have low freight rates that are detrimental to the company itself if such rates are viewed as facilitating or increasing trade levels. An early example of this was the 1985 bankruptcy of Sanko Steamship, one of the largest shipping companies in the world at the time. While the government of Japan lost hundreds of millions in what was the largest business collapse in postwar Japan, a more cogent analysis pointed to tens of billions that the Japan economy benefited over the years. This resulted from lower rates by Sanko Steamship, which were in turn followed by all shipping companies moving cargo to and from Japan also lowering their rates. When you measure all the effects, Japan's experience with Sanko was clearly a very large net positive.

In my view, another ownership aspect related to shipping companies that weighs negatively on the industry's financial performance is the majority of the industry remains privately owned. That is a striking contrast to the public ownership structure that predominates in most other large industries. Of the shipping companies that are publicly traded, many are still operated as if they were private due to control retained by a majority owner.

Without the transparency resulting from companies reporting detailed operating results and metrics each quarter, the shipping industry doesn't have the financial benchmarks that are readily available to other industries. Chief among these is a credible awareness of where your cost and performance levels are relative to other shipping companies. Without a clear awareness of where you stand and rank on various metrics, you are flying blind on major operating and investment decisions. These benchmarks allow for numerous comparisons by internal and external audiences that result in greater awareness of relative performance and more informed and efficient decisions by all parties.

The broader disclosure that results from being publicly traded results in changes at the under-performers and copying the practices of the over-performers, both of which have a beneficial effect on most industries. Without this, many companies in the shipping industry are truly operating without any real awareness of their relative standing.

Having internal and external audiences looking over your shoulder may be annoying, but it rarely impedes performance and more often than not has the opposite effect. I've often had this discussion with folks in the shipping industry who will steadfastly claim that they can perform better as a private company. Stated reasons such as long term focus and desire to keep their plans confidential fall by the wayside when they are logically scrutinized. My strong opinion is that the shipping industry would perform much better collectively if it had the public ownership structure of other large industries. This would make the industry more subject to the disciplines and transparency that the financial markets impose on publicly held companies.

In addition to lacking the information content from public disclosure, a number of other adverse consequences flow out of the mostly privately owned nature of the shipping industry. Foremost among these is corporate governance and management selection. The governance practices of the shipping industry as a whole are poor. One window into this comes from the disclosure of companies with limited public ownership. Almost all of these companies will have certain transactions with the majority owners that involve commissions, payments or side deals that wouldn't be allowed by a truly independent board of directors. It is not unheard of for a shipping company to pay a commission to a company affiliated with its CEO when it builds a new ship or enters into a long-term charter. That such commissions are viewed as normal rather than a clear conflict that often leads to decisions not in shareholders interest is itself an indictment of the industry's corporate governance.

In almost all private shipping companies, management selection and succession is a function of bloodlines. This pattern is also evident in many shipping companies with limited public ownership. While this carries on a family tradition, nepotism is rarely in the financial interests of shareholders and management competence often declines with each succession. Such structures also do not attract qualified outsiders who see the lack of meritocracy limiting their own upside. There are some exceptions but they tend to be few and far between. Noteworthy among those are descendants of Y.K. Pao and C.Y. Tung, two of the individual giants discussed in other chapters, who have lead successful shipping companies with well above average performance.

Given this private ownership structure, it sometimes results in an autocratic CEO who is less than qualified, with little management depth and a weak board. Those situations hardly lead to good performance. Poor performance is often unrecognized and unacknowledged. Even if it is eventually viewed as sub-optimum, the governance structure makes it difficult to make meaningful changes in an expeditious manner. In most other large industries, almost all of the major companies are broadly publicly held. Independent boards oversee professional managers with a sole focus on the best way to maximize shareholder wealth. Everyone is fully aligned on this singular goal. Those structures result in transparency and disclosure and the relative performance of the company is known to all. If that performance is sub-optimal or deemed to not be aligned with shareholder interests, changes can and will occur at various levels.

The market place mechanisms existing at most publicly owned companies are self-correcting and make those companies better performers. There are, unfortunately, far too few examples in the shipping industry where the companies are broadly publicly held with professional management and a strong independent board. If there were one macro change that could significantly improve the overall performance of the shipping industry, it would be the transition in ownership structure from effectively privately held to mainly broadly publicly held.

The shipping industry is one of the few, perhaps the only, major industry someone can become immediately involved with in a significant way solely by writing a check. There are outside firms that can handle every facet of the business for the owner, from overseeing the construction to crewing and operating the vessel to seeking employment for the vessel in the spot market. That ease of entry is not a good thing for the shipping industry as it promotes excess supply funded by someone without an in depth knowledge of shipping demand. While the various entities he is aligning with are no doubt promoting the efficacy of the investment and often underscoring it with a co-investment themselves, their larger economic interest lies in their vendor role. Owning a ship has a certain cocktail party panache, not unlike writing a check to purchase a racehorse or fund an off-Broadway play. But as many have learned, if you get involved in the shipping industry just by writing a check, your returns will be significantly weighed down by assorted vendors just as they are in those other two examples.

Now that I've framed some of the macro aspects related to the performance economics of the shipping industry, let's review tangible examples of the major cost items by sector to better explain the cost economics of the industry.

The table below shows the total daily costs of the largest ship size category in each of the four segments reviewed earlier. The total costs are comprised of operating, fuel and capital, which are detailed for each segment. The largest ship size in each category are also almost always the most cost efficient in terms of moving cargo due to the inherent operating leverage in the shipping industry. In other words, these ships result in the least shipping cost relative to cargo value and smaller ships in each category will be incrementally higher.

Segment	Container	Tanker	Dry-Bulk	General
Vessel Category	ULCV	VLCC	VLOC	Car Carrier
Daily Vessel Cost:				
Operating	$10,534	$9,438	$8,986	$8,932
Fuel	$72,733	$35,527	$17,863	$35,167
Capital	$50,685	$28,767	$19,726	$18,630
Total	$133,952	$73,733	$46,576	$62,729

The first observation worth highlighting in scanning the table above is both the similarity and relative smallness of operating costs. This cost item is mainly comprised of crew compensation. On large modern ships across categories, it is typical to have a total crew of approximately 20 people. While compensation obviously varies with the licensed officers at the top, an across the board average of $300 per day per person is a realistic overall average to use. By extension, that works out to $6,000 per day in crew compensation costs. When you add in food, supplies and consumables as well as vessel maintenance costs totaling some $2,000 per day, you get to $8,000 per day. That amount is a reasonable figure to use for almost any modern large ship that is typically registered under one of the flags of convenience. The only other vessel operating cost item that the vessel owner is responsible for is insurance cost. This cost is driven by the insured value of the vessel. As a rule of thumb, an amount equal to one half of one percent of vessel value will be paid for hull insurance and miscellaneous other insurance generally maintained. The differences in the operating costs per category in the table above result from the difference in vessel values. They range from a large container ship at the high end to a large dry-bulk ship at the low end.

Significantly more than operating costs across categories is the fuel cost related to powering and propelling the vessels. These average fuel costs per day were calculated starting with the fuel consumption per day at sea for each vessel and using a typical 85% time at sea for each vessel. Many factors go into fuel consumption, but key factors include the design speed of the vessel and its fully loaded draft. Speed is the variable that particularly effects fuel consumption.

Not only does daily consumption increase proportionately with speed, but consumption per mile also increases as vessels go faster. Container ships are the racehorses of cargo vessels and this is reflected in their relatively high fuel consumption. In general, a vessel in port uses one-tenth as much fuel to power its utilities and various other functions compared to what it burns at sea. The resulting average consumption figures were then multiplied by $462 per ton, the current price of residual fuel in Singapore, the busiest bunkering port for vessels in the world. Note that this price is actually below the price of crude oil because the residual fuel primarily for vessel fuel contains various foreign elements.

Residual fuel is literally what is left over after crude oil has been refined and is therefore dirtier and has less energy than crude oil. While its price discount relative to crude oil varies, residual fuel typically sells for 15-20% below crude oil and almost half the price of refined petroleum products. This has been a significant economic benefit to the shipping industry for decades. As we will see later, this will change in 2020 when new worldwide fuel cleanliness standards promulgated by the International Maritime Organization (IMO), the division of the United Nations with control over various aspects of international shipping, go into effect. Vessel owners will either need to switch to cleaner fuels or install expensive scrubber systems on their vessels which often bring with them the problem of how to dispose of the scrubber system residue. Most ships are expected to switch to cleaner fuels that are expected to cost 50% to 75% more than residual fuel.

The third cost item that is also several times higher than operating costs but generally below fuel costs is capital costs. This item represents the physical deterioration of the vessel along with interest cost on the capital deployed to buy the vessel. Today, it is unusual to see vessels operating after they are more than twenty years of age as costs related to mandatory special survey and dry-docking every five years and routine maintenance costs go up sharply. Both of these facts are driven by the corrosive effect of salt water on steel and the wear and tear on the hull and a wide array of components that most vessels get from traveling more than a million miles in harsh environments.

Once a vessel reaches twenty years of age, it is typically worth only a single digit percentage of its construction cost as its high maintenance costs and related non-dependability make it non-competitive and uneconomical to operate. In most cases, it is sold to scrappers at prices that are driven by the price of steel but almost always less than 10% of construction cost. In other words, the physical deterioration portion of capital costs generally approximates a 5% annual factor. The interest component will vary based on both capital market conditions and the specific credit worthiness of the individual ship owner. After you include this interest component, the total actual capital cost is equivalent to an annual factor ranging from 8% to 12% cost per year. The daily equivalent capital costs in the above table are based on a midpoint annual factor of 10% applied to the new construction cost of each vessel category.

A recap of these cost items as a percent of total costs by vessel category is shown in the table below. The table also includes the fuel consumption figures per day at sea along with the new construction cost of the respective vessels.

Segment	Container	Tanker	Dry-Bulk	General
Vessel Category	ULCV	VLCC	VLOC	Car Carrier
% Daily Vessel Cost:				
Operating	7.9%	12.8%	19.3%	14.2%
Fuel	54.3%	48.2%	38.4%	56.1%
Capital	37.8%	39.0%	42.3%	29.7%
Total	100.0%	100.0%	100.0%	100.0%
Fuel Tons/Day @ Sea	182.0	88.9	44.7	88.0
Build Cost In Millions	$185	$105	$72	$68

When you reflect on these costs and the ability of management to control them, you gain a greater understanding on the factors that drive the economics and competition in the shipping industry. While there are clear divergences across the various categories, there are also some broad similarities that will be addressed first.

Across all categories, the daily operating cost item that is most influenced by day to day management is also the smallest cost item. If management is able to secure a meaningful 10% advantage in this item, a daunting accomplishment itself, in the grand scheme of total costs, that hardly moves the needle in terms of relative cost competitiveness. Daily operating costs accrue at the same rate whether a vessel is at sea or in port and whether it is full of cargo or half empty.

To achieve an advantage and leverage their fixed operating costs as much as they can, ship owners are obviously drawn to minimize port time and maximize cargo load factors to achieve better vessel utilization. As crew sizes do not vary materially among ocean going vessels of different sizes within categories, another way ship owners have sought to obtain an advantage in this area is by operating ever-larger vessels. Except for insurance costs that tend to be proportionate to vessel value, the operating costs for ships half as large as those in the table above are very similar. This reality has been a key catalyst in the postwar growth in average vessel size across categories.

While the larger cost items of fuel and capital costs do increase with vessel size, they don't increase proportionately. Both offer economies of scale that have also supported the postwar growth in ship size across all categories. Almost all vessels burn the same type of residual fuel whose commodity price ship owners have no control over. Similarly, the consumption characteristics of the handful of different types of marine engines used by shipyards around the world have nearly identical consumption per horsepower hour metrics. Electing to build a larger vessel is the primary method for a ship owner to achieve a competitive advantage related to fuel costs because horsepower requirement doesn't increase proportionately with size. My analysis of a broad range of different sizes of container ships shows that with a given percent increase in size, fuel costs increase at approximately half that percent. Capital costs have similar economies of scale characteristics as fuel costs. Unlike fuel consumption where there is a defined relationship, capital costs have the potential for differences due to initial building place and timing as well the resulting interest cost differences where financing is involved.

With dozens of major shipyards across the world, the pricing variances due to differences in their underlying costs sometimes offer a competitive advantage in the area of capital costs. This has particularly been true for early customers of shipyards in countries with major shipbuilding initiatives. For instance, in the postwar period the early customers of Japanese, Korean and Chinese shipyards in successive twenty-year or so periods all achieved an initial competitive advantage related to capital costs. This relative advantage dissipated as others followed their example.

In addition to differences related to where a ship is built, the shipbuilding industry has a cycle similar to the shipping industry itself that affects its pricing structure. The prices and terms offered by shipbuilders are at their best when the industry is performing poorly. These macro factors can often result in swings as much as 20% for the construction price of a new vessel. The new construction cost of a ship is just the initial component of capital costs, which are significantly affected by the interest rate and term of debt financing that is almost always employed by ship owners. While the financial condition and creditworthiness of the ship owner first influence these, they are also affected by general economic conditions in the capital markets.

When all these factors that can influence capital costs are taken together, it is easy to see that this is the cost item that many ship owners believe offers the best way to achieve a competitive cost advantage. Some of these differences relate to negotiating skills, but most of these differences relate simply to perceived timing.

A ship owner who contracts to build a vessel at the bottom of the cycle will have a meaningful competitive cost advantage compared to a ship owner who contracts to build a vessel at the top of the cycle. Achieving that, however, requires success in anticipating the cycles in shipbuilding and the overall shipping market. While that is easier said than done, there are many ship owners who time their new construction contracts, as well as purchases and sales of existing ships, to seek to achieve a cost advantage based on their own view of these cycles.

Shipping is a largely fixed cost business with all cost items showing little variability. Once a ship is fully crewed, daily operating cost is more or less the same whether it is in port or at sea and regardless of cargo volume. The only way to significantly reduce that cost is to lay-up the ship, but even then a skeleton crew, maintenance and docking costs and ongoing insurance costs can add up to over one-third of normal operating costs. This inability to completely eliminate operating costs plays a role in making the lay-up of a ship, excluding any possibility of revenue, less attractive to ship owners.

Fuel costs at sea are minimally affected by cargo volume. However, overall fuel consumption per mile is very affected by vessel speed. It is not unusual to use 25% less fuel on a given voyage if a vessel elects to slow-steam instead of cruising at its design speed. That results in a significant difference across categories. In fact, there has been a meaningful reduction in average vessel speed since the financial crisis in 2008. Across all categories, today vessels are moving at a speed approximately 30% below speeds before the financial crisis. While resulting in significant fuel cost savings, the larger beneficial impact on the shipping industry was that slower speeds had the effect of reducing excess vessel supply. We'll discuss the impact of a potential unwinding of these slower speeds in another section.

The third major cost item, capital costs, economically has little variability once a vessel is purchased and is driven by the initial outlay and related financing. Obviously it is not affected at all by cargo volume and accrues at the same amount each day whether a ship is in port, at sea or in lay-up. Because it is inevitable, many ship owners often view capital costs as sunk and not affected by their decisions. In addition, most ship owners don't think of capital costs based on their daily equivalent amount. Whether because interest and principal payments are typically made on a quarterly schedule or because there is no debt, the real capital cost that accrues each and every day is not top of mind. Unfortunately, the economic cost element of capital costs is often not given the attention it deserves by ship owners.

Reflecting on all of these cost items and the limited ability of ship owners to develop a competitive cost advantage, it should be fairly easy to see that the focus is on maximizing revenue. Getting more cargo loaded for a given voyage and having more revenue producing voyages are key to overall financial performance. As everyone has the same goal and the revenue per unit in most shipping sectors is commodity like, pricing is significantly affected by supply and demand.

When shipping capacity exceeds shipping demand in any category, the price competition will be severe. Likewise, when shipping demand exceeds shipping capacity, pricing will move up quickly and sharply. There is no industry whose pricing is so immediately and dramatically affected by supply and demand. For the shipping industry, unfortunately, much more often than not the former exceeds the latter.

Costs related just to the ship itself represent varying percentages by category of the total costs that the ship owner is typically responsible for in the underlying movement and these differences affect overall cost economics. For instance, in container shipping the ships themselves are usually only 25% of the total costs for which the owner is responsible. Terminal costs, loading and unloading costs, equipment costs, inland transportation and general and administrative costs are all significant and part of the overall service provided by the container owner. In that sense, container shipping is less about ocean shipping and more about logistics related to the entire end to end movement.

On the other side of the spectrum are tankers where the ship itself represents almost all of the costs the ship owner is responsible for as well as the underlying movement. The loading and unloading of tankers is fairly automated after simple pipe connections are made between the ship and shore-side terminals. Those terminals are in turn connected with pipeline networks where crude oil and most petroleum products move autonomously from initial origin and final destination points. In between those two extremes lies the dry-bulk shipping category, although it is closer to the tanker category in terms of how much that business is purely related to shipping.

In the dry-bulk category, the ship does in fact represent almost all of the costs the ship owner is typically responsible for. However, the loading and unloading of dry-bulk vessels does require labor and costs. While not as involved as the labor to work container ships, it is not an inconsequential cost, particularly related to the relatively low value of some dry-bulk cargoes. Loading cargoes required less labor, as most cargoes are gravity loaded via chute or conveyor built. Equipment designed to most efficiently move the cargo is utilized in the unloading operation, but it does generally require more labor and time. Except for the times a dry-bulk ship owner contracts for a voyage charter or a contract of affreightment rather than a time charter, the loading and unloading costs are paid directly by the customer.

The general cargo ship category skews more towards container ships on the shipping business spectrum as the loading and unloading costs are typically well above the dry-bulk category.

The variance in costs the ship owner is typically responsible for as well as the overall cost of the underlying movement all play a role in the cost economics of the various categories. In general, the more the costs are just related to the ship itself, the more control and flexibility the owner has during extreme market conditions in both directions.

Tankers and dry-bulk vessels are most frequently employed under a timecharter where fuel costs and non-vessel voyage costs are paid directly by the customer. This results in the timecharter payment in effect covering daily operating costs and capital costs, which includes profit. That framework results in daily operating costs usually being a floor for timecharter rates. Even in the worst market conditions, accepting a timecharter rate below operating costs would result in negative operating cash flow for an owner. Confronted with this, an owner may choose to lay-up his ship and not reactivate it until rates would at least cover his operating costs.

Actual lay-up costs, desires to position a vessel and drydocking schedules may alter this equation, but as a rule of thumb, operating costs set a floor for tanker and dry-bulk ships and companies operating in those sectors generally have a positive operating cash flow. If and when that cash flow isn't sufficient to service underlying debt service and that condition isn't expected to improve, the company will usually be reorganized with some or all of the debt converted into equity.

Container ship owners and operators do not have the same flexibility as other ship owners. They operate multi-vessel networks where the vessels are only a portion of their overall costs. Many of those other costs, such as lease payments for terminals and container equipment, are fixed and continue whether the vessels operate or not. These owners do not have the same option as tanker and dry-bulk owners to lay-up ships because that doesn't impact their overall network costs as much. As such, operating costs are by no means a floor. In extreme market conditions with excess supply, container ship operators will experience negative operating cash flow even before significant capital costs.

For instance, in 2016 when supply exceeded demand in the container shipping, the sector showed a collective net loss of $9 billion before one-time charges and a net loss of $14 billion including those charges. At that performance level, the operating cash flow of the entire sector was negative. It is unusual for an entire industry to report such a large annual net loss. It is even more noteworthy for a capital intensive industry to experience an annual operating cash deficit with nothing generated to service its very significant capital investments.

The financial performance of the entire shipping industry since the financial crisis of 2008 has been less than satisfactory and the overriding culprit is excess supply. For many years prior to the crisis, volume growth across the board had been well above average and ship owners were experiencing record revenue and profits.

The key catalyst was China and the so-called super cycle of trade growth it experienced after joining the World Trade Organization in 2001. Just prior to the crisis the largest tankers were being chartered for $200,000 per day, the largest dry-bulk ships were being chartered for $100,000 per day and container ships were sailing near full capacity with ever increasing container rates. Profits were sufficient to pay for a new ship in two years even though it has a physical life ten times longer.

With this heady backdrop, orders for new ships, which had already been strong for years, were ratcheted up even more. Many ship owners believed that demand growth would continue to accelerate. Then the financial crisis came. Demand across most categories declined some 15% the first year, driven by trade financing difficulties as banks around the world experienced balance sheet trauma.

When growth resumed, it was at a much lower trajectory across categories. However, years worth of ships ordered in the heady days were being delivered. Where possible, ship owners sought and paid for delays in delivery dates and in some cases reached settlements to cancel construction contracts. Even with these actions, the actual growth in capacity swamped growth in demand for several years. Rates plummeted from their pre-financial crisis levels across categories.

A mitigating factor that kept rates from going even lower following the financial crisis was the adoption of slow steaming by ship owners and charterers. Container ship operators implemented this practice first as they always pay for fuel and the savings from slower speeds were significant. While it was telegraphed as a cost saving initiative driven by high fuel prices, the primary reason was to absorb new capacity as it was being delivered. A string of eight vessels providing weekly service first became a string of nine vessels and then strings of ten vessels and eleven vessels.

These slower speeds effectively absorbed capacity and at the same time reduced fuel costs. For charterers of tankers and dry-bulk ships who control vessel sea speeds, they would often choose the optimal speed that minimizes overall voyage costs. Arriving at that speed is a simple algebraic function based on the daily timecharter rate, the fuel consumption curve and fuel price. The lower the timecharter rate, the more attractive it is for charterers to engage in slow steaming. While their focus is on minimizing total voyage costs, by engaging in slow steaming they are also effectively taking actions that absorb capacity.

This combination of less excess capacity and lower fuel costs has played an extraordinary role across all shipping categories since the financial crisis and it continues to do so today. To put that into context, the average speed of most types of vessels is now 30% less than it was before 2008. In effect, this is shadow capacity that would automatically come back if vessel speeds increased.

One catalyst for that would be lower fuel prices, which would change the equation for charterers and ship owners in terms of speeds that would minimize total voyage costs. Even with no material changes in fuel prices, this overhang has a clear dampening effect on rates across categories. This occurs because when supply and demand factors start to push up rates, the optimal speeds increase and that has the effect of increasing capacity. This becomes a circular equation. It will potentially burden the entire shipping industry until cumulative demand growth is sufficient to fully absorb cumulative capacity growth. What has been a mitigating life preserver for the industry since the financial crisis is now an albatross burdening its future.

Fuel costs are expected to increase 50% to 75% for the entire shipping industry in 2020 when new IMO standards go into effect requiring ships to use cleaner low-sulfur fuel. While some believe this may usher in even more slow steaming, many observers note the consumption curves show diminishing benefits and end users would object to slower supply chains. At the very least, however, this sharp increase in fuel prices will blunt any incentives to increase vessel speeds.

With the change resulting from the IMO regulations, fuel costs will go from something approaching half of total operating, fuel and capital costs of a ship to something approaching two-thirds of such total costs. More than ever, fuel costs will be the dominant cost factor for ship owners and charterers alike. With little ability to impact the price of this commodity, more efforts will be focused on new technologies to improve overall fuel consumption. Main engine performance may be marginally improved with design changes to optimize fuel consumption at lower speeds. In addition, power and propulsion assists from solar power cells and rotor sails, among other existing technologies, could play a more meaningful future role.

All of the cost items and factors discussed above feed into the development of revenue rates in all shipping categories. However, the overriding catalyst in the determination of rates is and always will be supply and demand dynamics. When supply growth exceeds demand growth over a given period, there is downward pressure on rates. The opposite results when demand growth exceeds supply growth. Those changes influence behavior, like ordering new vessels or changing vessel speeds, which in turn feeds into the all-important supply versus demand equation. The resulting changes are often geometric in either direction, particularly when a tipping point is reached. Supply and demand dynamics are everything in terms of shipping rates and they in turn drive the economic performance of the industry.

For better and worse, each shipping category has a different set of factors that affect its supply and demand characteristics. Vessel cost, cargo value versus freight rates, customer base and ease of entry, among others, all influence this key dynamic. At one end of the spectrum is the dry-bulk sector which has the worse supply demand dynamics. Relatively simple ships built by dozens of shipyards, low cargo value, diverse customers and easy entry into a sector with little economies of scale all tend to work against the economic interests of ship owners. At the other end of the spectrum is the container sector. Expensive ships and the requirement for multiple vessels and significant investments in container equipment and terminal facilities result in major barriers to entry. The container sector rarely sees new entrants, a recurring capacity issue problem with most other shipping categories. The tanker and general cargo shipping categories fit within the other two categories, with the former closer to the dry-bulk sector and the latter closer to the container sector.

A case can be made that the container sector has more of the elements of a sustainable business model than the other shipping sectors. The fundamental reason for this is that the ship itself is less a part of the entire business. A container operator pulls together a broad array of elements to provide a service that can't be readily duplicated by its customers. In doing so, it can develop comparative advantages that may result in sustainable performance leading to a business valuation beyond the value of the discreet assets. On the other hand, the other sectors that are all much more ship-centric are subject to more duplication. As such, its more of a challenge to build a business model with a value beyond that of the discreet assets.

While the supply and demand characteristics vary somewhat across categories, a shared characteristic is that much more often than not, supply has exceeded demand. In fact, during the period I've been involved with the shipping industry, my observation is that for every favorable year where demand exceeded supply, there have been four or five years where supply exceeded demand.

The reasons behind this chronic over capacity situation are multi-faceted, but there are a few ones that are the key drivers. First and foremost are the attractive terms and financing that adroit ship owners have historically been able to obtain from shipyards and banks. When combined with corporate structures that limit the ship owners risk, the ship owner often ends up with a heads I win, tails you lose situation that is made even more attractive by the inherent financial and operating leverage in building a new ship. Once that ship is built, it doesn't go away even if the initial venture fails. Another ship owner will buy it, typically resulting in a much lower effective capital cost, which further exacerbates market conditions.

As to the initial decision to build a new ship or series of ships, the industry certainly doesn't suffer from a shortage of big picture thinkers who look at their crystal ball and firmly believe that it is the right time in the cycle to build. They often have a valid basis for thinking they are right. Unfortunately, they aren't alone and the collective orders typically swamp whatever actually unfolds.

My contention is that this macro, long-term focus of many ship owners, when not balanced out by a firm and analytical grasp of supply versus demand realities, is a fundamental source of much of the industry's performance problems. There is certainly a groupthink in the industry, with some owners even ordering because they learn other owners are ordering. The secretive nature of both the shipping and shipbuilding industry also makes accurate and reliable figures on ship orders not generally available on a timely basis so decisions aren't made with the best information.

In addition to inaccurate factual information on the newbuilding order book and coming supply, some ship owners are often too optimistic on their expectations of demand growth. The heady years of the China supercycle from 2001 to 2008 left some with the view that such growth would be the new normal.

The two-year lag from ordering a ship to taking delivery of a ship also complicates matters as economic conditions may change significantly. Ship owners are sometimes motivated to build new ships because they see vessel size or fuel consumption differences making them more cost effective than their current ships. That may be true, but when they sell their existing ships to other owners, the net effect of their decision is to increase supply while demand has remained constant.

When the shipping cycle is at a low point, shipyards reduce their prices to levels that some owners view as too attractive to pass up. As noted above, some owners think that building new ships at what they perceive as the lowest prices in the cycle is the best way to achieve a sustainable competitive cost advantage. Sadly, that strategy hasn't always worked well for ship owners but it still results in more capacity.

There are many things that go into the initial decision to build a new ship, but often those reasons don't stand up to scrutiny. In the end, the shipping industry only has itself to blame for this chronic over capacity situation.

The best way to solve this problem is to make more informed decisions when contemplating ordering new ships. It is almost as if the shipping industry has a collective fear that demand may exceed supply and they need to take steps to meet customer needs. However, only good things happen for the shipping industry in those infrequent times that demand exceeds supply. The shipping industry could stand to have more situations where that occurs.

One catalyst that continues to unfold that will help is the massive losses banks have and are experiencing in their shipping loan portfolios. With the withdrawal of some banks and changing requirements of the banks that continue to make loans to the sector, ship owners' ability to make irrational decisions will be constrained. Nevertheless, even with less financing, there will still be decisions by ship owners to build new ships that turn out to be bad decisions. Unfortunately, once such a ship is built, it becomes part of the over capacity problem.

While the economics and performance of the shipping industry is driven by market forces as in all other industries, there is another factor at work today that often skews and impacts the effect of those market forces. This factor is the direct government ownership and support of shipping companies. This is a growing phenomenon and its effect on the economics and performance of the shipping industry is decidedly negative.

The critical importance of shipping services to many economies, particularly those with significant exports and imports, is the reason behind governmental involvement. In many of those cases, the government is willing to accept a sub-optimal return on its shipping company investment if that is seen as being supportive of its larger agenda and goals for the economy. Even where there isn't direct direct equity ownership, governments may support shipping companies through subsidies and other means that skew the effect of normal market forces.

There have been situations where governments have supported low freight rates that are detrimental to their shipping company interests if such rates are viewed as facilitating exports or imports. In other words, what they lose in shipping they more than make up in other areas. The yardstick they are using to measure results goes beyond their shipping industry investment.

Governments that are actively involved in shipping also tend to be involved in shipbuilding. Shipbuilding may be the most government-supported industry because it achieves multiple goals. It is an industry with national security, labor employment and steel consumption attributes that most countries embrace. Unfortunately, too often that leads to government supported shipyards pushing unneeded ships onto government supported shipping companies, exascebrating the capacity situation.

While the involvement of governments in shipping companies may be rational for them, it injects irrationality into the economic performance of the shipping industry. This is a major detriment to market forces alone driving the results of the industry. As such, the increasing involvement of government entities in the shipping industry is a major negative in terms of overall financial performance.

The cost economics of the shipping industry played a direct role in the postwar specialization and ever-increasing vessel size across segments. In seeking to improve those cost economics, the individual giants discussed in other chapters took steps that eventually resulted in the remarkably efficient worldwide conveyance system we have today.

20. Shipping Versus Other Transport Modes

There are four fundamental modes by which cargo can be transported. One way to think of the various modes is to consider the trade-off between cost and speed. An axiom throughout the transport business is that costs move up as speed is increased. That cost difference between modes is typically geometric.

The fundamental transport modes by which cargo moves are water, rail, road and air. That broad classification moves from lowest cost to highest cost and also from slowest speed to fastest speed. Every cargo movement has at least two different transport modes that theoretically can be utilized. Many movements of goods, particularly those involving large countries like the U.S., have three and even four transport modes that can be utilized. In many cases, two or more modes will be used within an entire freight movement. The mode or modes that will be used will be based on various factors, with the trade-off between cost and speed a key factor. In general, the large majority of freight will flow to the lowest cost mode available.

If you look up the definition of freight in the dictionary, it is defined as something added to the cost of the product. Most producers of products are very focused on minimizing the overall costs of serving their customers. That definition of freight was one of Malcom McLean's favorite sayings and it framed his lifelong quest to develop better methods for moving freight from one point to another. Malcom would often say "Freight is something added to the cost of the product. If your focus isn't on minimizing that cost, you won't be in the freight business for long".

Goods moving internationally between continents usually only have the water and air modes to choose from. Only 15% of trade between countries is handled by land modes, with most of that concentrated in North America and Europe. By air, there are 1,690 planes exclusively dedicated to moving cargo and they account for 56% of total airfreight movements. The balance is represented by freight moving in the bellies of a much larger number of passenger planes. Another way to think of it is that airfreight cargo keeps the equivalent of 3,018 full freighter planes busy worldwide. That's a lot of planes, and when they are flying they move at 30-40 times the speed of ships.

However, in terms of average cargo carrying capacity, even the largest plane hardly moves the needle compared to a typical ship. You can see this by looking at the aggregate data. Total annual air cargo is now running at 47 million tons worldwide. That is equal to just .44% of the 10.6 billion tons of cargo now moved each year by the world's merchant marine fleet. The air tons also include domestic movements such as express mail. Therefore, even that low percentage is overstated if the focus is solely on cargo moving in international trade movements. On the other hand, the ship tons include dry and wet commodities moving in bulkers and tankers that should never move via air.

World trade can be viewed as a pyramid, with most of the volume in terms of weight made up of lower value bulk commodities. Some 63% of total trade in weight tons is represented by crude oil, iron ore and coal that move in the largest tankers and bulkers. The next 22% is made up of wheat, corn, steel, chemicals and an array of other bulk products that move in smaller bulkers and tankers. Then the next 14% is represented by manufactured goods moving in container ships. At the top of the pyramid is the very small sliver of trade in terms of overall volume that moves via air.

In terms of total ton-miles, worldwide air cargo was equivalent to 149 billion ton-miles in 2014. In comparison, in 2017 container ships moved some 10.6 trillion ton-miles of cargo. That works out to air cargo shipments equaling just 1.4% of the ton-miles represented by shipments on container ships, which is the primary shipping segment with any overlap with air. Compared to all shipping segments, air ton-miles are only .23% as the average distance is less owing to significant amounts of shorter intra-continental air cargo shipments and the straightline routes of air. By any measnure, air shipments are an inconsequential amount of overall cargo volume compared to what routinely moves on the giant ships that literally and figuratively deliver almost all world trade across the seas.

The trade-off between speed and cost across modes will depend on the particular unit sizes being compared. Across all modes, there is a fair amount of operating leverage, meaning the larger the unit size, the lower the underlying total cost per unit. A larger plane has a lower cost per ton-mile than a smaller plane, a truck moving more cubic feet of trailer space has a lower cost per cubic foot than a smaller truck, a 125 car train has a lower cost per ton than a 50 car train and a 21,000 TEU container ship has a lower total cost per TEU than a 5,000 TEU container ship. Each mode has different degrees of operating leverage. However, given the different cost attributes of the various transport modes and how those costs change as capacity per unit increases, shipping has the highest degree of operating leverage because no mode can match its unit size and ability to scale up capacity.

In order to quantify a rough approximation of the typical trade-off between speed and cost, the table below was developed. It shows for each mode the typical speed while in operation between points and the percent of total time around the clock spent moving between points. The table also includes an approximation of the relative linehaul costs by mode, excluding any setup costs on either end. This comparison was developed based upon the typical unit sizes in each mode as currently used in the U.S. today.

Mode	MPH Speed	% Linehaul Time	Relative Cost
Water	15	85%	1.0
Rail	25	65%	4.0
Truck	65	35%	12.0
Air	550	20%	36.0

As the table shows, there is a geometric relationship between speed and cost. The effective speed differences narrow somewhat when you take into account the fact that the faster the mode is, the smaller the percent of total available hours that are typically spent moving between points. Some of this is accounted for by the time needed to load and unload, but more of the differences are due to various constraints on usage such as hours of service and time of day. This relationship where the slower the mode the more time that is spent actually moving brings to mind the classic story of the tortoise and the hare.

The fastest mode, air, spends the least amount of available time moving. This was something I became keenly aware while performing a detailed analysis of block hour costs by plane type at cargo airlines and found that most planes were in the air five hours or less each day. On the other hand, ships typically spend 85% of their time at sea where they are moving 24 hours per day. The table was developed based upon how each mode is typically utilized today. The water mode is the slowest but has, by a very large margin, the lowest relative cost. The air mode typically operates at a linehaul speed that is 37 times faster than water, and 9 times faster if you adjust for the percent time in air or at sea, but it has a cost that is 36 times higher.

While merchant marine vessels are engaged almost exclusively in international trade, trucking and rail are primarily involved with domestic freight movements. There is some competition between trucking and rail, but more typically a cargo tends to be mostly if not entirely linked to one mode. The level of that competition is increasing as railroads have succeeded in getting more shippers to accept longer overall transit times in exchange for meaningful savings. Much of course depends on the specific cargo situation, but the increasing predictability of rail schedules and the higher service in the form pickup and delivery of intermodal container shipments continues to result in some switching from road to rail.

Because vessels are engaged almost exclusively in international trade while rail and trucking are almost exclusively in domestic trade, there is relatively little competition between those modes. In the situations that lend itself to such competition, vessels will have a linehaul cost advantage even on relatively short routes. However, the setup costs on either end, primarily the costs of loading and unloading the cargo unit from the ship, can change the comparison. The main routes where either rail or trucking could prevail against ships are those geographical situations where the distance is much shorter to go over land versus the over water distance, given the significant linehaul cost per unit mile advantages of water. Of course, transit time and non-ship related costs also factor into the equation.

When it comes to most international trade, the only two modes that are really involved are water and air. As shown earlier, total air shipments are virtually meaningless in terms of volume compared to water shipments. If you were to measure that based on shipment value, that would change the comparison as all air freight shipments are typically high value, low volume such as smart phones, software and prescription pills. The data shows that trade moving by air has a value equal to approximately 18% of the combined value of total trade moving by both water and air. Cargo value has little or no impact on the underlying costs of the freight provider as that cost is largely driven by the space you occupy in any given mode. However, higher cargo value does typically translate into less underlying price sensitivity by the cargo owner.

One underlying cost for the cargo owner that is affected by transit time is inventory carrying cost. The longer the transit time, the higher the inventory carrying cost. This can be readily calculated using cargo value and the respective company's cost of capital.

It is interesting to note that such a calculation will rarely justify, based just upon combined freight and inventory carrying costs, going with a faster mode in situations where you have a choice. Despite this incontrovertible fact, there is a bias towards quicker transit times, particularly if the price difference is perceived as reasonable. This bias was also supported by the fact that historically faster modes had more predictable transit times while the slower modes showed more variability. Those differences, however, are much less so today and the predictability of slower modes has substantially closed this inconsistency gap.

Earlier we had referred to just the container ships operating in the world today as moving 10.6 trillion ton-miles of cargo each year. If you take into account the other vessel types, that figure would go up by a factor of six to 63.9 trillion ton-miles of cargo each year. To put that into perspective, that figure is more than ten times the total U.S. domestic freight movement across all modes.

That comparison is worth reflecting on as it underscores the enormity of what the largely invisible fleet of ships does compared to a more tangible benchmark. Millions of trucks, thousands of locomotives and countless barges and miles of pipeline, and yet collectively they only move just 8.3% of the cargo moved in the 17,546 giants at sea.

That staggering comparison is based on U.S. Bureau of Transportation Statistics estimates that total domestic freight across all modes is 5.293 trillion ton-miles in the latest available year. Domestic truck and rail were the largest modes at 1.997 and 1.852 trillion ton-miles, followed by pipeline, water and air at .928, .504 and .012 trillion ton-miles, respectively. Note that in terms of domestic U.S. transportation, barges towed on inland waterways represent the water mode almost exclusively. While such barge tows are a very efficient mode compared to other domestic modes, they are significantly less efficient across all measures when compared to deep-sea cargo vessels.

Total U.S. domestic transportation represented a $1.2 trillion revenue industry in 2014. The breakdown of that revenue by mode is shown in the table below where the amounts are in billions of dollars.

U.S. Transport Modes	Revenue (Billions/Year)	% Total Revenue
Trucking	$715	59.9%
Rail	$178	14.9%
Water	$104	8.7%
Pipeline	$94	7.9%
Air	$44	3.7%
Other	$58	4.9%
Total	$1,193	100.0%

The split in total revenue by mode can be compared to the split in total ton-miles by mode to get some insight into relative pricing in the domestic U.S. transportation sector. That comparison is shown in the table on the next page where any revenue to ton-mile ratio above one indicates pricing higher than the overall domestic freight average. Note that these are broad comparisons across overall modes and there are subcategories within each mode. For instance, the revenue to ton-mile ratio for the truckload segment would be well below the same measure for the less than truckload segment.

Transportation Mode	% Revenue	% Ton-Miles	Revenue/Ton-Mile
Trucking	59.9%	37.7%	1.59
Rail	14.9%	35.0%	.42
Water	8.7%	9.5%	.92
Pipeline	7.9%	17.5%	.45
Air	3.7%	0.2%	18.50
Other	4.9%	na	na
Total	100.0%	100.0%	1.00

From this data, a related economic comparison can be developed that underscores the extraordinary efficiency of those 17,546 vessels. Using the figures above, the worldwide merchant marine fleet would represent a $12 trillion per year industry if it generated the same per ton-mile revenue as the entire domestic U.S. freight industry did.

Fortunately for shipping company customers and consumers, and unfortunately for the shipping industry itself, its annual revenue is something on the order of 2% of that amount. On the basis of how efficiently it moves a ton-mile of freight, the worldwide freight system comprised of 17,546 vessels is more than 50 times more cost efficient than the U.S. domestic freight system comprised of trucks, rails, pipelines and all other modes.

The 17,546 vessels move much more freight than all the trucks, railroads, pipelines, barges and planes in the world taken together. And they do it in a manner that makes them by far the most cost-efficient mode in which to move freight.

21. Geography and its Impact on Shipping

When you participate in the shipping industry, you develop a strong awareness of and appreciation for geography. It is fascinating to reflect on all the various ways geography affects and impacts shipping. In some cases, efforts related to improving shipping have also had a meaningful impact on actually changing geography.

My greater appreciation for geography began just from the contents of my mentor Malcom McLean's office when I started in shipping. A massive floor to ceiling world map dominated one of his office walls. In addition, next to and within reach of his office table was a rotating globe with a four-foot diameter.

I would come to find many discussions related to analyzing costs of various potential deployments would start with looking at the map or globe. Malcom would then reach for a decades old book never far from his side that contained nautical distances between all combinations of hundreds of ports worldwide. The starting point in developing the cost of moving something from point A to point B by ship is the nautical distance from point A to point B. That distance is of course totally driven by geography.

Historians often refer to the tyranny or randomness of geography and its impact on world events and history. Sigmund Freud believed that with humans, anatomy is destiny. Likewise, in the affairs of countries, geography is also destiny. Just as the close proximity of many countries in Europe has been a contributing factor to military invasions over the centuries, the isolation of America has prevented invasions. The oceans have protected America just as the Alps have protected Switzerland.

When reflecting on the interaction between geography and cargo shipping, there are three factors that initially come to mind on how the latter actually impacted our knowledge of and eventually even the contour of the former.

First, it was ships on mercantile voyages during the Age of Discovery that literally began to make mankind aware of the entire geography of the world. The only way these long voyages were possible was with ships. Second, it was the advent of much faster ships starting a couple hundred years ago that effectively shrank the globe and acted as a catalyst to broaden world trade. Third, in pursuit of shrinking distances and improving the efficiency of maritime trade, some of histories greatest civil engineering projects were undertaken that literally changed the geography of the world.

Water covers some three-quarters of the planet. That is the maritime geography in which ships have always operated. The maritime geography of the world can be loosely divided into three regions. Those regions are brown water, green water and blue water. Brown water is defined as navigable rivers and their estuaries, green water is defined as coastal waters, ports and harbors and blue water is defined as the open ocean.

The first cargo shipping began in the Nile over five thousand years ago. From that and other brown water regions, cargo shipping would then expand into green water regions. But the real effect and impact of cargo shipping on the world would only begin to take hold when it expanded into blue water regions over five hundred years ago during the Age of Discovery.

Whether it involves brown water, green water or blue water, shipping has for the most part been constrained by the geography within which it operates. On brown water, vessels have no choice but to go where the river goes. On green water, vessels move from one safe harbor to another by generally following the coastline. One thing that shipping on both brown water and green water have in common is that generally the cargo it moves can also be moved by either truck or rail modes.

This substitutability across modes means that even with the linehaul cost per mile advantage the water mode has, cargo may still move on the other modes. First, the linehaul cost advantage can be mitigated or sometimes even eliminated if the water distance is more than the land distance. Many rivers snake along in a way that results in distances well above nearby road or rail distances. That ratio of course is case specific and depends on the contours of the rivers or coastlines. That same ratio also drives time differences that play a role in determining the modal choice. With shipping, the loading and unloading costs at each end can also mitigate its lower linehaul cost per mile advantage. This is particularly true on the relatively short distances typically involved with cargo movements on brown and green water regions.

With the blue water cargo movements that are the domain of the 17,546 ships we focus on, for the most part there is no ability to move that cargo by either truck or rail mode. In the few cases where those land modes can be utilized, the long distances involved along with the extraordinary linehaul cost per mile advantages of shipping typically make those land modes less economical.

It is in this blue water region which covers 70.8% of the globe that the 17,546 ships are not only the dominant mode for moving freight, they are effectively the only mode for moving freight. While in fact planes also move freight over the same areas, since that represents a fraction of 1% of total freight movements, in the grand scheme of things from an actual ton-mile basis, the air freight market is virtually irrelevant.

The distances on these blue water voyages are geometrically more than the distances when cargo is moved over either brown water or green water. With the former, the voyages generally involve movements of a few hundred miles. With the latter, distances typically range from a few hundred miles to a few thousand miles.

In contrast, the average round-trip voyage distance by the 17,546 ships is now at 12,068 nautical miles. Note that a nautical mile is equal to 1.151 statute miles, so that distance is equivalent to 13,890 miles with which most people are familiar. To put that into perspective, the average roundtrip voyage of these blue water ships is a distance equivalent to driving between New York City and Los Angeles more than five times. There are slight differences in average voyage distances across the various vessel categories, which are shown in the table at the top of the next page.

Segment	Container	Tanker	Dry-Bulk	General
Ave Voyage Distance	14,227	11,229	12,389	10,409
Voyages/Year	6.1942	6.1942	6.1942	6.1942
Nautical Miles/Year	88,126	69,554	76,738	64,474
Ave Speed In Knots	10.06	7.94	8.76	7.36

These average voyage distance figures were determined based on the current average overall speeds of each vessel category. Those speeds come from actual readings of transponders on all ships and are averages including all time in port. Those speeds then determined the nautical miles traveled each year. Using the 10,596,000,000 total cargo tons moved in 2017 and comparing it to the 1,710,628,408 cargo carrying capacity of all 17,546 ships resulted in an estimated 6.1942 average voyages per year. We determined the average voyages per year using the most credible aggregate data. While some differences among categories exist, they are not particularly material.

The total nautical miles per year divided by that number of voyages resulted in the average voyage distance figures above. Note that those figures are roundtrip voyage miles determined based on the simplifying assumption that ships are fully loaded in one direction and completely empty in the other direction. While neither of those assumptions is completely accurate, particularly as it relates to ships in the container segment, they mitigate each other and the voyage distance estimates are accurate.

The variance in actual speeds across categories fits with what you would expect. At the low end of the speed spectrum is the general cargo vessel category. Despite including vessels such as car carriers that have highly efficient cargo operations, that category is weighed down by a majority of traditional general cargo ships being tied to less efficient cargo operations. Even though they are relatively small vessels, the longer time they spend in port pulls down their average overall speed. At the other end of the spectrum is the container ship category. Their average speed of 10.06 knots is 37% above the 7.36 knots average for general cargo ships. This difference is a combination of more efficient cargo operations as well as the faster at sea speeds associated with high value container cargo.

The 10.06 knots average speed for container ships can roughly be broken down as follows. If you assume that 30% of total time is spent in port and other activities not involving at sea transit such as canal passages or piloting into ports, the average speed at sea works out to 14.4 knots. With the slow steaming tactics almost all container ships now engage in, that speed can then be divided into the average speed in the headhaul direction and the average speed in the backhaul direction. Container ships operators typically concentrate their slow steaming in the less important backhaul direction. For instance, one way that average speed of 14.4 knots could be broken down is a speed of 18.0 knots in the headhaul direction and 10.8 knots in the backhaul direction.

Speed at sea was a primary way the cargo shipping industry addressed the challenges of geography. Columbus and other early explorers discovered new worlds, but their voyages were measured in years. Faster ships had the effect of bringing distant lands across the oceans closer together. While this was well known, it really didn't start to come into play until the advent of the magnificent clipper ships in the late 18th century. The term 'clipper' derives from the verb 'clip', which meant to run or fly swiftly. Clipper ships were built for speed and were intended to 'clip' over the waves rather than plough through the waves.

There is no single definition of the characteristics of the clipper ships built mostly by shipyards in America and England, but a marine author described them as follows: "To sailors, three things make a ship a clipper. She must be sharp-lined, built for speed. She must be tall-sparred and carry the utmost spread of canvas. And she must use that sail, day and night, fair weather and foul."

Built and optimized for speed, clipper ships were too fine-lined to carry much cargo. A typical clipper ship had a total cargo capacity of 200 tons. To put that in perspective, the average cargo capacity of the 17,546 ships profiled herein is 435 times the cargo capacity of a clipper ship. Just one modern cargo vessel could move many times the total cargo that moved on all the clipper ships at their height.

However, when it comes to speed, clipper ships can more than hold there own with modern cargo ships. Clipper ships averaged 250 nautical miles per day, or slightly more than 10 knots. That speed was more than twice as fast as sailing ships prior to the introduction of clipper ships. Those were the average speeds across all weather conditions and most clipper ships would reach 15 or 16 knots in good weather. There developed an active competition to achieve and surpass various speed records and this resulted in the development of even faster clipper ships. In addition to overall transit time between various ports, they competed to see who could cover the most distance in a full 24-hour day. In 1854, the *Sovereign of the Seas* covered 528 nautical miles in one day, setting the record at a blistering 22 knots.

For much of the 1800's, these graceful clipper ships crisscrossed the world, moving trade between countries to a higher level everywhere. They focused on high value cargoes such as tea, opium, spices, silk and other goods. China to England and the rest of Europe and China to America were the most important trade routes for the clipper ships. The arrivals and departures of clipper ships from ports like New York, Boston, London and San Francisco was front-page news and resulted in hundreds if not thousands of people to go to the docks to see the ships. The lore of and fascination with clipper ships by the citizenry of the day is hard to overstate. These fast ships literally made the geography of the world more familiar and introduced millions to the concept of trade.

The routes of the clipper ships would later play a direct role in the global extension of another transport mode. In the 1930's, Juan Trippe, the founder of Pan American Airways, wanted to expand into international markets. He visited the New York City Library and spent days researching himself the routes of the clipper ships.

This research led him to conceive of a network of strategic stopping points for planes he was developing that had a range of 3,000 miles. At one point, Trippe told an associate, while placing his finger on a seemingly open expanse of ocean, "I need to find an island right here". His further research on a more detailed map would turn up the small and barely inhabited Midway Island where Pan Am established a stopover facility. These large, four-engine propeller planes were designed as amphibious planes that could land on water. With this network and those planes, Pan Am launched the first ever America to Asia flight service. From there, what others called flying boats were utilized to open up other long distance international air travel markets. Trippe, however, would name the largest passenger planes flying the Pan Am Clippers, in honor of where they traced their heritage.

Getting back to the blue water regions and the 1800's, with the development of steamships, the clipper ships started to see increasing competition. While they were generally faster, the vagaries of the wind also made their schedules less predictable. Some customers began to prefer the more consistent steamships, which were also growing in size. As they scaled up in cargo capacity, this allowed steamships to start offering better economics.

What marked the beginning of the end of the clipper ship era, however, was the opening of the Suez Canal in 1869. It is ironic that the decline of clipper ships, an early way cargo shipping challenged geography by cutting sea transit time in half, was ushered in by the first major effort at tangibly changing geography to benefit cargo shipping in blue water regions.

Prior to discussing the Suez Canal, it is worth noting the constraints related to shipping in the blue water regions. While they aren't as significant as the constraints in the brown and green water regions, they also exist. While the former have tangible boundaries and contours, the blue water regions have similar but less recognizable constraints. Their origins go back to Pangea, the single supercontinent that existed 325 million years ago.

As the continental plates shifted, Pangea was transformed into the continents and oceans we have today. The Atlantic Ocean was formed when what is now the Americas were ripped apart from what is now Europe and Africa. Look at a map and you can see the similarities in the contours, particularly where the bulge in South America is symetrical with the recess in Africa. When large deposits of iron ore were found in the former, geographically astute entrepreneurs surmised the same must exist in the latter and they were recently proven correct.

When all these landmasses were ripped apart, random boundaries and contours were created. Think of the Atlantic Ocean as a very wide river running vertically east of the Americas. Similarly, the Pacific Ocean can be seen as a very wide river running vertically west of the Americas. Many of the most direct, longer blue water routes are primarily vertical, following the direction of these hypothetical rivers. Many of the primarily horizontal blue water routes across these hypothetical rivers were also fairly direct.

Where marine routes became convoluted and less direct is where they involved voyages in two or more oceans. Invariably, such voyages needed to go around landmasses represented either by the Americas or Eurasia and Africa. As trade patterns developed more around east-west routes, these landmasses became increasing obstacles to more efficient shipping. The Suez Canal was the first major attempt to dramatically change world geography in order to make cargo shipping more efficient.

In the 1800's, the Asia to Europe trade lane was the busiest in the world. Clipper ships would typically take some 40 days in each direction and all voyages sailed around the Cape of Good Hope, the southern tip of Africa. Regular sailing vessels would take almost twice as long, or 80 days in each direction.

Mariners had long known that a shorter route could be created if a canal could be built connecting the Mediterranean Sea with the Red Sea via the Isthmus of Suez. In fact, there was a smaller ancient canal built more than two thousand years ago that linked the Nile River with the Red Sea making use of various intermediary lakes.

After conquering Egypt in 1798, Napolean sent surveyors with a plan to construct a canal connecting the Red Sea directly with the Mediterranean. Such a route would reduce the one-way distance by some 3,300 nautical miles, cutting voyage time by one-third. However, Napoleon's surveyors erroneously determined that the sea level difference was 38 feet, making the project unworkable based on the lock technology available at that time. As trade continued to increase, however, finding a way to build such a canal continued to be studied by many, particularly the French.

With improvements in lock technology, a new survey was undertaken by the French in the mid-1800's. Those surveyors determined that such a project would not require locks and it would be a sea level canal. Active planning ensued and construction began in 1859 by a company underwritten by the French. With some 30,000 laborers working at all times, progress was slow at first as pick and shovel dug everything.

Two years into the project, however, the invention of steam-powered shovels resulted in hundreds of the new machines being shipped to Egypt. Making use of the intermediary lakes as well as some of the remnants of the ancient canal, but driven by the efficiency of the steam shovels, the canal would be completed ahead of schedule some ten years after construction began. In total, more than 75 million cubic meters of sand were excavated to build the canal.

The Suez Canal opened in 1869 and with that event the clipper ship dominance in the Asia to Europe trade route quickly dissipated. This was partly affected by this more protected route not having the same open ocean tradewinds that helped sailing ships and hindered steamships. The main catalyst, however, was consistent improvements in the size and speed of steamships and their ability to offer lower freight rates. Within a few years, steamships dominated the Asia to Europe trade route. The clipper ships they displaced were redeployed in long Australia and South America to Europe trade routes where favorable tradewinds mitigated their increasing cost disadvantages.

Early in my shipping career I had the opportunity to see the Suez Canal while in Port Said, the northern terminus of the canal, managing the discharge of a vessel loaded with bulk wheat. It is certainly an impressive site. In particular, driving along a desert road that ran parallel to but a few miles away from the canal and seeing convoys of giant ships that appeared to being floating on the sand is something that is remarkable.

As meaningful a change in shipping geography as the Suez Canal was, an even bigger change would begin to take hold not too long thereafter in Panama. With its strategic location as a narrow isthmus separating two large oceans, the concept of a canal to connect those oceans had been talked about for centuries. In 1534 King Charles V of Spain ordered a survey for a route through the Americas that would shorten the distance for ships moving between Spain and Peru. Such a route was also seen as giving Spain a military advantage over its archrival Portugal.

In 1668, British philosopher Sir Thomas Browne actively promoted the idea of a canal to shorten voyages between England and Asia. This westbound route would be shorter than the eastbound route around the tip of Africa. Thomas Jefferson suggested in 1788 that Spain build a canal to result in routes that were less treacherous than the long route around the tip of South

America. No active construction planning resulted from any of these and other initiatives, but the concept of a canal and the significant savings in voyage distance and time that would result from it were well known.

The discovery of gold in California in 1849 created renewed interest in building a canal across Panama to connect the Atlantic and Pacific oceans. The gold rush sharply increased the ships travelling between the East Coast and West Coast, as the transcontinental railroad didn't exist and was still twenty years away. Such voyages were very long and went around the tip of South America. For example, it was 13,277 nautical miles from New York to San Franscisco.

Beyond the long distance, these voyages involved rounding Cape Horn, the southern tip of South America, which consistently has some of the worst sea conditions in the world. The key reason for this is that this is the only place on earth where there is no landmass along the entire latitude. With nothing to break the effect of waves and wind at a narrow part of the globe, storms whip around almost endlessly in that area.

Ferdinand Magellan was the first European to experience this tumultuous passage in 1521 during his westward circumnavigation of the globe. Days after going through, he entered an unchartered body of water he named the "peaceful sea". That body of water is the modern Pacific Ocean and Magellan's name stuck. While most mariners don't view the Pacific Ocean as particularly peaceful, Magellan was undoubtedly thinking in relative terms compared to the wretched sea conditions he had just come through.

While avoiding the passage around Cape Horn would be an anicilliary benefit of a canal through Panama, the primary reason it continued to be focused on was the significant reduction in voyage distances it offered. For instance, New York to San Francisco via a canal would be 5,257 nautical miles, a reduction of 8,020 nautical miles or 60% compared to going around South America. In other words, a canal through Panama would typically reduce voyage distances more than twice the distances saved by the Suez Canal. With such benefits, and the growing trade that could and would take advantage of such a canal, the interest in building it continued to intensify.

The success of France in building the Suez Canal encouraged them to turn their attention to Panama. In 1877, French engineers surveyed a route that had been proposed by a 1855 study underwritten by the U.S. That study resulted in a book entitled *The Practibility and Importance of a Ship Canal to Connect the Atlantic and Pacific Oceans*. Confirming the project, the French outlined a plan to build a canal with an organization that would be headed up by the man who oversaw the successful construction of the Suez Canal.

After reaching an agreement with Columbia, which controlled Panama at the time, the French began constructing the canal in 1881. While only 40% as long as the Suez Canal, the challenges in Panama were extraordinary. Unlike the dry conditions in Egypt involving the excavation of mostly uniform sand, Panama was a wet tropical forest, carpeted with trees and vegetation resulting in non-uniform digging conditions. The rainy season resulted in flash floods and cuts needed to be constantly reworked and widened to minimize the ever-present danger of landslides.

While France had started the project with the plan of a sea level canal like in Egypt, experience with the rainy season and further studies would make it eventually realize that locks would be necessary. The hot and humid conditions made it a wretched environment for the workers, even though most of the excavation was being done with the aid of steam shovels and other machinery.

In addition, the dense jungle contained wildlife, snakes and insects at every turn. These conditions came together to result in yellow fever, malaria and other tropical diseases that were impacting thousands of workers. At the time, the role of the mosquito as a disease source was unknown. Measures to reduce the spread of these diseases were ineffective and by 1884 the fatality rate was over 200 workers per month. The workers weren't the only ones adversely affected by the climate as steel equipment rusted quickly.

Despite these difficulties, the French company spearheading the project kept sending money and workers to Panama. With some 800,000 French investors backing the venture, the leaders had little interest in admitting failure even after this had become apparent to them. The work plodded on but increasingly fell behind targets and eventually ran out of money.

In 1889, the company holding the franchise from Columbia went bankrupt, having spent $287 million and losing some 22,000 lives to disease and accidents. In total, the French had excavated 23 million cubic meters of material. With the bankruptcy wiping out the savings of many French citizens, the ensuing fingerpointing and scandal resulted in the prosecution of many prominent Frenchmen. A successor French company took over the franchise in 1894 and continued to operate the cross-isthmus railroad while it marketed its rights to continue construction of the canal to other entities that may be interested.

In 1902, the U.S. Senate voted in favor of moving ahead with building the canal. The following year the U.S. supported Panama's succession from Columbia and entered into agreements with the new government as well as the French company for its assets. The U.S. took control of a designated canal zone in 1904 and resumed construction.

The key first step was to address the disease problem, which had recently been shown to spread by mosquitos. With this new information, Colonel William C. Gorgas, the chief sanitation officer, implemented a series of measures resulting in largely eliminating mosquito-spread diseases after two years. The housing and infrastructure for workers was rebuilt and enhanced. Thousands of new workers were recruited from the U.S. and other countries. New, more efficient equipment, including over one hundred very large rail-mounted steam shovels, was brought in from the U.S.

With the yellow fever and malaria problem addressed, a revitalized workforce with the best earth moving equipment available moved ahead with many times the efficiency of the earlier French effort. At its peak, 40,000 people would be at work building the canal, with the majority of those workers coming from various Caribbean countries.

The Panama Canal, the largest engineering project the world had ever seen, was completed in 1914. The project included the largest dam, the largest man-made lake and the largest locks ever built. One section of the canal was literally cut through a mountain range. In total, the U.S. effort resulted in the excavation of 130 million cubic meters of soil.

When added to earlier excavations by the French, the Panama Canal required the removal of twice as much material as the Suez Canal, under much more challenging conditions. Even with much less disease, more than 5,600 workers would die from accidents and other causes. In total, the U.S. spent some $500 million to construct the Panama Canal, making it the largest construction project ever undertaken at that time.

World commerce benefits immensely today from the shipping cost and transit time advantages that result from the operation of the Suez Canal and the Panama Canal. In 2017, the Suez Canal had a total of 17,550 ships transit the canal. With $5.3 billion of revenue, the average canal toll was approximately $300,000 per ship. While that may seem high, it is still only approximately two and one-half sea days of total cost of large container ships that frequently use the Suez Canal. With the distance savings from using the canal typically 3,300 nautical miles, it is still very cost-efficient to use the Suez Canal. In 2017, there were 11,992 ships that transited through the Panama Canal. The $2.2 billion in total canal tolls works out to approximately $185,000 per ships. With the Panama Canal offering voyage distance savings of up to 8,000 nautical miles, the vessel cost savings from using the canal are many times more than the canal toll.

While these large canals are the most dramatic way that cargo shipping changed the geography of the world, they came after many smaller canals in brown water regions across the world that benefited commerce. China, Europe and the U.S. all had canals that were built to augment various inland waterways.

The Grand Canal in China, with portions built more than fifteen hundred years ago, is the longest canal in the world with a length of over 1,000 miles. It connects Bejing with various interior provinces and links the Yellow and Yangtze Rivers, China's two major inland waterways. In Europe, canals have long been used to extend and augment inland waterways that are used to move all types of freight. Two major cities, Amsterdam and Venice, are actually built around canals. The largest canal in the U.S. is the Erie Canal, which played a key role in the development of the young country. All of those canals physically changed geography and allowed maritime commerce that produced major economic benefits. Nowhere was this truer than with the Erie Canal.

The Erie Canal was started in 1817 after being proposed for several decades. When the 363-mile long canal was completed in 1825, it connected Buffalo and Lake Erie with Albany and the Hudson River. The canal connected the eastern seaboard with the western interior of the country in a way that cut transport costs by 95%. The economic impact of the Erie Canal on the Hudson Valley and New York City cannot be overstated. With its completion, towns developed on the Hudson River between Albany and New York City that became the industrial center of the young country.

The impact on New York City, specifically activity in the port, was equally dramatic. The port grew geometrically as it became the gateway for everything coming from or going to the Erie Canal. Prior to the canal opening, there were several cities, including Philadelphia, Baltimore and Boston, which were on par with New York City in terms of population and port activity.

With the growth that came from the canal opening, New York City catapulted ahead of all cities on the eastern seaboard in terms of both population and port activity. The Erie Canal would eventually be displaced by railroads and highways that were more efficient compared to the small canal boats, but its pivotal role in the 1800's is undeniable. Its hard to think of a single event in American history that has been as much of an economic catalyst for growth of a single city as the Erie Canal was for New York City.

In addition to building actual canals, there are more subtle ways that maritime commerce leads to changes in geography. In green water regions, dredging harbors and docks allow larger deeper draft ships to be utilized, resulting in major cost benefits. In brown water regions, augmenting those waterways with levees and locks increases their navigability. In the U.S., the U.S. Army Corps of Engineers, the same organization that successfully managed the construction of the Panama Canal, actively manages the inland waterway system. As a result, today the inland waterway system of the U.S. has almost as many miles of navigable rivers as the rest of the world combined.

That efficient inland waterway system is the sole reason the U.S. is a large exporter of grain and other commodities. While our cost of producing those commodities is higher than in many countries, nobody can match our low cost of transporting those commodities from the interior to export ports. That extraordinary inland waterway system is our underlying competitive advantage.

When you think about the settlement of the New World during the Age of Discovery, you can't help but to develop an appreciation for the intersection of shipping and geography and how that drove economic development. The very choice of where to start a settlement was completely driven by where these explorers found a harbor where mercantile ships would be safe. It is by no means a coincedance that the two largest New World cities founded by the Spainards also had the two best natural harbors in the Caribbean.

Havana has a narrow channel that connects a large inner harbor with the Caribbean Sea. The precision of the cut through a six hundred foot mountain makes it look like a modern man-made project, but it is natural. It results in a safe harbor fully protected in all weather conditions and one impervious to attack by enemy ships if canons are placed on each side of the channel as the Spainards did. With these maritime related geographic advantages, Havana grew into the largest city in the Caribbean and the capital of Spain's empire in the New World.

Similarly, San Juan had a large oval shaped harbor with a narrow entrance offering protection from the weather and the ability to be fortified. The Spainards were so taken with the port and the commerce they saw it supporting that they named it Puerto Rico, for rich port. A mapmaker maker would later transpose that and the name the Spainards had given the island, San Juan, and that is how they are known today. With the foundation of nothing more than excellent natural harbors, Havana and San Juan have continuously grown to the cities with populations over two million people that they are today.

While it is obvious the role maritime geography played in those and other New World cities, the same holds true for the development of many cities around the world. Almost all of the largest cities in the world are either on coasts or on major inland waterways. This too is no coincidence and has nothing to do with a desire for waterfront views, a modern day preference. These locations had everything to do with proximity to ships and other waterborne vessels.

At the time many of these cities were initially settled, the water mode was effectively the only mode for moving cargo and that was the prime catalyst for site selection. If you could choose any site within a large expanse of land, why wouldn't you choose a site adjacent to a natural harbor or navigatable waterway? Whether its New York, Shanghai, Sao Paulo or London, a shared trait of these and many of the largest cities in the world is that the roots of their existence go back to their initial discovers and early settlers who appreciated their maritime geography.

Today 40% of the world's population lives within 100 kilometers of a coast. If those coastal distances are extended to 200 and 400 kilometers, the percentages grow to 54% and 67% respectively. These statistics underscore the continuing role proximity to water and maritime commerce plays in the world today. While the widest band of 400 kilometers or 248 miles from a coast represents just 10% of total land area, it is home to two-thirds of the world's population.

There is a multitude of ways geography continues to impact shipping and vice versa. In addition to impact the cost efficiency of shipping has had for world trade, Asia experiences a secondary benefit that has the effect of lowering its manufacturing costs. That, in turn, is a catalyst that drives even more trade. The major manufacturing centers in Asia are mostly located in coastal cities. Manufacturing in Asia frequently involves components made in various places with final assembly in another place. This specialization lowers actual manufacturing costs at each stage. And it is ships that move most of these goods through the various stages of production.

For instance, in the container sector, the dozens of intra-Asia routes constitute the largest container trade in the world. Sometimes just a few hundred miles, the combination of the linehaul cost efficiency of ships and the relatively low cargo handling costs in Asia translate into little added transport cost. Those transport costs are generally much less than what transport costs would be for a similar truck or rail movement. Ships are the trucks of Asia. That results in meaningful cost benefits for products manufactured in Asia.

The physical changes that created the continents and oceans continue to occur, albeit at rates that won't affect mankind for milleniums. As the plate under Africa moves northbound, it will eventually close off the Gibraltar strait. Without the inflow of seawater from the Atlantic to compensate for the high evaporation rate in the Mediterranean Sea, it will almost completely dry-up approximately one thousand years later.

We know this will happen because it happened six million years ago. The passage closed, the sea dried up and it remained that way for hundreds of thousands of years. However, more plate activity resulted in a fissure that opened up what it now the Gibraltur strait. The waters from the Atlantic rushed in at incredible speed in what was the biggest flood in history. Many researchers now believe that today's Mediterranean Sea was refilled in as little as two weeks with water rushing in at 200 miles per hour at volumes many times the largest rivers.

Obviously macro changes like these, had they not occurred or occurred at different times, would have dramatically changed maritime geography and in so doing the entire spectrum of world history would be different. With no Mediterranean Sea, centuries of pivotal cargo shipping developments wouldn't have occurred, Columbus and other explorers wouldn't have sailed and the Suez Canal wouldn't have existed. Human endeavor and progress would have been tilted in dramatically difference ways on which we can only speculate today.

Another macro change that will change maritime geography and which the data suggests is closer at hand relates to climate change and the fabled Northwest Passage. For centuries, early explorers sought to find routes to connect Europe with Asia that were shorter than the long sailing trip around Africa. That effort focused on ways to get to the Pacific Ocean by going through portions of what we now know is the Artic Ocean. The desire to find such a passage motivated many early explorers such as John Cabot, Marco Polo and Sir Francis Drake.

Attempts to find such a passage would drive voyages of exploration along both coasts of North America. Henry Hudson would sail up what is now the Hudson River, convinced it would lead him to the Northwest Passage. In the 1700's, the British dispatched separate expeditions led by Captains James Cook and George Vancouver to explore the artic region and find a passage.

With the knowledge gained from these and other explorations, finally by the mid-1800's a shorter route was discovered, but it was not entirely navigatable by ship. It would not be until 1903 when Norweigen explorer Roald Amundsen would sail the Northwest Passage entirely by ship. Even then, some portions were extremely shallow, with drafts of only three feet, making it commercially impractical.

Further exploration and surveying would result in refinements to the route allowing passage of deep draft vessels, but the constant obstacle was ice floes and seasonal conditions. In 1969, the 105,000 DWT ice reinforced tanker *Manhattan* successfully navigated the Northwest Passage with the support of icebreakers as a test of whether it could play a role in moving newly discovered oil from Alaska. Stavros Niarchos, one of the individual giants, owned the *Manhattan*. While it succeeded, the time and cost involved with the route made it cost ineffective. The Alaskan pipeline was built instead to move oil.

Even with the assistance of icebreakers, the Northwest Passage can only be transited during the warmer months. However, climate change is resulting in consistent reductions in artic ice based on various measurements. Recently, a ship was able to go through the Northwest Passage earlier than anytime previously. Several studies are now predicting that based on current trends, the Northwest Passage will be open year round to cargo ships by 2100. Given that Asia to Europe and Asia to North America are the two biggest trade routes in the world, and both could have voyage distances between many port pairs cut in half, the impact on shipping will be pronounced. The cost of shipping would come down further and both the Suez and Panama Canals would find their relevance significantly reduced.

The cause and effect and broad interplay between geography and shipping have been present at all times throughout history and continue to this very day. It was ships, after all, that first made mankind aware of the geography of the world. Beyond the shipping-related engineering projects that have changed geography, shipping has figuratively shrunk the globe and brought countries closer together by the ties resulting from trade.

22. Shipping Cost Versus Cargo Value

The dictionary defines freight as something that is added to the cost of the product. That definition was one of Malcom McLean's favorite observations. I suspect that was the case because the business thesis of his life was really reducing the freight cost of moving something from point A to point B. Neither Malcom nor the other individual giants could have anticipated that by the steps they took to make shipping more cost-efficient, they were laying the foundation for the explosion in trade the world has experienced.

As it turns out, the data since the post-war revolution in shipping cost efficiency highlights that world trade is in fact very elastic to shipping costs. One straightforward measure of this is shipping cost relative to cargo value. In the pre-war period, it was typical for shipping costs to be 50% or more of the value of the cargo being moved.

Those real world costs were friction that significantly added to the cost of the product. It is fairly obvious to understand the barrier that such shipping costs would be to trade. However, when those relative costs come down by more than a factor of ten, its equally obvious to understand how that would be a catalyst for trade.

The relationship between shipping cost and cargo value varies sharply by vessel category. This relationship impacts a number of variables affecting each segment, not the least of which is the pricing power and related profitability of the segment.

The table below shows the total daily cost at sea of the largest vessel types in each segment and the roundtrip voyage days of one of the most frequent routes for each vessel. The total resulting port to port cost of that voyage is then compared to cargo value, assuming the vessel is fully loaded in one direction and the cargo is valued using current rates. As the table shows, at the low end of the spectrum is the container segment where direct vessel costs are equal to 1.82% of cargo value. At the other end of the spectrum is the dry-bulk segment where direct vessel costs are 31.34% of cargo value.

Segment	Container	Tanker	Dry-Bulk	General
Vessel Type	ULCV	VLCC	VLOC	Car Carrier
Total Daily Cost	$133,952	$73,733	$46,576	$62,729
Origin Port	Shanghai	S Arabia	Brazil	Tokyo
Destination Port	Rotterdam	Shanghai	Shanghai	Rotterdam
Distance Miles	10,525	5,938	10,857	11,192
RT Voyage Days	103	73	122	149
Total Vessel Cost	$13,739,554	$5,406,037	$5,659,340	$9,351,874
Cargo (Millions)	$756.2	$153.2	$18.1	$250.0
Vessel Cost/Cargo %	1.82%	3.53%	31.34%	3.74%

The voyage costs above include only the direct vessel costs and exclude any costs of loading and unloading cargo. On the other hand, vessel costs include all capital costs, which often aren't recovered by ship owners in periods of excess supply. The port pairs used are among the longer voyages in each segment and shorter voyages would have proportionately less cost. Taking all these factors into consideration, the resulting percentages in the table above are reasonable representations of shipping cost relative to cargo value by segment that can be used to make a number of observations.

In particular, the container shipping example showing shipping cost to cargo value of 1.82% is worth reflecting on. This segment is the one most connected to the postwar explosion in world trade and the concept of globalization. First, a simple comparison of the segment's total revenue to the goods it moves confirms the efficacy of the example. With revenue of $140 billion and goods moved worth $7.0 trillion in 2017, the total cost was 2.00% of value. That is almost approaching an inconsequential cost for many products. When compared to a 50% cost to value ratio for many manufactured products in the prewar period, that is a reduction in relative costs by a factor of twenty five times.

More so than any segment, the extraordinary cost efficiency of container shipping has propelled world trade in the postwar era. By reducing real world transfer costs to a near frictionless level, container shipping has figuratively shrunk the world and made distance almost irrelevant. In doing that, manufacturing has transitioned to locations with the lowest labor and materials costs.

In general, the lower the relationship of shipping cost to cargo values, the greater the pricing power of the ship owner. It stands to reason that, everything else being equal, customers will be more resistant to pricing increases when they have a more pronounced impact on their own final delivered cost. That, however, is a relative statement that is almost always overshadowed by the supply and demand dynamics at any given point in time.

While the dry-bulk segment has the highest relationship between shipping cost and cargo value, it also has the most variability among the different commodities that move on those vessels. For instance, wheat and corn will have much lower relationships than the iron ore example used in the above table. However, wheat and corn collectively are less than half the volume of iron ore shipments that move on dry-bulk vessels.

Iron ore is the largest seaborne dry-bulk commodity and the exclusive cargo of the largest dry-bulk ships. The large majority of seaborne iron ore shipments are destined for China, which now produces more than half of the world's steel. For each ton of steel, just over 1.5 tons of iron ore are required. The iron ore voyage from Brazil in the table above is among the longest iron ore voyages.

Significant amounts of iron ore also come from Australia, where the distance to China is one-third the distance from Brazil. Recognizing the shipping cost disadvantage that distance would result in, the largest miner in Brazil constructed a new class of ships. Known as Very Large Ore Carriers or VLOC's, they move almost twice as much iron ore as Capesize vessels, previously the largest dry-bulk carriers.

That comparison between iron ore from Brazil and iron ore from Australia brings up a basic point regarding shipping that is worth re-emphasizing. Demand in the shipping industry isn't driven by cargo units, but by cargo unit-miles, whether the units are containers, tons or barrels.

To move the same volume of iron ore from Brazil would take three times as many similar sized ships as to move that same volume of iron ore from Australia. While Australia is still the largest exporter of iron ore, Brazil is a close second and is growing faster as steel producers like its high-grade ore. To the extent that the source of a given amount of iron ore shifts from Australia to Brazil, it would have no effect on absolute iron ore production, but it would have a pronounced effect on related demand for large bulk carriers.

This truism that for shipping it is all about unit-miles and not just units is something that has always affected the shipping industry for good and bad. For instance, that is why various closings of the Suez Canal have resulted in such immediate and pronounced increases in various shipping rates. Overnight, those closures increased the distance and time for routes between Asia and Europe by 50% and between the oil exporting Middle East and Europe as well as North America even more.

With these longer supply lines, effective capacity literally shrunk overnight and the supply demand dynamic swung sharply in favor of ship owners. The impact of dramatic changes in unit-miles even when units remain unchanged will continue to effect all shipping sectors going forward.

The large majority of the final delivered cost of both iron ore and coal, which collectively represent 57% of the cargo volume moving on dry-bulk vessels, is actually represented by transportation. From moving from the mine to the railroad to the export terminal to the import terminal, transportation is the main input to its value at each stage. While they are tangible products, their economic value is a function of the transportation services that go into moving them.

This characterization of the two largest dry-bulk commodities as largely the sum total of transportation services to their final delivery point also explains the dominance of the water mode for iron ore and coal as well as other dry-bulk cargoes. Whether via inland barge or ocean-going ship, the cost economics of moving these cargoes is vastly superior per unit-mile compared to anything that can be achieved with rail or road. When all these factors are kept in mind, they mitigate the dry-bulk segment's high shipping cost to cargo value ratio and its adverse effect on pricing power.

An example involving China highlights this. China has a very large domestic iron ore industry with further iron ore reserves that could be mined. However, much of the growth in its demand for iron ore has been satisfied with imports of iron ore from Australia and Brazil. While China's iron ore has half the iron content of imports and this is a meaningful factor, another key factor is that the transportation cost economics of moving iron ore on giant cargo ships is often less than moving it from interior points in China to where it is needed.

For a country known for its manufacturing cost efficiency, China's system for moving freight to and from interior points via barge, rail and road is at present relatively inefficient. However, this is rapidly changing with massive investments in infrastructure which themselves will impact the shipping industry in the future.

If you take the shipping cost to cargo value ratios for all four segments and consolidate them based on aggregate total value moved by segment, you get 4.35% as the overall composite ratio of direct vessel cost to cargo value. This is shown in the table below. As indicated above, the dry-bulk segment is somewhat unique, as much of the final delivered cargo value is comprised of the various transport modes. If you do a similar calculation on just the container, tanker and general cargo segments, you get 2.47% as the composite direct vessel cost to cargo value.

Segment	Container	Tanker	Dry-Bulk	General	Total
Vessel Type	ULCV	VLCC	VLOC	Car	
Vessel Cost/Cargo %	1.82%	3.53%	31.34%	3.74%	
Total Value (Bill)	$7,027	$1,925	$766	$1,994	$11,712
% Total Value	60.0%	16.4%	6.5%	17.0%	100.0%
WA Cost/Value %	1.09%	.58%	2.04%	.64%	4.35%

The low shipping cost to cargo value ratios today help explain the staggering increase in postwar trade that has been driven in large part by the corresponding increase in shipping cost efficiency. Prior to World War II, it was not unusual for shipping costs to be 50% or more of the value of manufactured goods. With what in effect is a high cost barrier, many manufactured products just did not move interenationally and were sourced domestically.

For many dry-bulk commodities, they didn't even move in much volume across the oceans in the prewar period as they were locally sourced in order to minimize transport cost. In testimony to this, the dry-bulk shipping segment, today the largest with 7,849 ships over 600' long and 9,420 ships over 300' long, didn't even exist prior to the postwar cargo shipping revolution.

While the sharp rise in shipping cost efficiency has benefited all the segments in ways that are similar, the striking difference in current shipping cost to cargo value ratios across segments says something about the relative structural barriers to profitability in the various segments. Put simply, the lower your direct vessel cost to your customers' end product, the more pricing power you have. Similiarly, the higher your direct vessel cost to your customers' end product, the less pricing power you have.

This relationship is supported by any one of a number of basic practices in our professional and personal lives, yet isn't recognized as much as it should when owners and investors are thinking about the various shipping segments.

While overall supply and demand dynamics can and often do swamp the impact of the shipping cost to cargo value ratio, it is a key item to keep in mind when contemplating relative constraints to future performance. This metric has the container segment ratio 17 times lower than the dry-bulk segment. That large difference suggests the former will outperform the latter, with the other two segments between those two.

A similar metric just comparing cargo value by ship type to the cost of building each new ship is shown in the table below. With that metric, the container segment ratio is 13 times lower than the dry-bulk segment, with the other two segments similarly positioned between those two as shown in the following table.

Segment	Container	Tanker	Dry-Bulk	General
Vessel Type	ULCV	VLCC	VLOC	Car
Cargo Value (Mill)	$756.2	$153.2	$18.1	$250.0
Newbuild Cost (Mill)	$185.0	$105.0	$72.0	$68.0
Cargo/Newbuild %	409%	146%	30%	368%

These pricing power metrics and how they rank the various shipping segments are largely borne out by actual market experience. The dry-bulk segment not only has the largest number of ships, but by far the largest number of ship owners. There are literally thousands of ship owners in the segment as many owners have just one or two ships. Even the largest owners of dry-bulk ships barely crack one percent of total capacity in terms of segment ownership.

Despite constant expectations over the years of consolidation, little such activity has occurred in the dry-bulk segment. This lack of concentration in and of itself reduces the pricing power of owners. Even with more concentration, however, the fact that the service provided by these ships is a relatively high percentage of cargo value makes customers particularly intense negotiators. All these factors come together to make the dry-bulk segment the most commodisized in terms of pricing. An individual ship owner can't really impact pricing, and ever-present structural conditions are constantly placing downward pressure on segment pricing.

The other shipping segments share some of these characteristics, but not to the degree they are present in the dry-bulk segment. At the other end of the spectrum, the container segment and the car carrier part of the general cargo segment will always be buoyed by the high value of the cargoes they move. Both also represent the most concentrated segments with multiple ship owners having double digit percent market shares.

These factors come together to give these segments more pricing power, both collectively and by individual ship owners. Again, this can still be overpowered by supply and demand dynamics, as it has been in the container segment since the financial crisis. However, this metric argues for more favorable relative long-term performance by the container and car carrier segments.

Given the above, why would anyone go into the dry-bulk segment and why wouldn't they always prefer the container segment? The answer for that goes back to initial capital investment and other barriers to entry. The easiest shipping segment to get into is the dry-bulk segment. They are the least expensive ships to build, one ship can get you into the business and all your operations and marketing activities can be outsourced. If charter rates aren't sufficient to generate revenue in excess of operating costs, the ships can be laid-up and an active secondary market would allow you to sell.

These factors come together to make for an easy entry with a fairly protected downside. In contrast, container ships are not only among the most expensive, but multiple ships are required and the equipment needs add to the large investment requirement. Not surprisingly, the new entrants into the container segment are few and far between.

The historical trend in the ratio of shipping cost to cargo value helps explain an underlying catalyst in the phenomenal growth in world trade in the postwar period. By going from a number that made trade uneconomical to a number that is now often inconsequential, the flood doors of trade were opened up. As it turns out, the volume of world trade is much more elastic to the ratio of shipping cost to cargo value than any economists would have thought.

23. The Flags Ships Fly

The beginning of the modern cargo shipping era coincided with a shift in the flags ships fly. Up until World War II, ships flew the flag of where they were based and owned. British owned and operated vessels flew the Union Jack, American owned and operated vessels flew the Stars and Stripes and so forth and so on. The flags of merchant ships were broadly consistent with countries ranking in the industrial world. Those ships and their owners were subject to the laws and regulations of the country whose flag they flew, including ones related to income taxes, vessel inspection and crew manning.

Throughout history, the flag that flew on the stern of a cargo ship has been important and involves various legal principles that go beyond a simple identification of the vessel's home country. Wherever the ship is, the laws of the flag state apply to it, whether it relates to crew composition and compensation, vessel inspection and safety rules, income taxes and fees and even criminal matters. While laws of other countries may also apply when the vessel is in port in their jurisdiction, for all practical matters the vessel is treated as if it is an appendage of the country, much like an embassy on foreign soil is viewed as part of the sponsoring country.

The flag state is extending its implicit protection to all ships under its umbrella no matter where they are in the world. For this reason, any attack on a cargo ship has historically been considered an act of war against the country whose flag flies on the vessel. Likewise, any salute to or respect for a cargo ship is considered doing the same to the flag state.

The very first salute to America by a foreign government occurred on November 16, 1776 when a merchant ship flying the flag of the Continental Congress entered the port of St. Eustatius, a Caribbean island that was the center of Dutch trading in the New World. Wanting solely to trade and engage in commerce with that ship, the Dutch governor ordered the guns of the local garrison to fire a welcoming salvo as the ship entered the port.

The traditional alignment between ship ownership and flag was in part marketing as customers in a particular country, given a choice when they viewed everything else as generally equal, would want to use ships that flew their countries flags.

In large part this was also influenced by regulations that certain cargoes could only move on vessels that flew their countries flag. For instance, many countries have cabotage laws covering cargo moving between domestic ports. Approximately two-thirds of the countries with maritime coastlines have laws or regulations that are supportive in some manner of ships registered in their own country. In addition, there were often special rules requiring that government controlled and military cargoes move on ships that fly the flag of that country. All of these cargo preference laws and regulations are rooted in the view that a country's merchant marine is an important element of national security.

History is filled with examples of important roles played by merchant marine vessels in supporting the military. None are more dramatic than World War II where more than one military leader said America couldn't have won without the Liberty ships.

In times of war or conflict, the only cargo ships a country can completely rely upon are ships that fly their flag because governments have the legal ability to requisition such vessels. Without cargo vessels that can be controlled, there is no way to assure the necessary supply lines that are required for any military to function.

In addition, a robust merchant marine results in large numbers of trained crewmen, including a large population of people who formerly sailed who could man cargo ships held in reserve in the event of a national emergency. An active merchant marine builds ships in domestic shipyards, which makes for a more vibrant shipbuilding industry and those benefits flow over to shipyards building actual naval vessels. Across the board, there has always been a symbiotic relationship between a country's merchant marine and its national security.

Panama was the first country to establish what would become known as a flag of convenience registry in the mid-1930's. The initial reason behind and attraction for registering ships under the Panama flag was to reduce income taxes. Most countries taxed owners of ships flying their flag using their typical corporate tax rate applied to the net income of the ship. In establishing its registry, Panama put in place an income tax rate for international shipping that was significantly lower than any corporate income tax rate and this was attractive to ship owners.

Greek ship owners such as Onassis and Niarchos were the first to make use of the Panama registry and reducing income taxes was what drew them initially. While the tax rates appeared attractive to other ship owners, their insurance companies were leery of the vessel inspection regime for Panamanian flag vessels and it would take several years before participation began to increase.

The catalyst for broader participation in the Panamanian registry in particular and flags of convenience registries in general was actually the U.S. government. President Roosevelt, who had previously served as Assistant Secretary of the Navy, was familiar with the U.S. shipping industry and involved even as President in policies related to the industry. He championed the Merchant Marine Act of 1936, which broadly restructured all of the regulation related to the sector.

Roosevelt's desire to avoid having any shipments from the U.S. going to Germany or Italy had resulted in the Neutrality Act. However, he now recognized that in 1939 this same act would prevent U.S. flagged ships from moving supplies to Great Britain and France who were now almost at war with Germany.

To get around the Neutrality Act, the government quietly gave certain American ship owners permission to transfer some of their ships to foreign registry. With a foreign flag, these ships would not be subject to U.S. law and would be free to move cargo to Great Britain and France. Panama, where the U.S. owned the Canal Zone and still exerted considerable influence since its separation from Columbia earlier in the century, was chosen as the country to host foreign registered but U.S. owned vessels.

In order to encourage American ship owners to re-flag in Panama, the Roosevelt administration exerted its influence to have the Panamanian government impose few restrictions and limited inspection and maintenance standards for the ships it registered. It also pressured Panama to further reduce taxes related to shipping, resulting in ship owners paying only token taxes if they flew Panamanian flags. These incentives made Panama very attractive as a place to register ships.

This behind the scenes effort achieved its initial purpose of allowing the U.S. to provide critical supplies to Great Britain and France without technically violating U.S. neutrality. It was also the catalyst for the cost savings benefits that continued after World War II and to this day for ship owners who choose a flag of convenience registry. The rules and regulations that were adopted by Panama became the model for other countries as they developed their own flag of convenience registry.

In 1948, Edward R. Stettinius founded the Liberian registry in partnership with the Liberian government. Stettinius had served as Secretary of State under President Roosevelt from 1944 to 1945 and as the first U.S. Ambassador to the United Nations. The Liberian registry was created at a time when the Panamanian registry was becoming less attractive due to heightened criticism by labor unions, political unrest in Panama and increases in fees and regulations.

Liberia was founded in the early 1800's as a settlement in Africa for blacks who relocated from the U.S. because they believed it offered a better life for them. It became a separate country in 1847 with a constitution and flag modeled after those in the U.S. The flag looked exactly like the U.S. flag except that it had one white star instead of stars equal to the number of states. The capital city of Monrovia was named after President Monroe who was a prominent supporter of the initial settlement.

Liberia consistently aligned itself with the U.S. and was an ally during World War II. This historical closeness had much to do with the establishment of the Liberian registry. In addition, the close resemblence of the Liberian flag to the U.S. flag also made it an attractive registry for U.S. flag vessels. At the time the Liberian registry was established, U.S. flag vessels comprised the largest merchant marine fleet in the world.

The first ship registered in Liberia in 1948 was owned by Greek shipowner Stavros Niarchos. The Liberian registry prospered and by 1967 it had passed the United Kingdom to become the largest flag registry in the world. The fact that the Liberian flag has such a striking similarity to the U.S. flag no doubt played a key role in the success of the Liberian registry, particularly with ship owners who were switching from of the U.S. registry.

Driven by the transition of the Liberty ships to commercial service, the peak of the U.S. flag merchant marine in terms of its representation worldwide was 1950. At that time, U.S. flag vessels represented some 43% of worldwide cargo vessel tonnage. That relative position has been in steady decline ever since then.

While preferable income tax treatment was an initial catalyst for owners switching to these new registries, the lower operating costs that often resulted from such registries was also very attractive. These new registries were open registries that allowed the ship owner complete flexibility on where to source crewmembers from. The regulations were typically less stringent than the regulations ship owners were accustomed to.

As more open registries developed, the competition between them to get ship owners to switch resulted in even more attractive operating cost economics for the ship owner. While operating costs are a relatively small part of the total cost of a ship when fuel costs and capital costs are included, they are an area offereing differentiation. If a ship owner wants to develop a competitive cost advantage, operating costs is the primary area on which to focus. This dynamic resulted in fairly intense competition among the growing number of open registries which were now being referred to more as flag of convenience registries.

With civil war and unrest in Liberia, by 1990 it was overtaken by Panama, which regained the title of the largest registry in the world. There was no country that was as focused on the ship registry business as much as Liberia as the sector provided 70% of the government's total revenue. With its expertise on the sector and continuing civil unrest in Liberia, the government of Liberia joined with the Republic of the Marshall Islands to develop a new open registry.

The Marshall Islands registry grew quickly and was particularly attractive to ship owners based in the U.S. The Marshall Islands is a republic in free association with the U.S., which provides defense. In other words, it is as close as you can get to the U.S. without being the U.S. There is a view among some ship owners that a Marshall Islands flag brings with it the implicit protection of the U.S. government due to various defense treaties, but the open registry results in lower, competitive operating costs.

A vivid example of a reflagging driven by military protection goals occurred in 1987 during the Iran-Iraq conflict. Kuwait, an American ally, had tankers that it believed were at risk in the Persian Gulf. With the support of the Reagan administration, Kuwait reflagged 11 tankers to U.S. flag. This resulted in those tankers being escorted by warships from the U.S. Navy's Seventh Fleet. Because an attack on any of those tankers would have been considered an act of war and responded to accordingly, there was no attack. When that conflict ended, those tankers were transferred back to their previous flag of convenience registry.

The intense competition among the largest open registries also exerted an effect on the other registries as they took steps to avoid having ships switch out from their registry. While this didn't result in any meaningful reduction in their own regulations or standards, in part because the insurance firms and classification societies would act as a check on any wholesale deterioration, they also weren't looking to unilaterally add new regulations. Any registry that moved outside of the norm could expect to experience defections.

One area in particular where something initially adopted by the open registries eventually flowed through to all registries relates to income taxes on shipping. The initial lower tax rates at open registries were eventually replaced by a modest fixed annual tax on the vessel based on its deadweight tonnage. Because this was used to attract new ships that would not result in any related government revenue loss or expenditure need, the host country viewed it as a windfall and the amounts kept getting lower at the open registries.

Almost all registries eventually adopted a tonnage tax regime where vessels operating in international commerce that fly their flag pay a fixed annual amount based on deadweight tonnage regardless of the economic earnings of the vessel. One rationale that supported this transition was the view that ships primarily operate in international waters and that results in difficulty in apportioning in whose jurisdiction the earnings actually occur.

The tonnage tax is really more of a license fee in lieu of an income tax than a pure income tax. The reason for this is that it does not vary regardless of how well or how poorly a ship performs in a given year. For example, it is not unusual today for a large modern ship to pay an annual tonnage tax of $25,000 in lieu of all income taxes, whether the vessel operated at a loss or made $1 million or $10 million for the year.

With tonnage tax regimes now prevailing in almost all registries, the shipping industry now collectively enjoys a tax benefit unheard of in almost all other industries as it can effectively operate taxfree without paying any real income taxes.

Today the top three flags of convenience are Panama, Liberia and the Marshall Islands and collectively almost half of the worldwide cargo fleet in terms of deadweight tonnage flies one of those flags. The table below lists the top twenty flag registries ranked in terms of overall deadweight tonnage. The table also shows how overall tonnage at each flag registry is broken down in terms of vessel type.

Flag Registry	Grand Total	Container	Tanker	Dry-Bulk	Other
Panama	324,589,815	38,288,715	61,794,924	199,822,215	24,683,961
Liberia	198,749,031	45,526,085	71,142,555	74,817,171	7,263,220
Marshall Isl	189,448,831	13,679,649	77,850,684	85,926,693	11,991,805
Hong Kong	163,588,980	29,572,210	35,366,167	91,541,021	7,109,582
Singapore	119,961,433	25,104,975	37,226,565	51,273,472	6,356,421
Malta	95,638,923	14,935,791	30,599,252	44,558,274	5,545,606
Greece	72,000,613	906,957	45,362,228	23,799,082	1,932,346
Bahamas	67,553,798	1,451,407	36,651,959	16,353,965	13,096,467
China	64,962,740	6,727,202	12,679,094	40,774,910	4,781,534
Cyprus	32,520,442	4,748,642	4,745,841	21,269,121	1,756,838
Japan	28,996,541	406,840	6,996,278	18,306,430	3,286,993
Isle Of Man	21,948,545	1,312,860	8,276,356	9,840,949	2,518,380
Norway	17,206,155	5,202	7,649,166	4,670,614	4,881,173
Denmark	16,905,673	11,436,515	4,447,803	357,648	663,707
South Korea	16,422,544	1,318,941	1,670,944	10,760,646	2,672,013
Italy	15,734,349	622,861	6,488,625	5,724,207	2,898,656
Indonesia	15,206,755	1,696,554	6,345,482	2,788,033	4,376,686
India	14,717,865	392,049	8,467,110	4,784,868	1,073,838
UK	13,299,591	7,989,588	2,331,298	1,751,553	1,227,152
United States	10,616,525	3,101,484	3,818,990	1,893,394	1,802,657
Top 20	1,500,069,149	209,224,527	469,911,321	711,014,266	109,919,035
Other	204,443,593	35,326,475	73,359,160	45,756,808	50,001,150
Grand Total	1,704,512,742	244,551,002	543,270,481	756,771,074	159,920,185

Some 88.0% of the worldwide cargo fleet is registered in one of the top twenty registries, of which the U.S. is the smallest with only 0.6% of the worldwide fleet. The table on the next page breaks down each registry in terms of its percent of the total in each category. While Panama is the largest flag registry overall, it is second in the container category and third in the tanker category. Liberia is the largest flag registry in the container category and the Marshall Islands in the largest flag registry in the tanker category.

Flag Registry	Grand Total	Container	Tanker	Dry-Bulk	Other
Panama	19.0%	15.7%	11.4%	26.4%	15.4%
Liberia	11.7%	18.6%	13.1%	9.9%	4.5%
Marshall Isl	11.1%	5.6%	14.3%	11.4%	7.5%
Hong Kong	9.6%	12.1%	6.5%	12.1%	4.4%
Singapore	7.0%	10.3%	6.9%	6.8%	4.0%
Malta	5.6%	6.1%	5.6%	5.9%	3.5%
Greece	4.2%	0.4%	8.3%	3.1%	1.2%
Bahamas	4.0%	0.6%	6.7%	2.2%	8.2%
China	3.8%	2.8%	2.3%	5.4%	3.0%
Cyprus	1.9%	1.9%	0.9%	2.8%	1.1%
Japan	1.7%	0.2%	1.3%	2.4%	2.1%
Isle Of Man	1.3%	0.5%	1.5%	1.3%	1.6%
Norway	1.0%	0.0%	1.4%	0.6%	3.1%
Denmark	1.0%	4.7%	0.8%	0.0%	0.4%
South Korea	1.0%	0.5%	0.3%	1.4%	1.7%
Italy	0.9%	0.3%	1.2%	0.8%	1.8%
Indonesia	0.9%	0.7%	1.2%	0.4%	2.7%
India	0.9%	0.2%	1.6%	0.6%	0.7%
UK	0.8%	3.3%	0.4%	0.2%	0.8%
United States	0.6%	1.3%	0.7%	0.3%	1.1%
Top 20	88.0%	85.6%	86.5%	94.0%	68.7%
Other	12.0%	14.4%	13.5%	6.0%	31.3%
Grand Total	100.0%	100.0%	100.0%	100.0%	100.0%

The widespread use of flags of convenience by many countries can be seen in comparisons of flag registry to where the vessel owner actually resides. Not surprisingly, ownership is more skewed towards developed countries. Only three countries among the top ten in terms of flag registry, Singapore, Greece and China, show up in the top ten in terms of vessel ownership values. Countries that aren't in the former category are high up in the later category. For instance, the U.S. is fourth overall in ownership value with 7.3% of the total. That is almost twelve times its representation in terms of flag registry.

Collectively, the top ten countries in terms of vessel ownership represent 78.0% of the value of cargo ships in the world, or almost four times their representation in terms of flag registry. The only country within that group with similar representations in both categories is Singapore. The table on the following page shows the top ten countries in terms of vessel ownership and how they compare to their respective flag registry representations.

Country	Value (Bill)	% Value	% DWT	Value/DWT
Greece	$93.6	15.3%	4.2%	3.6
Japan	$84.9	13.9%	1.7%	8.2
China	$73.5	12.0%	3.9%	3.2
U.S.	$44.6	7.3%	0.6%	11.7
Singapore	$42.4	6.9%	7.0%	1.0
Norway	$38.1	6.2%	1.0%	6.2
Germany	$31.6	5.2%	0.5%	10.4
U.K.	$23.7	3.9%	0.8%	5.0
Denmark	$22.2	3.6%	1.0%	3.7
South Korea	$21.4	3.5%	1.0%	3.6
Top 10	$476.0	78.0%	21.6%	3.6
Other	$134.5	22.0%	78.4%	0.3
Total	$610.5	100.0%	100.0%	1.0

As discussed in more detail in another chapter, daily operating costs of a cargo ship, of which crew wages and benefits are a large majority, are typically a single digit percentage of total costs of a ship when fuel costs and capital costs are taken into account. While relatively small, however, those operating costs are subject to meaningful variation depending on where a ship is registered as well as the ship owner's decisions related to crew manning.

As such, daily operating costs are often the primary area of differentiation in terms of total costs as larger items such as fuel and capital costs typically are in tighter ranges. Fuel is a commodity and all ship owners pay the same price in a given area and at a given time. The similar ships they operate have similar fuel consumption rates. Even the capital cost that needs to be amortized will be similar as shipbuilders offer little variation in pricing for the construction of similar ships at a given time.

When recognizing all of these factors, it is easy to appreciate the relative importance of having the lowest possible operating costs as that is the primary means of developing a competitive cost advantage. In the highly competitive shipping markets where the end product is mostly viewed as a commodity by customers, the only sustainable competitive advantage is lower overall costs in the movement of a given cargo from origin to destination.

How those lower overall costs are distributed between the customer and the ship owner is a separate issue, but the path to first achieving these lower costs usually involves having lower operating cost. That reality is the catalyst that gave rise to the flag of convenience registries and that sustains those registries today.

Shipping is by definition a highly mobile industry where the primary assets can and are readily re-deployable. That extends to what flag the ship is registered under as switching registries is something that can be readily done with a few documents. Many ship owners have ships that are registered under different flags, which creates tension and competitiveness among the registries. If a registry makes a change that results in lower or higher operating costs, ship owners can and do change where their ships are registered. This dynamic tends to have ship owners moving to the registry that will allow them to minimize their overall operating costs.

The main check to a downward spiral in regulations comes from the insurance companies who insure the vessels and the classification societies who inspect the vessels. Both are focused on safety and if they view changes in regulations and policies at the registries as going beyond acceptable norms, they will make their displeasure known in the form of changes to their own policies. Data is maintained on the overall safety performance of all vessels within each registry. The ultimate power of an insurer or classification society to neither insure nor issue necessary classification documents keeps the various registries in check. Without both insurance coverage and classification documents, a ship can't really operate anywhere in the world.

The pros and cons of autonomous shipping are discussed in more detail in a later chapter. However, it is likely to play a role in the future of shipping and the ramifications will be broad. If autonomous shipping were to become widespread, one ramification would likely be a reduction in the role of flag of convenience registries.

In a completely autonomous vessel, what was operating cost in the form of crew wages and benefits would now be replaced by capital cost in the form of computers, software and sensors. The ability to differentiate and develop a competitive cost advantage based on the crew selected by the ship owner would disappear. With that gone, much of the reason for flying a Panamanian or Liberian or Marshall Islands flag would also be gone. Ship owners would still want to have the most favorable regulations related to income taxes and inspection requirements and those items would still be very important in determining registries, but the crew wage issue that drives much of the registry decisions today would be off the table with autonomous ships. Almost all countries now have favorable income tax regulations for ships flying their flag in international commerce. Likewise, the impact of insurance companies and classification societies tends to result in similar inspection and technical requirements among registries.

In a future environment with significant autonomous vessels, it is fair to say that the influence of flag of convenience registries will be less. There will be more of a return to ships flying the flag of the country where their owners reside and in whose commerce they are involved. In other words, the mix of flags would be similar to what it was in the past as it would be more tied to economic interest than to minimizing crew costs.

24. The Yards that Build Ships

The first step in engaging in maritime commerce is of course to build a ship. Shipbuilding fits hand in glove with shipping with a cause and effect role that continues to this very day. However, what proceeded as the first step has changed and shifted over time. A strong case can be made today that there is still circularity between the two that exists and affects each that we will highlight later.

Phoenicia didn't grow sturdy cedar trees because the Phoenicians were great sailors. Similarly, Scandinavia didn't grow tall hardwood trees because the Vikings were excellent navigators. The ready availability of significant amounts of strong timber was the precedent that made both the Phoenicians and the Vikings the extraordinary shipbuilders of their time. That, in turn, led to the development of skilled sailors who would take those ships on voyages across far-flung trading routes.

Over time, most large countries with a seacoast would develop some type of shipbuilding industry. The key driver of this related to building ships for exploration as well as military ships for its navy. Having the ability to build its own naval vessels was an important issue for countries in the past. It remains a key national security issue supporting domestic shipbuilding in many countries today.

With the dawning of the Age of Exploration, many countries in Europe developed large shipbuilding industries. That period was a catalyst for many events, but a largely under reported affect was the widespread deforestation that resulted.

Before the fourteenth century, hardwood trees blanketed much of Europe to form a forest comparable in size to the Amazon Basin. Forest density was intense and the wood was a staple for many manufacturing processes, of which shipbuilding was the largest in the world at that time. With the sharp growth in shipbuilding beginning with the Age of Exploration, the production of ships put extreme pressure on the oldest and largest trees in the forests of Europe. The massive tree trunks that were decades and even centuries in the making had the best timber that was well suited for the large hulls of ships.

Wooden ships typically had a physical life of only ten years, so just the replacement needs were taxing on the European forests. One of the first applications of petroleum was to use the heavy tar that washed up on shores to make joints between wooden planks more watertight. We now know that such tar is natural seepage from the ocean bottom that floats to the top and washes ashore because petroleum is lighter than water.

Centuries later, of course, this substance, formed from plankton and algae that fell to the bottom of ancient oceans and was compressed by layers of sediment over millions of years, would power ships and the world. In addition, it would become the major cargo for one of the key shipping segments. It is ironic that something that would become so central to mankind played almost no role five hundred years ago and among its first uses was to waterproof wooden hulls.

The key reasons for the limited life of wooden hulls were parasites and dozens of different kinds of shipworms that were a constant threat. In addition to the wood needed to build ships, the use of iron in fittings and weaponry on ships consumed large amounts of wood in the high temperature fires needed for various metallurgical processes. The deforestation directly related to shipbuilding was widespread across Europe, with the most extreme example being Spain in the sixteenth century.

Not surprisingly, no country was building and sending to sea as many large ships during that period as Spain. However, that activity took a devastating toil on Spain's forests. A contributing reason for the subsequent decline in the influence of Spain on world affairs was the depletion of wood to build new ships.

Iron and steel began to replace wood in ship construction in the mid-1800's. This transition would occur almost simultaneously with the move from sail power to steam power. The growing scarcity of wood was a factor, but the increasing metallurgical skills resulting in strong, longer lasting metal ships was the main factor. The new steam engines also required significant metal components and once you made the decision to go with the better propulsion method, the logic of a full metal ship became clearer.

Nowhere were these transitions more prominent than in England. The lack of timber in England was more than mitigated by its leading role in the industrial revolution. While already a large shipbuilder, with these changes England quickly became the leading shipbuilder in the world with an expertise well ahead of all other countries. That leadership was needed to provide the ships for what was the largest naval fleet and the largest merchant marine fleet in the world. These British flag merchant ships were primarily involved in moving goods between England and the far-flung British Empire.

The 1800's are broadly defined by most historians as the British century as they were the most influential, powerful country in the world. In a 2004 book entitled "To Rule the Waves: How the British Navy Shaped the Modern World", a noted historian made the case that the British Empire was the foundation of the modern world and that the foundation of the British Empire was the Royal Navy. In a related sense, the foundation of the Royal Navy was Britain's extraordinary shipbuilding industry and expertise.

It is hard to overstate the role that shipping and shipbuilding played in Great Britain in the 1800's. Collectively with the commerce that moved on those ships, it was by far the largest industry in the British economy. At its height, some 44% of the merchant ships in the world flew the British flag. The financing of those ships and the related trade led to the development of a large banking and insurance industry in London.

While shipping and shipbuilding were the very foundation for the development of those financial services, they would grow well beyond those industries. This foundational role that shipping and shipbuilding played in the banking industry and in the broader economy in Great Britain would be a pattern that would repeat itself in other countries.

Britain's supremacy in shipping and shipbuilding would continue well into the next century, only to be dethroned by the U.S. when it ramped up shipbuilding during World War II. Legendary shipyards such as Thames Ironworks and Shipbuilding, John Brown & Company and Harland &

Wolff provided a steady supply of high quality merchant marine ships to serve the trading needs of the British Empire. As late as the 1930's, British flag vessels made up more than one-third of the tonnage in the world's merchant marine fleet.

The ramp up in shipbuilding production capacity in the U.S. as a result of World War II was extraordinary. In the ten years before 1940, the U.S. built a total of just 23 cargo ships. In the five years after, the U.S. would build 4,600 cargo ships. Without these ships, it would not have been possible for the U.S. and its allies to prevail. After those ships won the war, many of them transitioned into commercial service where they became the foundation for the cargo shipping revolution that would later unfold. The amazing story of these ships and the roles they played is covered in detail in other chapters.

As U.S. commercial shipbuilding waned following the war, the mantle would eventually pass to Japan. As discussed in the profile of D.K. Ludwig, the beginnings of this can be traced to exporting processes he used at his U.S. shipyard to Japan where he was able to build ships for his own fleet more efficiently. There is a direct thread flowing from the Liberty ships Henry Kaiser built to Ludwig's Virginia shipyard and on to the establishment of the Japanese shipbuilding industry.

The modular construction processes and steel welding and cutting techniques that had been developed in the U.S. were refined in Japan. With these straightforward innovations, the two primary inputs to manufacturing ships of steel and labor became even more important. Japan was increasingly well positioned in both of these areas. Its shipbuilding industry grew even more than its fast growing steel industry.

The focus on training and quality control by Japan with its labor teams resulted in unprecedented labor productivity when it came to building new ships. Many of the processes Japan used in shipbuilding were then used in other industries where it became succesful. By the early 1960's, Japan had become the largest commercial shipbuilder in the world and would retain that title for decades. While some of the ships Japan built were used to satisfy its own large volume of imports and exports, the majority of the ships it built were exported to owners outside of Japan.

Beginning in the late 1970's, South Korea became more of a factor in worldwide shipbuilding. Just as it followed in Japan's footsteps in developing a steel industry, it followed in developing and growing a shipbuilding industry. By the mid-1980's, South Korea was challenging Japan in many of the shipbuilding segments. The contract that underscored South Korea's arrival was one in which I was intimately involved.

In 1984, Malcom McLean finalized a contract with a Korean shipyard to build 12 container ships for $570 million. It was the largest shipbuilding contract in history and involved the construction of the largest container ships in the world at that time. The Korean shipyard offered the lowest price that resulted from a rigorous, disciplined approach to managing their labor force. When touring large shipyards in South Korea, visitors often remarked that it was run with the precision of a military facility.

I remember a dinner with a South Korean shipyard executive where he observed that Korea needed to be diligent so that they did not become lazy like the Japanese. While hardly an apt description, it did underscore the intense focus and competitiveness South Korea was giving to the shipbuilding industry. Not surprisingly, by the mid-1990's, South Korea had displaced Japan as the world's largest shipbuilder.

As China's steel industry grew, so did its involvement in shipbuilding. The pattern of Japan being followed by South Korea, which was then followed by China, seen in steel and cars among other industries, was also seen in the shipbuilding industry. In the same way it developed other industries, China focused on the shipbuilding industry through state-owned enterprises, or SOE's. In 1990, China represented less than 2% of worldwide deliveries of ship tonnage. By 2000, it was up to approximately 7%, but almost all of that was for SOE shipping companies with few exports.

China's entry into the WTO in 2001 was a major shot in the arm for its shipbuilding industry. In addition to sharp increases in demand by Chinese shipping companies, it started to become more of a factor in the international export market. However, while China had the steel and wage rates that allowed it to be competitive, the quality of its product wasn't up to Korean and Japanese standards.

As a result, China's initial focus was on standard size dry-bulk ships, which are the simplest vessels to construct. As their expertise in meeting international quality control standards grew, they migrated into tankers. Finally, they would become a factor in building container ships, which are the most complicated of the major segments to construct owing to more exacting technical standards. For example, the cell guides that align containers in the holds have tolerances measured just in millimeters.

By 2010, China was building almost 30% of the world's cargo ships and was competing with South Korea to be the largest shipbuilder. The largest, most sophisticated ships were generally built in South Korea. This included LNG carriers, the most expensive cargo ships, and the ultra large container vessels. South Korea had all but abandoned building ships at the lower end of the quality spectrum, such as standard size dry-bulk ships. While China and South Korea were neck and neck in terms of total tonnage delivered, the composition across segments was different.

China's approach to shipbuilding benefited from the central planning that came from an autocratic government. Most of what were now hundreds of shipyards were controlled by two large SOE's that directed the type of vessels in which each shipyard should specialize. Recognizing more than a decade earlier that China was lacking in both quantity and quality of naval architects, it established a new university solely focused on that area that quickly grew to 20,000 students. These and other initiatives took hold and allowed China to continue to move up the quality spectrum even as they continued to build ever more cargo vessels.

In 2017, China was the largest shipbuilder in the world and delivered over 36% of total shipbuilding tonnage. The top three producers collectively represented 91% of total deliveries in 2017. The table on the next page shows shipyard deliveries by country based on gross tonnage, a measure of the volume of cubic meters of total enclosed space on a cargo ship. Gross tonnage is the measure that shipyards have traditionally utilized. The more meaningful measure of deadweight cargo capacity varies by ship but is typically 150% of gross tonnage. As gross tonnage across all categories is generally twice the actual weight of the steel used to build vessels, approximately 2.0% of the steel produced in the world in 2017 was used to build cargo ships.

2017 Production	Gross Tonnage	% Of Total
China	23,682,160	36.3%
South Korea	22,616,947	34.7%
Japan	13,113,388	20.1%
United States	225,593	0.3%
United Kingdom	0	0.0%
Other	5,534,349	8.5%
Total	65,172,437	100.0%

In further recognition of its climb up the shipbuilding quality ladder, in 2017 Chinese shipyards signed a contract to build nine 22,000 TEU container ships. These ships will not only be among the largest container ships in the world, but will be capable of being propelled by cleaner LNG fuel. China also now builds sophisticated LNG, LPG and chemical tankers, among other technically complex vessels. Its prowess in building naval vessels was similarly improving. China converted a former Russian aircraft carrier for its own use and is now in the process of building its first completely home built aircraft carrier.

As the table shows, neither the U.S. nor the United Kingdom, each the world's largest commercial shipbuilder before the ascendancy of the Asian shipbuilders, were meaningful commercial shipbuilders in 2017. It would be impossible for the U.S. to compete in such a labor-intensive sector when its per capita income and wages are more than five times the rest of the world.

However, while it lacks in the quantity of ships built, the quality of the U.S.'s commercial shipbuilding continues to be at the forefront. LNG powered vessels and diesel electric engines are among the recent commercial innovations where U.S. shipyards led the way.

Separate from but clearly related to commercial shipbuilding is naval shipbuilding. In this specialized and highly technical area, no country comes anywhere close to the U.S. today. The U.S. is the largest naval shipbuilder in the world and is also unmatched in quality. The largest naval vessels are aircraft carriers and the U.S. Navy mans 11 of the 15 carriers now operating in the world.

With the cummulative experience from building 78 aircraft carriers, no country can approach the capability and sophistication of the U.S. in building these complex vessels. The U.S. has a similar dominance in building nuclear powered submarines, the most important naval vessels for maintaining peace in the world today.

From a technical standpoint, it is undeniable that today the U.S. has the most advanced shipbuilding capability in the world, but that capability is focused more on building vessels for the U.S. Navy. However, it is not a meaningful participant in international commercial shipbuilding and the construction of commercial vessels will be primarily related to vessels used in the various Jones Act trades.

The largest commerical shipbuilding countries will continue to be in Asia based upon labor productivity and efficient steel manufacturing. China's dominance will grow as it moves up on the quality spectrum. In addition to its advantages in the core steel and labor factors that go into shipbuilding, its position as the largest user of shipping services will result in further benefits for its shipbuilding sector. Just as China effectively consumes half of the world's shipping services, there is no reason that it will not soon be building half of the world's ships. The symbiotic relationship between shipping and shipbuilding continues to this day.

25. The U.S. Flag Merchant Marine

It is irrefutable that everything that led to the development of today's modern cargo shipping industry has its roots in and flowed from the U.S. It started with shipbuilding innovations pioneered by Henry Kaiser. From there the genius of McLean, Ludwig and Skaarup put in motion the development of the giant container ships, tankers and bulk carriers that fueled world trade.

Unfortunately, for understandable structural reasons the actual number of vessels flying the U.S. flag has consistently declined during the postwar period. The relative peak in terms of the U.S. flag merchant marine fleet was in 1950 when 43% of the world's cargo vessel tonnage flew the U.S. flag. Liberty ships that had transitioned to commercial service represented the majority of that tonnage.

As highlighted in other chapters, many of those Liberty ships were sold to allied nations as they developed and rebuilt their own merchant marine fleets, while some of them remained U.S. flag. The table below shows the total number of U.S. flag vessels along with their average deadweight in five-year increments since 1955. In addition to the consistent decline in number, the U.S. flag vessels have not grown in average size like international flag vessels. The latter are more than twice the typical size of the former.

Year	Number of Vessels	Average DWT
1955	1,075	12,648
1960	1,008	13,976
1965	948	15,454
1970	793	18,166
1975	580	25,910
1980	578	36,521
1985	477	44,434
1990	408	50,909
1995	316	47,411
2000	282	44,000
2005	231	41,575
2010	221	43,199
2015	170	45,529

Just after World War II, the U.S. flag fleet was carrying 60% of U.S. foreign commerce in 1947. As the world economy recovered and the U.S. government sold off much of its Liberty and Victory class vessels, that had declined to 40% by 1951. It would decline steadily thereafter. By 1980, the U.S. flag fleet was carrying only 5% of U.S. foreign commerce, or around the same amount carried before World War II. Today, that figure is less than 2%.

Most countries have long accepted that a merchant marine fleet flying its flag provides both economic and national security benefits. The U.S. recognized this national security aspect as early as 1785. John Jay, the Secretary of Foreign Affairs in the federal government, asked "whether it would be more wise in the United States to withdraw their attention from the sea, and permit foreigners to fetch and carry for them, or to preserve in concerting and pursuing such measures as may conduce to render them a maritime power".

The U.S. learned hard lessons in the late 19th and early 20th centuries regarding the limitations of projecting sea power when you had to rely on foreign flag vessels to "fetch and carry". Admiral Dewey's expedition, the Spanish American War and Roosevelt's Great White Fleet were all significantly impeded by reliance on foreign flag vessels.

The event, however, that most underscored the need for a strong U.S. flag merchant marine was World War I. In the period leading up to the war, the Allies chartered every vessel that they could, but the Germans sank many of those vessels. The U.S. economy suffered because of a lack of available tonnage to carry U.S. products.

This led to a series of laws, including the Shipping Act of 1916 and the Merchant Marine Act of 1920, and a program to build vessels to support both the U.S. economy and the war effort. It became accepted doctrine that a strong U.S. flag merchant marine was a key element of national security. The policies that came out of that philosophy were evident and played a role in the shipbuilding revolution led by Henry Kaiser. There can be no question that the thousands of Liberty and Victory class vessels built during World War II had a direct and pronounced impact on the outcome of the war.

Following the war, the transfer of these military cargo vessels to the world's merchant marine fleet coincided with the development of open registry or flag of convenience vessels. These registries effectively broke the link between vessel ownership and what flag the vessel was to fly along with the traditional link of much of a country's foreign commerce moving on its merchant marine. There is no industry whose hard assets are as so easily and readily re-deployable as shipping.

The various open registry countries, which required no real link to that country as a condition to registry, sought to be attractive to ship owners by limiting income tax and crewing regulations. There is a direct linear effect between those regulations and the cost to the ship owner.

Not surprisingly, ship owners gravitated to the open registries that resulted in the least cost to operate their vessels. That structural change negatively impacted the U.S. as well as most other developed countries in terms of their flag registries. Open registries such as Panama, Liberia and the Marshall Islands took hold. They would become the dominate place where vessels with U.S. owners and owners from other developed nation would be registered.

Life at sea has always entailed risks and this too has played a role in the crewing and flagging of cargo vessels. An additional risk for merchant seaman that started in World War I and increased in World War II entailed cargo ships being sunk by submarines. In addition to the effectiveness of submarines in sinking enemy naval ships, they were particularly effective in sinking cargo ships and thereby disrupting supply chains.

During World War II German U-boats sank thousands of allied cargo vessels. Each sinking was fraught with danger for the lives of the crewmembers. This was particularly the case during the early part of World War II when large amounts of supplies were being sent from the U.S. to Europe. Those convoys did not have the benefit of the better protected convoys that would follow later in the war. Most of the cargo ships that were sunk by the Germans were U.S. flag.

In striking testimony to the dangers American merchant marines were exposed to, their mortality rate was twice as high as the sailors on actual naval war ships. In total, 9,497 American merchant marines were killed when 733 cargo ships were sunk during World War II. As 243,000 mariners served during the war, that translates into a 1 in 26 mortality rate which was actually a higher rate of casualties than experienced by any of the armed services.

The national security benefits of an American merchant marine recognized centuries ago by John Jay were certainly demonstrated by World War II. It is incontrovertible that the U.S. couldn't have prevailed as it did without the sealift capability provided by the thousands of Liberty ships U.S. shipyards built and the extraordinary sacrifices by the brave seaman that manned those ships. General Dwight D. Eisenhower underscored this in 1944 when he said, "When final victory is ours, there is no organization that will share its credit more deservedly than the Merchant Marine". That is a strong, unequivocal statement by someone who was clearly a subject matter expert.

Today the U.S. flag merchant marine fleet is primarily centered on vessels serving the domestic Jones Act markets. These include tankers moving petroleum products and crude oil in coastwise routes as well as container vessels serving the non-contiguous markets of Hawaii, Alaska and Puerto Rico. To serve those markets, these U.S. flag vessels must be built in U.S. shipyards and manned and owned by U.S. citizens. The construction and repair of such vessels represents much of the commercial order book of domestic shipyards.

There are a few dozen U.S. flag vessels that are currently deployed in international trade routes. All of these vessels have contracts with the U.S. government that results in payments that are designed to mitigate the higher operating costs of U.S. flag vessels. Under the Maritime Security Program, those contracts are offered only to vessels that were deemed to have particularly useful military sealift capabilities that could be utilized in times of national emergencies. Another form of support comes from government impelled cargoes that must move on U.S. flag vessels.

For U.S. flag vessels operating in foreign trade lanes, there is no requirement that these vessels are built in the U.S. and as such they are newer vessels. Today, the daily operating costs of a U.S. flag vessel are typically three times the costs of a similar foreign flag vessel. Given the significant difference in operating costs and the hyper competitive nature of the shipping industry, there simply would be no U.S. flag merchant marine presence in international markets in the absence of these government support programs.

Today the U.S. flag merchant marine fleet is relatively small and ranks twentieth among all countries based on total deadweight tonnage in the respective registries. Vessel owners based in the U.S. have geometrically more vessels that are flagged under open registries. Based on total deadweight tonnage ranked by where the owner is domiciled, the U.S. controlled fleet is the seventh largest worldwide. If you base the rankings on where the owner is domiciled but use vessel value rather than deadweight tonnage as the metric, the U.S. controlled fleet moves up to fourth worldwide.

The vessels flying the U.S. flag in the Jones Act trades are concentrated in container movements to the non-contiguous areas of Alaska, Hawaii and Puerto Rico as well as coastal movements of petroleum products. It is in that area where I had decades of experience that have influenced my views. The Jones Act and its related cost impact has been a much-discussed topic throughout my entire career. The law comes with an economic cost, but I'm always struck by the hyperbole that comes with many claims of what that cost is, particularly in the container sector. Allow me to outline the facts as I see them on this issue.

It is incontrovertible that cargo ships can be built for much less overseas and that those ships can also be manned by foreign crews which cost much less. This is the case across all labor-intensive industries for the simple reason that wages are higher here. For example, per capita income in the U.S. in 2017 was 5.66 times worldwide per capita income.

This is actually higher than the differences in both ship construction and ship manning costs. Based on actual construction contracts and reported crewing costs, the difference in both areas is less than a factor of four. Critics of the Jones Act frequently reference larger differences, up to eight times, but those figures lack credibility. The larger mistake made by those critics, however, is to imply that rates would change in that same proportion if the Jones Act did not exist.

Across most shipping segments, the largest vessel related cost item is fuel expense. Whether a ship is a U.S. flag vessel or a flag of convenience ship, the price per ton it pays for fuel will be the same. Even if there were no Jones Act, this large cost item would not change. That fact mitigates the impact of the Jones Act difference related to total vessel costs.

More importantly, in the integrated systems offered by container shipping companies, costs related to the ship are as small as 25% of total costs. Cargo handling, terminal, equipment, trucking, inland transportation, maintenance, sales and G&A costs make up the large majority of costs in container shipping. All of these costs are unaffected by flag registry.

When you exclude these costs along with fuel costs, the vessel capital and crewing costs that are affected by the Jones Act amount to some 12% of total costs based on my experience. Applying a 4 to 1 relationship to those costs, the use of foreign flag vessels would reduce costs by 9%. Without minimizing the effect of a 9% cost reduction, that difference is a far cry from the 80% to 90% implied difference that is often bandied about by critics of the Jones Act.

The blue water Jones Act market is approximately $3.5 billion in total annual revenue. It can be broken down into $2.5 billion represented by the container carriers serving Hawaii, Alaska and Puerto Rico and $1.0 billion from non-container vessels, mostly tankers, in primarily coastwise movements of both petroleum products and crude oil.

The container markets are similar in that they are heavily imbalanced in the outbound direction with consumer staples. The largest tanker lanes are crude moving from Alaska to the West Coast, gasoline and other refined products moving from the Gulf Coast to Florida and the East Coast and, more recently with shale oil growth, crude moving from the Gulf Coast to Philadelphia area refineries. There are some two dozen container vessels deployed in the non-contiguous trades and approximately 60 tankers, the majority of which are product carriers, in the bulk petroleum trades.

Despite the rhetoric, competition within the Jones Act is intense and the sector often operates at breakeven with total costs close to revenue. For the container segment, the 9% cost savings would translate into $225 million per year. The cost differences for tankers operating in the smaller Jones Act niche, however, would be higher as almost all of the costs with tankers relate to the vessel. There are no externalities like in container shipping and the cargo handling and terminal function is little more than connecting pipes and vessel capital and crewing costs. Applying the 4 to 1 relationship to 50% of total daily tanker costs because the balance is primarily fuel costs that are not affected results in an expected cost reduction of 38%. For the tanker segment, that translates into annual savings of $380 million.

In total, these calculations show that the direct cost impact of the Jones Act is $605 million annually, or 17.3% of the sector's revenue. While that is a meaningful absolute figure, at just 9/100ths of 1% of the involved areas gross domestic products, the Jones Act is hardly the scapegoat it is claimed to be by critics.

An immediate consequence of any repeal of the Jones Act would be the complete withdrawal of U.S. flag vessels as any profit margins are typically below the cost savings percentages. A likely consequence of foreign flag carriers serving some of these domestic markets is that direct shuttle service will be replaced by en-route service. Because the Jones Act container markets are heavily imbalanced in the outbound direction with consumer staples, the ships return with mostly empty containers. Therefore, the rates on those inbound shipments are extraordinarily low.

In the case of Puerto Rico and Hawaii, it would be very attractive for foreign flag carriers to make port calls en-route to South America and Asia, respectively, as those directions are the weaker legs. However, to move domestic cargo in the inbound direction, customers would now need to pay more than what those carriers presently get with their foreign cargo. Because of the different dynamics, those rates are many times what those shippers now pay. While such stop-by service is less likely for Alaska, it is also possible in that domestic market.

The potential cost increases to shippers in these smaller inbound domestic lanes might not be enough to mitigate the cost savings estimated above, but this is a factor that needs to be taken into account in any factual analysis of the impact of the Jones Act. It also points out that any repeal of the Jones Act will result in both winners and losers. The latter group would likely include companies that ship to the mainland rum from Puerto Rico, pineapple from Hawaii and seafood from Alaska.

Before getting to the national security aspects that are the policy underpinnings of the Jones Act, it is worth reflecting on the fact that it involves domestic commerce. As such, many domestic laws and regulations related to labor, taxes, wages and hours of service apply. Much of the cost differences can be directly linked to these various laws and regulations. The balance of the cost differences can be explained by structural factors such as trade lane size, ship size, trade lane imbalances and seasonalality. Those are just basic economic facts.

I can understand folks who say they don't support laws or regulations that result in increased costs, whatever the level of those costs. That is a basic philosophical view shared by critics of the Jones Act. What I don't understand is that they make the strongest application of that philosophy to the domestic shipping industry. Perhaps because the activity occurs offshore and out of sight, they seem to be willing to accept a suspension of laws and regulations they would never propose for an onshore industry.

Across all industries in the U.S., our labor cost is many times more than it is in most countries. The three times higher crewing costs on U.S. flag ships is directly related to those differences and is fueled by a multitude of laws and regulations. The Jones Act critics who readily call for a suspension of those laws and regulations for labor activity occuring on a vessel never promote the same thing for onshore sites. They no doubt recognize that such proposals would go nowhere. Yet they loudly rail against the Jones Act, not recognizing the basic illogic in a position that rips at the fabric of our economic system. They never seem to realize the whats good for the goose is good for the gander effect in the unlikely event they succeed in their quest. How long would it be before a bright entrepreneur would have a floating plant moored most of the time in the U.S. if activities onboard what was technically a vessel were largely exempt from our laws and regulations?

Legal experts have noted that even if the Jones Act were repealed, foreign-flag ships that engaged in domestic commerce would automatically be covered by some of these laws and regulations. The U.S. Congress would also likely attach new regulations to any repeal of the Jones Act. The impact of existing and new laws and regulations would need to be taken into account in any factual analysis, as they would result in reductions, perhaps significant, to existing crewing cost differences.

Despite the critisism the Jones Act gets, it is hardly a unique law. Laws that restrict various marine movements to ships that fly that country's flag are broadly referred to as cabotage laws. In a just released study, some two-thirds of the countries in the world with maritime coastlines were found to have cabotage laws that support their merchant marine.

Most observers see the beneficial national security aspects of a U.S. merchant marine. With Jones Act vessels now the majority of the fleet, it's continuation is more important than ever. Ships provide sealift, train mariners and support the shipyard base, all of which result in clear national security benefits. In my view, these components tie together and support each other along with a network of professionals and vendors. Changes that seem to impact just one component, such as the Jones Act, will actually have a ripple effect through a very large supply chain.

While the Jones Act comes with an economic cost, the relatively modest level of that cost is hardly reason enough to unwind a framework that has served our nation so well. I believe any thorough analysis of all the economic and national security aspects would conclude that the Jones Act continues to serve its purpose today. Even if I didn't believe that, a case could be made to support the Jones Act to honor the legacy of what the U.S. merchant marine has done for our country in the past.

Let me share a story involving someone with subject matter expertise in the national security area. He is a senior executive at General Dynamics, the largest defense contractor. In a speech a number of years ago, this executive spoke before a shipping industry group in the U.S. Even with this partisan audience, he certainly got folks attention when he made the statement that his view was that the Jones Act won the cold war.

After pausing for effect, the executive said specifically that it was their Electric Boat Division, and its development of quiet propulsion technology for nuclear submarines that could not be duplicated by the Soviet Union in the 1980's, that was primarily responsible for winning the cold war. He then went on to explain that in his view the development of that technology would not have been possible without an array of naval architects, engineers and vendors here who are also supported by the Jones Act. That is why he directly connected the Jones Act with winning the cold war.

That is certainly a strong statement to say that the Jones Act is not only important from a national security aspect, but that even in recent times and today it continues to play a pivotal role. There is no doubt that the executive was biased given the shipyards his company controlled and there was likely some hyperbole in his statement. However, the gentlemen that made the statement is certainly a subject matter expert.

The U.S. merchant marine makes sense for our country and the Jones Act is a key pillar supporting our merchant marine. Rather than focusing on cost disadvantages compared to foreign-flag ships, the focus should be on cost advantages that new domestic marine networks can achieve compared to rail and truck modes. That issue, however, goes well beyond the subject of this book.

The American merchant marine has a proud history and it has served our country well. Various initiatives that would result in impairing the sector ignore this legacy and make no sense.

26. China's Recent Effect on Shipping

Ross Perot, when running for President in 1992, famously used the colorful phrase "giant sucking sound" to describe what he believed would be the negative effects of the North American Free Trade Agreement, or NAFTA. Mr. Perot opposed NAFTA and believed that it would result in a massive shift of jobs to Mexico as industry relocated.

The accuracy of his forecast regarding NAFTA and Mexico is debatable, but his colorful phrase would prove to be prescient in terms of the effect China would begin to have on the shipping industry only a few years later.

Before China began transitioning in a massive way to a capitalist economy, its effect on shipping was muted. The economies driving cargo shipping in Asia were Japan, Korea, Taiwan, Hong Kong and Singapore. As it related to container cargo, what moved to and from China generally went through Hong Kong. The major container ship operators did not even call directly on any ports in China. That remained the case well after I began my career in container shipping.

But change was already beginning to percolate in China as its leadership took notice of the economic forces that were shaping the world in the postwar era. They may have been socialists, but it turned out that those leaders were incredibly good at studying and learning from what was going on in capitalist economies.

Mao Zedong, the founder of modern China, was an astute observer who closely followed the economic policies of other countries in Asia. Copying individual initatitives that seemed to work in Japan and elsewhere, he began nudging China towards more economic development in the 1950's. In what was a very prescient call in the late 1950's as China's nascent steel industry was beginning to grow, Mao observed that there is no reason why China should not one day become the largest steel producer in the world.

Deng Xiaopong succeeded Mao in the late 1970's and he put in place far reaching market economy reforms that accelerated China's transition. One of Deng's closest outside advisors was Y.K. Pao, one of the individual giants. Indeed, Deng listened to and bonded with Pao's broad worldview and grasp of long term trends and this made him a valued and influential adviser at a pivotal time in China's history. One of the subjects that they undoubtedly discussed was shipping and the key role it played in import and export cost efficiency.

With the long term plans outlined by these leaders, China increasingly transitioned into a capitalist, market-based economy in the 1980's and 1990's. There were two events related to international trade that would prove to be extraordinary events fueling increases in China's growth.

In 1995, China gained membership in the General Agreement on Tariffs & Trade, or GATT. With that, its international trade began to expand. This growth turned into a gallop beginning at the turn of the century. The key catalyst that drove this was when China became a member of the World Trade Organization, or WTO, in 2001. Economists point to 2001 as the beginning of China's period of extraordinary growth. That began something often referred to as the commodities super cycle and almost no industry was as profoundly impacted as shipping.

Few statistics highlight what has occurred in China as much as its annual steel production. For much of the 20th century, one of the most followed measures of relative economic activity among various countries was annual steel production. It was a tangible measure of what a country was building and manufacturing, as initially almost all steel produced was consumed locally.

Even after the cargo shipping revolution, exports of finished steel were relatively small, in large part because of tariff barriers many countries had erected to protect what is still viewed as a key domestic industry. In fact, for most large steel producers, exports of products partially made with their steel contain most of the steel used beyond their borders.

Before getting to the amazing story of China's unprecedented growth and its effect on the shipping industry, it is useful to go back to the time when the cargo shipping revolution was in its infancy. In 1950, the U.S. produced 46.5% of the total steel produced in the world. The Soviet Union was second with 14.4% of total production. Both countries had large domestic sources of iron ore and they therefore resulted in little volume for the shipping industry. For the next couple of decades, these two countries would remain the two largest steel producers in the world.

The competition between the two became an adjunct of the cold war and the Soviet Union gained bragging rights when it surpassed the U.S. to become the largest steel producer in the world in the early 1970's. Around then, Japan emerged as a major steel producer and in fairly short order became the largest steel maker in the world.

Korea would follow in Japan's footsteps and also become a major steel producer. Neither Japan nor Korea had meaningful iron ore or coal resources and the growth in their steel industries resulted in significant shipping demand to move the raw materials needed to make steel.

Throughout most of this period, China wasn't even a factor. In 1950, its steel production was just 0.6% of U.S. production and less than 0.3% of world production. Although it was the most populous country in the world, with 563 million people representing 22% of the world's 2.6 billion people, it was an agricultural economy. The large majority of its people lived on communal farms and eeked out a subsistence living. But the leadership of China had a long-term vision that was quite different.

Mao first and Deng later envisioned a China that was less rural and more urban with factory jobs replacing farm jobs. They were keen students of Japan and Korea's growth, both in their overall economy and as large exporters. Implementing those policies that made the most sense to achieve their goals, and benefiting from the decisiveness of autocratic rule, the transition to what they envisioned began. Slowly at first, but the momentum grew in the 1980's and 1990's.

In a speech in 1996 at an event commemorating the 40th anniversary of Malcom McLean's invention of container shipping, Henry Kissinger emphasized that westerners do not appreciate the long-term focus of Chinese leaders. He characterized them as thinking in terms of decades and centuries and implementing policies focused on that long-term view.

With the aid of hindsight, it is clear that both Mao and Deng had clear economic visions. The central planning aspect of China's governmental structure allowed that to be successfully implemented. The extraordinary economic growth China has experienced since 1950 can be seen in the table below showing its annual steel production in tons every ten years and including the latest annual figures and how that compared to the U.S.

Steel Production	China	U.S.	China/U.S. %
1950	500,000	87,900,000	0.6%
1960	18,000,000	90,100,000	19.8%
1970	18,000,000	119,300,000	15.1%
1980	36,000,000	101,500,000	35.5%
1990	66,300,000	89,700,000	73.9%
2000	127,200,000	101,800,000	125.0%
2010	626,400,000	80,600,000	777.2%
2017	813,200,000	81,600,000	996.6%

As you can see in the table, China's absolute and relative growth in steel production has been extraordinary, particularly over the last several decades. By 2017, China was by far the largest steel producer in the world. Its 813.2 million tons of steel represented 50.0% of worldwide production and was many times the amount of steel produced by Japan and India, the distant second and third largest steel producers.

More than 91% of the steel China made in 2017 stayed in China. The largest domestic uses of steel in that and earlier years was in construction. Residential buildings, office buildings, factories, warehouses, bridges, roads and rail lines all require large amounts of steel to be constructed. Most of the new construction was directly related to the migration of what would become hundreds of millions of people from rural areas to urban ares. Those people needed housing and the entire infrastructure that came with what was the largest migration in world history.

In the new cities and urban areas that sprung up, tens of millions went to work in new factories and offices. Farm jobs were replaced by industrial and professional jobs. As this happened, income levels increased which resulted in domestic demand and consumption soaring. By 2000, China had transformed itself into a large capitalist economy. One tangible indication was that in that year it produced 127.2 million tons of steel, making it the world's largest producer.

As impressive as China's growth through 2000 was, it moved into overdrive when China joined the WTO in 2001 and its trade activity began to increase exponentially. In quick order, China became the manufacturing center of the world with companies across most industries switching some or all of their manufacturing to take advantage of low wages and a productive workforce.

Almost all of this relocated manufacturing activity was export focused and China quickly became the largest exporter in the world. This sharp increase in industrial activity created tens of millions of new jobs, drawing in more people from rural to urban areas. This in turn resulted in the need for even more residential and infrastructure construction.

China was hitting on all cylinders on what was essentially a virtuous circle of economic growth. The period between 2000 and 2008 become known as the supercycle during which China

274

experienced unprecedented growth. The transformations that had taken many decades at other countries were squeezed into just a few years in China. In a tangible indication of the growth China experienced, its steel production quadrupled between 2000 and 2008. The table below shows China's steel production in tons per year compared to worldwide steel production from 2000 through 2017.

Steel Production	China	World	% China
2000	127,200,000	743,600,000	17.1%
2001	150,900,000	749,300,000	20.1%
2002	181,600,000	801,300,000	22.7%
2003	220,100,000	854,100,000	25.8%
2004	269,300,000	816,700,000	33.0%
2005	348,100,000	957,800,000	36.3%
2006	421,500,000	1,145,900,000	36.8%
2007	487,500,000	1,315,000,000	37.1%
2008	497,900,000	1,304,000,000	38.2%
2009	566,400,000	1,197,000,000	47.3%
2010	626,400,000	1,394,000,000	44.9%
2011	684,300,000	1,491,000,000	45.9%
2012	708,800,000	1,510,000,000	46.9%
2013	774,600,000	1,578,000,000	49.1%
2014	822,700,000	1,670,100,000	49.3%
2015	803,800,000	1,620,400,000	49.6%
2016	786,900,000	1,606,300,000	49.0%
2017	813,200,000	1,626,700,000	50.0%

The financial crisis in 2008 negatively impacted most of the world, but it barely impacted China. While growth post financial crisis wasn't as high as during the supercycle period, it was nevertheless well above the rest of the world in most areas. For instance, China's steel production in 2017 was almost two-thirds higher than it was in 2008.

The world has never witnessed the amount of concentrated growth that occurred in China during the last few decades. The key driver to this was the relocation of hundreds of millions of people from rural to urban areas and the resulting effects of that monumental change can be seen in the per capita steel production figures.

World steel production was equivalent to 484 pounds per capita in 2017, or almost five times the 101 pounds per capita in 1935 when the world was more agricultural and less urban and industrial. In 2017, China's per capita steel production was 1,318 pounds, or 2.7 times higher than the world averages. Those statistics underscore the new construction and expanded export activity that underpins China's remarkable economic growth.

While it wasn't altogether different than transitions other countries went through, it was compressed into a significantly smaller period of time and its world impact was exacerbated by

China's 1.4 billion population. The effect that China has had and continues to have on all segments of the shipping industry is impossible to overstate.

Today, by a large margin, China is both the largest importer of goods and the largest exporter of goods in the world. On the import side, resources like iron ore, coal, crude oil and grain are all more destined to China than any other country in the world. For instance, the total seaborne movement of iron ore, the largest commodity moved by the dry-bulk segment, was almost 1.4 billion tons in 2017. Given China's steel production along with its domestic iron ore production, the numbers show that approximately 59% of the iron ore shipments moved by ship were destined for China.

While that commodity could be on the high side, in one commodity after another, China is the destination for a moderate to medium two-digit percentage of the total amount of almost all commodities moving by ship. Whether its crude oil from the Middle East, meteorological coal from the U.S. or soybeans from Brazil, the flow of these and other commodities into China is voracious.

In addition to satisfying domestic demand fueled by what is becoming the largest consumer market in the world, many of these commodities are directly related to manufacturing products for export. In that regard, imports also include a significant amount of sub-assemblies and semi-finished products that are completed in China. Those items were typically imported into China in containers. The intra-Asia market is by far the largest trade lane in terms of the number of containers moved. The large majority of these intra-Asia movements involve China either as an importer or an exporter.

On the export side, most of what flows out of China are manufactured products that move in containers. Beyond that similarity, what moves in those containers covers almost the entire breadth of manufactured products. In 2017, Asia represented 56.5% of worldwide container exports and China was involved in the large majority of those shipments.

In product after product, China has emerged as the dominant manufacturer based on a labor cost and productivity that is unmatched in most countries. The cost efficiency of container shipping, which we estimated resulted in a shipping cost of only 1.82% of the cargo value, allowed China to quickly displace less efficient manufacturing in many countries. As a further indication of its manufacturing dominance, in 2017 seven of the ten largest ports in the world in terms of total container volume were located in China.

China also benefits immensely from centralized planning and an autocratic system that establishes priorities and minimizes internal competition. With this focus, the best export markets to target are determined and the results are predictable. In many product categories, nobody can effectively compete with China. Not surprisingly, today almost all of the actual containers that carriers use to move cargo on ships are made in China. Similarly, the majority of goods flowing into and out of China today move on ships that were built in China.

Closer to home, a walk through any Walmart gives a sense of the broad array of products made in China. The example that is always amazing to me is bicycles, where a new nice looking multi-gear, feature-loaded children's bike will sell for $72. When considering the steel, rubber, paint, accessories and labor that go making such a bike, its flabbergasting to realize that it can be made and delivered to consumers on the other side of the world for just $72. Not surprisingly, almost all the bicycles made in the world today come from China and those that are exported are all shipped out in containers.

Few trips are as eye opening as to see China firsthand today. On my first trip to China, I was amazed by everything I saw in both Bejing and Shanghai. The modern skyscrapers are astonishing, particularly in Shanghai where they seemed to just go on for thirty minutes even in a fast cab ride from the airport.

The high-speed train between Bejing and Shanghai provides insight into the development going on in the interior, albeit that moving close to 300 miles per hour requires that you look fast. The dozens of large new cities being developed near new train stations and the new four lane highways all have the imprint of well thought out long range planning.

While a trip to China doesn't allow you to see firsthand everything that has occurred there, it certainly gives you a sense of the extraordinary changes that have occurred in a compressed time. It is fair to say that the world has never seen as much concentrated economic growth as has occurred in China this century. It is also hard to imagine that level of concentrated economic growth being surpassed in the future. The reason is that no other country offers the possibility of migrating hundreds of millions of people from rural to urban areas which is the fundamental catalyst that resulted in China's economic transformation.

There are many product categories where China is a dominant producer, but where strong domestic demand has precluded meaningful involvement in exporting that product. A key example of that is the car market. China is now the largest passenger car market in the world, with sales of 24 million cars in 2017, almost all of which were produced domestically. Right now, China's middle class population in the hundreds of millions is catching up with the rest of the world regarding cars and various consumer products.

That won't always be the case, and when a tipping point is reached that significant productive capacity will in all likelihood be turned to the export market. While China isn't a factor in the car export market today, at some point it will almost certainly become the largest car exporter in the world.

In addition to its very large volume of imports and exports that benefits shipping immensely, most of the shipments to and from China involve relatively long voyages. For shipping, it is unit-miles rather than units that are the key demand metric.

If you were to consider all of the factors together, there is another coincidental metric that may be the best way to capture China's impact on shipping today. I'm referring to the statistic that China produced 50.0% of the world's steel in 2017. Similarly, it's reasonable to peg China's effective utilization of worldwide shipping capacity today at 50.0%. In other words, today half of the shipping industry owes its very existence to China's extraordinary economic activity.

The world has never seen as much economic activity compressed into a short period of time as what has occurred in China these last few decades. Almost no industry has been as directly and dramatically affected by this phenomenon as the shipping industry.

27. Shipping and the Environment

In terms of overall fuel use per unit mile of cargo, there is no other transport mode that comes even close to the efficiency of the shipping industry. To put that into context, the table below compares the fuel efficiency of the shipping industry to that of the U.S. truckload and rail sectors, both of which are generally recognized as the most efficient land modes of transport in the world. The comparison is framed in terms of the equivalent miles one gallon of fuel will move a 40' container on the respective modes.

Mode	40' Miles/Gallon	Efficiency Vs Truckload
Truckload	6	1.0x
Rail	21	3.5x
Shipping	176	23.9x

Land modes generally do not compete with the shipping mode, but the comparisons above highlight the extraordinary fuel efficiency involved with shipping. While it is physically posssible for the air mode to compete with shipping, large ships are some one hundred times more fuel efficient than even the largest cargo planes. This is just one of the cost factors that explain why planes move only .44% as much cargo as ships.

The shipping industry moves many times more ton-miles of cargo than all the other transport modes in the world combined and that obviously takes lots of fuel. Collectively, cargo ships consumed 305 million tons of fuel in 2017, which was equal to 5.8% of worldwide petroleum production.

As technology has improved and as ships have increased in size, the shipping industry has consistently become more fuel-efficient. Greenhouse gas emissions are a direct function of fuel consumption and relative to the other transport modes, it's hard to see the shipping industry as a primary culprit. In terms of climate change which is the major environmental issue today, shipping is much less of a contributor than the other transport modes.

However, despite what the shipping industry delivers in terms of the efficient quantity of fuel used to move cargo, the quality of that fuel has resulted in an environmental issue that has nothing to do with climate change.

The fuel historically used by cargo ships is an unrefined residual fuel. Because this fuel is literally what is left over after crude oil is refined into gasoline and other lighter products, it concentrates the particulate matter impurities found in crude oil. A key impurity in residual fuel is sulfur, which typically makes up 3.5% of the residual fuel used by cargo ships. While it combusts and helps to propel the ship, it produces sulfur dioxide emissions which are a toxic particulate matter.

The residual fuel used by cargo ships is heavier and dirtier than crude oil and therefore its uses are limited. As a result, it has always typically sold for 10% to 20% less than crude oil. For instance, crude oil was recently selling for $78.80 per barrel, which is equivalent to $544 per ton. By comparison, residual fuel was 14.3% less at $466 per ton. Obviously the price difference compared to various refined fuels is much wider. This relative price discount, of course, explains why the shipping industry has historically used residual fuel.

In my view the fuel quality issue has been the defining environmental issue that makes all other environmental issues facing the shipping industry pale in comparison. I became involved with the issue almost two decades ago. One key observation is the issue has consistently been conflated with climate change by both sides. With apologies to Dickens, it really is a tale of two cities. It is the best of times regarding fuel quantity, it is the worst of times regarding fuel quality.

Fortunately, the fuel quality issue has now been solidly addressed with a phase-in for the use of cleaner fuel, with the final global phase-in taking effect in 2020. I'm proud of my role in increasing awareness of this issue. Before we get to that and the current situation, more background is in order.

The key to understanding this subject is to first know what the issue is about and what it isn't about. It is about raw, toxic air pollution and it has almost nothing to do with carbon emissions and the broader climate change issue that dominates current environmental discussions. Whatever your perspective on the latter, an area where reasonable people can disagree on the role human actions are playing in climate change, shipping scores well in terms of carbon emissions per ton-mile of freight moved. That is not the issue. The issue is that vessel fuel includes a toxic substance unlike anything in any other fuel that is burned. When it is released into the atmosphere, it is poisonous to humans.

The closest analogy to the effect on humans of sulfur in vessel fuel goes back to when gasoline still contained lead more than 40 years ago. Before anyone worried or even talked about climate change, a ground-breaking study showed that lead in gasoline was a pernicious air pollutant that killed 6,000 Americans each year. This discovery resulted in the elimination of lead from gasoline in the U.S. in what was the first major initiative by the EPA. In fact, that study was really the main catalyst for the establishment of the EPA. Prior to this change, lead represented approximately .09% of gasoline, or less than 1,000 parts per million.

Since the transition from sail to power, cargo ships have generally always burned residual fuel which typically contains 3.5% sulfur, or 35,000 parts per million. This residual fuel is much dirtier than crude oil as it is literally what is left over after distilled products are refined. While refined fuels were consistently getting cleaner, there has been no change in the quality of the residual fuel used by vessels. The impetus for a change in vessel fuel quality was a groundbreaking study in 2007 by Dr. James J. Corbett of the University of Delaware College of Earth, Ocean & Environment and other leading academic experts.

In that study, they linked the particulate matter emissions in ship fuel with 60,000 deaths annually with projected growth to 84,000 in 2012. This study was the main catalyst for the establishment by the International Maritime Organization in 2008 of a decade long phase-in plan to cleaner fuel beginning in 2010. The IMO is a division of the U.N. that regulates safety and environmental issues related to international shipping. The new requirements would first apply to defined coastal areas, with the allowed sulfur levels declining to no more than 0.5% throughout the world by 2020.

The residual fuel used in vessels today contains 35 times as much sulfur as compared to the amount of lead in gasoline that was deemed unacceptable over 40 years ago. Even without knowing the precise toxicity of those two chemical elements, that is a comparison that should give any reasonable person pause.

One measure of the known toxicity of sulfur can be seen every time you fill up your car with gasoline. The plaque on the side of the pump says there are no more than 15 parts per million of sulfur in the gas. In New York, that is the only at the pump environmental disclosure that regulators require. It has nothing to do with climate change and everything to do with raw, toxic pollution that can kill humans. Health experts have determined that sulfur is so toxic to humans that it must be severely limited in gasoline. And vessel fuel currently contains more than two thousand times as much of this known toxin per equivalent unit compared to gasoline.

While the climate change effect of ship emissions may be marginal, the more basic sulfur dioxide pollution those emissions produce is anything but. Starting with fuel that has a sulfur content of 35,000 parts per million, when burned in high horsepower engines that operate almost continuously, the typical cargo ship emits more sulfur dioxide in a year than 9.4 million cars. It takes only 64 cargo ships to equal the annual sulfur dioxide emissions of the world's 600 million cars. And there are 17,546 cargo ships more than two football fields long operating in the world today. In other words, these cargo ships emit more than 250 times the amount of sulfur dioxide as all the cars in the world.

Vessels are now the source of the majority of particulate matter emissions, the largest of which is sulfur dioxide, in many port cities and coastal regions around the world. Comparing the number of cargo ships worldwide to the mortality estimates in the 2007 study, you reach the uncomfortable conclusion that the emissions of each vessel can be associated with five deaths per year. To paraphrase Ralph Nader, vessels burning high sulfur fuel are unsafe for mankind at any speed.

It is laudable that the IMO recognized these facts and crafted the phase-in plan adopted in 2008. An argument could be made that the standards should be more stringent and the implementation schedule swifter, but the plan recognized various industry concerns and provided a long timetable in order to adapt to these changes.

I first became aware of of this issue in the late 1990's. The company I led moved containers to and from Puerto Rico with giant barges towed by large ocean-going tugs. Our business model was patterned after truckload carriers on the mainland that resulted in a number of unique characteristics, including 53' equipment and an integrated truckload operation that allowed us to handle the inland movement also.

While we were the smallest carrier, we were growing more than anyone else as our focus on costs allowed us to deliver a better value proposition to customers. Tug/barges rather than self-propelled vessels were a key part of our cost difference. They could be built at more cost-efficient shipyards on the Gulf Coast, required substantially less crew and because they traveled at half the speed of self-propelled vessels, used much less fuel per unit mile.

That last characteristic, however, was often a constraint to potential customers who otherwise liked what we offered. The at sea transit time difference was always highlighted by our competitors, even though the gap between our six day voyage and their three day voyage was often mitigated by our inland transit time superiority. We were constantly encountering prospects where this at sea transit time was an obstacle and we sought ways to counter their concern.

In various comparisons, we noted that our slower speed resulted in using half as much fuel as our competitors and that was a positive. That speed also resulted in a fuel cost advantage, although the higher cost fuel tugs used mitigated much of that difference. Our tugs had higher speed engines that required a distillate fuel similar to what was used in our over-the-road tractors. The residual fuel typically used in a self-propelled vessel just was not even an option for our tugs.

As we systematically focused on and analyzed the granular differences in our business model compared to our self-propelled vessel competitors, we began to view the fuel quality issue as a differentiating factor that may assist in obtaining additional business.

While there was data available on emissions related to different fuels, there wasn't anything analogous to our situation. We would come to realize that our situation where cargo vessels using distillate fuel competed with vessels using residual fuel was somewhat unique. Our research into the area led us to be put in contact with Dr. Corbett.

Further discussions with Dr. Corbett resulted in his supervising the installation of monitoring equipment on our vessels to precisely measure various emissions. Our clear goal was to obtain the most credible data on our emissions differences for our own marketing purposes. Dr. Corbett was focused on the same data, but for research and scientific purposes. That work resulted in a paper presented at a 2001 environmental conference in Brazil comparing our emissions to those of competitors using residual fuel. Dr. Corbett was kind enough to show me as a co-author of the paper, but the work was almost all his.

The study concluded that our sulfur and other emissions were geometrically lower, in part to do slower vessel speed, but primarily due to using a cleaner distillate fuel. As our tugs only worked with that fuel, it wasn't a specific decision we made to be more environmentally friendly, but we still sought to use this new data to our advantage.

My contention was that our having 94% less sulfur emissions based on Dr. Corbett's research paper was a meaningful differentiating factor that could appeal to shippers with publicly stated environmental goals. In press releases and meetings with shippers, I highlighted this difference. Along the way, as I learned more about the toxic first derivative effects of vessel sulfur emissions, I became an accidental environmentalist. We even subsequently elected to use cleaner fuel than the then-current regulations required.

With regard to shippers, it was disappointing that major differences in our emissions metrics, by two and even three digit multiples, were not considered particularly relevant at the time. Even at large companies that professed a commitment to environmental stewardship in their ads, the traffic departments were largely indifferent to our environmental overcompliance. While shippers did not seem to care, my competitors certainly took notice and my environmental initiatives were ridiculed and vilified.

On Earth Day in April 2007, we issued a release that highlighted our emissions differences using the data provided by Dr. Corbett. We noted that cargo moved on our vessels resulted in 94% less sulfur oxide, 90% less particulate matter and 64% less carbon dioxide than the same amount of cargo moved on self-propelled vessels using residual fuel.

Shortly after that release was issued, the CEO of Horizon Lines, our largest competitor, sent me an email with the subject line of *Comments about ships bunkers* that read as follows: *I don't understand why you continue to divide the industry with this rhetoric. It is not going to help us be profitable and reinvest!* He also elected to copy the CEO's of Sea Star Line, Totem Ocean and Saltchuk Resources on his email. The first two companies provided service to Puerto Rico and Alaska, while Saltchuk Resources is the parent of both Sea Star Line and Totem Ocean.

Several hours later, the CEO of Saltchuk responded to all parties with the following email: *Chuck- You are on the wrong page. Tommorrow we will announce that SSL & TOTE will be converting to bio-diesel, including using human waste from our ships to provide over 80% of our fuel needs. We will place at least 5 containers of beef on each of our voyages and are providing a financial incentive for our crews to eat as much meat as possible. Watch out John.-Mark*

Less than a year later, the FBI would raid the corporate headquarters of both Horizon Lines and Sea Star Line in what would end up being one of the largest and most widespread examples of price fixing and other antitrust activity in U.S. history. This resulted in large fines and civil settlements by both companies and was the catalyst for the subsequent bankruptcy and liquidation of Horizon Lines. As part of that investigation, I imagine somebody came across that email. While they would not have been interested in the environmental issue, I suspect that resulted in inquiries that may have been uncomfortible for the two gentlemen on the email thread.

I could write a book on that investigation and its resulting impact. In fact, if I write another book, that would make for an interesting subject. However, I don't want to get off the key subject of this chapter. More on subject, the CEO who sent the sarcastic email has apparently matured on his environmental views and is highlighting the benefits of new LNG powered ships now operating in the Puerto Rico trade lane.

It is fair to say that while our efforts to highlight environmental differences didn't really land us additional business at the time, it did increase awareness of the issue. More importantly, the study that Dr. Corbett did was getting more attention in the academic community and it served as a catalyst for additional studies. All of these studies ultimately resulted in the new IMO fuel cleanliness regulations.

In addition to switching exclusively to distillate fuel with no more than 0.5% sulfur, the IMO regulations allow for the possibility of companies to be in compliance by installing scrubbers which remove sulfur from exhaust gases. These scrubber systems cost approximately $2 million per vessel to install. In closed systems, you have the not inconsequential problem of storing and ultimately disposing of the scrubber slurry residue. In open scrubber systems fed by salt water, residue that is claimed to be inert is discharged into the sea.

The effectiveness and allowability of scrubbers over the long term is questionable. A number of ports have said they will not allow ships with open system scrubbers and some charterers have indicated they will not use such ships. While some shipping companies have announced they are opting for installing scrubbers to meet the IMO regulations, the majority of companies and ships are expected to meet the regulations by switching to cleaner fuel.

Not surprisingly, for the most part the shipping industry resisted the establishment of the IMO regulation. Even after it was established, there was a concerted effort recently to postpone the global implementation from 2020 to 2025. However, the IMO has held to its timetable even though most companies in the shipping industry believe the regulation is excessive.

The reason, of course, for the shipping industry's resistence is that the IMO regulation will result in a sharp increase in its largest cost item. Residual fuel can be purchased for $466 per ton, but the cleaner distillate fuel that meets the new IMO regulations costs $696 per ton, or 49.4% more. The relationship between the prices of these different fuel types varies, but typically the cleaner fuel has ranged from 35% to 65% more than residual fuel.

Many shipping industry folk argue that the sharp increase in demand for this cleaner fuel will push its price up further and the difference in prices between the two fuel types will be well above the current gap. At current prices, the $230 per ton difference translates into an additional annual cost of $70 billion based on the shipping industry using some 305 million tons of fuel per year.

For an industry that is already performing poorly, another $70 billion in annual costs that someone must absorb is concerning at several levels. By adding what amounts to some 25% to the total operating, fuel and capital costs of all vessels, it may make the movement of some cargo uneconomical. Beyond that macro effect, it presents real challenges for all shipping segments to recover this added cost from customers.

In those cases where vessels are chartered out and the fuel is paid directly be the charterer, it will be less of an issue. However, even in those cases, it will undoubtedly put more downward pressure on the charter rates. The most adverse effect of this sharp cost increase will be felt by the container shipping segment.

In container shipping, the vessel operator pays directly for all fuel costs. The contracts with customers include a surcharge mechanism that seeks to adjust rates for changes in fuel prices. Historically, however, these mechanisms have usually disadvantaged container operators.

Given the sharp cost increase this regulation represents, it will not be surprising to see the shipping industry lobby the IMO for a postponement. Many claim that there won't be sufficient distillate fuel to meet the sharp increase in demand in 2020. Others observe that enforcing the regulations at sea will be difficult and compliant vessel owners will be at a disadvantage relative to non-compliant vessel owners.

Even if they succeed in getting the IMO to postpone implementation, however, it may prove to be a Pyrrhic victory. Regulators worldwide, with the support of major environmental groups, will take note of such action. They will see it as evidence that the industry's form of self-regulation as it relates to vessel emissions is not working and mandatory official governmental standards will be imposed. This will result in a hodge podge of varying standards that will likely be even more stringent than the IMO plan.

Despite my affinity for an industry I spent decades in and care for, with what I've learned about this issue, I will stand squarely with the environmental groups calling for direct regulatory intervention should the IMO regulations be postponed.

It would be constructive for the shipping industry to recognize that in the view of most environmental groups and regulators, the industry so far has been accorded very lenient treatment on an issue that isn't debatable to them. Unfortunately, the shipping industry too often seems to conflate its excellent score in terms of carbon emissions per freight ton-mile with its abysmal score in terms of the toxicity of those emissions. As a result, it feels victimized, collectively believing that it has done nothing to deserve such scrutiny and interference.

Having done nothing, of course, is a fundamental part of the problem. While there has been no basic change in vessel fuel quality for decades, all other fuel types have consistently become cleaner over time. The environmental background against which the industry is being measured has changed immensely.

There may be an argument related to an opinion on the role human actions are playing on climate change, but there is no argument justifying the current sulfur levels in vessel fuel. Unless, of course, you think sulfur isn't dangerous to humans. But then if you think that, you might as well show your contempt for science and call for putting lead back in gasoline, arsenic back in paint and mercury back in hat making. The issue is that basic.

When you focus on this issue, what resonates is the extraordinary amount of sulfur in vessel fuel. At 3.5% sulfur, the 305 million tons of fuel used annually contains some 11 million tons of sulfur that is released into the atmosphere. That is the equivalent of 3 pounds of sulfur annually for each person on the planet. By any measure, this sulfur is hazardous to human health.

The change to low sulfur fuel globally is coming. In addition to the significant environmental benefits, however, this change can also be a catalyst for an improvement in financial performance that is so desperately needed in the shipping industry. This goes beyond the obvious rate increase that should accompany any cost increase. Let me explain why.

Pricing across shipping sectors is set at the intersection of vessel supply and demand. Since the financial crisis in 2008 supply has consistently exceeded demand. This has pushed down rates and resulted in dismal financial results. Fuel remains the largest single cost in a typical voyage and the global transition to more expensive low sulfur fuel will make it even more so. Total voyage cost is a function of per day operating and capital costs along with fuel costs, with slower speeds resulting in greater fuel efficiency but also more voyage days. The tradeoff is determined by the specific cost factors of each vessel, but given the various cost factors, the ideal speed that results in the lowest total voyage cost can be algebraically determined.

Whatever the current ideal speed, the increase in fuel costs accompanying the global switch to low sulfur fuels will push that down further. In the drybulk and tanker sectors where fuel costs are frequently paid directly by charterers, they can also be counted on to act in their best economic interest by reducing vessel speeds. The collective reduction in average speeds will result in a similar reduction in capacity. This will put upward pressure on rates and benefit the financial performance of the shipping industry.

In addition to this capacity reduction effect, the container sector has another tool that should be adjusted in the face of this major cost increase. The present fuel surcharge mechanism in the industry is archaic and opaque. With its round numbers, major differences among carriers and timing inconsistent with underlying fuel cost changes, it is not surprising that the present subjective mechanism has no credibility with customers.

First and foremost, container carriers should fully embrace the concept that fuel surcharges solely relate to a pass through of cost changes. That concept was long ago embraced by the U.S.truckload sector and precise formulas tied directly to weekly published DOE diesel fuel prices are automatically and immediately embedded in invoices.

Why not have credible independent parties prepare a transparent calculation that shows the total vessel fuel cost per FEU by trade lane using actual consumption data for the largest vessel in the lane at say 90% utilization? This advantages the most fuel-efficient operators as it should and establishes a clear transparent benchmark formula against which real time additions and subtractions can be made to contract rates.

For instance, if the benchmark for the Asia to U.S. West Coast lane was $231.27 when a customer entered into a contract and $248.61 the week its container was loaded, the invoice shows the initial contract price adjusted up $17.35 per FEU. A simple, straightforward mechanism is in everyone's best interest. If the cost increase accompanying the transition to cleaner fuel is a catalyst to making that happen, it will put the container sector on better and firmer financial ground.

There are of course other environmental issues that involve the shipping industry, but today the fuel quality issue dwarfs them all. The one the public is most aware of is oil spills, primarily resulting from tanker casualties. Due to the massive civil liability resulting from such spills and an array of new regulations and operating procedures, however, these mishaps are much less frequent.

Ballast water treatment systems on ships are addressing the problem of invasive species being transported to an area where they can upset and damage local ecosystems. For example, zebra mussels that found their way from the Caspian Sea to the Great Lakes through ballast water discharge have wreaked havoc, eliminating native species and clogging outlet cooling pipes.

The scrapping and recycling of ships is now subject to additional regulations to deal with various dangerous and toxic substances. As awareness increased about the environmental issues related to substances like asbestos, this was incorporated into shipbuilding standards. As a result, the environmental issues encountered in recycling a ship today are less than they were in the past.

All of these environmental issues have been subject to oversight and regulations by the IMO. However, except for the carbon dioxide emissions or climate change issue, they are inconsequential from a public standpoint relative to the fuel quality issue.

The shipping industry's effect on climate change is a companion to the fuel quality issue but the two are often conflated. In all other transport modes, fuel quality isn't really an issue as it was typically addressed long ago.

In effect, the shipping industry is where other transport modes were many decades ago, except that their fuel was never quite as dirty. The fuel quality situation needs to be fully addressed by the shipping industry before more attention can be turned to the climate change issue. In a similar vein, regulators and environmental groups should focus on this foundational issue as success with fuel quality yields dividends for the companion climate change issue.

The climate change effect of transportation is fundamentally related to the amount of fuel used to move a given amount of cargo. As noted earlier, the shipping industry already scores relatively high on that metric. That being said, there is still room for further improvement.

There continue to be minor improvements in engine and propeller technology that allow a given amount of fuel to propel a ship a slightly longer distance. Refinements in hull design can have the same marginal effect. All the engineering components of a vessel are configured to optimize fuel consumption at the designed speed at sea. With the slow steaming that is now occurring across all shipping segments, many owners are tasking their naval architects and engineers to refine components on new ships to optimize consumption at these slower speeds.

Beyond improvements in traditional shipping technology, there are a number of new technologies that offer ways to augment main engine power and therefore reduce consumption. Two of these are innovative modern day uses of wind power that harken back to how ships were originally propelled. Several shipping companies have added rotor sails, which are large vertical rotors attached to vessel decks that spin with the wind. The spinning produces something known as the magnus effect that leads to propulsion force perpendicular to the direction of the airstream. Another way that wind power is being harnassed is with very large kite-like sails that can be automatically deployed when conditions are right. These sails, tethered to a control arm that automatically adjusts to varying conditions, typically fly at 500' or more above sea level to take advantage of more consistent high altitude winds.

In several actual cases where rotor sails or kite sails have been used, main engine fuel consumption reduction in the 10-15% range have been achieved. Solar power panels also offer a way of providing electricity to a ship that reduces the power demand on the main engine. However, the placement of panels can not interfere with cargo handling operations and that limits the potential in many shipping segments. These renewable power examples are primarily viewed as augmenting the propulsion provided by the main engine.

Fuel cell technology has great potential across all transport modes, but a case can be made that it is highest in shipping because the larger scale helps to justify the initial capital investments. In discussions related to how shipping may move away completely from fossil fuels in the long term, hydrogen or ammonia fuel cells are the best candidates. With those technologies, the only emission is water vapor.

When we get to 2020 and all ships are in full compliance with the IMO standards, will that be enough? Those regulations will require the use of fuel with no more than 5,000 parts per million of sulfur globally and no more than 1,000 parts per million of sulfur in certain defined coastal areas. With reductions equivalent to 86% and 97%, respectively, compared to fuel used before the IMO regulations, the shipping industry will view that as a significant change.

However, many will still see that as fuel that is still too dirty as those levels are 333 and 67 times higher than the U.S. limit for sulfur in gasoline. At 5,000 parts per million, the typical cargo ship emits more sulfur dioxide in a year than 1.3 million cars and the 17,545 cargo ships emit 36 times as much sulfur as all the cars in the world. Even at the 1,000 parts per million of sulfur requirement in a limited number of coastal areas, the sulfur emissions relative to any comparison to other transport modes is daunting.

Confronted with the situation that will likely exist beyond 2020, it is easy to envision various parties calling for further action on shipping emissions. After all, continuous reductions have been made in the emissions of other transport modes and it is reasonable to assume this will continue. As everything else gets cleaner, the emissions of the shipping industry, even after it has significantly reduced emissions, will stand out.

Ever increasing attention is being paid to the health impact of particulate emissions, the largest of which is sulfur dioxide. In port cities and coastal areas the awareness of the impact of shipping continues to grow. This may well result in demands for further regulation and the bodies that could effect change go well beyond the IMO.

Indeed, various European Union regulatory bodies are viewed as more aggressive than the IMO. They along with environmental regulators in populous states like California could effect much of the worldwide fleet by requiring specific emissions limits on all vessels calling at ports within their jurisdiction. As ship owners make decisions on how to meet the known environmental regulations and to plan long term, they should also take into account the likely further direction of such regulations. Beyond the current IMO regulations, this is a particularly important consideration for ship owners when they are making decisions related to building new vessels.

Considering all the various cost and environmental factors, it is likely that shipping will move to LNG as the primary fuel and the transition will happen faster than proponents are predicting. As the cleanest fossil fuel available, it addresses the extraordinary fuel quality issue the shipping industry will have even after the final IMO regulations go into effect. Importantly, LNG also has 27% less carbon dioxide emissions compared to the same energy amount of distillate fuel. As such, it is also making a considerable reduction related to the shipping industry's impact on climate change. LNG can be utilized as the fuel in traditional main engines with some modifications.

The cost to build a ship capable of using LNG, or to modify an existing ship, adds something in the range of 15-20% to the cost of the ship. The price relationship between LNG and distillate fuel varies, but at times the energy equivalent amount of LNG has been less. In other words, it has made economic sense regardless of the very favorable environmental aspects.

Perhaps more importantly, from a purchaser's standpoint, the long-term pricing outlook for LNG looks very favorable as most forecasts show the supply of natural gas and LNG growing at rates well above all the other petroleum segments. This continuous growth and likely consistent over-supply will ironically let ship owners benefit from the same supply versus demand dynamic that has adversely impacted the shipping industry for too many years.

A ship owner wanting to make the strongest environmental statement based on existing technology would build a ship propelled by a LNG powered fuel cell, which would be augmented with rotor sails and solar panels. Such a vessel would be the cleanest cargo vessel in the world from an emissions standpoint. That vessel could also end up being the most cost-efficient based upon various long-term forecasts of the price of LNG relative to distillate fuel. Sometimes things do actually come together in a virtuous circle that is both environmentally and economically friendly.

As we go to press, however, it is increasingly looking like that while LNG will be the next fuel making major inroads into shipping, it may be overtaken quicker than once thought by zero carbon emissions fuel sources such as hydrogen and ammonia. The only emission from such energy sources used in fuel cells is water vapor. With 97% of the known universe comprised of hydrogen atoms, its fair to say there is an endless supply whether it's used to power traditional ships or spaceships of the future. However, hydrogen is highly flamable and explosive and advancements in an array of technologies are needed before it can safely be used. Ammonia is a by-product of hydrogen that is not flamable but it is highly toxic and processes will need to be developed for its safe handling and use. Those, however, would likely appear sooner and its reasonable to envision that ammonia powered ships will be the first zero carbon emission ships.

The shipping industry is by far the most fuel efficient transport mode, but that has been mitigated by its historical use of dirty residual fuel. However, that is being addressed and the industry is on the path to a cleaner future. In terms of recent improvement and trends, you would be hard pressed to find an industry more on an upward environmental trajectory than the shipping industry.

28. Shipping and Globalization

Shipping makes globalization possible. Without the efficiency of cargo ships today, globalization simply wouldn't exist. The extraordinarily cost-efficient networks created by the 17,546 ships over 600' long are the lifeblood and enabler of world trade.

The post-war revolution orchestrated by the nine individual giants we profile took shipping costs as a percent of cargo value from 50% or more to where they are 2% or less in many cases. With such a sharp reduction in transfer costs, barriers to trade around the world collapsed and goods and commodities could be sourced from places with comparative advantages in producing particular products.

Freight costs are the real world friction that has acted to constrain trade. Efficient shipping costs are the lubricant that resulted in business decisions to go overseas. As ships became more specialized and larger and their operating processes became more efficient, the business decisions to go overseas accelerated. David Ricardo's economic theories on trade have been more than proven out. However, it is likely that even he would be surprised by the massive elasticity in trade volume that has occurred as shipping costs as a percent of cargo value have plummeted.

In most of the largest trade lanes in the world, the only modes to choose between for moving cargo are ships or planes. In 2017, ships moved 226 times as much cargo as planes. If planes were the only option, much of the trade that now moves would go away because the air cost mode would render that trade uneconomical. Airfreight costs are on average 36 times higher than moving cargo on ships. If that was the only option you go back to pre-war times when costs as a percent of cargo value were 50% and higher.

One tangible metric of the elasticity of trade to decreases in relative shipping costs is the fact that the dollar amount of U.S. trade has increased almost 800 times from the end of World War II to today. While some may say those metrics are coincidental, they are missing the basic causal effect. Shipping efficiency is the cause and world trade growth is the effect.

In 2017, the world's merchant marines collectively moved $11.7 trillion in goods representing 15.0% of 2017 gross world product of $78.0 trillion. With 63% of that gross world product represented by services, the net result is that cargo moved by vessels equates to 40.6% of tangible goods worldwide. Almost half of what can be tangibly touched across the entire global economy makes its way in part on one of these vessels.

The shipping segment that is most associated with globalization is container shipping. Container ships moved $7.0 trillion worth of goods in 2017, representing 60% of the total value of shipborne trade. With intricate supply chains moving components, semi-finished products and finished products to and from all corners of the world, container ships moved 161.7 million twenty-foot equivalent units in 2017.

No segment is as directly involved with and responsible for world trade as container ships. With total revenue of approximately $140 billion in 2017, or 2.0% of the total value of goods moved, the container shipping segment performs its key logistics role very efficiently. That extraordinarily low transport cost for goods is what greases the skids and makes trade possible. Indeed, container shipping is the primary supply chain for globalization and the main catalyst for world trade.

In terms of what it makes possible, shipping is clearly one of the most important industries in the world because the service it provides can't be displaced or substituted by something else. Without cargo ships, world trade and the world economy as we know it today would simply grind to a halt within a matter of weeks. How many other industries are so critical and irreplaceable? When you reflect on what much bigger industries provide, you can still readily envision substitutes and alternatives if they didn't exist.

There is, however, no viable substitute for the 63.9 trillion ton-miles of tangible goods moved by cargo vessels in 2017. That underscores the staggering amount of cargo moved by the largely invisible network of cargo ships. To put that figure into more perspective, it is useful to compare it to more visible freight networks with which people are familiar. The 63.9 trillion ton-miles of cargo moved by merchant vessels is 34 times larger than the freight moved by all the U.S. railroads and 32 times larger than the freight moved by all the U.S. trucking companies.

If it is a tangible product, the likelihood is that either it or something that played a role in its manufacture moved on one of these giant cargo ships. When you reflect on other industries where shipping is a key component of their supply chain, you are hard pressed to find many exceptions.

The relative role of shipping varies from industry to industry and from company to company. For instance, the retailing industry in the U.S. is particularly dependent on container shippiing. Companies like Walmart, Home Depot and Target simply wouldn't exist anywhere near the scale they are today without container shipping.

At a higher macro level, the key role of shipping in the growth and development of many countries and their economies in the postwar period is undeniable. The first country to materially benefit from shipping was Japan. One of the first prominent industries developed in Japan after World War II was shipbuilding, which also became the model for building other industries in which Japan became prominent.

Japan was really the first country to be labelled an export economy and as such relied on ships to bring in raw materials and to also take out finished products. Among other shipping firsts as it grew, Japan was the first country outside of the U.S. to move cargo on the early container ships. As ships in that and the other segments grew in size and efficiency, Japan was a primary beneficiary. The success of Japan became the model for other export economies such as Korea, Taiwan, Singapore and Hong Kong.

Those economies that were advantaged by shipping, however, would pale in a comparison to shipping's impact on China over the last few decades. This was also a symbiotic relationship that made the shipping industry even more efficient. The massive amount of raw materials that poured into China resulted in new classes of more efficient dry-bulk vessels. As China transitioned to the largest manufacturing center in the world, container ships grew significantly in size and scope to handle the unprecedented growth in container volume.

290

Seven of the ten largest volume container ports in the world are now in China. Shipping and China are both cause and effect and tied together in recent times in a virtuous circle that benefits each other. It is reasonable to say that half of the world's shipping capacity is used in moving cargo to and from China. Likewise, without the extraordinary cost efficiency of these ships, China could not have an economy anywhere near as large as it has today.

To go a step further, it is also clear that globalization has also played a direct role in making the world safer. Beyond the financial benefits of trade which are irrefutable, mutually beneficial commerce has lessened tensions between countries that otherwise may have been expressed in conflict and even war. Without the economic ties resulting from trade, disputes could easily flare into military confrontations.

The rules for engaging in trade put in place by various organizations established a framework that moderates sovereign behavior. A key goal of Nixon and Kissinger with regard to their China initiative was that having a stake in the world economy would make for a better and calmer overall relationship. That is largely exactly what has played out. Even in the face of serious issues like the territorial claims in the South China Sea, the communications framework and ties related to trade has almost everybody agreeing that the likelihood this escalates into military conflict is minimal.

In addition to the contributions the world's merchant marine fleet makes to commerce, the bonds resulting from that commerce contribute directly to the security and well being of everyone. There is a thread directly linking shipping to globalization and globalization to world peace.

Up until recently, the economic and political benefits from a growing interconnected global economy seemed to be self-evident and recognizable by all. Most business, political and academic leaders embraced trade and globalization. The view that cross border competition resulted in giving consumers the best products at the lowest costs was broadly shared.

All credible economists believe that by having countries focus on producing products where they have relative comparative advantages, the collective benefits to the world are measured in the trillions of dollars each year. All countries benefit from trade, but how those benefits are distributed within countries was a different matter and one not typically addressed by economists. The implicit assumption was that policy makers in countries would take steps to have the collective benefits from trade distributed equitably.

Unfortunately, that has not happened and as trade continued to grow, the sectors and individuals experiencing disruption became more of a political force here and abroad. Instead of coming up with proposals to more equitably distribute trade's collective benefits some politicians demagogued the issue and challenged the overall benefits of trade. The very concept of globalization became a culprit in some circles. With China's entry into the WTO and its subsequent growth into a manufacturing powerhouse, the pros and cons of globalization were increasingly debated. The financial crisis and its aftermath exacerbated these tensions in many Western economies. This became one of the key issues in recent elections in the U.S. and the U.K. that resulted in both countries withdrawing from previous trade agreements.

As must be clear, I am an unabashed supporter of the economic and political benefits of world trade. While my involvement in the shipping industry obviously makes me biased, the objective facts are squarely on my side. It is the misrepresentation of basic facts related to trade that is most disappointing. Recent tariff initiatives by the U.S. have been justified by referring to specific goods with high tariffs, implying that country has much higher tariff levels for our products than we do for theirs.

However, the actual data simply does not bear that out. The reality is that today the WTO framework results in a largely free trade environment among most nations. In 2017, the average tariff across the trading world was just below 2% or inconsequential. The average tariff for imports coming into the U.S. was 1.6%, identical or slightly higher than most of our long term allies in Europe and twice the average for Canada, our largest trading partner. The average tariff for goods going into China is slightly higher but still only 3.6%.

This low tariff framework has allowed goods to flow freely to the significant economic benefit of the countries involved. The imposition of 10% and 25% tariffs into this equilibrium has been highly disruptive and has been met with guaranteed and predictable responses. The end result has been that everyone loses.

Without a doubt, there are issues related to trade that need addressing, but it should be done with a scapel and not the blunt force of 25% tariffs on a wide range of products. Taking such steps is nonsensical and incredibly wrong-headed at so many levels. The retaliation that it invites makes it analogous to taking the first shot in a circular firing squad.

At the very least, tariffs impose unnecessary taxes on consumers and reward less efficient manufacturers. Furthermore, the very notions that trade deficits are bad and equivalent to a transfer of value is nonsense. First, it ignores the obvious that in exchange for cash a consumer is getting a car or bicycle or some other tangible product that the consumer values more than either cash or the same domestically produced product. Rhetoric implying a trade deficit equates to a direct transfer of value is ludicrous.

In addition, with the dollar the reserve currency of the world, this creates international demand for our currency that has the effect of almost guaranteeing U.S. trade deficits. Our status as the world's reserve currency results in meaningful economic and political benefits. Initiatives to reduce the U.S.'s trade deficit not only bring illusory benefits, but risk tangible damage to this status which in turn will weaken our economic and political standing.

When a complete factual analysis is done, you can not help but conclude that no country has collectively benefited as much from world trade in the postwar period as America. After all, the U.S put the systems that govern trade and much of the global economy in place. To take steps that may result in dismantling systems that have served America well would be shortsighted and extraordinarily misguided.

Globalization has brought enormous economic benefits to the U.S. and the world, although it is clear that such benefits have not been distributed as equitably as they could be. The latter is a matter for policy makers, but the former is undeniable. Another tangible indication of this is statistics on world poverty maintained by the World Bank. They show a significant drop in poverty levels around the globe just in the recent past.

In 1990, some 1.85 billion people or 35% of the world's population lived in poverty, which is defined as less than $1.90 per person per day. Twenty-five years later in 2015, poverty levels had been reduced to 768 million people or 10% of the population. Much has been written about this staggering and unprecedented reduction in world poverty levels. However, not enough credit has been given to globalization as a catalyst. I believe there is no other causal relationship to explain the tectonic shift in world poverty levels that is as important as the geometric increase in world trade.

Shipping made globalization possible as it has consistently reduced the cost and time barriers which acted as friction in preventing or impairing trade. There has be no instrument as key to globalization than the efficiency of the modern shipping industry. The thousands of giant cargo vessels and the extraordinarily efficient distribution network they form are what make world trade possible. While performing their core task, those ships also created conditions that make the world safer and brought hundreds of millions out of poverty. That is quite a legacy for a largely invisible industry.

Just recently there was an appropriate recognition by a leading Washington D.C. think tank that squarely recognized this legacy. The Cato Institute's Human Progress project is chronicling major events that significantly benefited mankind. As part of that project, every few weeks they profile someone they refer to as a Hero of Progress. So far, they have identified more than forty individuals including luminaries such as Johannes Gutenberg, inventor of the printing press, and Jonas Salk, discoverer of the polio vaccine.

In April 2019, the Cato Institute announced that its 17th Hero of Progress was Malcom McLean. In their profile, they saw a direct link between Malcom's invention of container shipping sixty-three years earlier, the trade it enabled and the worldwide reduction in poverty that resulted from that trade. Malcom is the only businessperson who has been recognized as a Hero of Progress, a group populated mostly by vaccine discoverers and others whose individual efforts improved the lives of countless millions. Cato's selection of Malcom and the analysis that went into that selection was impeccable.

Globalization has been very good for mankind, and shipping has been very good for globalization.

29. Challenges Facing Shipping Industry

First and foremost among the challenges facing the shipping industry is its financial performance. The dictionary defines industry as a distinct group of productive or profit-making enterprises. While the productivity of shipping related to world trade is indisputable, its consistent lack of profits could lead some to question whether it really is an industry in the true definition of the word. Few if any industries have a cumulative income statement since they started that would show worse results than shipping.

The bottom line results of the industry are very poor and they have been for over a decade since the financial crisis of 2008. While most of the industry is privately owned and a comprehensive income statement of overall results is not possible, much insight can be gained from the results of publicly reporting companies.

The most visible segment is container shipping where companies representing almost two-thirds of total vessel TEU capacity report their results. Over the last three years, the twelve companies that release results showed a cumulative loss of $5.3 billion. This was ongoing loss and excluded the impact of non-recurring charges totaling in the billions.

Below is a recap of the overall bottom line results reported by container operators for 2016, 2017 and 2018 along with three-year totals. The companies are listed in order of their total current TEU capacity. The table takes the reported results and assumes the remaining non-reporting operators had similar per TEU results to develop overall sector results. With those estimated results included, the container sector had an ongoing net loss of $8.6 billion over the last three years. All amounts in the table are in millions of U.S. dollars.

Company	2016	2017	2018	Total 2016-18
Maersk	-381	524	202	345
CMA CGM	-454	701	34	281
China Cosco	-982	81	-26	-927
Hapag Llloyd	-150	35	41	-74
Evergreen	-282	243	10	-29
Orient Overseas	-219	138	108	27
Yang Ming	-492	11	-219	-700
Mitsui OSK	129	146	89	363
NYK	-274	-214	-170	-658
Neptune Orient	-105	na	na	-105
Hanjin Marine	-721	na	na	-721
Zim	-168	11	-127	-284
Hyundai Merchant	-848	-691	-603	-2,142
K Line	-612	87	-169	-694
Subtotal	-5,559	1,071	-831	-5,319

% Public	62.2%	64.5%	64.5%	na
Estimated Total	-8,937	1,661	-1,288	-8,565

With total industry revenue in the $140 billion range per year, the overall net loss over the entire period was equivalent to 2.0% of revenue. In 2016, it was more than three times that at 6.4% of revenue. With the total container ship capacity of the sector at 22,689,243 TEU's, the total net loss over the period was $377 per TEU of capacity, or an average of $126 per TEU annually. The net loss in 2016 was much higher at $394 per TEU of capacity.

When you measure results against asset and equity investments in the container sector, the story gets even bleaker. This capital-intensive sector requires a minimum profit just to meet its cost of equity capital and to provide an adequate return on those substantial equity investments. The container ships themselves represent asset investments of at least $10,000 per TEU, resulting in a total sector investment of approximately $227 billion. Container and chassis equipment investments push that figure considerably higher. Capital structures vary by company, but collectively the equity investment in the sector readily tops $5,000 per TEU, or $100 billion in aggregate.

Just to meet its cost of equity capital, the container shipping industry needs to have real economic profits of $10 billion and $500 per TEU of capacity each year. Over the last three years, on an average annual basis it has been $12.9 billion and $569 per TEU of capacity short of that measure. Simply to meet those minimums, rates would have needed to be 9.2% higher over the entire period. The gap, of course, was much higher in 2016.

The most recent actual results in the container shipping sector are similar with those over the entire three year period shown in the table, so we will use the longer period to benchmark the current annual run rate results. In other words, we will peg container shipping as now running at annual revenue of $140 billion with a net loss equal to 2.0% or $2.9 billion.

Getting the current run rate results of the other shipping segments is more difficult as the large majority of those companies are privately owned. However, there are a number of benchmarks we can use to develop reasonable estimates on the size and performance of each segment. Chief among them is our data on the breakdown of vessels by segment and current timecharter equivalent rates. With that data, annualized market size can be estimated. From there, using estimated total costs for the entire segment, net performance can be broadly estimated.

When you go through those calculations, you come up with an annualized market size of $133 billion for the three non-container segments combined. Note that unlike the container segment, which has significant non-vessel related costs it is responsible for, these segments primarily revolve around the ships themselves.

Using the timecharter equivalent revenue, total equivalent costs were estimated based on operating costs plus a reasonable estimate for depreciation and interest costs as well as general and administrative expenses. The daily amounts are aggregates for the entire segment and were built up from averages in each subsegment. Using this approach, the non-container segments collectively have an annual run rate loss of $2.6 billion, or 2.0% of revenue as detailed in the table below.

Segment	Tanker	Dry-Bulk	Other	Subtotal
Revenue (Billions)	58	46	29	133
TCE Rate/Day	16,207	13,986	11,017	na
Est Total Costs/Day	17,092	13,716	11,127	na
Est Net Income/Day	-885	270	-110	na
Net Income/Revenue %	-5.5%	2.0%	-1.0%	-2.0%
Net Income (Billions)	-3.2	0.9	-0.3	-2.6

While the container shipping segment is clearly performing very poorly, the estimated data shows that all of the other shipping segments are also performing poorly. Most are showing net losses and the overall loss as a percent of revenue is the same as that measure in the container segment. We estimate current net losses in the tanker segment are equal to 5.5% of revenue while the dry-bulk segment has a slight profit and other segments come in slightly below the container segment loss ratio. In the case of the dry-bulk segment, its current performance is well ahead of recent large losses. The tanker segment is the opposite as it experienced small and short-lived profits recently.

The limited numbers of publicly traded companies in both segments have reported their most recent results on both sides of our estimates. For the six months ending June, 2018, Euronav, International Seaways and DHT Holdings, three of the larger publicly traded tanker companies, reported actual losses equal to 18.3%, 25.9% and 12.5% of revenue, respectively. The 18.9% average loss of those three is many times our segment estimate of 5.5%. On the other hand, for the same period, Genco, Dryships and Diana Shipping, three of the larger publicly traded dry-bulk companies, reported actual profits equal to 6.5%, 6.5% and 4.9%, respectively. The 6.0% average profit of those three is slightly better than our segment estimate of 2.0% profit.

Looking at the composite annual results of those three companies in both segments as a further check, they generally confirm that losses have often been higher than our current estimates. The table below shows the average loss as a percent of revenue for both 2017 and the five year period from 2013 to 2017. Note that in all cases the ratios exclude the effect of extraordinary and non-recurring items that would have negatively affected all companies.

Net Loss/Revenue %	2017	2013-2017
3 Tanker Company Average	-11.7%	-0.7%
3 Dry-Bulk Company Average	-9.6%	-43.1%
6 Company Overall Average	-10.6%	-21.9%

As a further indication of consistently poor results, each of the three dry-bulk companies above reported net losses in every year over the 2013 to 2017 five-year period. Excluding non-recurring items which would have made the ratios worse, those net losses ranged from 0.5% to 143.8% of revenue. The tanker companies weren't as consistently loss making, but still reported net losses in the slight majority of the years involved. The worse performance among the tanker companies involved a net loss equal to 71.8% of revenue, while the best performance was net income equal to 41.4% of revenue.

Needless to say, the financial results across the entire shipping sector have recently been both poor and volatile. Unfortunately, that volatility tends to have a downward bias with the entire sector having losses in a magnitude and consistency that are rarely seen in other industries.

The current container segment results shown above are solid and driven by the recent actual reported results. The current estimated results of the non-container segments detailed above are reasonable approximations. If anything, they may understate current losses based on the actual results of companies that likely perform better than most of the other companies in the segment.

If both the container and non-container segments are combined, the total annualized revenue for the cargo shipping industry is $273 billion, resulting in a net loss of $5.5 billion or 2.0% of revenue as shown in the table below.

Segment	Container	Non-Container		Total
Revenue (Billions)	140	133		273
Net Income (Billions)	-2.9	-2.6		-5.5
Net Income/Revenue	-2.0%	-2.0%		-2.0%

The current poor results are indicative of actual performance for much of the last ten years since the 2008 financial crisis. Just as the decade prior to the crisis saw the best overall financial performance ever by the shipping industry, the decade since the crisis is at the other end of the spectrum. Actual results have bounced around between small profits to losses much larger than the $5.5 billion loss above.

Relative financial performance varied across segments, but all have seen cumulative losses since the financial crisis. I believe an accurate accounting would show that over the last ten years, the combined loss in the shipping industry is as much as $100 billion, wiping out most if not all of the profits in the decade leading up to 2008.

The rather unique income tax situation of most companies in the shipping industry is ironic. By virtue of where ships are registered, the industry effectively pays no tax on income and instead typically pays a relatively small fee based on vessel tonnage. The actual benefits from that envious position have unfortunately been almost non-existent in the recent past.

In fact, the fixed tonnage tax amounts paid by most shipping companies in lieu of income taxes have likely cost most companies more recently than if they had been taxed like regular corportations. The industry with what could be called the best structural income tax loophole among all industries has by its own performance shown that it can take advantage of that less than almost any other industry, at least recently.

Despite these losses, the industry has managed to limp along as most companies are still generating cash flow to service at least part of their debt. EBITDA is the acronym that stands for earnings before interest, taxes, depreciation and amortization. Unfortunately, too many ship owners have grown to view this metric as a substitute for profit. In the extraordinarily capital intensive shipping industry, that sets an incredibly low bar.

Just as banks should not measure their results before interest to depositors and other capital providers, shipping companies shouldn't measure their results before the real economic cost of ships that physically depreciate each year. The bottom line losses in the shipping industry represent a destruction of shareholder value. Furthermore, as highlighted earlier, a minimum profit level is required just to cover the minimual cost of capital related to substantial shareholder equity investments.

The poor performance of the shipping industry has also adversely affected the banking sector. Of the approximately $400 billion in shipping loans held by commercial banks around the world, $150 billion are non-performing. Many banks have adopted a "kick the can down the road" approach, entering into serial deferrals and restructurings with the hope that industry conditions will improve. By not addressing the problem directly, this is just pushing the overcapacity problem forward from the standpoint of the industry. There is, however, an even more serious problem overhanging the shipping industry that is largely unrecognized and that is constraining its future financial performance.

Across almost all the segments, ships are traveling at around 30% less speed than they were prior to the financial crisis. This resulted from new ship deliveries well exceeding demand growth over the past decade, particularly in the first half of that period. The collective response of the shipping industry was to engage in "slow steaming" which had the effect of absorbing that capacity. Such practices also reduced fuel usage so it had a double benefit, particularly during much of the period when fuel prices were at historic highs.

While many in the shipping industry see slower speeds as a permanent change, that is not borne out by the data. In time after time, when market conditions lead to an uptick in rates, average speeds bump up almost immediately. That has the effect of increasing capacity, which then exerts downward pressure on rates. This circularity in the form of this shadow or phantom capacity remains a much-underappreciated dynamic in the shipping industry today. It is a meaningful negative catalyst going forward.

The root cause of the shipping industry's financial performance issues is hardly a secret. The culprit, as always, is excess capacity as new deliveries have been in excess of increases in demand. In the heady decade prior to the financial crisis, overall demand growth was stronger and more consistent than any period in history.

Driven primarily by what was occurring in China, demand was growing 10% per year or more in many segments. Charter rates for VLCC's were hitting $200,000 per day and Capesize bulkers were getting $100,000 per day. At these rates, the cost of newbuildings could be fully recovered in less than two years. Delerious with the potential, existing and new ship owners over ordered vessels in all segments.

This multi-year ordering binge slowed down with the financial crisis, but almost all segments are still suffering from the overhang. Even with delays and some outright cancellations negotiated by owners, ship deliveries consistently exceeded the slower demand growth after 2008. Intermittent spikes in demand and shipyard incentives in subsequent years even had some owners even return to short-lived ordering booms.

Unfortunately, the combined effect of all of these factors is that the real over-capacity situation got worse each year in almost all of the shipping segments. This occurred even with better than average demand growth, particularly in the dry-bulk and container segments. While not at pre-crises levels, growth in those sectors was around 4.5% per year. Much of this excess capacity was absorbed in the various markets in the form of slower vessel speeds.

The capacity growth in the container sector was different and came in the form of much larger vessels in addition to more vessels. The super-sizing of ships in the container sector is a more recent phenomenon compared to the other sectors. The biggest ships today are literally five times larger than the largest vessel before the beginning of the second container revolution, which effectively began with Malcom McLean ordering his Econships.

This trend to ever-larger container ships has continued unabated even after the financial crisis. Once a carrier introduced a new ship that is significantly larger into a given trade route, the resulting cost-efficiency from scale economies was such that other carriers needed a similar size ship if they wanted to stay in that trade lane and compete.

As a result, overall capacity expanded well beyond demand growth even in recent years in the container sector. The industry began using the term "cascading" to describe when a larger vessel replaced a smaller vessel that was then deployed in another route where it replaced an even smaller vessel. This process typically continued for several iterations, often increasing capacity well beyond demand in numerous routes. A key aspect was that all vessels remained deployed and this drive to match competitor's economics resulted in container sector capacity growing above the other sectors in recent years.

For example, there was a recent news story that highlights the capacity problem in the container sector today. Hyundai Merchant Marine, the largest Korean operator, entered into an agreement with Korean shipyards to build 20 large vessels for $3 billion. As shown in the earlier table, HMM lost $2.1 billion over a three year period.

Putting aside why anyone would finance such a project for company that has been the worst performer in an under-performing sector, this is a prime example of how chronic oversupply in the container sector develops. As this story developed, it was reported that the Korean government was providing financial assistance to both HMM and the shipyards that made the agreement possible. Obviously the governmental decision-makers here are thinking about what is good for

Korean shipbuilders, shippers and national pride with little or no regard for this company and the broader sector.

Despite the most recent data showing an $5.5 billion annual run-rate loss for the overall shipping industry, there are two events looming in the near future that will result in even more pressure on the financial results of the shipping industry. Those events are slower growth rates in most segments and the worldwide implementation of cleaner fuel standards in 2020.

Over the last six years, the growth rate in total ton-miles for all cargo has been 3.8% per year. Going forward until 2030, that overall growth rate is now forecast to decline to 2.0% per year. For the 20 year period from 2030 to 2050, the overall growth is forecast to decline further to 0.2% per year, driven by less growth in all segments and an actual contraction in crude oil and petroleum products shipments. These growth rates are discussed in detail in the next chapter.

When the new cleaner fuel standards go into effect at the beginning of 2020, overall annual vessel costs based on historical relationships will go up by $70 billion, or an average of around 27%. This will undoubtedly change the economics of some cargo moves and in that sense result is a one time structural negative change to demand even if all of the increased cost is borne by customers. It is likely that customers will resist paying all of the increased cost. In the case of ships that are employed under timecharter, there will be more pressure for lower charter rates to absorb a portion of the increased fuel costs.

The fuel surcharge mechasism in the container sector does not even work now for the carriers. Without some fundamental changes, it is difficult to see the container operators succeeding in passing along all of this cost increase. However, in the absence of the container operators passing along the cost increase, their already poor financial performance will become even worse.

The forecast slowdown in demand growth assumes no fundamental changes in the largely free trade environment under the WTO framework that exists among most nations. In 2017, the average tariff across the trading world was around 2% or almost inconsequential. For imports coming into the U.S., the average tariff was 1.6%. That is identical or slightly higher than most of our long term allies in Europe and twice the average 0.8% for Canada, our largest trading partner. The extraordinary efficiency of container ships that carry the majority of foreign trade by value has reduced overall shipping costs on many products to an equally inconsequential percentage. These facts have allowed goods to flow freely to the significant economic benefits of the countries involved.

Unfortunately, the China trade issue has now become highly politicized and tariffs of 10% to 25% have been imposed and even higher tariffs are being talked about. Furthermore, the rhetoric continues to increase with discussions of expanding the goods covered by such tariffs. The imposition of these tariffs into this equilibrium has been highly disruptive and has led to predictable responses that result in everyone losing.

Tariffs are simply taxes paid by the importing consumer if the cargo still moves. However, because they are aimed at making that product less economical to the consumer, they often achieve their goal and stop that movement. Obviously the industry that will first feel the effect of this is the shipping industry. Indeed, a case can be made that no industry will be as harmed by an escalating trade war as the shipping industry.

Determining the impact on cargo volume from a potential escalating trade war is speculation and difficult to discern now. However, the decline in overall shipping volume following the financial crisis in 2008 provides one benchmark. During that period, cargo volume across sectors declined some 10% largely due to relatively short-lived difficulties with trade financing.

In my view, it is easy to see tariffs in effect and being discussed as having one and a half times the impact, or a 15% decline in cargo volume. Any reduction in cargo volume from tariffs would be permanent for as long as the tariff was in place. As bad as slower growth is, it is still growth. The shipping industry has not really experienced any permanent declines in cargo volume and the impact of that would be extraordinarily adverse.

A full fledged trade war, while still highly unlikely, could have a much more devastating effect. While the comparisons are limited, it is worth noting that the imposition of the Smoot-Hawley tariffs by the U.S. in 1930 were the catalyst for igniting a worldwide trade war. The impact on U.S. trade was dramatic as by 1933, compared to 1929, imports had declined 66% and exports had declined 61%.

While the shipping industry is still struggling to come to terms with the major cost increases that will result from the new fuel standards in 2020, the industry can expect further environmental regulations that could also result in additional cost increases. For instance, at some point the IMO will likely lower the worldwide sulfur cap from 0.5% to 0.1% to equal the current cap in emission control areas. Even at 0.1%, the sulfur content would still be 67 times the current sulfur limit in gasoline. It would not be surprising to see the IMO revisit the sulfur issue and call for lower limits, particularly as other fuels continue to get cleaner.

One sign of the dysfunctional economics in the shipping industry is the current lack of actual vessel ownership by large users of maritime transport such as major oil companies, grain companies and miners. After all, shipping companies are not generally able to obtain higher utilization in these one way cargoes, which is the primary reason where outsourcing transport is a win-win for both parties. Without that difference, cargo owners generally prefer to own the transport assets. By doing this, they capture what would otherwise be profit going to the carrier.

While it was once the case that major oil companies, grain companies and miners owned vessels their products moved in, that was decades ago. Those companies control the vessels they need mainly through spot charters. When relatively efficient shipping companies lose money, that value in effect accrues to their customer. If you can get all the ships you need with short-term charters that are lower cost than owning, there is little reason to tie up capital by owning vessels.

When investing in transports at a large hedge fund, I prepared an analysis that drove home how many of these large customers address their shipping needs today. Using VLCC's as an example, I did a comparison that went back over the latest twenty-five years. For each year, I first calculated the average spot timecharter rate as the short-term charter cost. For the ownership case, I took the average newbuilding cost each year and amortized that amount less estimated scrap value over 25 years at 6% interest to get a daily equivalent capital cost. To that I then added daily operating costs of the most efficient operator to arrive at the total daily ownership cost.

Even with the ownership case determined at a nominal 6% interest rate, it was higher than the short-term charter cost in 20 out of the 25 years. In fact, to have the ownership case equal the charter case over the entire 25 year period, the interest factor needed to be in the 2% range, effectively meaning that there was almost no return on capital for a very capital intensive asset. I suspect similar analyses on the dry-bulk and general cargo segments would show the same thing. These analyses support the notion that large customers have lower costs from relying on short-term charters rather than owning vessels. While this is counter intuitive, it is explained by the dyfuntional economics that exist in the shipping industry today.

It is generally recognized that the first phase of dealing with a problem is to recognize the existence of the problem. The shipping industry is in a financial crisis today, in no small part due to many self-inflicted wounds. A case can be made that no single industry has as poor a cumulative income statement since it began as the shipping industry. That cumulative result may very well be negative. With four or five years of loss making or barely scraping by for each year of acceptable profits, it is no wonder that it is in the shape that it is in today.

The poor financial results of the shipping industry were quantified in a recent study by McKinsey & Company of the container shipping sector and how its returns compare to related sectors it interacts with. Using data over the past twenty years, McKinsey calculated the average return on invested capital as well as the returns of companies in the top 25% or quartile in each sector. Not only were the average returns in container shipping the lowest, but also the returns of companies in the top quartile were poor and clustered near the average. The actual returns on invested capital from 1995 to 2015 are shown in the table below.

Sector	Average ROIC	Top 25% ROIC
Container Shipping Companies	2.6%	4.0%
Container Terminal Companies	8.7%	11.0%
Freight Forwarding Companies	6.4%	14.0%
Intermodal Rail Companies	6.8%	9.0%
Intermodal Trucking Companies	5.7%	10.0%

Note that return on invested capital is before interest expenses and measured against both equity and debt capital. The container shipping sector has significants amounts of debt. Therefore, the 2.6% annual average and even the 4.0% for the top performers generally would not be sufficient to even cover interest expense, let alone result in an economic profit. In other words, the McKinsey study indicates that over the twenty years, a period that included the largest expansion of container trade the world has ever seen due to the China supercycle, the entire container shipping sector operated at a meaningful economic and accounting loss.

It is a rather staggering statement to realize that the container shipping sector operated at a loss even during a period when it had macro tailwinds that will likely never be duplicated. As seen in the table, however, its not that the entire activity of moving containers was without profits. All of the sectors which fundamentally rely on the container shipping companies performed much better than those companies, some quite handsomely.

For example, the best performing freight forwarding companies had returns three and one half times better than the best performing container shipping companies. It is clear from the data in the table that the way the economic pie is split between the container shipping companies themselves and the businesses they literally put in business needs serious re-examination.

Similar actual and relative performance data on the other shipping segments over the last twenty years is not as readily and reliably available due to their generally private ownership structure. However, I suspect that those segments would show similar under performance financially. With the collective losses that have occurred over the last ten years since the financial crisis, the shipping industry has likely displaced the airline industry as the one with the worst cumulative financial performance in history.

This financial underperformance has carried through in how the stocks of those publicly listed shipping companies have performed. With some minor exceptions, in period after period those stocks have performed poorly. Since the financial crisis, most of these stocks have been decimated as companies struggle to stay afloat and investors flee the industry. Even in a longer term study of stock market performance by industry from 1900 to 2014, a leading investment bank ranked shipping stocks as the single worst performers over that long term period.

The disillusionment of the shipping industry by the equity capital markets is itself a challenge that is impacting the industry and it goes beyond affecting just the publicly held companies. Equity investors often fund the innovation and improvement that comes into most industries. When this source of funding is constrained, so too is innovation and improvement. While too much capital is also problematic, that is usually in the form of debt. A case can be made that the reduction in shipping loans as banks reduce their involvement in the industry is a positive catalyst, as less creditworthy projects will not move forward. However, the same can not be said of additional constraints on equity capital, as it is really what makes positive changes possible.

In the absence of new equity capital, the status quo and everything that goes with that is likely to be maintained. For the shipping industry, that is not a good situation. There is unfortunately a groupthink mentality within the industry that blinds it to more constructive interaction with the capital markets. That groupthink typically involves some version of how outsiders do not understand the industry.

I will always remember a conference hosted by a major investment bank promoting the establishment of a derivatives market for container shipping rates. Responding to a question from a young investment banker, an industry veteran said the banker did not understand the business and if he did he would realize that derivatives could not work. The young banker retorted that he certainly had no experience in the business, but had immersed himself in the financial statements of the industry the last few months and that the business model is broken.

Similarly, in conference after conference I have attended over the years where executives of shipping companies make presentations and answer questions, the refrain is that Wall Street does not understand our business. There is a consistent rejection of outside observations and forecasts without providing a cogent alternative.

At conferences shipping executives have actually relished in the view that the future is fundamentally unknowable. By effectively presenting the case that shipping is an un-analyzable industry, the equity capital markets loose interest and move on to other industries. Investors do not need to invest in shipping. The biggest loser from this lack of equity capital market interest in the shipping industry is of course the industry itself.

A recent conversation with the CEO of a publicly held maritime company comes to mind. He suggested that, with the exception of the container shipping segment where there are multiple elements that can be pulled together to build an actual business model, that the other segments are more like commodities than an actual business. To the extent that there is little or nothing those segments can do to differentiate themselves from one another, there is much truth in his observation.

The shipping industry needs to honestly reflect on the way it does business, recognize the parts of its business model that are broken and move quickly to change and improve them. There are structural flaws in the way it does business that should be corrected to get the industry on a more firm financial footing.

As highlighted above, the macro issues of slower growth, higher fuel prices and potential tariff barriers will put even more financial pressure on the industry. To remain a viable business, it needs to be operated much more like a business. In the next chapter, we attempt to offer some solutions to the challenges the shipping industry is facing now and in the future.

30. Future of the Shipping Industry

Prior to looking into the crystal ball of what the future may hold for the shipping industry, the discussion should be framed in terms of a long-term forecast for shipping demand. Among the more credible long-term forecasts for shipping demand is the one from a recent report by DNV GL of Norway. In that report, they forecast ton-mile demand by segment over various periods through 2050. After framing the outlook for growth in shipping demand, we highlight its implications and then discuss various other factors that will affect the future of shipping. We also discuss potential solutions to challenges and problems of the shipping industry.

DNV GL is the world's largest classification society, providing services for some 13,175 vessels across all segments. DNV GL also provides technical consultancy to the oil and gas and renewalable energy industries. The table below shows DNV GL's forecast of total ton-mile demand in both 2030 and 2050 along with actual demand in both 2010 and 2016. It includes a further breakdown of the tanker segment by its three primary components of crude oil, products and natural gas such as LNG and LPG. In my view the best analysis and forecasts related to the tanker segment in particular and oil usage in general come out of Norway because its economy is primarily driven by the exploration for and transportation of petroleum. When so much of a country's economy is focused and dependent on one area, you develop considerable expertise in analyzing and forecasting that area.

Billions of Ton-Miles	2010	2016	Est 2030	Est 2050
Crude Oil	8,608	9,580	11,380	6,570
Petroleum Products	2,591	3,040	3,760	2,800
Natural Gas	1,147	1,460	3,670	4,520
Subtotal Petroleum	12,346	14,080	18,810	13,890
Dry-Bulk	21,007	27,200	34,320	37,890
Container	6,589	8,580	12,690	16,250
Other	3,985	5,190	6,680	8,140
Grand Total	43,927	55,050	72,500	76,170

The annual growth rate in terms of total ton-miles moved in all cargo ships was 3.8% from 2010 to 2016. The dry-bulk and container segments grew above that rate while the growth in the tanker segment, particularly the movement of crude oil, was below that rate.

Going forward until 2030, all segments are forecast to grow at slower rates except for LNG and LPG which are being driven by shale exploration in the U.S. In the 2030 to 2050 period, the forecast growth rates for all segments are anticipated to go down sharply with some segments actually declining. The table at the top of the next page shows the actual annual growth rate in ton-miles for the 2010 to 2016 period along with the forecast annual growth rate for the 2016 to 2030 and 2030 to 2050 periods.

Ton-Mile Growth/Year	2010-2016	Est 2016-2030	Est 2030-2050
Crude Oil	1.8%	1.2%	-2.7%
Petroleum Products	2.7%	1.5%	-1.5%
Natural Gas	4.1%	6.8%	1.0%
Subtotal Petroleum	2.2%	2.1%	-1.5%
Dry-Bulk	4.4%	1.7%	0.5%
Container	4.5%	2.8%	1.2%
Other	4.5%	1.8%	1.0%
Grand Total	3.8%	2.0%	0.2%

Economic activity is the primary driver of shipping demand. That activity can be measured by world GDP growth, which in turn is inextricably correlated with world population growth. During the decade preceding the financial crisis, it was not unusual to see demand for shipping to grow at three and four times the growth rate in world GDP.

In the more recent 2010 to 2016 period, overall growth in shipping demand was approximately twice world GDP growth. From the end of that period to 2030, it is expected to be around the same as the growth as GDP growth in mature economies. From 2030 through 2050, DNV GL forecasts that growth in all segments will slow down further and will barely equal the world population growth rate in most segments. In all periods, the movement of crude oil and petroleum products is the laggard, consistent with DNV GL's view of a global transition towards greater use of renewable energy and less use of fossil fuels. The only relative bright spot in the tanker segment is the movement of much cleaner LNG and LPG.

This serial deceleration across shipping segments will be a departure from the recent past, but can be better understood when all the relevant factors are considered. The energy transition away from fossil fuels will have direct effects such as 42% and 26% absolute declines in the movement of seaborne crude oil and petroleum products, respectively, from 2030 to 2050. The forecast calls for even larger absolute declines in coal movements. The electrification of vehicles and further improvements in fuel efficiency along with the transition to more renewable power sources by utilities will be major contributors to reduced demand for petroleum.

As consumers and countries become even more environmentally conscious, the second order benefits will also impact shipping ton-miles. For instance, nearshoring, the practice of transferring a business operation to a nearby country from a more distant country, does not change trade volume, but can result in a geometric decrease in the ton-miles that define shipping demand. The movement to more regional trading agreements and patterns can have a similar effect.

Technology itself will have a leveling effect across countries, in some cases reducing the reason for or even the need for trade in some situations. The cargo shipping industry exists because commodities are produced and products are manufactured in locations other than where they are consumed, but technology can impact this.

As more robotic processes are used in manufacturing, for example, labor is disintermediated and previous labor cost differences disappear. Another technology that could disrupt the shipment of manufactured goods is 3D printing. If advances are made to reduce the cost of 3D printing, an array of products could be produced in the precise location of where they are consumed, obviating the need for any shipping services at all.

While the downward slope in the long-term movement of crude oil and petroleum products is driven by the transition to renewable energy, there is an existing technology that could make the future of tankers even bleaker. The U.S. has recently become the largest energy producer in the world by virtue of exploiting its shale oil reserves. This phenomenon has already significantly impacted world energy and shipping markets and will continue to do so.

While the U.S. has the largest shale deposits in the world at an estimated 539 billion tons, it is certainly not alone. China has an estimated 48 billion tons of shale oil reserves. There are another 105 billion tons of shale oil reserves in the rest of the world, including many countries that are presently large oil importers. As these shale oil reserves are exploited using new technology and drilling techniques, the distances between production and consumption will narrow or even disappear, adversely affecting tanker shipping demand.

The impact of slower growth rates across all shipping segments will have a stabilizing affect on the industry. With reduced expectations related to growth, ship owners will order less new vessels and those that are ordered will be more focused on replacing existing vessels. This across the board deceleration in new vessel orders will lead to a sharp reduction in shipyard capacity.

That capacity was built up to serve the halcyon days when shipyards were delivering vessels every year equivalent to 10% or more of the capacity of a segment. Only modest structural reductions in that capacity have occurred to date. The excess capacity overhang in the shipbuilding industry has consistently exceeded that of the shipping industry for decades. This excess shipyard capacity has long been a catalyst for excess vessel capacity and a reduction is long overdue. Similarly, the reduction in bank financing to the shipping sector will continue with less new vessel construction and that will also stabilize the past excesses of the shipping industry.

These slower growth rates will play out over decades, with population growth rates generally acting as a floor. With world population expected to grow at 0.9% annually over the long term, demand growth in that range will hardly be welcomed by ship owners who are accustomed to growth at some multiple of GDP growth, which itself is typically at least twice population growth. While the overall population growth rate will remain fairly constant compared to historical levels, the composition of that growth will have far-reaching affects on the shipping industry over the long term.

For instance, the biggest absolute and relative changes in world population going forward will occur in Africa. Between now and 2100, its population will almost quadruple to 4.4 billion, going from 16% of the world's population to 39%. In 2100, the three most populous cities in the world will be in Africa, with Lagos at 88.3 million, Kinshasa at 83.5 million and Dar es Salaam at 73.7 million. While Africa just has one city among the fifteen most populous cities in the world today, by 2100 nine of those fifteen cities will be in Africa. The implications for shipping with all of these relative changes in population will be significant. Whether they will be positive or negative, however, is nearly impossible to deduce at this stage because there are too many variables that are at work.

In contrast to the gradual rollout of slower demand growth and its related impact on revenue, the shipping industry is facing an immediate expense shock in the form of the worldwide IMO fuel cleanliness standards that go into effect at the beginning of 2020. Converting to distillate fuel will add $70 billion annual to the cost of operating cargo ships. Needless to say, an immediate cost increase of $70 billion per year for an industry losing $5.5 billion per year is a near term financial shock. The effect of this change will vary by sector.

Charters dominate the tanker and dry-bulk sectors where the fuel is usually paid directly by their customers, so this cost increase does not affect them directly. In practice, however, it will impact them by putting downward pressure on the charter rates their customers are willing to pay based upon their reassessing overall voyage costs. Furthermore, in some cases that reassessment will result in cargoes not moving, reducing overall cargo volume. This will be particularly true in the dry-bulk sector where the increased fuel costs will be largest relative to the underlying value of the cargo.

In the container sector, the fuel price increase is a more direct problem as it is included in the service a container operator provides to customers. Historically, the container shipping sector has dealt with changes in fuel prices with a fuel surcharge mechanism that is adjusted from time to time. However, because these adjustments are neither transparent nor real time and often vary widely by carrier, most customers view these surcharges as lacking creditabilty. The largest customers seek and often obtain contracts that state no fuel surcharge shall apply or that they are capped at a certain amount.

The net result is that in periods of rising fuel costs, container shipping companies almost never recover all of their increased fuel costs through such surcharges. Indeed, a meaningful part of the container sector's $8.6 billion loss over the last three years is the impact of fuel prices not fully recovered with surcharges.

With the present fuel surcharge mechanism clearly not working in the container sector, and an additional $19 billion of annual fuel costs that must be paid directly by the container carriers, the sector must come up with a different approach. In my view, a better approach for the container sector would be a real time, transparent formula.

The contract would specify fuel consumption per load, which could be determined using budgeted volume in both directions and total fuel consumption to get average consumption per load, and that the contract rate is based on that consumption and the fuel price in Singapore on the effective date of contract. As the world's largest bunkering port, daily Singapore prices are credible and widely available.

All billings would reflect adjustments in both directions based on changes of Singapore prices between the contract effective date and the sailing date of that load. The carrier may elect to have fuel consumption per load figure different than their experience for competitive reasons. However, the two-way nature of adjustments should have them circling in on consumption of their most efficient ship on the route.

For example, assume a situation where consumption is pegged at 1.375 metric tons per FEU and Singapore's low sulfur marine gas oil is $761 per metric ton on the contract effective date. If the same fuel index is $805 some 52 days later when the shipper's 40' load departs Shanghai,

$60.50 is added to the bill. Likewise, if that fuel index was $743 when the shipper's 40' load departs Rotterdam, $24.75 is deducted from the bill.

While many will say that such a process is too complicated, it is real time, equitable, transparent, and auditable, all characteristics absent in the current methods. This dynamic approach is a move away from the static, round-number approach that the container shipping industry has historically used. Fortunately, there are computers and software that can seamlessly handle the math and lead to a much better system.

Ironically, as shipowners come to terms with the inevitable slowing of demand growth in the future, the financial results of the shipping industry will probably improve. The main driver of this will be less speculative building, as the case for pell-mell growth ahead can not be made. This along with more constrained financing should result in overall supply growth being better aligned with overall demand growth.

In addition, a variety of subsidiary bottom-line benefits for the industry should flow out of a lower growth environment. Instead of building new ships to grow, companies will turn their attention more to acquisitions and consolidation. This action in and of itself will alleviate some of the ruinous price competition.

Furthermore, in periods of strong volume growth, companies often do not pay as much attention to expenses as they should and this has certainly been the case in shipping. Slower growth will allow more focus on and management of expenses. It should also usher in more long-term contracts and less spot business as shipowners see less volatility in the future. Even a partial return to an industrial shipping model that was how the industry started would improve sector results. While some of these changes may make it a less exciting industry, it will be a more stable and better performing industry financially.

In the future there should be more recognition that many of the financial ills facing the shipping industry have resulted from self-inflicted wounds. Simply put, for too long the shipping industry has not been operated like a real business. Instead it has had too many people making large bets on what their gut told them was the right point in the cycle. An asymmetric heads I win, tails you lose framework for the decision-maker encouraged such risks, often assisting to make a casino-like environment.

The most swashbuckling of today's shipowners have probably been influenced by the stories they have heard about the individual giants profiled here. Some maybe even believe they are just one deal away from duplicating similar successes. All of those men, however, had first mover advantages that are almost impossible to duplicate today. Times have changed for a variety of reasons, not the least of which is the increasing direct involvement in shipping by state-owned enterprises.

The way shipping companies are managed needs to adapt to the changed circumstances of today and the future. The corporate governance at shipping companies should be much better. Boards need to be much more diligent in risk oversight and checking newbuilding plans. Promotion and succession due more to demonstrated competence than bloodline would be a welcomed change.

Leadership driven more by detailed financial analysis rather than salesmanship would also move the results of the shipping industry in the right direction. The shipping industry would have benefited from more of the former in the recent past, but as the industry moves into a future that will have slower overall growth and more stability, that transition is absolutely required. An early test of whether it is moving in the direction of being managed more as a business will be who pays the $70 billion in additional annual costs arising out of the new fuel standards. Under any objective review, all of those costs should be borne by the recipients of shipping services.

Technology will play an increasing role in the shipping industry in the future. Most of the improvement in shipping cost efficiency has come from specialization and scale economics. While technology has played a role at the margins, the shipping industry has been less blackbox and much more analog than digital. For instance, the biggest technology advancement in propulsion was from steam to diesel decades ago. While there has been some refinement, the diesel engines of today are fundamentally just much larger versions of the first such engines. Driven entirely by environmental considerations, we are now on the cusp of major technological changes in both the fuel used in ship engines and the types of propulsion systems used in ships.

Ships will transition to using LNG as a fuel for both environmental and economic reasons. LNG is the cleanest fossil fuel with a significantly better emissions profile than even the distillate fuel ships are mandated to switch to by 2020. It is reasonable to assume that emissions standards for vessels will continue to increase, particularly since using LNG to fuel vessels is now a fully proven technology.

Starting in the U.S., there are currently many examples of ships now in service built to use LNG. The cost of constructing such a vessel adds approximately ten percent to the total cost. A meaningful percentage of the large container ships now being built will be capable of using LNG as a fuel. With these contracts, a framework for supplying LNG at various ports is quickly being developed. To date, the lack of this infrastructure has been a constraint. The price of LNG has been at times a lower cost alternative than distillate fuel. This comparison should get much more attractive in the future as the natural gas supply expands from increasing shale production and distillate fuel prices increase due to the 2020 mandate.

All of these developments will lead to a much quicker transition to LNG as a ship fuel source than the industry currently anticipates. Within a couple of years, most new vessels will be built to be LNG capable. An increasing percent of the world fleet will use LNG each year and within twenty years when most of the existing vessels have been scrapped, the only fossil fuel being used in ships will be LNG.

Even as that transition to LNG occurs, there will be research and progress on ways to reduce shipping's carbon footprint. The most promising long-term soluation will involve fuel cells. Through a chemical reaction between a feed stock and a catalyst, fuel cells act like a battery to provide electric power. Fuel cells fed by hydrogen or ammonia, whose main ingredient is hydrogen, will probably be the preferred method of propelling ships at some point in the future. Hydrogen is a readily available element and the only exhaust from a hydrogen fuel cell is water vapor. They would achieve the Holy Grail of zero carbon emissions and make ships the most environmentally friendly form of transport.

Autonomous vessels will be part of the future. If autonomous control of any transport mode makes sense, the case for vessels should be relatively high on the list. The technologies to make that happen are already being tested in a number of applications. Some argue that the labor cost that autonomous vessels would save is such a small portion of total costs that it does not make sense. In some situations, that is certainly a valid point.

However, there is an array of benefits that can accrue from autonomous vessels that are not as recognized as much as they should be. The increase in cargo carrying capacity for a ship of a given size can be meaningful if space does not have to be provided for crew. This is particularly the case with container ships where line of sight visibility from the bridge is often a major constraint in terms of containers loaded on deck.

Beyond fully autonomous vessels, there are a number of iterations that would result in hybrids involving automation to reduce costs. Entire functions that have been traditionally handled by crewmembers could be turned over to automation. Many engine rooms are now fully automated with no crew present during parts of the day. The trends in this area will continue and the time will come when engine rooms operate unmanned around the clock.

Technology can also be used in small ways to reduce costs. With the voice control technology that exists today, a bridge officer's command related to navigational heading can be used to automatically turn a the wheel and rudder of a ship. That change would lead to up to three less crewmembers needed.

A broader hybrid use of automation would involve a traditional vessel traveling alongside one or more fully automated vessels. This mother ship, daughter ship arrangement addresses the concern that human eyes are needed on the scene. Possible remote control of the daughter ship by the mother ship, and even a hard wire connection between the two for further redundancy, are further options. Such an arrangement also potentially allows crewmembers to board the daughter ship if that was deemed to be necessary. Within such a framework one could envision a mother ship escorting multiple daughter ships, with additional crewmembers standing by to provide emergency maintenance or navigation activities.

Obviously any remote control of autonomous vessels would have to be via secure systems. This of course is not unique to vessels and will be a key requirement for all methods of autonomous transport. There are many examples of secure systems that have been developed to handle important information and transactions. For example, hundreds of billions of dollars are moved each day between accounts at various financial institutions without any reportable losses.

My own view is that concerns regarding the hackability of systems related to autonomous transport are not fact based and that fully secure systems to control vessels can be developed. I hold a patent on a process we developed to control the engines on an unmanned barge that was tethered to another barge being towed by a tug. In this example of a semi-autonomous vessel, the engines were controlled remotely from the tug and a hard wire control for redundancy was attached to the tether.

The future will see an array of existing technologies deployed on ships to improve their environmental characteristics. While the transition to LNG fuel will make emissions dramatically cleaner, other environmental initiatives will be targeted at carbon emissions which will still be significant with LNG. Regulatory groups are already focusing on the carbon emissions of the shipping industry even before the 2020 mandate which just addresses sulfur oxide emissions goes into effect.

Maersk Line, the world's largest shipping company, has announced that by 2050 it plans to reduce its net carbon emissions to zero. This in effect means moving completely away from any type of fossil fuel. Technologies that will be used include hydrogen and ammonia fuel cells, rigid metal sails, rotor sails, solar cells, electric power and engines running on biomass fuel. The ships of the future will rely on a combination of these and other technologies to achieve stronger environmental targets that will almost certainly be mandated by regulators at some point.

One of the likely consequences of fully automated ships would be an increase in U.S. flag ships involved in international commerce. With no crew and the varying operating costs that arise related to them, the operating cost disadvantage of U.S. flag ships goes away. In general, there would be less incentive for shipowners from high income developed countries to use of flags of convenience. The registry of vessels in a future with many autonomous vessels would likely become more aligned with the shipping company headquarters, just as it was in the prewar period.

The increasing use of technology will not be limited to the vessel itself. In many ways, other parts of the maritime supply chain will benefit even more from overdue digitization. Cargo operations to load and unload ships will become increasingly automated. This will particularly be true in the container sector where fully automated terminals are not too far away.

With GPS and optical character readers, fully automated vehicles can already retrieve containers from terminal stacks and deliver precisely to where a fully automated crane will takeover and place the container in the vessel. These operations reduce labor costs and also increase productivity. Because three-quarters of the accidents on vessels and in terminals are due to human error, those accidents and the economic damage they cause can be avoided with fully autonomous operations.

For some time, digital technology has been used to book, track and trace physical shipments on vessels. However, it grows in sophistication each year along with being further integrated into larger supply chain and information systems. The 1999 article in Wired Magazine, *The 20 Ton Packet*, referred to container shipping as the biggest realtime datastreaming network in the world, so the analogy between digital and physical is on point.

This digital twin of the physical movement will continue to grow in importance. In many cases the digital twin will become more important than the movement and even product itself. The value of this information goes well beyond inventory control. Having precise knowledge of where a product is often determines if it and similar products will result in revenue and profits. It is in this information technology area related to shipping that significant digital value continues to be created. Unlike the application of technology to vessels where the industry is more analog than digital, in this area the broader shipping and logistics industry is doing some very interesting things.

In an indication of the digital transformation that is sweeping across the shipping industry, a recent report by Danish Ship Finance identified 160 startup companies that are involved in the maritime space with digital initiatives. The four categories the efforts of these startups are focused on are performance management, capacity optimization, value beyond the vessel and reinventing the operating model. The first two categories identify how new technologies can increase industry efficiency while the latter two are focused on transforming the business models of the industry by creating new streams of revenue.

The shipping industry is still in the early stages of a digital revolution that has dramatically changed other industries. Many of these startups will survive and prosper, bringing with them disruptive change to the shipping industry. For example, one company in the third category is Flexport. Founded in 2013, Flexport is a freight forwarder with a robust digital platform that is dominating less digital incumbents in the freight forwarding industry and is already valued at over $3 billion.

If there is any takeaway from this book, it is that the revolution in shipping cost efficiency has been extraordinary in the postwar period. From an economic standpoint, however, unfortunately in most years all of that value and a little bit more has been transferred to customers.

It is very clear that the shipping industry has to re-access the pricing framework in which it deals with its customers. The shipping industry has made substantial investments in vessels and hard assets and this commitment needs to be better balanced with meaningful contractual commitments from customers. The days where the shipowner is more bound than the customer needs to end.

Just as the shipping industry's revenue has been adversely impacted by what has really been a dysfunctional relationship with its customer base, value has also been lost at the other end in its relationship with vendors who are aligned with it in the broader supply chain. This is apparent in the McKinney study referenced earlier that compared returns on capital over a recent twenty-year period. Without exception, all of these groups which rely on the shipping industry for all of their business perform significantly better in terms of return on capital.

That simply is not the way it is supposed to work. The return on capital for the shipping industry should be at least as much as those that are in business because of the industry. These relationships need to be reflected on and examined. Where it is evident that profit has been exported by outsourcing the function, companies need to consider handling that function themselves. Intermediaries that constrain and reduce return on capital need to be dis-intermediated as soon as possible.

Malcom McLean was not a fan of outsourcing any of the core activities performed by container shipping companies. His repeated observation on that subject was "If you outsource your headaches, you outsource your profits". The leaders today in the container shipping industry would do well to reflect on that statement by the man who invented container shipping.

Against the backdrop of a slowdown in demand growth across all segments, technological advancements and a geometrically cleaner environmental signature will mark the future of the shipping industry. It will continue to be the driver that makes world trade possible. It can be the industry's brightest period ever.

However, a key requirement is that the industry needs to start getting its own financial house in better order first. The world needs the services it provides, as there is no substitute. Recognizing this should make it easier to address the financial challenges facing the industry today. As the video on the airplane says, you need to always put the oxygen mask on yourself before attempting to assist someone else.

The shipping industry helps billions around the world each day by its very existence. If it augments that clear and tangible accomplishment by managing itself better in ways that are really already known, the industry may truly be on the cusp of the golden age of the shipping business.

Bibliography

Primary Data Sources:

    Bloomberg Terminal BMAP
    Container Trade Statistics
    U.S. Bureau of Transportation Statistics
    United Nations Conference on Trade and Development
    World Bank
    Encyclopedia Britanica

Books:

Batio, Christopher. *Super Cargo Ships.* Osceola, WI: MBI Publishing Company, 2001

Conners, Michael and Alice King. *C.Y. Tung: His Vision and Legacy.* Hong Kong: The Seawise Foundation, 1984

Cudahy, Brian J. *Box Boats: How Container Ships Changed the World.* New York: Fordam University Press, 2006

Donovan, Arthur and Joseph Bonney. *The Box That Changed The World.* East Windsor, NJ: Commonwealth Business Media, 2006

Evans, Harold. *They Made America.* New York: Little, Brown and Company, 2004

George, Rose. *Ninety Percent of Everything.* New York: Henry Holt and Company, 2013

Geroux, William. *The Matthews Men: Seven Brothers and the War Against Hitler's U-Boats.* New York: Viking, 2016

Gilford, Steve. *Build 'Em by the Mile, Cut 'Em Off by the Yard.* Richmond, CA: Richmond Museum Association, 2011

Ignarski, Sam. *The Box: An Anthology Celebrating 25 Years of Containerization and the TT Club.* London: EMAP Business Communications, 1994

Johnston, Mark. *The Sugar Trade in the West Indies and Brazil Between 1492 and 1700.* University of Minnesota

Krieger, Michael. *Where Rails Meet the Sea.* New York: Friedman Fairfax Publishers, 1998

Labarree, Benjamin W., William M. Fowler, Edward W. Sloan, John B. Hattendorf, Jeffrey J. Safford and Andrew W. German. *America and the Sea: A Maritime History.* Mystic, CT: Mystic Seaport Museum, 1998

Lavery, Brian. *Ship: The Epic Story of Maritime Adventure.* New York: DK Publishing, 2004

Levinson, Mark. *The Box: How the Shipping Container Made the World Smaller and the World Economy Bigger.* Princeton: Princeton University Press, 2006

LaRocco, Lori. *Dynasties of the Sea.* Stamford, CT: Marine Money, 2012

Lilly, Doris. *Those Fabulous Greeks: Onassis Niarchos and Livanos.* New York: Cowles Book Company, 1970

Mostert, Noel. *Supership.* New York: Alfred A. Knopf, 1974

Nersesian, Roy. *Ships and Shipping.* Tulsa: Penn Well Publishing Company, 1981

Newby, Eric. *The Last Grain Race.* London, England: Martin Secker & Warburg Ltd, 1956

Newton, John. *A Century of Tankers.* London: Intertanko, 2002

Paine, Lincoln. *The Sea and Civilization.* New York: Alfred A. Knopf, 2013.

Pao-Sohmen, Anna. *Y.K. Pao, My Father.* Hong Kong: Hong Kong University Press, 2013

Rife, James P. *Talking Globally: Forty Years of the Box Club.* Washington, D.C.: International Council of Containership Operators, 2014

Sauerbier, Charles L., Meurn, Robert J. *Marine Cargo Operations.* New York: John Wiley & Sons, 1985

Shields, Jerry. *The Invisible Billionaire Daniel Ludwig.* Boston: Houghton Mifflin Company, 1986

Thubron, Colin. *The Venetians (The Seafarers),* New York: Time-Life Books, 1980

Tuchman, Barbara. *The First Salute,* New York: Alfred A. Knopf, 1988

Villiers, Capt. Alan. *Men Ships and the Sea.* Washington, DC: National Geographic Society, 1962

Woodman, Thomas. *The History of the Ship.* London: Conway Maritime Press, 1997

9 781087 902760